# POLI

# IN THE

# MEDIA AGE

# POLITICS IN THE MEDIA AGE

## Ronald Berkman

Associate Professor of Political Science
Brooklyn College

## Laura W. Kitch

Professor of Sociology
Brooklyn College

**McGRAW-HILL BOOK COMPANY**

New York   St. Louis   San Francisco   Auckland   Bogotá
Hamburg   Johannesburg   London   Madrid   Mexico   Montreal   New Delhi
Panama   Paris   São Paulo   Singapore   Sydney   Tokyo   Toronto

This book was set in Optima by The Graphix Group, Inc.
The editor was David V. Serbun;
the cover was designed by Rafael Hernandez;
the production supervisor was Diane Renda;
Project supervision was done by The Graphix Group, Inc.
R. R. Donnelley & Sons Company was printer and binder.

**POLITICS IN THE MEDIA AGE**

1 2 3 4 5 6 7 8 9 0 DOCDOC 8 9 8 7 6

ISBN 0-07-004882-7

**Library of Congress Cataloging in Publication Data**

Berkman, Ronald.
 Politics in the media age.

 Includes bibliographical references and index.
 1. Mass media—Political aspects—United States.
I. Kitch, Laura W.  II. Title.
P95.82.U6B47  1986   302.2'34'0973   85-12784
ISBN 0-07-004882-7 (pbk.)

# CONTENTS

# PREFACE

The election of 1984 may be remembered as the year of tribute to the power of the mass media. On the day after his crushing defeat in the presidential election, Walter Mondale admitted what virtually everyone in the country knew—that he had been devastatingly ineffective in using television. He had failed to master the art of "imageship." In a moment of candor, Mondale seemed to signal the end of an era as he proclaimed that it would probably be impossible for anyone who could not perform well on television to be elected President of the United States.

Ronald Reagan used the campaign to demonstrate that he truly deserved the title of "Great Communicator." While Ronald Reagan never publicly paid tribute to the success of his media campaign in generating the tremendous public support he received in the election, his mastery before the cameras was widely recognized. 1984 should be recorded as the year that politics took a giant step out of the "machine age" and plunged into the "media age."

Our interest in the media developed some years ago as the influence of the news media on the political process grew and as the media became center stage for an intensified struggle to win the hearts and minds of the American people. The conditions that permitted the mass media to rise to a preeminent position on the American political scene were rooted in the political, cultural, and technological changes that took place during the 1960s and early 1970s. Traditional affiliations and political loyalties were shattered during that period, and there were deep doubts about the adequacy of many traditional political arrangements. The electorate became more independent and unpredictable. Voters were less likely to use the old cues, such as their families' political affiliation, to decide how to vote. Since traditional arrangements could not guarantee support, it was necessary for candidates to mobilize much of their own support. It soon became evident that using the mass media was the most effective way to gain such support. While the mass media were initially used to gain electoral support, they soon became an important means to mobilize support for certain policies and ideological beliefs.

Even without the changes occasioned by the political wars of the 1960s and 1970s, the mass media were destined to become a potent political weapon. How could any political actor ignore a technology with the ability to transmit political messages into virtually every American household? The 1960s produced new opportunities for the media and accelerated their rise. As the media become more widely used, their power grew. As their power grew, the power of more traditional instruments of mobilization, such as the political party, declined.

By the mid-1970s, there was a new American political landscape. This book is an investigation of the media's place in that landscape. The task of investigating power is always complicated by the fact that it is shifting, changing the relationships as the seasons change a landscape. So the task of examining the power of the news media, which is a prime feature of the book, is complicated. In the last decade, for example, the triangular relationship between the news media, the political establishment, and the general public has undergone some significant changes. In the early 1970s, the news media's investigation of the Watergate affair helped unravel political corruption at the highest levels. At the time, there was public acclaim for the work of the media. Politicians feared encountering the wrath of the media or becoming the subject of investigation. Today, there is a very substantial degree of public hostility toward the media. Many politicians have used this opportunity to go on the offensive against newspapers, magazines, and television stations. A large number of libel actions have been instituted by politicians seeking redress for purported injustices. Many politicians no longer fear the "long arm" of the free press the way they did ten years ago.

The power of the news media is one important feature of the new political landscape, but there are others. Politicians, interest groups, and private interests have used the mass media to communicate an ever-increasing variety of overt and covert political messages. The effects of these messages, from standard campaign commercials to advertising campaigns in support of nuclear power, are also difficult to evaluate definitively. What is certain is that these paid and unmediated political messages are reaching millions of American homes and becoming a potential force in the public opinion arena.

We begin the book with a brief description of the two basic questions that guide the investigation: How do the news media cover the political world, and how does the political world use the mass media? This is followed by a discussion of what is known about the general effects of the media on political behavior. Specific effects are discussed in the individual chapters.

Part One of the book, which follows an introductory chapter, contains a comprehensive examination of the organizations that collect and disseminate news. Chapter 2 begins with a description of the historical evaluation of the mass media, particularly the television industry. This chapter illustrates the fact that the news is, in essence, a business, which operates in essentially the same environment as other businesses. Its operation and its product can be understood only when the news media are considered in this context. The discussion of the evaluation of the news industry is followed by a chapter that chronicles the development of government regulatory apparatus designed to control the operation of the media. Since the Federal and Supreme Courts have been consistently called upon to interpret these regulations, there are reviews of some pivotal cases in which the courts have spelled out the meaning of regulatory doctrines. Part One concludes with an analysis of the most important factors that determine what becomes news.

Part Two is devoted to the way the media cover political campaigns. Much attention is focused on the industry that consults, directs, and produces the campaign commercials and media appearances, which are a large part, if not the heart, of the modern American political campaigns. To what degree are media consultants and pollsters able to fashion the form and control of a political campaign? What is the significance of these consultants' ascent from campaign work to governing? These are a few of the questions analyzed in the chapters in Part Two.

Part Three provides a systematic discussion of the relationship between the news media and various political actors and institutions. The routines that have been established to cover the activities of particular branches of government are a prime focus. The means adopted by various political actors to engineer favorable coverage are described and critically evaluated. This section contains an unprecedented chapter on the coverage of corporate activities and on the corporations' use of the mass media to achieve certain political goals. Since the corporation is an important participant in the struggle for power, it is also an important player in the media age. This chapter provides a comprehensive picture of the interrelationships between public and private bastions of power and the media. The chapters in this section contain material collected in numerous interviews with journalists (print and electronic) and press secretaries, as well as a number of case studies which highlight the role of the media in the modern political process.

In the final section of the book, the overall impact of the new political alignments is evaluated. Here, in general terms, there is an attempt to tackle the most complex, perplexing, and crucial questions of all: How will the democratic process be changed by politics in the media age?

As always, there are many people to thank for their contributions. When the project was first conceived, Star Sandow helped Ronald Berkman clarify his ideas and focus the project. Professor Mark Fishman, of the Brooklyn College Sociology Department, provided Laura Kitch with the basic framework for the study of the mass media. Several colleagues in the Department of Political Science of Brooklyn College read parts of the manuscript or participated in discussions about issues in the book. Professor Morton Berkowitz read the early chapters of the book. Professor Philippa Strum read the material on regulation and the courts. Professors Jiman Tagavi, Archibald Singham, and Martin Fleisher provided much-needed doses of theoretical assistance all along the way. Professor Roberta Satow, of the Sociology Department, read the material on political campaigns with an unerring eye for detail and organization. Over the years, our students in Media and Politics and in the Sociology of Mass Communications have discussed and examined many of the ideas contained in this book and have provided some ideas of their own. They have been a continuing source of inspiration.

Many journalists and press secretaries gave us generous portions of time and candor. Their aid was truly invaluable. We would particularly like to thank Lou Peck, of Gannett, and Sam Donaldson, of ABC, who asked as many important questions as they answered and who led us to many other valuable sources.

Thanks also go to our editors at McGraw-Hill: Eric Munson, who signed the project, Christina Mediate, who stayed with it through some troubled times, and David Serbun, who continually showed interest in the subject matter of the book and brought the project to a successful completion.

There are many people who reviewed all or part of the manuscript. Many of the reviewers provided new ideas, important suggestions for revisions and organization, and a wealth of knowledge about the subject. Their generosity is greatly appreciated. The list is long and distinguished: Sheldon Wolin and Jamison Doig, both of Princeton University; Shanto Iyengar, Yale University; Herbert Schiller, the University of California at San Diego; Michael Robinson, George Washington University; Bertram Gross, C.U.N.Y.; Michael Krasner, Queens College; Ben Page, the University of Texas at Austin; Earl Shaw, the University of

Minnesota-Minneapolis; Gregory B. Markus, the University of Michigan; Charles Atkins, Michigan State University; Michael Traugott, the University of Michigan; Gerry S. Tyler, the University of Rhode Island; James Clotfelter, the University of North Carolina; Marilyn Hoskin, the State University of New York at Buffalo; George Watson, Arizona State University; Michael Delli-Carpini, Rutgers University; Stephen Bennett, the University of Cincinnati; Hal Rhodes, the University of New Mexico; John Hocheimer, the University of Iowa and Brent Berkman, the University of Michigan.

Many secretaries at Brooklyn College typed parts of the manuscript. Doris Glassman not only did the bulk of the typing with incredible precision but also called our attention to many problems in the manuscript. Thanks are due to Lorraine Lange for her assistance. Special thanks go to Tricia Maddox, who typed, proofread, organized, and transcribed hours of interviews, and to Jack Kitch, who proofread and edited the manuscript at every stage and through every draft. Finally, we thank both Tricia Maddox and Jack Kitch for providing love and support throughout the entire project.

*Ronald Berkman*
*Laura W. Kitch*

# CHAPTER 1

# INTRODUCTION TO POLITICS AND THE MEDIA

## THE INFLUENCE OF THE MEDIA

### Early Research

The relationship between the mass media and politics has been a concern of social critics since the first mass medium, the penny press, hit the streets of New York City in the 1830s. Some, at the time, thought that the increased dissemination of information would enhance the democratic process by expanding the audience and the range of public debate. The press was seen by some as the mechanism which could produce a truly "informed" public. As C. Wright Mills pointed out, "early observers believed that the increase in the range and volume of the formal means of communication would enlarge and animate the primary public."[1]

From the very beginning, however, others had attacked the popular press. Throughout the nineteenth century, there was a growing concern about the potential power of the mass press to persuade and manipulate the public and perhaps undermine the democratic process. By seeking the sensational and by simplifying the political issues of the day, the press was thought to divert the attention of the masses, arouse irrational passions, and lower the level of political debate. However, it was not until World War I, when the twin spectors of government news management and propaganda became realities, that the relationship between the mass media and politics began to come into focus. Government news management during the war was seen as necessary to the war effort.

Journalists accepted the notion of secrecy when it came to such things as the movement of troops. Peace was to bring with it a more open relationship between the government and the press. The press was to be free to collect news about national policy. However, the Paris Peace Conference of 1919 did not fulfill the promise of a more open relationship; it signaled a new relationship between the press and the government. The negotiations were shrouded in secrecy, as the government "controlled" the news in an organized, self-conscious fashion. What particularly disturbed journalists was not so much keeping negotiations confidential from the public as it was keeping them secret from the press.[2]

Even greater was the concern engendered by the reality of wartime propaganda and the seemingly overwhelming potential of the mass media to control the minds of men. The propaganda used during World War I was the first attempt at large-scale persuasion of entire populations through the skillful use of the mass media. The apparent success of propaganda led to a widespread acceptance by social scientists of the "hypodermic needle" theory of the effects of the media. This theory is not so much a specifically articulated hypothesis as it is an underlying assumption. Simply put, this theory assumes that everyone is exposed to the media messages equally, everyone interprets them in the same general way, and everyone is affected uniformly by them. Thus, a cleverly designed message could produce a more or less uniform response from everyone in the population.

The hypodermic needle theory was not based on empirical research but instead reflected the social and psychological theories of the day. It reflected Emile Durkheim's vision of modern industrial society, made up of isolated individuals no longer held together by tradition and thus susceptible to manipulation. It also reflected the insights of Sigmund Freud, who portrayed human beings as subject to irrational instincts and unconscious motivations. The hypodermic needle theory was further supported by the emerging advertising industry, which appeared to be transforming America into a consumer society through the use of subtle and not-so-subtle psychological appeals. The hypodermic needle model assumes that information is transmitted directly from the mass media to the individual, without taking into account the social context within which the message is received. It also assumes that the individual, in modern industrial society, is prone to be manipulated, is irrational, and is governed by unreasonable passions—traits that are themselves threats to democracy.

Given this unhappy picture, it is somewhat surprising that it was not until 1940 that a systematic study of the political effects of the media was undertaken. This study, entitled *The People's Choice*, was restricted to investigating the relationship between the mass media and voting behavior.[3] Contradicting earlier assumptions, the authors found that information on candidates running for office received through the mass media had very little effect on voting behavior. Information received from the media tended to reinforce a voter's already-formed opinions. If a voter was predisposed to vote for a Democratic presidential candidate, he or she would use the mass media to reinforce that predilection. Mass media, according to the authors, tended to reinforce political choices rather than create political choices, because people exercised what the researchers called "selective exposure" and "selective attention." What people tended to do when they read newspapers or listened to the radio was to pay more attention to information which reinforced their preconceived political ideas and dismissed that information which contradicted those ideas.

Where did these preconceived ideas come from? Political attitudes and voting patterns were found to be heavily determined by community, family, and group affiliations. This was a time when affiliation with a labor union, for example, would probably result in an individual's voting for a Democratic candidate. Groups transmitted political beliefs, held the allegiance of their membership, and acted as a buffer against the direct impact of the media.

The most important insight to emerge from this early research was that when the respondents were asked to report on their recent exposure to campaign communication of all kinds, "political discussions" were mentioned more frequently than exposure to radio or print. This led to the concept of the "opinion leader" and to a new hypothesis: "the two-step flow hypothesis." This hypothesis presumes that information flows from the mass media and is absorbed by opinion leaders, who, in turn, transmit the information to the audience—a two-step flow of communication. Opinion leaders were found to be distributed throughout the social structure and were not necessarily formal leaders. Each stratum of society seemed to have its own opinion leaders. Most important, opinion leaders were more fully exposed to the mass media campaign than were nonleaders. Thus, the opinion leaders were mediators, or intervening variables, between the mass media and other people in their group.

From this point of view, the threat to the democratic process posed by the mass media seems to be minimized. Human beings are not simply "injected" with a message and do not uniformly respond to the messages they receive. From the point of view of American democratic ideology, this is good news indeed. It appeared as though the very existence of opinion leaders insured the free flow of ideas. Following the initial findings, research in the mass media continued in the direction of comparing media effects with patterns of personal influence. The research moved away from interest in opinion leaders and voting behavior to patterns of influence in a number of decision-making areas—from choosing to get a new haircut to buying furniture or applying for a job. In general, this research found that personal contacts had the greater influence on decision making, with the mass media playing only a contributory role.[4]

While the two-step flow hypothesis was receiving support from sociologists during the 1950s and 1960s, the psychologists were looking at media effects from the point of view of individual differences. Joseph Klapper's (1960) influential summary of survey and social psychological research on media effects proposed a "reinforcement theory," which added a psychological dimension to the two-step flow theory.[5] Klapper suggested that people will avoid exposure to media messages that conflict with their predispositions and will selectively perceive other messages in order to reinforce their predispositions. From this point of view, psychological mechanisms are the intervening variable between the media message and the audience response. Thus, media messages necessarily have differential effects based on differential personality characteristics. The individual is protected in two ways from direct manipulation by the media. On the one hand, media messages are received indirectly through opinion leaders and group affiliations; on the other hand, psychological predispositions will select only those messages which are congenial.

### Recent Research Trends

Taken together, the two-step flow hypothesis and the reinforcement theory constituted the generally received wisdom of the field throughout the 1960s: the media merely reinforce existing opinions and attitudes or activate predispositions; or, more to the point, they have only "minimal effects." It would, however, be incorrect to say that everyone who thought about the media held so sanguine a view of their effects. C. Wright Mills, in 1956, spoke of the media as creating a "sort of psychological illiteracy" through "violent banalization" and stereotyping. Mills stated, "No one really knows all the functions of the mass media, for in their entirety these functions are probably so pervasive and so subtle that they cannot be caught by the means of social research now available."[6]

Of course, the findings of the early researchers were limited to the effects produced by newspapers and radio. Television had not yet become an affordable commodity. By the middle 1960s it became evident that television had revolutionized the mass media. Today there are television sets in 96 percent of American homes, which is a higher percentage of homes than those with indoor plumbing. On the average, during winter months, the television set is on six hours a day. Television serves up healthy portions of political programming, including news, documentaries, political talk shows, interviews, and extensive coverage of political campaigns. Most entertainment programs also contain subtle and not-so-subtle political messages. Candidates and interest groups buy time on television to promote their causes. The power of pictures makes the messages received more powerful and often more believable. Television changed the media landscape. Combined with other social and political factors, it enhanced the ability of the media to influence political attitudes. Television would become, as Daniel Schorr has observed, not merely the witness to a contest but also the arena for a contest, and perhaps the arbiter.[7]

Research on the effects of the media conducted in the early 1970s recognized the role of television. Additionally, the research began with the presumption that previous studies had made a mistake in narrowly defining effects as changes in attitudes, opinions, or voting behavior after exposure to some message. It was thought possible that attitudes, opinions, and predispositions might be conditioned over years of exposure to the media and without recognition by the individual.

Modern research has also considered the role of the media in "setting the agenda."[8] Whether information received through the mass media changes attitudes or merely reinforces preexisting beliefs might be less important than the role the media play in determining what people will think about. Existing attitudes about the Soviet Union, for example, could be reinforced or remain dormant, depending on the significance that the media chooses to give to various Soviet foreign policy actions.

The recognition of the agenda-setting elements of the media has its roots in Walter Lippmann's book, *Public Opinion,* which was published in 1922. In his opening chapter, "The World Outside and the Pictures in Our Heads," Lippmann pointed out that political responses are reactions to the pictures we have of the real world and that such pictures are selected and arranged by the media.[9] It might be said that current research on agenda setting is an attempt to verify Lippmann's hypothesis empirically.

Maxwell McCombs and his colleagues take the position that research that found the media to have minimal effects is valid only if you define effects as a change in attitude, opinion, or behavior. If, on the other hand, effect is looked upon in terms of changes in attention, awareness, and information, a different picture emerges, in which the effect of media is far from minimal. The media may not be able to change an attitude or an opinion, but they can effect *cognition.* McCombs and Shaw assert:

> People do learn from mass communication. Not only do they learn factual information about public affairs and what is happening in the world, they also learn how much importance to attach to an issue or topic from the emphasis placed on it by the mass media. Considerable evidence has accumulated that editors and broadcasters play an important part in shaping our social reality as

they go about their day-to-day task of choosing and displaying news. In reports both prior to and during political campaigns, the news media to a considerable degree determine the important issues. In other words, the media set the "agenda" for the campaign. This impact of the mass media—the ability to effect cognitive change among individuals, to structure their thinking—has been labeled the *agenda-setting function of mass communication.* Here may lie the most important effect of mass communication, its ability to mentally order and organize our world for us. In short, the mass media may not be successful in telling us what to think but they are stunningly successful in telling us what to think about.[10]

In this view, media have the ability to set the public agenda and to influence the relative importance (salience) of any issue in the public mind. Political responses are made to political reality as the individual understands it. The agenda-setting role of the media is the process by which the media define important issues around which the individual can formulate an opinion. Inevitably, news is edited reality, since news directors and editors select which events or issues are to be passed on to the public. The amount of emphasis given to a political event or issue will function to construct the individual's concept of what is important. Variations in headline size, placement, and length are cues to the newspaper reader. Whether or not an item is a television lead-off signals its importance to the viewer. Regular and extended coverage implies significance. Instead of focusing on attitudes for or against some political issue, the agenda-setting research focuses on the knowledge or belief *about* political issues.

Besides the media's determining what the public thinks is important, the particular way in which topics, events, issues, or persons are presented will have an effect on our image of the attributes to be attached to them. One has only to remember the coverage of Iran during the hostage crisis to realize that we received more than straight information. We received an image of Khomeini as a fixated religious fanatic and an image of a people who acted out of blind emotion. These secondary messages are very powerful and point directly to the media's ability to confer status, to create a stereotype, and to construct an image.

While recognizing the variety of governmental bodies, interest groups, lobbyists, and political leaders who also contribute to the process of political agenda building, it is clear that the media have come to be a major force in focusing public opinion and creating issue priorities. The power of the media to impose their agenda has been enhanced by the dissolution of organizations and groups which had the ability to offer alternative agenda. Trade unions, civic organizations, and political parties have lost participants and have difficulty getting their agenda before the public. At one time, these organizations could not only create items which often got incorporated into the national agenda but could also mobilize strong constituencies ready to support the agenda. There were alternative sources of information and alternative worldviews. Without these additional sources of information and without the cohesion and direction that results from party or group allegiances, individuals are adrift in the tumultous and confusing world of politics and turn increasingly to the media to sort out the political puzzle for them.

This realization has led researchers to believe that the importance of the media's agenda, this ability to create political priorities and beliefs, is directly related to the degree to which the audience is dependent on the media for information and direction. Recent research has been based on a new premise about causes and effects. Investigators are now attempting to determine what the audience does *with* the media rather than what the media do *to* the audience. Dubbed the "uses and gratification approach," this new slant emphasizes what needs are being satisfied or what gratifications are being derived through attention to the mass media.[11] DeFleur and Ball-Rokeach have used this approach as a basis for a "dependency theory." As these writers see it, the key variable in understanding when and why media messages alter beliefs, values, opinions, and behavior is the "degree of audience dependence."[12] The media can be used to get information about the world, to get reassurance, to escape through fantasy, or just to fill time. The greater the need, the stronger the dependence, and thus the likelihood of effects.

As the media have taken on more information delivery functions and have increasingly become the sole source of information about the world, the audience has necessarily become more dependent. This would suggest, on the one hand, that those individuals who do not have alternative agenda will be more dependent on the media and more directly influenced.[13] On the other hand, if most, though not all, individuals are, in effect, isolated from direct and reliable sources of information (about, say, events in foreign countries), then dependency may exist on a societal scale.

McCombs and his associates have recognized some of the factors that influence audience use of the media, particularly the "need for orientation." The need for orientation is created when interest in the message is high and there is uncertainty about the meaning of the message. Thus, a message of high interest and uncertainty, like the shootings of President Reagan and Pope John Paul II, or the assassination of Anwar el-Sadat, are bound to increase media use on a large scale. Increased media use, in turn, leads to increased effect of the media. On an individual level, "persons with a high need for orientation about political matters are more susceptible to mass media agenda-setting influence with regard to national political issues...."[14] This need for orientation, combined with the more general need for information, links the agenda-setting approach with the uses and gratifications approach.

The assertion of the media's agenda-setting effects on the public is thus modified by examining the way people use the media. Looking at agenda setting from the point of view of audience needs, interests, and preferences allows us to see what conditions enhance or reduce the agenda-setting role of the media. Thus, the media's impact is enhanced by "exclusive dependence" on the media for information and is reduced by group affiliations and "involvement in interpersonal communication flows."[15] Within this context, it is necessary to recognize that some issues, like inflation, concern everybody, and are experienced personally. Some issues, like recession and unemployment, concern some groups in the society more than others. Some issues are experienced only through the media, such as the Iranian hostage crisis and the loss of American lives in Lebanon.

In experimental studies done in 1980 and 1981, researchers demonstrated the agenda-setting effects of television news programs by manipulating the amount of attention news programs gave to specific issues. They found that people exposed to a steady stream of information about a specific national issue came to see that issue as more important than they had prior to exposure. However, on the issue of inflation, they found that media exposure had no impact. Inflation was ranked as a very important national problem before the experiment and remained in first place after the manipulated media exposure.[16]

As we shall see in Chapter 4, a variety of internal and external pressures on news organizations contribute to the press's agenda and to what becomes "news." However, some events or issues (like inflation) are so compelling that they influence the public's perception independently of the media. Actual conditions ("real-world" events) may determine what media users pay attention to.[17]

Those who would like to influence the media's agenda also have to confront the impact of real-world events. Clearly, President Carter in 1980 would have liked to remove the Iranian situation from the agenda, but he could not. On the other hand, in 1984 the Reagan administration managed to get Attorney General-designate Edwin Meese off the agenda after reports were spread that he had received financial help from people who later got presidential appointments. (Presidential attempts to influence the agenda for news organizations are discussed at length in Chapter 7.)

The same 1980-1981 experiments revealed some evidence that the agenda presented on network news programs determined the way the audience evaluated the President's general performance and, to a lesser degree, his competence. The researchers called this process "priming," in that the media may alter the standards by which people evaluate governmental institutions by focusing their attention on one issue rather than another. Thus, if the media focus on a foreign crisis rather than on a domestic crisis, such as unemployment, the President's success or failure in foreign policy will be more important in evaluating his performance than his success or failure at home.

As Lippmann pointed out over fifty years ago, the "pictures in our heads" are gained from the media. These pictures are not just information; they are our experience of what is real. As we shall see, much of what constitutes the contemporary political process is the competition to define the public's reality among a number of agenda-building institutions, including political officials, lobbies, citizen groups, and, of course, the media.

Although there are unremitting efforts to shape the agenda, the issues and events which finally compose the various news media's agenda are strikingly similar. Once an issue is determined to be part of the agenda by the largest and most influential news organizations, it is accepted by virtually all news outlets in the country. The public is not confronted by a variety of competing "pictures" and agenda, so that we can compare and evaluate the relative merits of each. Rather, we are presented with a fairly uniform and simplistic picture of reality, "a repertory of stereotypes," as Lippmann so aptly called it.

The media's ability to direct or divert attention toward or away from problems, solutions, individuals, and groups has several implications. As we shall see, a politician can safely ignore or postpone action on issues that are not receiving public attention. A candidate not taken seriously by the media may not be taken seriously by anyone else. Inevitably, some politicians will benefit from the media's priorities, while others may be destroyed.

The effect of the media on citizenship is very difficult to measure. In subsequent chapters, we will examine particular effects, such as the impact of campaign coverage on electoral behavior and the impact of congressional coverage on the public's perception of Congress. In general, we shall see that media priorities have a greater impact on the politically naive, who do not have enough prior or independent information to counter the news organizations' definition of the political reality.[18] The individual need not even recall a specific piece of political information to be affected by extended media coverage of some political issues and not others. Much of what is learned from the media is incidental and unconscious. In fact, research indicates that "casual attention" to media messages may be the most favorable condition for manipulation by the media.[19] As we shall see, when voters are committed to a political party or a candidate, they tend to perceive media messages selectively, so that their own views are effectively reinforced. However, voters who have little interest in or commitment to a political point of view may allow their perceptions to be determined by the media messages they receive. People, in general, do not learn much by way of specific information from the media. However, through casual attention to the media, they often come to understand the major political issues and problems of the day, as well as their relative significance.

People differ in the ways they use the media and in the types of media they use. For example, high-income people, who are usually better-educated, use newspapers more than the rest of the population. Although people with low incomes and less education spend more time with the media, particularly television, they extract less political information. The well-informed absorb more political information than do the poorly-informed. Thus, those with little political information are likely to remain politically naive or ignorant.[20] (The implications for democracy of information-rich and information-poor segments of American society are discussed in our conclusion.)

There are, of course, a host of additional factors that must be considered in assessing the media's power to define political reality for the individual. While it may be true that the media remain the only consistent source of political information for most citizens, this does not necessarily mean that the public believes what it hears and reads in the media. Consistent with the difficulty in empirically verifying how the media affect a cross-section of the population is the difficulty of verifying how much people believe the information that they get through the media.

Opinion polls are the most commonly used method to survey American attitudes about the credibility of the mass media. The evidence only suggests certain generalizations. Until recently, most polls tended to indicate that people were more likely to believe news received from television than the news read in newspapers. Throughout the 1960s and 1970s, as television became the premiere medium for news, the percentage who gave television higher marks on credibility continued to increase.[21] Recent studies show a reversal in this trend.[22] Even during these two decades, different groups have had varying perceptions of the credibility of newspapers versus television. Political influentials, those who are more politically involved, have regarded newspapers as a more reliable source of news by a very large margin. This would confirm the general insight of researchers (the dependency and uses and gratification groups) who maintained that different groups within the society use the media for different purposes.

Polls also indicate that journalists are not held in particularly high esteem. Although certain polls register low marks for the media on credibility, the media actually do relatively well in this regard, when you compare them to other groups. A 1981 Gallup poll, for example, found that television reporters and commentators and newspaper reporters enjoyed higher marks on credibility than lawyers, senators, executives, congressmen, local political office-holders, labor union leaders, state political office-holders, and advertising practitioners.[23]

Attitudes about the credibility of the media are, like other attitudes, subject to change. There is evidence that the media's star is falling from its relatively high orbit in the middle 1970s. The National Opinion Research Center reported that the percentage of the population who had "...a great deal of confidence in the press dropped from 29% in 1976 to a new low of 13.7% in 1983."[24] It took the exclusion of the press from covering the American invasion of Grenada to bring the issue of the public's attitude toward the press out of the darkness and onto the national agenda.

If the press assumed that the American public would rise up against the censorship imposed by the Reagan administration, they were roundly disappointed. Rather than rushing to the barricades to support the press's right to know, the public seemed to rejoice at the decision to exclude the media from covering the invasion of Grenada. *Time,* which ran a cover story in its December, 1983 issue on public attitudes toward the news media, concluded that the exclusion of the press seemed a cause for something approaching celebration by the American population. It revealed a deeply felt and, evidently, quickly growing hostility toward the press.[25]

This was not the first demonstration of public hostility toward the press. Former President Richard Nixon found a hidden vein when he sent Vice President Agnew forth to deliver a speech criticizing the media's coverage of his administration. One of the reasons cited for the public hostility toward the press is a generalized fear about the power of the press, including its paramount concern with profit. There is also a growing distaste for some of the ghoulish tactics used by journalists in the name of collecting the news.[26]

It is very difficult to sort out conclusively the picture of public attitudes about the media. In part, the hostility which the public feels results from the fact that people are dependent on a number of giant news corporations to present them with a reliable vision of reality. While they may report that they do not have a great deal of confidence in the media, this does not necessarily mean that their notions of what is politically important are not conditioned by the cumulative effects of reading newspapers and watching and listening to the news.

## MEDIA AND POLITICAL CHANGE

It is our belief that the mass media play a dominant role in defining political reality. Their influence over what people think politically has continued to grow. Ownership of the means of production and dissemination of the news is, in and of itself, a formidable source of power. This control of news collection and dissemination gives the media the additional power to exercise choice over what to report and how to report it, which gives them the ability to influence what people know and believe. Perhaps there is no better tribute to the belief in the power of the media to affect political choice than the vast amount of time, energy, and money which virtually every political actor invests in getting the most favorable coverage.

Of course, the power to disseminate political information is no longer strictly the province of the news media. Those with the resources to buy commercial time on television, radio, or cable TV, or commercial space in newspapers and magazines, also have the ability to influence public opinion. The political and corporate worlds are increasingly utilizing a variety of techniques, from the production of political commercials to the creation of entire television and radio programs, with the hope of using the mass media to influence public political judgment.

The growth in the power of the news media and the vast increase in the use of the mass media for campaigning, organizing, and propagandizing has changed the American political landscape. The media's increased political role results from a combination of factors. Economic conditions and a tendency toward greater centralization in the marketplace hasten the concentration of ownership in the media industry. Government regulatory schemes did nothing to stop giant media corporations from extending their control. Over the years, the networks have adopted a course which has increased their political visibility. In 1963, NBC and CBS expanded their national news coverage to 30 minutes and gave the news a regular prime-time slot. By the early 1970s, network news was appearing on 600 local stations, with an estimated audience of 60 million. It is now rumored that the network news will soon be extended to 60 minutes. The last decade has seen a virtual explosion of the time allotted by local stations to air news programs.

The media's power to influence a candidate's electoral chances has multiplied as voting patterns have changed, partly as a result of the breakdown of political parties and partly as a result of certain basic demographic, social, and economic changes. Many fewer individuals are willing simply to cast their votes for the Democratic or Republican candidate, no matter who he or she might be and what he or she might advocate. The number of voters identifying themselves as Independents rivals the number who are registered Democrats. Ticket splitting has almost become common practice. Some recent research indicates that issues have become more important in determining voting behavior. With traditional loyalties playing a much more limited role in decisions about how to vote, individuals use the information, pictures, advertisements, and commentaries they get from the media to make voting decisions to a much greater degree than they did twenty, or even ten, years ago.

The media have not only been the beneficiaries of some of these economic, social, and political changes, but have also been agents of change as well. As news organizations became more powerful and more politicians saw the media as the place to conduct business, the pace of change accelerated. At times, the media have independently been responsible for political changes. For the most part, however, the ability of the media to create political change is dependent on other factors. In order to understand the nature of the media's power, it is essential to determine the factors that affect this power, and the effects that they produce. It is simply impossible to study the media in a vacuum. Throughout the book, we attempt to provide the historical, political, and social backdrops needed to appreciate the role of the media in different historical periods. Although the power of the media to create a change is dependent on other political forces, it is an exceedingly powerful agent. The astonishing capacity to bring the news to every household and the opportunities for political actors to use the media to further their political ends have dramatically changed the balance of power in America. It is no longer sensible to consider the media as standing outside the political system, observers and guardians of the public trust. Media now constitute the central stage for the political drama. Media corporations and journalists who report the news are political actors in their own right. As the political stage has changed, so have the traditional scripts.

The media have set off a powerful chain reaction, one change producing another. Changes in campaigning for office have led to changes in organizing strategies and finally to changes in the manner in which political leaders govern. The first political arena where the media had an identifiable impact was in the process of selecting candidates. Theodore White's classic treatise on the path to the presidency, The Making of The President (1960), brought attention to the media's growing ability to decide who would be a viable candidate for office. If the media did not consider a candidate viable, according to White, it would be next to impossible to gain the momentum necessary for success. If a political campaign, on the other hand, received serious coverage by the media, the chance of being a significant contender was almost assured.

Those politicians who early recognized this growing power of the media to determine political success, sought means to influence the choices made by news organizations and methods to use the mass media technologies to promote their candidacies. In the 1952 presidential campaign, both candidates hired media advisors to work on getting desirable coverage. Dwight D. Eisenhower broke through a barrier and used televised political advertisements to promote his candidacy.

As the potency of televised politics grew and more candidates turned to television to promote their own candidacy, the power of the party to determine who would receive the nomination was threatened. Candidates now had an independent means to try to create the popular momentum necessary for primary victories and electoral success. In order to use television to its fullest, candidates increasingly turned to media consultants for help. Experienced in using marketing and advertising techniques to sell products through the mass media, these consultants helped package the candidates and teach them the skills needed to take advantage of the mass media. Media consultants became a new group of power brokers, as the seriousness of the candidacy was judged by the media advisor who worked on the campaign. The stage shifted from the streets, factories, and churches to the television studios.

If the skilled use of the media could make the difference in an election, it was only a small step to conclude that the media could also be used as a tool to help an elected official govern and maintain a good public profile. Richard Nixon sought to take advantage of these opportunities by appointing many of the people responsible for designing the election year media campaign to top positions in his administration.

By the middle 1960s, political actors from other branches of the federal government and from state and local governments began to spend more time considering how to use the media effectively. Today, members of Congress devote probably more time and energy to activities that are likely to result in good coverage at home than to the routine activities associated with serving in the House or Senate. Even members of the Supreme Court, which still operates in relative obscurity, have shown signs of sensitivity to the way they are portrayed in the media.

There is an unnoticed beneficiary of the changes in the political system—the corporation. Virtually every aspect of this newly-arranged political scenario, from the reliance on marketing techniques to the dissolution of traditional party coalitions, has provided an opportunity for the corporation to alter its political role. Now that politicians have legitimized the use of the media to wage a political campaign and to serve as an instrument of governance, the corporation is prepared to use the media as a legitimate means for political agitation.

This very brief description of some of the changes produced by the media illustrate how one modification in political practice changed others. Throughout the book, we describe the measures taken by political actors to influence their portraits, the practices of journalists who cover the political world, and the changes in the distribution of power produced by this interaction.

The development of the mass media created the potential for strengthening democratic institutions. The mass media made it possible for all citizens to gain political information, virtually at will. The activities of governing bodies and political officials now take place with the whole world watching. Political leaders have gained the means to communicate with their constituencies with regularity. The media have held forth a promise of expanded political communication and political debate. The media have created the possibility of a better-informed public and leadership accountability. Our task in this book is to distinguish that promise from the reality.

## NOTES

1 C. Wright Mills, *The Power Elite*, Oxford University Press, New York, 1959, p. 311.

2 Michael Schudson, *Discovering the News*, Basic Books, New York, 1978, pp. 164–165.

3 Paul Lazarsfeld, Bernard Berelson, and H. Gaudet, *The People's Choice*, 2d. ed., Columbia University Press, New York, 1948.

4 Elihu Katz and Paul Lazarsfeld, *Personal Influence*, Free Press, New York, 1955.

5 Joseph Klapper, *The Effects of Mass Media*, Free Press, New York, 1960.

6 Mills, *The Power Elite*, p. 311.

7 Daniel Schorr, *Clearing the Air*, Houghton Mifflin, New York, 1977, p. 17. Copyright © 1977 by Danial Schorr. Reprinted by permission of Houghton Mifflin Company.

8 Maxwell McCombs and Donald Shaw, "The Agenda-Setting Function of Mass Media," *Public Opinion*, vol. 36, Summer, 1972, pp. 176–187.

9 Walter Lippmann, *Public Opinion*, Macmillan, New York, 1922.

10 Maxwell McCombs and Donald Shaw, *The Emergence of American Political Issues: The Agenda-Setting Functions of the Press*, West, St. Paul, 1977, p. 5.

11 Elihu Katz, Jay Blumler, and Michael Gurevitch, "Uses of Mass Communication by the Individual," in W.P. Kavison and Frederick T.C. Yu (eds.), *Mass Communication Research*, Praeger, New York, 1974, pp. 11–35.

12 Melvin DeFleur and Sandra Ball-Rokeach, "Toward an Integrated Theory of Mass Media," *Theories of Mass Communication*, McKay, New York, 1975, pp. 255–280.

13 L. Edwards Mullins, "Agenda-Setting and the Young Voter," in *The Emergence of American Political Issues*, Maxwell McCombs and Donald Shaw, 1977.

14 David H. Weaver, "Political Issues and Voter Need for Orientation," and Lee B. Becker, "The Impact of Issue Saliences," in McCombs and Shaw, 1977.

15 Lutz Erbring, Edie Goldenberg, and Arthur H. Miller, "Front-Page News and Real-World Cues: A New Look at Agenda-Setting by the Media," *American Journal of Political Science*, vol. 24, No. 1, February, 1980, p. 29.

16 Shanto Iyengar, Mark D. Peters, and Donald R. Kinder, "Experimental Demonstrations of the 'Not-So-Minimal' Consequences of Television News Programs," *American Political Science Review*, December, 1982, pp. 848–858; also see Michael B. McKuen and Steven L. Coombs, *More Than News: Media Power in Public Affairs*, Sage, Beverly Hills, 1981.

17 Erbring, et al., pp. 16–49.

**18** See S.T. Fiske, D.A. Kenny, and S.E. Taylor, "Structural Models of the Mediation of Salience Effects on Attribution," *Journal of Experimental Social Psychology*, vol. 18, 1982, pp. 105–127; and see S.E. Taylor and S.T. Fiske, "Salience, Attention, and Attribution: Top of the Head Phenomena," in *Advances in Experimental Social Psychology*, vol. 11, L. Berkowits (ed.), Academic Press, New York, 1978.

**19** See J.G. Blumler and D. McQuail, *Television in Politics: Its Uses and Influence*, Faber, New York, 1968.

**20** Doris Graber, *Mass Media and American Politics*, Congressional Quarterly Press, Washington, D.C., 1980, pp. 124–130.

**21** Burns W. Roper, *Public Perceptions of Television and Other Mass Media: A Twenty-Year Review 1959–1978*, April 1, 1979.

**22** See Peter Clarke and Eric Fredin, "Newspapers, Television and Political Reasoning," in Dan Nimmo and William L. Rivers (eds.), *Watching American Politics*, Longman, New York, 1981, pp. 251–256; Lawrence W. Lichty, "Video Versus Print," *The Wilson Quarterly Special Issue*, 1982, pp. 48–57; Ronald Mulder, "Media Credibility," *Journalism Quarterly*, Autumn, 1980, pp. 474–477; Thomas E. Patterson, *The Mass Media Election*, Praeger, New York, 1980, Chap. 6, "The Audience for National News," pp. 57–66; Robert L. Stevenson and Kathryn P. White, "The Cumulative Audience of Network News," *Journalism Quarterly*, Autumn, 1980, pp. 477–81.

**23** *New York Times*, July 30, 1981.

**24** *Time*, December 12, 1983.

**25** *Time*, December 12, 1983.

**26** *Time*, December 12, 1983.

# PART ONE

# POLITICS, BUSINESS, AND THE NEWS

# CHAPTER 2

# A BRIEF HISTORY OF THE DEVELOPMENT AND GROWTH OF THE MASS MEDIA

It is difficult to imagine a time when we were not surrounded by a constant flow of information. We read the newspapers at breakfast, turn on the car radio as we drive to work, and return home at night to be entertained, informed, distracted, or soothed by the ubiquitous television set. On the coffee table may lie *Time, Newsweek,* or *U.S. News and World Report.* Almost everywhere we go—the dentist's office, the beach, an airplane flight, a bus ride—some medium of mass communication is either there or we carry it along. It is hard to imagine that just 150 years ago news of events in Washington came, if at all, days, weeks, or even months after the events themselves.

In order to understand the role of the mass media in contemporary society, it is necessary to examine their development within specific economic and political conditions of American society. The power of the mass media to affect, mold, and shape the political process in modern society must be seen against the backdrop of their own development. We will see the mass media of communication gradually come to change their relationship to the political process. We will see them first largely reporting political events, only occasionally becoming active in public affairs. We will see the gradual emergence of political commentary and analysis. We will observe the politician's growing awareness of the power of the media to bypass traditional political institutions. Finally, we will see the media become *the* political arena in modern American society.

The first hundred years or so of this history is largely the history of individual men, who, through creativity and innovation, often motivated by the desire for personal wealth and power, molded the direction and laid the foundations for the modern communication industry. Reflecting the more general patterns of industrial growth of the nineteenth and early twentieth centuries, the mass media grew, and power tended to become concentrated in large, increasingly faceless, corporate structures. The media of communication once reflected the individual, often eccentric, styles of individual men. By the end of World War II, the mass media were big businesses of enormous wealth and power run increasingly by carbon-copied media professionals. This is not to say that the voice of a David Sarnoff (NBC), or of a William Paley (CBS), could no longer be heard. Rather, such individual styles had to be filtered through the needs and the realities of the modern corporate structure. Where once a William Randolph Hearst could be accused, with some reason, of fomenting the Spanish-American War, now we can only accuse the anonymous media of setting the public agenda.

## THE PRINT MEDIA

### The Penny Press

We can mark the beginning of the mass communication revolution with the first issue of Benjamin Day's *New York Sun*, on September 3, 1833. For the first time a newspaper was sold to an anonymous and heterogeneous audience on the street corners of New York City for the price of one penny. The "penny press," as all of these early mass-marketed newspapers came to be called, signaled a major change in the way the average citizen came to find out about his or her world. The earlier colonial press consisted of small papers and pamphlets directed toward an educated elite and specific economic or political interests. They were distributed largely by subscription, and they cost six cents a copy, which was well beyond the means of the average man or woman. In contrast, the penny press was for anyone who had a penny to spare. The penny press did not appeal to any specific interest, but aimed at the newly-literate and growing middle and working classes. The penny press developed as part of the emerging urban-industrial society of the nineteenth century. As Americans and immigrants flocked to the cities to find work in the new industrial order, traditional sources of information were weakened. Few could know local leaders directly. People from a variety of backgrounds were crowded together, without ties of family, religion, or tradition. In contrast to their rural or European experience, city life was a world of strangers and of the strange and colorful. The penny press offered local news, human interest stories, and sensational reports of crime, disaster, and other lurid happenings. This was information and entertainment of a new sort.

Like the other mass media to come, the mass press emerged and flourished within a context which included technological, economic, political, and demographic developments. The major technological developments included rapid printing and cheap paper. Other advances, like the improvement of home lighting, which encouraged nighttime reading, contributed to the growth of the first mass medium of communication.

Without such developments, the mass circulation newspapers could not have come into being. However, although technology may have made the mass press possible, it did not necessarily make these newspapers desirable. There had to be an audience or a market. Unlike later broadcast media, the mass press needed a new market that had not existed previously. By the time of radio and television, the mass media markets were already established. A historian of American journalism, Frank Luther Mott, suggests four reasons for the growth of the audience for the mass press: population growth, increase in literacy, widened political participation, and reduced price.[1] Michael Schudson goes further, suggesting that the emergence of a market for the mass press is embedded in the political realities of the "Jacksonian era" of democracy, when the ideal and fact of mass democracy replaced the political rule of the landed gentry. The emerging and increasingly prosperous middle class led to the growth of public education and the extension of political and economic rights.[2] This was the age of the skilled craftsmen, the merchants, and the tradesmen, who constituted the audience for the penny press of the 1830s—and the audience grew. After two months, the circulation of Benjamin Day's Sun rose to 2000, after five months to 5000, and after six months to 8000. By 1837, 30,000 copies a day were sold. Rivals to the Sun emerged almost immediately, and the penny press quickly spread to other urban, commercial centers: Philadelphia, Boston, and Baltimore.

In the 1840s, the telegraph came into use and changed the nature of news gathering. The first "wire" story was sent in 1844. In 1846, Polk's presidential message was transmitted by wire. The Associated Press was formed in 1848 as a cooperative enterprise by six New York newspapers. The main objective was to cut the costs of news gathering. They each had equal access to the pooled news, and they sold news to clients in other cities.

The financial success of these early papers depended on their appeal to advertisers. Advertisers assumed that the size of circulation determined the amount of profit they could anticipate. Thus, the battle for the largest share of the market was on. Here is the foundation of the link between advertiser, media professionals, and audience which has come to determine the nature of much of mass-communicated content.

In order to attract the advertiser, the papers needed to increase circulation. They rivaled each other with extras and competed to be the most sensational (Day's staff even went so far as to invent a hoax about "life on the moon"). The "human interest" story became typical. Crime was regularly covered.

Day's most successful competitor was James Gordon Bennett. The *Herald* (1835) was to a large extent a scandal sheet, but it also reported on politics and finance. The *Herald* became the most widely-read American newspaper until the Civil War. Bennett was the forerunner of sensational journalism; his copy was blatantly vulgar, covering the high life and the low life. He created what we now call "society news." The private habits of public officials were grist for his mill. However, he also offered financial reporting with his regular "money articles." Bennett's emphasis on gathering news began to be imitated and adopted by the other papers. As newspapers began to seek out news, reporters became more important and more specialized. The surveillance function of the press was firmly established. Although seeking out news became the norm, the idea of "making news" by promoting or creating events which could be called news did not immediately come into existence. Even the mildest form of making news—the interview—did not appear as a journalistic ploy until the 1860s.

Horace Greeley established the *New York Tribune* in 1841, and Henry Raymond established the *New York Times* in 1851. (It is interesting to note that Bennett's capital investment was $500, in 1835; Greeley's investment was $2000, in 1842, and, by 1851, Raymond's capital investment was $100,000.) New York City came to be the center of the emerging information industry. Around the country, other newspapers printed articles under the designation "From the *Herald*" or "From the *Times*," and everyone knew that meant from New York City.

With the exception of Horace Greeley's *Tribune*, most of these early newspapers were overtly nonpartisan. They reported political events as part of the general flow of events. Politics was news, and the newspapers competed for the "scoop," the inside story, in much the same way as they covered any event.

The Civil War was, by far, the biggest story of the nineteenth century. Up until that time, advertisements appeared on the front page. The coverage of the Civil War permanently changed that practice, as news directly from the battlefield commanded the front page. The newspapers expanded to eight pages. The number of reporters rose, as did circulation and the number of extras. Sunday papers were printed for the first time by the *Times* and the *Tribune*. The newspapers were eyewitnesses to war that people followed closely.

### Yellow Journalism

At the end of the nineteenth century, two more newspapers became important to the information industry: the *World* and the *Journal.* The

*World* had been established in 1859, but was revived by Joseph Pulitzer in 1883. The *Journal* was established in 1882 by Pulitzer's brother, but was bought and revitalized by William Randolph Hearst in 1895. Together, Pulitzer and Hearst ushered in the era referred to as "yellow journalism."* The popularity of the *World* and the *Journal* was based on a combination of sensationalism and crusading. Sensationalism came in the form of illustration, cartoons, larger and darker headlines, the use of color, and the promotion of exclusive features. At the same time, Hearst and Pulitzer repeatedly focused attention on political machines and big-business monopolies. They understood their working and lower middle class audience and knew how to appeal to both their desire for the sensational and their political interests. The established newspapers treated the *World* and the *Journal* with moral horror—much the way they had been treated at their inception.

The *Journal* and the *World* came to be the embodiment of news as entertainment. Even as the *World* exposed the abuses of power in big business and in politics, it sent Nelly Bly around the world in eighty days. Color comic strips appeared first in the *World*. The Sunday *World* included romantic fiction as well as advice columns on fashion and etiquette. While Pulitzer's editorial page championed the cause of the workers and the small businessman, the news emphasized sex, violence, and corruption.

In contrast to Pulitzer, who was an Hungarian immigrant and a self-made man, William Randolph Hearst came to journalism from a background of great wealth. When Hearst was 24 years old (1887), his father gave him control of the San Francisco *Examiner,* which he patterned after Pulitzer's *World*. In 1895, he entered the New York market and bought the *Journal*. With his enormous wealth, he was able to buy a first-rate staff of writers and artists, and the circulation battle between the *World* and the *Journal* ensued. Like Pulitzer, Hearst supported the causes of the working and lower middle classes. He advocated women's suffrage, crusaded against corruption in high places, and pressured for the eight-hour work day. However, he outdid Pulitzer in news which was shocking, vulgar, and often lurid. Circulation rose accordingly.

The journalism of Pulitzer and Hearst was active in public affairs and politics. Although both the *World* and the *Journal* played a role in inflaming the public against Spain in the 1890s, it is Hearst who is credited with the greater journalistic manipulation. In an often-recounted episode, Hearst sent an artist, Frederic Remington, to Cuba to cover the conflict between Spain and Cuba. Remington found only rumor and minor incidents. He wired Hearst that there would be no war. Hearst is supposed to have responded, "Please remain. You furnish the pictures

*Named for the "Yellow Kid," a comic strip printed in color.

and I'll furnish the war."[3] Eventually Hearst came to control twenty-nine newspapers in eighteen major cities.

The excesses of yellow journalism came under attack from leaders in religion, education, law, and government. Faced with the very real possibility of government regulation, the industry began to develop a code of ethics to put some limits on the mass press. Although the code which eventually was established is very vague and abstract, it served to ward off government regulation and did bring the period of yellow journalism to a close for the time being.

The period of yellow journalism also saw a change in the relationship between newspapers and advertisers, largely brought about by Pulitzer. He began the practice of selling advertising space based on actual circulation rates and at fixed prices, which made circulation even more firmly the measure of a newspaper's standing (much as the Nielson Ratings measure a TV network's standing today). Advertisers were now directly buying markets; they bought a readership as well as space. Pulitzer encouraged the use of illustrations and disregarded the old rules which put ads in solid columns of small type. A new graphics industry was on its way.

In this same period, advertising was developing into an independent institution, as an intermediary between the press and the business that advertised. The first modern advertising agency, N.W. Ayers and Son, initiated an "open contract" system in 1875, which made the advertising agent the sole representative of the advertiser for a given period of time. The agent bought space in the newspapers and guided and directed its use. Since the seller and his agent could no longer know potential buyers or what they wanted, techniques to collect facts about the desires and habits of consumers were developed. Market research, at first called "commercial research," came into being, and another media profession was established.[4]

### The *New York Times*

While Pulitzer and Hearst competed, another type of newspaper was developing and beginning to thrive: the *New York Times*. In 1896, Adolph Ochs took over the *Times*, and a new presence in the information industry began to be felt. In contrast to the *Journal* and the *World*, the *Times* was a Republican newspaper. Ochs found his audience by appealing to the wealthier classes. The *Times* expanded its financial reporting, reported real estate transactions, listed out-of-town buyers in the city, produced a weekly financial review, and included more financial advertising than the other newspapers of the day. The *Times* became the "Business Bible."[5]

The *Times* eventually came to set the standards for "good journalism." Ochs used the *World* and the *Journal* as foils in promoting his newspaper as morally superior. To a large extent this stance worked. Although the *Times* did not reach the circulation levels of the *World* and the *Journal*, it became the "respectable" paper. Ochs emphasized objectivity, decency, and fairness, and he produced a newspaper that appealed to the more conservative elements of society. Its "snob appeal" attracted the upwardly mobile and the newly-educated.[6]

Although dull by the standards of yellow journalism, the *Times* did provide the broadest news coverage of the day. News was information and not entertainment. Ochs announced, under his motto "All the news that's fit to print," his newspaper policy:

> It will be my earnest aim that The *New York Times* give the news, all the news, in concise and attractive form, in language that is parliamentary in good society, and give it as early, if not earlier, than it can be learned through any other reliable medium; to give the news impartially, without fear or favor, regardless of any party, sect or interest involved; to make the columns of The *New York Times* a forum for the consideration of all questions of public importance, and to that end to invite intelligent discussion from all shades of opinion (*New York Times,* August 19, 1896).

The prestige and influence of the *Times* grew over the years, making it "must" reading for the better-educated classes and for the politicians. However, in the early years of the twentieth century, the *Times* and the other newspapers had to confront new realities which were to have a profound effect on journalism: public relations agents, the press release, and wartime propaganda.

With the emergence of public relations, news was increasingly filtered to the newspapers through publicity agents representing the interests of their employers. Publicity agents were first used by business to sell its image and its product. It did not take long for politicians and government agencies to see the advantages of this new media professional. Although Congress made some feeble attempts to stop the use of "publicity experts" by federal agencies, government public relations proliferated during and after World War I. Reporters now had ready access to information, but this access was formal and easily manipulated. The idea of the scoop, the inside story, was being replaced by the press release and the press conference.

An even greater threat to Ochs's idea of presenting "news impartially, without fear or favor, regardless of any party, sect or interest involved" was the success of wartime propaganda. The *New York Times* described World War I as the "first press agents' war."[7] In 1918, President Wilson created the Committee on Public Information, which churned out 6000 press releases favorable to the war effort.* The success of this propaganda

---

*The committee also sent 75,000 "Four Minute Men" to deliver short speeches in public places. In a few years, radio would take the place of this human chain of mass communication.

stimulated the growth of more public relations firms in the 1920s. By 1930, Peter Odegard, a political scientist, estimated that 50 percent of all news items originated in the work of press agents.[8] The art of "making news," or what Daniel Boorstin calls the "pseudo-event," became a reality thirty years before he coined the term.[9]

This full-scale effort to control what facts reached the journalist and, eventually, what reached the people led journalists like Walter Lippmann to question the notion of the objectivity of facts.[10] The problem of objectivity emerges when there is doubt that the facts *can* speak for themselves. Reporters of the nineteenth and early twentieth centuries did not worry about objectivity. They saw themselves as trained observers, reporting facts as they developed. Wartime propaganda, press releases, and public relations firms cast this naive approach to facts and objectivity into doubt. One of the responses of journalism was the development of interpretive reporting, or news commentary and analysis.[11] Probably the most important interpretive journalism was that of the syndicated political columnist. Walter Lippmann's "Today and Tomorrow" appeared in the *Herald Tribune* in 1931. By 1937, it was syndicated in 155 papers. The political column began to have as much influence as, if not more than, the editorial.

The end of World War I, which began a period of greater American involvement and control in world affairs, made Washington increasingly the news center. Events of worldwide impact needed to be more than reported; they needed to be explained. The political columnist and, later, the radio commentator became important conduits between the politician and the public. As Frank Luther Mott noted, "The bald and exact fact was no longer enough to make the world understandable."[12]

The skepticism about facts and objectivity was to create a profound change in the nature of journalism. Nowhere was this change more obvious than in the history of the *New York Times*. As we have seen, the *Times* was, at first, clearly conservative. Later it became firmly, even staunchly, centrist, and, in the late 1960s, it was adversarial. The gradual awareness that news *can* be managed, and often *is* managed, by those in power changed the nature of the relationship between the journalist and the world he or she covers. Although most reporting still remains the routine reporting of facts as presented, the atmosphere of doubt finally led even the staid *New York Times* to question the official line and seek out the facts for itself. Harrison Salisbury's reports from North Vietnam, in 1966, exposed government lies. He reported on the bombing of civilians, which the American government had consistently denied. In 1971, the *Times* published the Pentagon Papers, a secret history of the Vietnam war compiled by Robert McNamara of the Pentagon, which again exposed government lies and news management.

It is important to note that the *New York Times* in many ways stands by itself in the information industry. It occupies a unique position in the sociopolitical reality of American society. As David Halberstam puts it, "Only the *Times* had the money and the power and the prestige to stand up to the government, to hire lawyers, to stand equal to the Solicitor General of the United States, to fight if necessary not just City Hall but 1600 Pennsylvania Avenue."[13]

While the *New York Times* is the dominant newspaper in America, it does not completely dominate the news. In the late 1960s, the *Washington Post* had, under the leadership of Ben Bradlee, become an important political force in its own right. During the period of the Watergate scandal, in 1973, the *Post's* investigative reporting set the political agenda across the nation. The *Post's* focus may be narrower than that of the *New York Times*, but it is world-famous, dominates the capital, and is taken seriously in the executive offices of New York. It now rivals the *Times* as an outlet for politicians who want to leak a story.

The *New York Times* and the *Washington Post*, along with the *Wall Street Journal* and the *Los Angeles Times*, dominate the news industry. Although these newspapers are not the largest in circulation or in profits, they are the most prestigious and politically influential newspapers in America. Together, these newspapers set the political agenda; what they say is news *is* news. What appears on the front pages of these newspapers often will be the lead stories on the evening network news. Political and economic elites, rightly or wrongly, perceive these newspapers as major forces with which they must contend. Whether these newspapers support, criticize, or investigate economic and political policies is of crucial significance to the structure of power in American society. As we shall see, major public and private institutions have developed strategies to deal with all the news media, and these prestige newspapers are a major target of their efforts.

## THE BROADCAST MEDIA

### Early Radio

While newspapers continued to develop and change, a new mass medium of communication emerged that would again transform the ways in which the average citizen came to know and understand his or her world—the radio. The evolution of radio was marked by conflicts: huge corporations fought over patent rights; rival transmitters competed on the same frequencies, forcing government regulations; radio fought newspapers for the right to broadcast news; and advertisers fought regulatory agencies. Since television grew out of radio, it shares a common history, financial base, and controls.

Radio has its technological roots in Guglielmo Marconi's telegraph, which he brought to England in 1897 because he thought that the British maritime needs would provide the greatest profits.[14] British Marconi was established, and the wireless was put to use sending messages from ship to shore, and from ship to ship. The wireless was obviously attractive to navies and shipping firms. In 1899, the *New York Herald* invited Marconi to use his wireless to cover the America's Cup Race. Marconi arrived on the scene just after the Spanish-American War, when, like England, the United States had acquired an overseas empire in need of swift communication. In 1899, American Marconi was founded as a subsidiary of the British company.

It was not long before the wireless became popular outside naval and shipping interests. Wireless amateurs, "hams," popped up everywhere, filling the air waves and listening in on shipping and naval signals. It was inevitable that someone would sooner or later see that there was a market here.

The next technological step was the transmission of the human voice, which was accomplished by Reginald Aubrey Fessenden in 1906. In that same year it was discovered that various kinds of crystals could detect radio waves. The "crystal set" could be built by anyone with fairly elementary skills. The market was widening.

The final technological step was taken by Lee de Forest, who invented the *audion* tube, now called the vacuum tube, since replaced by the transistor. Ultimately, the vacuum tube permitted the transmission of the human voice around the world. Radio receivers were improved, refined, and made smaller.

In 1912, radio received considerable public attention when a Marconi operator, David Sarnoff,* picked up signals from the sinking *Titanic*.[15] Supposedly, David Sarnoff decoded messages for three days and nights, recording the names of those who survived. President Taft ordered all other American transmitters to remain silent. Later, Sarnoff moved up into some of the most important positions in American Marconi. While there is some doubt about the actual truth of this story, the *Titanic* disaster did bring radio to the forefront and, incidently, promoted David Sarnoff.[16] It also turned out to be profitable for American Marconi; Congress made it mandatory for all ships with more than fifty passengers to carry and use wireless equipment.

World War I created the need for improved and coordinated radio systems. All patent litigation and restrictions were temporarily suspended. The war brought new cooperative efforts under the control of the

---

*David Sarnoff would become president of RCA and dominate NBC radio and later NBC television.

government. Amateurs were ruled off the air, and the navy took control of all privately-owned installations. The radio was used for coordination, intelligence, and for wartime propaganda. After the armistice, the navy recommended a government-controlled monopoly, but strong private interests prevented such a policy. Instead, General Electric bought up the British shares of American Marconi and gave it a new patriotic name: Radio Corporation of America (RCA). David Sarnoff was appointed commercial manager.[17] It has been estimated that the government retains about 50 percent of the spectrum for government and military use.[18]

For most Americans at the close of World War I, the radio was a hobby. Several amateur transmitters emerged around the country, and the airwaves were largely filled with amateurs talking to each other. One such amateur, Frank Conrad, who worked for Westinghouse, changed the broadcast pattern by transmitting phonograph music from the top of his garage. Enthusiastic listeners asked for scheduled broadcasts. Harry Davis, Conrad's superior, began to see a market in producing receivers based on the vacuum tube models Westinghouse had produced during the war. Westinghouse built a large transmitter in East Pittsburgh to stimulate the sale of home receivers and components. Station KDKA came into existence in 1920 and became the first broadcast station with regularly-scheduled programs.[19] Westinghouse gave birth to the household radio, but programming was largely of secondary concern. The sale of radios was to justify the expense of operating the station.

In 1921 AT&T, United Fruit,* and Westinghouse, each of which owned important patents, formed an alliance (patent pool) with General Electric and formed a joint ownership of RCA: General Electric (30.1%); Westinghouse (20.67%); AT&T (10.3%); United Fruit (4.1%).[20] General Electric and Westinghouse were to make receivers, 60 percent and 40 percent respectively. RCA would market them under its trademark; Western Electric, a subsidiary of AT&T, would produce transmitters. Wire or wireless transmission belonged to AT&T.[21] Under the guidance of David Sarnoff, RCA turned to broadcasting. RCA established stations across the country, still seeing its profits in the sale of receiver sets. Even in these early days, Sarnoff and others saw the future of broadcasting in television.

## Radio Networks

In 1922, AT&T linked stations by telephone wire, creating the basic condition for the modern network. A chain of stations could broadcast

---

*United Fruit used the wireless to coordinate its plantations and banana boats. It had acquired valuable patents.

the same program at the same time, each paying a fee for entrance into the system. AT&T's "toll station," WEAF,* was established. It carried the first commercial announcement, selling a ten-minute spot for fifty dollars. Such direct advertising called forth a major round of criticism; soon most WEAF sponsors used indirect advertising, what we now call "image advertising." They sponsored entertainment programs with no sales message. This "trade-name" publicity took the form of such programs as the Kodak Chorus, the Ipana Troubadors, and the A&P Gypsies.[22]

As broadcasting grew more popular, trouble appeared on the horizon from several sources; the American Society of Composers, Authors, and Publishers began to ask for royalties for the use of ASCAP-controlled material. Performers who had initially volunteered to perform free, for the publicity involved, began to ask for fees. Even more threatening to the new industry, in 1924, the Federal Trade Commission issued a formal charge that AT&T, RCA, General Electric, Westinghouse, and United Fruit had conspired to create a monopoly in broadcasting and in manufacturing radio receivers.[23]

In January, 1926 RCA approved the idea of a new company, The National Broadcasting Company (NBC), to be owned by RCA (50%), General Electric (30%), and Westinghouse (20%). It would lease AT&T wires. The new company bought WEAF from AT&T, and AT&T was out of the broadcast business, but with a steady and growing guaranteed income (almost one million dollars in the first year). In 1927, NBC established two national networks, the Red and the Blue (the Blue eventually became ABC, as a result of an antitrust suit).

The Red and the Blue networks were very different. The Blue adhered to a public service image and, in the beginning, sponsored an array of classical and semiclassical concerts. This was an image espoused by Sarnoff himself, who, although the founder of commercial broadcasting, had always disdained its vulgarity. In fact, he was always more interested in the technology of broadcasting than in its programming. The Red network inherited the WEAF commercial approach. Despite Sarnoff's public stance, the Red network, from the start, was given more publicity and fanfare than the more staid Blue network.[24]

The chaos on the airwaves still existed, and it was limiting the development of business. Finally, at the behest of the industry itself, Congress passed the Radio Act of 1927, which provided for a Federal Radio Commission, later to become the Federal Communication Commission, to license stations. Although the Radio Act was intended to put some controls on the commercial use of radio, it did nothing but side-

---

*WEAF later became WRCA and WNBC. By 1924, WEAF had connected 25 stations on a coast-to-coast hookup.

step the issue. It stated only that the person paying for or furnishing the program must be identified. The Act defined the airwaves as public, belonging to the people. Thus, no one "owned" a broadcast channel; the broadcaster merely licensed the use of it temporarily. The commission was explicitly forbidden to act as censor. The FRC was forbidden to license any firm judged guilty of monopoly. Radio broadcasting was to be regulated to best serve the "public interest, convenience, or necessity."

At this point, the broadcast industry's basic structure had been laid down:

- Government regulations are the key to stability
- Stations operate on temporary licenses
- The regulatory agency bases its decision on public interest, convenience, or necessity
- Networks of stations are linked nationwide by cables of telephone wires
- Networks are supported by advertising.

In 1928, a small, independent network, CBS, was bought by William Paley, a 27-year-old heir to a cigar fortune. Columbia Broadcasting System was only one station with affiliates. It had no parent company, like RCA, which produced receivers and equipment. It had only air time to sell. Its entire survival depended on advertising dollars. Paley had to sell sponsors on the potency of radio advertising. In the 1930s, most advertising dollars were spent on print advertising, magazines, and newspapers; he needed to prove that products advertised on radio sold better. To this end, he hired Professor Robert Elder of the Massachusetts Institute of Technology, who provided what appeared to be proof that people bought products advertised on the radio. Paley's director of sales promotion and Professor Elder began to research the market directly, breaking it down in terms of age, sex, and buying power. Although the techniques were rather primitive, the results were slickly packaged and presented to the would-be sponsor.

Faced with an emerging rival, NBC followed suit, competing in selling markets to the sponsor. At this stage, advertising and entertainment were intertwined. Radio stars became identified with a product: "This is Bob 'Pepsodent' Hope." Repetition and catchy jingles became the norm. Here radio had an advantage over print advertising. As radio increasingly became commercial, each network developed techniques to prove that it had the largest market. Each network attempted to prove its "rating" supremacy. Although the techniques were very unsystematic (for example, random phone calls), ratings became an obsession.

NBC's programs were dominated by comedians who had gained popularity in vaudeville, like Jack Benny, Ed Wynn, Bob Hope, Eddie

Cantor, Fred Allen, Burns and Allen, and the Marx Brothers.[25] CBS had the then unknown Bing Crosby and Kate Smith. Paley established the Columbian Artist Bureau to find and develop talent. In a bid for respectability, CBS aired the New York Philharmonic Concerts during unsponsored air time on Sunday afternoons.

NBC had other problems at this time. In 1930, the Department of Justice sued RCA, GE, Westinghouse, and AT&T. It demanded the end of interlocking ownership and directorates and the end of the 1919–1921 patent agreements. AT&T got out relatively quickly, withdrawing from the patent agreements which were expiring anyway. In order to avoid trial, GE and Westinghouse withdrew from RCA and NBC boards. NBC became a wholly-owned subsidiary of RCA. RCA, which had been a sales agent for GE and Westinghouse, was now a self-sufficient entity.[26]

It was not long before politicians realized radio's potential for reaching the public directly. President Franklin Delano Roosevelt was the first President to use radio to go directly to the people at a time of nationwide crisis. During the Depression, his "fireside chats" were used to inform and reassure the American people that the nation would indeed recover. They were immensely popular, and the networks were delighted. Roosevelt's use of the radio showed how powerful and effective it could be. At first, the President's use of the radio seemed non-partisan. However, it was soon apparent that radio could be used by a politician for partisan ends. When Roosevelt gave his 1936 State of the Union message, it was carried by CBS. Since it was an election year, it does not surprise us today that the speech had a decided partisan tone. Republicans demanded equal time, but CBS's response was that it was an official message from the President and not a message from a political party. The President's privileged relationship and access to the media were established.[27]

Profits for the networks soared throughout the Depression. In 1937, NBC grossed 38 million dollars in time sales, owned and operated fifteen radio stations, and had 135 affiliates. CBS grossed 37 million dollars, owned and operated nine stations, and had 106 affiliates. Together, they accounted for over half the time sales in broadcasting.[28]

During this period, Sarnoff concentrated on developing television. His plan was to use the profits from radio to subsidize the new technology. Sarnoff pressed the FCC to adopt industrywide standards in order to avoid repeating the early chaos of radio broadcasting. This pattern of dependency on the government to regulate the emerging industry set the pattern of cooperation between the government and the networks. Of course, Sarnoff was trying to get regulations which would assure RCA a prominent position in a market that was considered to have a limited number of channels.

**Radio Journalism**

While Sarnoff focused on television, Paley concentrated on competing with NBC. Paley was never interested in technology. He was the salesman and the programmer. CBS and Paley entered into the news business as a means to compete with NBC, which had the corner on the entertainment market. News was cheap to broadcast, it brought an aura of class, and, in the beginning, Paley had a lot of unsponsored air time to fill. Paley turned for help to Ed Klauber, trained in print journalism at the *New York Times*.[29] Klauber set the first standards for broadcast journalism, standards which were often above those of many newspapers of the day.[30]

CBS began to use much of its unsponsored time to cover the upheavals in the international scene. CBS built a news service which brought into every home the voices of such people as Edward R. Murrow, Eric Severeid, and H.V. Kaltenborn. CBS also produced dramas which touched on issues in the world scene. The most famous was Orson Welles' dramatization of *War of the Worlds,* by H.G. Wells, which created panic in many parts of the country. With the threat of a real war in the air, the idea of an alien invasion was, for many, far too real.

From the beginning of radio, news was broadcast to fulfill the license obligation of public service, to fill unsponsored time, or to gain prestige. Selling time to advertisers and the rules of the marketplace always took precedence; in the conflict between merchandising and public interest, public interest rarely won. However, the events of the 1930s—the Depression, the upheavals in Europe, and the threat of another world war—tipped the usual balance, and radio took on a major news function. CBS had the competitive advantage of already-established commentators and foreign correspondents.

In 1937, CBS sent Edward R. Murrow to London, where he created a staff which aggressively covered events leading up to America's entry into the war. When Hitler marched into Vienna in 1938, CBS correspondents were in place. CBS introduced its unprecedented "World News Roundup" with shortwave pickups around Europe. Eventually, Americans heard Mussolini, Hitler, and Chamberlain on CBS. As the war approached, Americans listened to two CBS foreign correspondents: William Shirer from Berlin and Edward R. Murrow from London.

Wartime broadcasting put radio into the news business. Edward R. Murrow's live broadcast from London symbolized radio's new role. Radio lent itself to commentary; print journalism was for the record. Murrow helped move America out of its post-Depression isolationism. He openly advocated an American commitment to the British. Many of his messages were nothing less than a call to arms. Murrow was not limited by a notion of objectivity or of balance in presentation. Part of this was due to the uniqueness of the radio coverage itself—a live broadcast from one man standing on the roof of the British Broadcasting Corporation (BBC) at 3:30 in the morning. On the other hand, the events Murrow covered were so big, so important, that the ideal of a balanced picture seemed irrelevant. For most Americans, this was a moral war; patriotism was at a peak, and the legitimacy of the Allied position was unquestioned. This was not a Vietnam. Murrow returned to America after the war a media hero and turned his attention to domestic affairs.

Other things were happening to the industry at this time. At the 1939 World's Fair in New York City, RCA demonstrated its television. However, World War II virtually ended television transmission when the nation's economy focused on the war effort. As with radio during World War I, television began to be refined and perfected during World War II. In 1941, the FCC ruled that RCA must divest itself of one of its networks. RCA sued to block the ruling but lost. In 1943, NBC's Blue network was sold, and it became ABC.[31] Naturally, Sarnoff sold off his weaker network. Ironically, the Blue network had been Sarnoff's public service network, which RCA could afford to support occasionally at a loss. By making it an independent network, ABC eventually had to become as commercial as NBC and CBS.

Meanwhile, Paley at CBS was gradually shifting his attention to entertainment, in preparation for television. Paley saw television as *the* entertainment medium. He believed that news would take a back seat, since it was, at the time, essentially nonvisual. In Paley's view, advertisers would flock to entertainment programming, and news would be reduced to merely a non-profit-making service. In contrast, Sarnoff concentrated his attention on the technology of television broadcasting; he never even met his biggest star, Jack Benny. Paley, on the other hand, loved the entertainment side of the business and moved into it as soon as he could. Sarnoff resented the big salaries that entertainers commanded. Paley consistently outbid NBC and eventually bought away even Jack Benny. Paley's gradual accumulation of stars was to serve him well when television emerged after World War II.

## EARLY TELEVISION

The years after World War II quickly accelerated the development of television. By 1948, there were about seventy stations and several million sets. Television technology had become quite sophisticated before the mass production of sets. There was no period like the "crystal set" period of early radio. Television did not have to work out controls; FCC regulations covering radio were simply expanded to cover television. The network idea was already in existence, and the public was accustomed to commercials. Radio could not continue with its format of drama, soap operas, westerns, variety shows, and amateur nights. The public turned quickly to television for such entertainment. Radio moved to the automobile, bedroom, kitchen, and beach. Now radio caters to an audience during times when television is inappropriate. Television did not destroy radio (there are now more than five radios per household), but it certainly changed it.

The transition from radio to television momentarily left in limbo the question of the place of news and commentary in this new, highly popular, and commercially successful medium. Rising audience statistics brought new sponsors to television. The notion of unsponsored time was gradually becoming a thing of the past. Audiences wanted entertainment, and advertisers wanted audiences. Programming was becoming increasingly expensive, and the relationship between the sponsor and the network began to change.

Advertising agencies had dominated network programming in both radio and television until the 1950s. In the days of radio, networks did not produce shows—the advertising agencies did. In the early days of television, one company sponsored a show completely, paying all costs. Networks gradually took control of their own programming and time schedules. As production costs rose, sponsors began to share the costs by alternating sponsorship.[32] Eventually sponsors became "participants," buying thirty- to sixty-second spots to go with a network production. The networks, or packaging agencies, took all the financial risks for their productions. When networks took over programming, the programming became even more commercial. Since the cost of an advertising spot was determined by the size of the audience, the higher the rating, the higher the cost to the advertiser. Rating competition became the name of the game. CBS captured the rating lead largely on the strength of the comedians raided from NBC. NBC had discovered Milton Berle, Sid Caesar, and Imogene Coca. It appeared that news would be swept away by the force of the commercially successful entertainment side of the broadcasting business.

There were other factors which led to a narrowing of the news function of broadcasting. The government was beginning to sense the power of broadcasting, and the fear of more extensive regulation was in the air. Broadcasters became wary of doing anything to offend the government. The combined pressures of government and Madison Avenue were pushing the networks away from an independent news function.

There were also internal pressures to limit the autonomy of news commentary. Television meant that the message would eventually reach more people—people who might never have been newspaper readers. Broadcasters sensed the power of visual coverage and the emotional impact of the immediacy of the picture. The platform being so big, personal opinions seemed almost dangerous. As Halberstam puts it:

> There is an unwritten law of American journalism that states that the greater and more powerful the platform, the more carefully it must be used and the more closely it must adhere to the norms of American society, particularly the norms of the American government; the law says it is better to be a little wrong and a little late than to be too right too quickly.[33]

## The Cold War

Perhaps the most powerful early constraint on television news came from the political atmosphere after World War II. The ideological hostility between the United States and the Soviet Union created a new political drift in Washington. When the Soviet Union developed the atomic bomb, suspicion turned to a fear bordering on paranoia. This fear created an increasingly conservative atmosphere that made opinion critical of the American government appear to be "left-wing" and threatening to our way of life. The "Cold War," as this era has come to be called, was felt by the networks. William Shirer's criticism of President Truman's loyalty program for government employees lost him his sponsor. Shirer was moved to a less popular time period, and he finally resigned. Any commentators suspected of "left-wing" leanings gradually disappeared from the airwaves. As political pressure on the networks began to grow, CBS, which had been considered the most liberal, was particularly sensitive and acquiesced more readily than the other networks.[34] To a large extent, this pressure was successful because of the networks' fear of investigation and government regulation.

Anticommunist pressure came in two forms: one from self-appointed vigilantes who were intent on flushing out communists in the networks, the other directly from Washington in the person of Senator Joseph McCarthy.

Vigilante organizations took many forms. One of the most influential was created by three ex-FBI men. They started a weekly publication, *Counter Attack: The Newsletter of Facts on Communism,* which offered to investigate any company for "suspicious" individuals. *Counter Attack* compiled a list of "communists" in broadcasting, *Red Channels: The Report of Communist Influence in Radio and Television,* which contained the names of 151 performers and writers in broadcasting and film. CBS was the most heavily hit and responded with a self-investigation which included asking all of its employees to answer the following questions:

**1** Are you now, or have you ever been, a member of the communist party, U.S.A., or any communist organization?

**2** Are you now, or have you ever been, a member of a fascist organization?

**3** Are you now, or have you ever been, a member of any organization, association, movement, group or combination of persons which advocated the overthrow of our constitutional form of government?[35]

These were, in fact, the very questions that Joseph McCarthy was asking in Washington.

As a public figure, McCarthy was news, and anything he said, even if it was known to be false or contradictory, was dutifully reported. As long as he was quoted correctly, the reporter was "objective." McCarthy made charges, and the press dutifully reported them. Careers and lives were destroyed. McCarthy became more extreme, vituperative, and, some would say, insane. Only very slowly did the media begin to be critical of McCarthy. Edward R. Murrow, who was nationally known and respected, was the first broadcast journalist to break the grip of fear and challenge McCarthy's activities.

After a brief stint as a news executive, Murrow had returned to radio broadcasting in 1947. He was initially wary of television, seeing it as mainly a vehicle for entertainment and disliking the teamwork required for television production. Radio broadcasters, in general, were suspicious of television, and it was not until Murrow started to appear on television that it became respectable. Murrow had teamed up with producer Fred Friendly on a radio program called *Hear It Now*. In November of 1951, they took it to television as *See It Now*. Because of his role during the war, Murrow occupied a unique position with regard to the anticommunist pressure emanating from Washington. In the beginning, even McCarthy wouldn't dare accuse Murrow of "communist sympathies." Nonetheless, Murrow was cautious in his new role as a television commentator, balancing his hard-hitting political coverage with a show called *Person to Person*, where he did informal interviews with celebrities.

Murrow was also cautious, or perhaps cunning, in approaching his confrontation with McCarthy. The first confrontation was indirect, in the form of a program entitled "The Case Against Milo Radulovich, AO58939," aired on October 20, 1953. Radulovich had been dismissed from the Air Force because of the suspected political sympathies of his family. Murrow questioned the assumption of "guilt by association," one of McCarthy's favorite ploys. Murrow took on McCarthy directly on March 9, 1954. In both cases, CBS and Paley were ambivalent. Although they did not interfere, they refused to give advertising support, and Murrow and Friendly themselves had to pay the cost of the ad in the *New York Times*. It did not carry the CBS symbol, the eye, and was simply signed Ed Murrow and Fred Friendly, as if it were their sole responsibility.[36]

The 1954 program created a sensation. Murrow exposed McCarthy by letting McCarthy speak for himself. McCarthy appeared on television to reply to Murrow and even further weakened his image. The Murrow program and the McCarthy reply were themselves news, and they set the stage for the televised Army-McCarthy hearings.

ABC broadcast the hearings initially as a way to fill up its daytime schedule. At the time, ABC was so weak that it had very little to lose. Surprisingly, the Army-McCarthy hearings boosted ABC's ratings. Starting in April of 1954, the nation had the opportunity to watch McCarthy close-up, and they were shocked. Coverage of the McCarthy hearings demonstrated the devastating power of broadcast journalism. By the end of 1954, the Senate voted 67 to 22 to censure McCarthy. Murrow was at this point at the height of his fame and had won more awards than any other broadcaster. Nonetheless, news and documentaries were being pushed out of prime time as game shows, the entertainment "spectacular," and the westerns took center stage.

CBS willingly accepted the praise that Murrow and See It Now brought, but there was an inherent contradiction between CBS's commercial success and Murrow. Paley moved to phase Murrow out. Murrow's program was expensive to produce, and, given its low ratings, it was hard to find sponsors willing to invest simply for the prestige that might result from being associated with the broadcast. Paley continued to be convinced that news programming, in general, was a drain on profits. Murrow's prestige made him almost independent of Paley's influence and pressure. Every time Murrow took on a controversial political issue, the shadow of government regulation loomed in Paley's mind. Murrow did not help his position. He took on deliberately provocative subjects, as in his two programs on the hazards of smoking. Murrow attacked the cigarette industry when cigarette advertising was one of the mainstays of network broadcasting. From the point of view of the industry, it was a blatant show of contempt for television's commercial interests.

Paley scheduled his very successful The $64,000 Question just prior to See It Now. That decision meant the end of a regularly broadcast See It Now. Since the cost of advertising is based on audience size, and The $64,000 Question drew the audience, the cost for advertising on See It Now would go up. It would cost a lot more now for the prestige of sponsoring See It Now. The escapist programming was making Murrow obsolete. Paley dropped See It Now in 1958.

During the 1950s, quiz shows were the big moneymakers. Prizes of money and/or consumer goods (cars, refrigerators, television sets, etc.) reflected the affluence and consumerism of the 1950s. Rumors began to circulate late in the decade that the quiz programs were "fixed." By 1959, the networks were faced with a major scandal and with a grand jury investigation. Government regulation was in the air again. The scandals forced the television industry to shore up its public image, which it did by expanding its public relations departments and by giving more attention to its news programming.

## Television News

From 1947 to 1956, NBC had been satisfied with John Cameron Swayze's *Camel News Caravan*, which amounted to fifteen minutes of newsreels and headlines, presented five times a week. CBS had fifteen minutes of *News with Douglas Edwards*, sponsored by Oldsmobile. Most foreign news came in headline form. Swayze used to end his program with "Now let's go hopscotching around the world for headlines."

Throughout the 1950s, the evening news programs were very limited. The use of the camera actually curtailed what was presented on the news. Television journalism could cover only places where the camera and lights could be set up. Commentary and news analysis, which had been so central to radio broadcasting, were shunted aside as nonvisual. Television relied on planned events, such as press conferences and speeches. Those who were in a position to plan such events had considerable control over news content.[37]

Television journalism was particularly weak on foreign news in these early days. To a large extent, Secretary of State John Foster Dulles controlled the headlines and the television coverage of foreign affairs in the 1950s. Dulles even had his own television and radio aide, who arranged "departure statements," "arrival statements," press conferences, and speeches. Dulles was a constant broadcaster.[38] Since cameras were not at the trouble spots in foreign countries, world events were seen through Dulles's eyes.[39]

Meanwhile, television coverage of domestic affairs began to change and enlarge. In 1956, Chet Huntley and David Brinkley covered the Democratic convention, where they attracted the attention of viewers and NBC executives. *Huntley-Brinkley Report* replaced Swayze that same year. For a while Huntley and Brinkley went unsponsored. In 1958, Texaco Oil took on the report. At CBS, news was still thought of as a drain on profits. News president Fred Friendly had to fight for time. Huntley and Brinkley of NBC were far ahead in the ratings.

A political drama that captured the attention of Americans occurred in 1960: the Great Debates between John F. Kennedy and Richard M. Nixon. All three networks cleared their schedules for the first televised presidential debates. The debates were unsponsored and attracted an estimated audience of sixty to seventy-five million viewers.[40]

Whether the debates lost Nixon the election or won it for Kennedy is an academic concern.* The real winner was television itself. Politics was moving into television, and a whole new set of media experts were needed for the new media politician. That year, each party bought more time than ever before for spots on television and radio (Republicans spent $7,558,809; Democrats spent $6,204,986).[41] Between 1960 and 1964, political candidates increased the amount of money spent on television advertisements by 300 percent, an increase that has not been matched since. Even though social scientists, at the time, continued to believe that television campaigning was only one factor among many, politicians began to see television as a major campaign vehicle.

Television began to move into politics with expanded news coverage of political events. In 1960, all three networks focused on the political conventions, but the strength of the Huntley and Brinkley team carried the ratings. In 1964, they repeated their performance. Walter Cronkite, of CBS, remained in second place until 1968.

Throughout the 1960s, competition between the networks' news programs continued in earnest. In 1963, the evening news was expanded to 30 minutes. News coverage was becoming profitable. By 1968, NBC news generated $100,000 in advertising sales each night. Its annual gross was almost 30 million dollars, the second largest of all NBC programs, including entertainment.

At the same time, television technology was improving news coverage. The smaller camera, the detached recorder, the wireless microphone, and the videotape recorder put television almost anywhere it wanted to go. President Kennedy permitted his press conferences to be telecast live. The networks began to focus on the presidency as a major news event; the presidency would come to be the "single most important story that the networks follow on a continuing basis."[42]

The 1960s also witnessed the Civil Rights Movement, and television coverage became an effective tool to bring its cause to national and world attention. The Civil Rights Movement, it could be said, was the first real issue covered by network journalism. Southern race problems, as audiovisual phenomena, were ideally suited to television. Racial practices in the South were so out of step with the purported values of the rest of American society that television journalists could afford to be heroes for a good cause. Television news and documentaries became a political force allowing access to people who were denied traditional means of being heard. By covering the early Civil Rights Movement, television journalism altered the public agenda. The coverage of the Civil Rights Movement gave television journalism prestige and legitimacy as journalism.

---

*It is interesting to note that those who heard the debates on radio thought Nixon had won, while those who saw them on television thought Kennedy had won.

In the 1960s, broadcast journalism became the new arena for social protest. Social protest movements in the past had had their own "underground" newspapers circulating, sometimes in large numbers, but, more often than not, only to the like-minded. The protests in the 1960s among blacks, students, and women had the network news, which reached millions. These movements came to rely on the broadcast media and, in turn, had to conform to the media's standards of newsworthiness in order to matter. Martin Luther King's march on Washington in 1963 was a television spectacular. King's "I have a dream" speech reached millions. The march was an event, and there was no question that it had to be covered.

During the 1960s, the war in Vietnam was *the* event, and television took the audience to that war. As protest against the war rose, the nation and the world witnessed demonstrations, marches, riots, and acts of government repression. The Students for a Democratic Society (SDS) sponsored a march on Washington in April of 1965 that made student antiwar protests news. At first, the coverage of the antiwar protests was negative, emphasizing the deviant aspects of the student movement: obscene language, draft card burnings, Viet Cong flag-carrying, American flag-burning, and many protestors' scruffy, bearded appearance. As the war lost its legitimacy in the eyes of many, antiwar activism became more understandable, and the media began to distinguish between the "respectable" opposition and "extremist," even "dangerous," radical student groups.* Although the implications of this distinction are far-reaching, the key issue, for our purposes, is that television became an important resource for groups denied traditional means to gain public attention.

The fact that wide-scale social protest attracted television, and the fact that politicians began to use television for political communication, politicized television news. Television's expanded news delivery function gave rise to new strategies to capture the attention of television news. Politicians saw the importance and power of television in campaigning and in governing, and protest groups developed techniques to make themselves "newsworthy." The expanded role of television in the 1960s signaled a change in modern politics, and the role of television in setting the public agenda became a fact of political life in the media age.

## MEDIA MONOPOLIES

Like other industries in the United States, the media have grown, and power has been increasingly concentrated in the hands of a few giant

---

*See Todd Gitlin, *The Whole World Is Watching,* University of California Press, Berkeley, 1980.

organizations. Such concentration poses a possible threat to a fundamental principle of a democratic society: access to a diversity of opinions and information. There are several ways that this concentration has taken place. The most important concentration is in types of monopoly ownership. These include:

**1** *Multiple Ownership of Several Media of the Same Type:* the ownership of several newspapers, or several radio stations, or several television stations.

**2** *Media Conglomerates:* cross-media ownership or ownership of a combination of media, such as owning a newspaper and a television station or a newspaper and a radio station.

**3** *Cross Industry Conglomerates:* ownership of media and other industries, or enterprises, unrelated to communications.

In each case, the number of persons or organizations who control the flow of information is reduced. Other kinds of concentration come from *joint operating agreements* and *interlocking directorates.* Joint operating agreements occur when two or more newspapers agree to do their printing in one plant and use one business office for advertising sales and circulation. By 1980, newspapers in twenty-four cities had such arrangements.[43] Interlocking directorates exist when a top executive of one corporation sits on the board of another corporation.

When we look at the development of the newspaper industry, we can observe a trend toward consolidation and concentration.[44] As newspapers became big business, they began to subordinate individual style to the rules of the corporation and the Wall Street investor. Reflecting the pattern in American business in general, newspapers, in the late nineteenth century, developed into chains, as the big newspapers bought up the smaller ones. The Scripps chain was started in 1880; by 1900, there were eight major chains, including the Hearst, Pulitzer, and Ochs papers. As newspaper chains grew, competition among newspapers within cities diminished. In 1923, 502 cities had two or more competing newspapers. In 1979, only 36 cities had competing newspapers. Only two cities, New York and Philadelphia, had three.[45]

The early chains concentrated on buying newspapers in major cities. The newer chains focused on the smaller cities. The peak of concentration was reached in 1946, when the seventeen Hearst newspapers had a circulation of 5.3 million or 10.4 percent of the daily circulation. Measured by circulation, Knight-Ridder is the largest chain today, with 3.7 million readers. Measured by the number of newspapers owned, Gannett is the largest, with seventy-eight, and accounts for 5 percent of the daily circulation.[46] However, the ten largest chains, taken together, account for 39 percent of all daily circulation. The four largest (Knight-

Ridder, Newhouse, Tribune, and Gannett) have 22 percent of the circulation.[47]

Although no single newspaper chain dominates the flow in information, recent patterns of ownership show that newspaper chains themselves may be part of much larger corporate structures, which include other media, as well as a variety of related enterprises. The *Tribune* Company, for example, owns the *Chicago Tribune* and more than forty different kinds of companies, including television stations. Graber points out that "Cox Broadcasting Corporation owned 17 newspapers, 10 radio stations, 5 television stations, and 36 cable systems; the *New York Times* company owned 15 newspapers, 2 radio stations, and 6 television stations, but no cable outlets."[48]

Perhaps the most important reality of modern print journalism is the pattern of affiliations between newspaper corporations and other major institutions in American society. Peter Dreier examined the board members of twenty-four of the largest newspaper chains in terms of their affiliation with a variety of elite institutions: corporations, business policy groups, nonprofit civic organizations, and social clubs. He found:

> ...the data indicate that the nation's major newspaper firms *are* heavily linked with the nation's power structure...the 24 newspaper companies have 447 ties with elite organizations, including 196 with *Fortune's* 1300 largest corporations, 97 with the 15 major business policy groups, 24 with the 12 major private universities, and 130 with the 47 elite social clubs.[49]

Dreier also points out that twenty-six board members have been, at one time or another, appointed to high-level federal government positions. Affiliations, in general, are concentrated: of the 290 directors studied, 25 account for 204 of the 477 elite affiliations.

Some newspaper companies, Dreier found, are more closely linked to the power structure than others: Dow Jones (*The Wall Street Journal*), New York Times, Washington Post, and Times-Mirror (*Los Angeles Times*) account for 41.6 percent of the elite affiliations. Although these companies do not own the newspapers with the largest circulation, it will be remembered that they own the most prestigious and politically influential newspapers.

There is even more concentration in television than there is in newspaper ownership. The FCC has, on occasion, tried to prevent concentration of ownership, with little far-reaching success. We have already noted that the FCC forced RCA to give up one of its two networks, only to have ABC grow into the third commercial media giant. In 1953, the FCC established rules which limited the number of stations that may be under the same ownership. The original ruling (called the 7-7-7 rule) limited ownership to seven AM radio stations, seven FM radio stations, and seven television stations, of which no more than five could be on regular wavelengths, VHF (Very High Frequency), which reach the largest audiences. UHF (Ultra High Frequency) reaches fewer people. Networks were forbidden to own cable systems.

However, the 1980s witnessed a move toward deregulation. In 1980, networks were permitted to enter the cable television market, and CBS and ABC did so. In 1984, the FCC increased the number of broadcast outlets that an individual or a company may own to twelve—a new 12-12-12 rule. The FCC decided to remove nearly all restrictions on ownership by 1990. The FCC noted that since 1953 the number of radio stations has tripled and the number of television stations has increased from 199 to 1169. Thus, the FCC reasoned that media competition had increased sufficiently to make the 7-7-7 rule unnecessary. Mark Fowler, chairman of the FCC, believed that relaxing ownership restrictions would encourage the creation of new networks and would increase program diversity. Critics of the new ruling were quick to point out that this action would increase competition for small stations, drive up their prices, and drive out ownership by small operators and minority groups, thus decreasing diversity.[50] It is too soon to tell what these efforts at deregulation will bring. However, the superior wealth and technological resources of the three major networks gives them a clear advantage over others in the radio and television market.

Clearly, the new rulings encouraged the Capital Cities takeover of ABC (for $3.5 billion), the largest acquisition in the communications business. The two companies had combined revenues of almost $5 billion in 1984 and now together own 12 TV stations, 11 AM and 13 FM radio stations, and 55 cable systems in 16 states.[51] The new rulings may also have encouraged Australian publisher Rupert Murdoch, whose properties already included the New York Post, New York Magazine, and the Village Voice, to buy half the shares of 20th Century Fox Film Corporation (for $250 million) and then, with his new partner, to go on to buy seven TV stations from Metromedia for more than $2 billion.[52] (This has given rise to speculation about the possibility of a fourth network.)

It should be noted that there are no limits on the size of the audience within the reach of a single owner. The audience for a broadcast station is all those people within reach of its signal. A station in a large metropolitan area may reach a market of several million. A station in Oregon will reach a much smaller audience. Each of the three major networks (NBC, ABC, and CBS) owns and operates five television stations, which are in the largest media markets. All three are in New York, Chicago, and Los Angeles. The rest of the stations are distributed among Philadelphia, Washington, D.C., St. Louis, Detroit, and San Francisco.

Networks supply most of the programming to their affiliates and even to independents, who regularly show reruns of off-the-air network productions. The majority of commercial stations are network-affiliated, about 550 affiliates to 90 independents. Most affiliates accept 95 percent of network programming, which means about 65 percent of their broadcast time.[53] The owned and operated stations almost always take all network programming.

The affiliate station signs a contract with the network in which the network agrees to offer all its programs to the affiliate. The affiliate agrees to base most of its programming on the network's productions. The affiliate has the right of refusal, and the network pays the affiliate a fee for each program it uses. It is in the network's interest to have as many affiliates as possible carrying a given program, so that the advertisements will reach the largest audience and keep the rates up. The affiliate gets the revenue only on local advertisements, so some time is given each network program for such local advertisements. Theoretically, profit for an individual station would be greater without network affiliation, since the station would receive all the ad revenue. However, the station would have to produce its own programs, compete with the network shows, and find enough local advertisers to carry the expense.

Since the mid-1970s, the FCC has prohibited cross-media ownership within the same market. This means, for example, that one owner could not own both a newspaper and a radio station in the same community. However, this prohibition did not affect combinations of radio and television prior to 1970, or newspapers and broadcast combinations prior to 1975. Network affiliation is limited to one station per network in a given market. Nonetheless, the three major networks, through their own stations and their affiliates, represent an awesome concentration of power in the communications industry.

If we look at the communication industry as a whole, including television, radio, and newspapers, fifty corporations control what Americans see, hear, and read.[54] These include Gannett, Knight-Ridder, Scripps-Howard, CBS, Capital Cities-ABC, NBC, Time Inc., Times-Mirror, Hearst, and media conglomerates such as MCA, Gulf & Western, and Warner. The concentration of ownership and control in the communication industry raises serious questions about the quality and diversity of public discourse.

## CONCLUSION

We have examined the growth and development of the mass media of communication. We have seen the media grow from small, independent enterprises to giant corporations and conglomerates. The media's growth and their increasingly sophisticated technologies have expanded the media's role in our daily lives and increased our dependency on them. We have noted the expanding political role of the media, both as the reporters of political events and as participants in the political process itself.

Newspapers experienced a gradual expansion of their coverage by stationing specialized correspondents in key locations around the world and by establishing extensive Washington bureaus. They expanded to include news analysis and commentary. Radio and television, which had initially provided entertainment whenever possible, gradually expanded their news coverage, both in terms of the time allotted to news and in the depth of coverage.

As we look at this history of the mass media of communication, three relevant trends are apparent. The media have gradually expanded their information-delivery function in all areas of social and political life. Political officials and political interests have become aware of the importance of the media in the political process and have attempted, with varying degrees of success, to manipulate them. Finally, political reality is defined for the citizen by what is covered by the news media.

## NOTES

1 Frank Luther Mott, *American Journalism: A History 1690–1960*, 3d. ed., Macmillan, New York, 1962, p. 214.
2 Michael Schudson, *Discovering the News*, Basic Books, New York, 1978, pp. 57–60.
3 Schudson, *Discovering the News*, p. 62.
4 Daniel J. Boorstin, *The Americans: The Democratic Experience*, Random House, New York, 1973, p. 151.
5 Meyer Berger, *The Story of the New York Times 1851–1951*, Simon and Schuster, New York, 1951, p. 109.
6 Schudson, *Discovering the News*, pp. 116–117.
7 Ray Eldon Hiebert, *Courtier to the Crowd: The Story of Ivy Lee and the Development of Public Relations*, Iowa State University Press, Ames, 1966, p. 243.
8 Peter Odegard, *The American Public Mind*, Columbia University Press, New York, 1930, p. 132.
9 Daniel J. Boorstin, *The Image: A Guide to Pseudo-Events in America*, Harper & Row, New York, 1964.
10 Walter Lippmann, *Public Opinion*, Macmillan, New York, 1922, p. 218.
11 Bernard Roshco, *Newsmaking*, The University of Chicago Press, Chicago, 1975, pp. 39–57; and Schudson, *Discovering the News*, pp. 121–159.
12 Frank Luther Mott, *The News in America*, Harvard University Press, Cambridge, 1952, p. 70.
13 David Halberstam, *The Powers That Be*, Dell Publishing, New York, 1980, p. 788. Copyright © 1980 by David Halberstam. Reprinted by permission of Alfred A. Knopf, Inc.
14 S. G. Sturmey, *The Economic Development of Radio*, Gerald Duckworth, London, 1958, p. 17.

**15** See David Sarnoff, *Looking Ahead*, McGraw Hill, New York, 1968, pp. 22–23.
**16** Laurence Bergreen, *Look Now, Pay Later: The Rise of Network Broadcasting*, New American Library, New York, 1980, p. 14; *also see* Carl Dreher, *Sarnoff*, Quadrangle, New York, 1977, p. 28.
**17** See Gleason L. Archer, *History of Radio to 1926*, American Historical Society, New York, 1938.
**18** Herbert Schiller, *Mass Communication and the American Empire*, Beacon Press, Boston, 1971, pp. 34–35.
**19** Bergreen, *Look Now*, pp. 27–29.
**20** Erik Barnouw, *Tube of Plenty: The Evolution of American Television*, Oxford University Press, London, 1977, p. 20.
**21** Barnouw, *Tube of Plenty*, pp. 37–40.
**22** Gleason L. Archer, *Big Business and Radio*, American Historical Society, New York, 1939, pp. 307–318.
**23** Erik Barnouw, *The Sponsor: Notes on a Modern Potentate*, Oxford University Press, London, 1980, p. 21.
**24** Bergreen, *Look Now*, p. 46.
**25** See Abel Green and Joe Laurie Jr., *Show Biz from Vaude to Video*, Holt, New York, 1951.
**26** Barnouw, *Tube of Plenty*, pp. 68–70.
**27** Halberstam, *Powers That Be*, p. 58.
**28** Bergreen, *Look Now*, p. 103.
**29** See William Paley, *As It Happened*, Doubleday, New York, 1979.
**30** Halberstam, *Powers That Be*, p. 53.
**31** Barnouw, *Tube of Plenty*, p. 95.
**32** Bergreen, *Look Now*, p. 166.
**33** Halberstam, *Powers That Be*, p. 198.
**34** Sarnoff, at NBC, eagerly cooperated with the government and consistently wrote of the communist threat. He cooperated in anticommunist broadcasting projects. NBC trained the staff for Radio Liberation, a C.I.A. operation. Barnouw, *Tube of Plenty*, p. 189.
**35** Bergreen, *Look Now*, p. 205.
**36** Barnouw, *Tube of Plenty*, pp. 174–179.
**37** Barnouw, *Tube of Plenty*, p. 169.
**38** Barnouw, *Tube of Plenty*, p. 222.
**39** During this period, the C.I.A. director was John Foster Dulles's brother, Allen Welsh Dulles. The two of them had enormous control over the flow of information.
**40** Bergreen, *Look Now*, p. 221.
**41** Barnouw, *Tube of Plenty*, p. 275.
**42** Michael B. Grossman and Martha J. Kumar, *Portraying the President*, The Johns Hopkins University Press, Baltimore, 1981, p. 259.
**43** Peter Sandman, David Rubin, and David Sachsman, *Media*, Prentice-Hall, Englewood Cliffs, 1982, p. 28.
**44** Ben Bagdikian, *The Information Machines*, Harper, New York, 1971.
**45** Benjamin M. Compaine, "Newspaper," in *Who Owns the Media?*, Harmony Books, New York, 1979, p. 18.
**46** Compaine, "Newspaper," pp. 20–22.

**47** Compaine, "Newspaper," p. 26.

**48** Doris A. Graber, *Mass Media and American Politics*, Congressional Quarterly Press, Washington D.C., 1980, p. 34.

**49** Peter Dreier, "The Position of the Press in the U.S. Power Structure," in *Social Problems*, vol. 29, no. 3, February, 1982, p. 302; *also see* Peter Dreier and Steven Weinberg, "The Ties That Blind: Interlocking Directorates," *Columbia Journalism Review*, vol. 18, Nov./Dec., 1979, pp. 51–68.

**50** *New York Times*, July 27, 1984, p. 1, and *New York Times*, July 29, 1984, p. E7.

**51** *Newsweek*, April 1, 1985, p. 54.

**52** *New York Times*, May 7, 1985, p. 1.

**53** Joel Swerdlow, "The Ratings Game," *Washington Journalism Review*, Sept./Oct., 1979, p. 38.

**54** Ben Bagdikian, *The Media Monopoly*, Beacon Press, Boston, 1983.

# CHAPTER 3

# ACCESS, LAW, AND THE MEDIA

One of the hallmarks of the American Constitution is the protection afforded the press. The First Amendment prohibits Congress from making any law which abridges freedom of the press or freedom of speech. These formal Constitutional protections reflect the importance of the press in the American political scheme and the early democrats' faith that the press would serve as an independent source of information, as a "watchdog" of government activity.

Newspapers, which were the only news media in the early days of the Republic, have always remained relatively free of any government regulation. The law specified civil remedies for those who believed they had been libeled by a newspaper, but there were no formal constraints on what newspapers could publish. Newspapers could be prosecuted for publishing government secrets, but the protections were interpreted to be so strong that it was very difficult to prevent newspapers from publishing these secrets, even when the government knew the newspapers possessed them. Except for some general economic regulations that were binding on the newspaper industry, newspapers were almost completely free from direct regulation.

The policy of leaving the press free of government regulation changed with the development, manufacture, and distribution of radio. The airwaves used to transmit radio signals were considered to be public property and were, therefore, subject to regulation by government. Since there were only a finite number of radio frequencies available, it was necessary to establish a means to select those who would be given a license to broadcast over the airwaves. In 1934, Congress passed the Communications Act, which created the Federal Communications Commission and empowered it to regulate and monitor the use of the airwaves. When television was created two decades later, the Act was extended to give the FCC power to regulate the use of television frequencies.

## FEDERAL COMMUNICATIONS COMMISSION

The seven commissioners who make all the important policy decisions at the agency are chosen by the President, with the advice and consent of Congress. The President also chooses the chairman of the Commission, who has traditionally had a very strong role in setting the regulatory tone for the agency. While Congress can exert some degree of influence over the direction of the agency through its control of the budget or through the legislative process, it cannot rival the strong role of the President in influencing agency policy. Presidents favoring strong governmental control over the industry will appoint commissioners who reflect that approach; Presidents wanting the industry to have wide latitude from government regulation will pick commissioners committed to that approach. Since the leadership of the FCC reflects the prevailing political view at the White House, the policy of the agency changes when a new President installs new leadership.

The most significant weapon in the FCC regulatory arsenal is the power to grant and rescind licenses. Since the airwaves are considered public properties, broadcasters must be licensed by the government. Licenses are granted only for three-year periods, at the end of which the FCC reviews the operation of the station to determine whether it is entitled to a license renewal.

The power to deny a license to a station, and thereby force the station to close up its operation, is the most important power available to the FCC. Losing a license to operate could result in the loss of millions of dollars. Not surprisingly, the FCC has rarely used this power. There is only one case in which the FCC has used its power to deny a license to a station, in order to lessen ownership concentration. In 1969, WHDH-TV, a station owned by a local newspaper company that also operated two local radio stations and owned a controlling share of a cable company, was denied a license renewal. This decision sent shock waves through the broadcasting industry, which soon succeeded in pushing a bill through Congress that guaranteed license renewal if the station performed satisfactorily.[1]

Although the FCC rarely uses its ultimate power, it does have a considerable range of other powers which it may use to influence broadcasting. It may promulgate rules which are binding on stations. It may announce in advance its intention to hold hearings on a challenge to an existing license and indicate its intention to give certain practices weight in deciding who should be given a license. Using administrative devices, the FCC may delay action on a license renewal, indicating its desire to see the station comply with certain practices. Epstein quotes the director of CBS News in Washington, who remarks: "The strength of the FCC is more in the threat it can pose than in actual action."[2] In these ways, the FCC can act as an important external influence over broadcasting and news practices.

Although the power of the FCC does not directly cover the operation of the networks, the Commission is in the position to apply pressure where it hurts. FCC decisions can significantly affect the profitability of network operations. Policy may limit the number of hours of network programs local stations may receive. Fewer hours of network shows mean fewer advertising dollars for the networks. The FCC may also promulgate rules limiting the types of media that one corporate group may operate. The "one to a customer rule," for example, limits ownership of radio stations in the same city where a corporate group owns a TV station. Because the FCC can hurt networks financially, it is in a good position to exert pressure on phases of their operation.

The work of the FCC is supposed to be guided by certain goals embodied in the Communications Act. The goals can be divided into two general categories. There is a mandate for television and radio to devote a share of their broadcasting time to informing the public about important issues of the day. The Act also directs the FCC to establish a means of providing access to the media for political candidates, ordinary citizens, or those holding beliefs that are contrary to positions espoused by broadcasters.

## Public Information

One of the goals of the Communications Act is to create a broadcast system that serves the public interest. Because stations are given a license to operate over a public property and receive income as a result of that operation, they have a responsibility to perform some degree of public service. Early Commission policy was very clear in establishing this priority, declaring that one of the basic purposes of broadcasting was "...the development of an informed public opinion through the public dissemination of news and ideas concerning the vital public issues of the day."[3] The Commission was specific in defining what it considered to be the needed ingredients for "development of informed public opinion": "News and information should emanate from as many different and competing stations as possible."[4] To meet this goal, the Act envisioned the development of broadcasting as a local, decentralized industry, where many different interests and views could be represented.

To encourage compliance with the goal of using broadcasting as a vehicle for the discussion of political and community issues, the Commission passed a series of regulations in 1973, and again in 1976, specifying the amount of time which stations must devote to public affairs programing. What has come to be called the "5-5-10 rule" stipulates that stations must devote a minimum of 5 percent of total programing to local affairs, 5 percent to news and public affairs, and 10 percent to nonentertainment programing.[5] Under the rule, stations are required to keep detailed logs of all programs that are aired, so the FCC can determine if they are complying with the regulation. Most stations' logs have surpassed the 20 percent figure in time devoted to public affairs programing since the rule was passed. While there are undoubtedly stations that are very flexible in what they list as public affairs programing, the rule has certainly encouraged stations to take their responsibility for airing public affairs programing more seriously.

In 1984, with the winds of deregulation howling at hurricane speed, the FCC all but abandoned its commitment to public affairs programing. In a unanimous decision, the Commission ruled "...that the nation's 850 commercial television stations were no longer required to file with the commission detailed logs of what they broadcast."[6] This action followed a 1981 order which freed radio from the obligation to keep programing logs. While the FCC ruling will not bring an end to news and political affairs programing, it is a signal to the ownership of television stations that the FCC will no longer monitor performance. Those who desire to reduce or eliminate public affairs programing will now have a free hand. With one wave of the deregulatory wand, the recent regime has reversed the commitment that has guided FCC policy since 1961.

While this action represents the most significant reversal of a goal established by the Communications Act to date, it is not the only instance in which the actions of the Commission have conflicted with some stated goal. In the 1960s, FCC policy supported the attempts of the three networks to gain a monopoly over national news programing. The FCC let it be known that it would look favorably on local stations that signed contracts to show the national news programs produced by the networks. Any station with a contract to carry national news programs would, according to the FCC, be considered as having fulfilled four-fifths of its tacit news requirement."[7] This gave the networks a very sweet sales incentive. By the middle 1960s, the networks had gained total control over the national news market and had increased the length of the national news from 15 to 30 minutes. Aiding the networks in their quest for control of the market did nothing to enhance the development of local programing or provide mechanisms for the expression of diverse opinions.

In general, the electronic landscape does not resemble the one envisioned by the architects of the Communications Act. Despite some sincere efforts by the FCC to lessen the concentration of ownership of the media and open up the airwaves to new voices, the corporations that control the industry have been successful in extending their empires. Although most stations are locally owned, a majority of their programing is provided by one of the networks. Each of the ten largest media groups commands an audience of five million households. Graber estimates that, based on an average of three to five people in each household, one of these major media corporations is capable of reaching an audience of thirty million.[8]

## ACCESS

The technical constraints of the broadcasting system, with only a limited number of U.H.F. frequencies available in each city, meant that the possibilities for ownership of television stations were to be very limited. Since the limited number of frequencies curtailed the amount of potential competition in each market, the structure provided the possibility for monopoly control by organizations owning stations in all major markets. The limit on the number of stations meant that there would also be severe constraints on the ability of potential users to get access to television time. Even in the 1950s, it was not difficult to imagine a situation where television was the prime medium for the expression of political views but was closed to all but a small number of participants. These concerns led the FCC to adopt a set of procedures that were supposed to insure a degree of fairness and equality of access.

The Equal Time Provision, one of the two pillars of the FCC's access policy, was not designed as a measure to increase diversity, but as a way to protect the political establishment from a potential electronic tyranny. Sensing the danger of private control of the airwaves, the political establishment opted to develop safeguards quickly for itself. The Equal Time Provision states that a station that sells commercial time to one candidate for office must sell time to other candidates. This measure protects the two major parties, which are generally the only political parties with the resources to purchase commercial time on television. The public can be said to benefit from the fact that it gets exposure to the messages of both major parties. However, this benefit must be weighed against the liability of a rule that effectively excludes other political parties from using the airwaves, limiting the public's exposure to different political points of view.

The conflicts that have arisen since the FCC's adoption of the Equal Time Provision point out the contradiction inherent in a system that is privately owned, with the express purpose of making a profit, and that is also supposed to serve a prime public function. At the point where the public purpose conflicts with the ability to make money, there are bound to be sparks. From the inception of the rule, television executives opposed the idea, claiming that it would be unprofitable for them to give over large chunks of advertising time, particularly to candidates for state and local office. They claimed that viewers would be bored by repeated commercials and switch to other stations; regular advertisers would not be able to get the desired time if the stations were forced to sell time to all political candidates. Many stations rebelled by refusing to sell time to any candidate. If they didn't sell time to any candidate, they assumed that they would not be compelled to sell equal time.

There was too much at stake for the political world to collapse in the face of this industry opposition. Politicians feared that station owners would be able to determine if or when they could use the media in political campaigns. Congress responded to the broadcasters' resistance by amending the Communications Act to make it possible for the FCC to revoke the license of a station that did not permit a legally qualified candidate for federal elective office to buy reasonable amounts of time on behalf of a candidacy. This raised the stakes involved in noncompliance, but it did not put an end to the struggle among the various groups affected by the Equal Time Provision. Some of the most important court battles over how the Equal Time Provision should be interpreted and applied are discussed in the next part of this chapter.

In 1983, the FCC made a major change in the Equal Time Provision. This change closed the only opportunity for smaller political parties to get some exposure through the use of the rule. Under the rule, broadcasters who aired political debates were obliged to invite all parties who were contesting the election to participate. Although there were certain exceptions, particularly for presidential debates, the provision did allow certain small parties a chance to join the dialogue. Under the new modification, broadcasters are now permitted to hold debates between candidates of their own choosing.[9] This will, in most cases, have the effect of limiting debates to the candidates of the two major parties and further tighten the networks' hegemony over the American political process. Although broadcasters were delighted with the decision, they vowed to continue to wage the battle for the total elimination of the Equal Time Provision.

The second pillar of the FCC's access policy is called the Fairness Rule. This rule requires broadcasters to provide reasonable time for the expression of opposing views on controversial issues discussed on the air.

The rule contains a rebuttal provision, which provides that any individual or group attacked in a broadcast is entitled to free time to answer the criticism. These two provisions are the only means for opposing views to get broadcast time.

The Fairness Rule contains goals but lacks specific standards for reaching these goals. In the absence of strong procedures, a considerable amount of latitude and discretion has accrued to the stations. There is, for example, no compulsion for television stations to broadcast opposing views near the time slot during which the original view was broadcast. A television station may show an editorial opposing nuclear power on one day, receive a request for time for a rebuttal on the next day, and schedule the rebuttal 2 weeks or a month later. Since the audience is usually unaware of the position that is being countered, the rebuttal policy does not provide an effective means for an audience to evaluate opposing positions. The provision of the rule which states that stations must provide "reasonable time" for a rebuttal does not provide any clue about what is to be considered "reasonable," leaving that decision in the hands of station executives. A station may show a 30-minute documentary on a particular topic and offer 3 or 5 minutes of rebuttal time. There are also no standards to help determine who, among a number of competing parties, ought to be chosen as the party to respond to a particular issue. In the absence of any standards, the decision about who should get time has generally been made by station executives.

In recent years, many stations have created a sort of ritual to satisfy the fairness requirement. Many stations now devote several minutes between the end of the local news and the beginning of the national news for broadcasting stations' editorials and for showing replies to previous editorials. Free time is regularly given to opponents of a station's editorials. This policy takes the pressure off stations to provide free time to respond to other topics that are discussed during the broadcast day. It also gives the stations the ability to create the agenda of issues for which rebuttal time will be offered.

Despite the considerable flexibility that the industry has developed over the years, it remains opposed to both the Equal Time and Fairness Provisions. The unhappiness of the industry is matched by that of other parties who believe that industry practice has made a sham of the equality and fairness policies. These parties regularly meet in the Federal and Supreme Courts, which have the power to determine whether FCC policy is consistent with the intent of the Communications Act, and whether certain practices violate Constitutional guarantees. The next section of this chapter reports on the legal wars between both the electronic and print media and groups and individuals seeking access to their audiences.

### Access to the Electronic Media

One of the most important cases in establishing the boundaries of fairness rules was heard by the Supreme Court in 1969 in the case of *Red Lion Broadcasting Co. v. F.C.C.*[10]

In 1964, WGCB AM-FM, in Red Lion, Pennsylvania, aired a program by the Rev. Billy Hargis, a right-wing clergyman. The program was part of a syndicated series of programs entitled "The Christian Crusade." On this particular program, Hargis launched an attack on the journalist Fred Cook, who had written a book on conservative Senator and Presidential aspirant Barry Goldwater. Hargis called Cook a liar and a left-winger and charged that Cook had written the book for the purpose of destroying Barry Goldwater's career.

Cook believed that the Hargis program constituted an attack and asked station WGCB to provide time for him to reply. WGCB answered Cook's request by sending Cook a rate card with the station's advertising rates. While the station seemed prepared to sell Cook advertising time, it was not at all disposed toward meeting the FCC's rule mandating free time to respond. After repeated efforts to persuade the station to provide free time, Cook filed a complaint with the FCC. The FCC ruled in Cook's favor. The FCC found the Hargis broadcast to be an attack on Cook and charged that the station "had failed to meet its obligations under the fairness doctrine."[11]

Losing this particular battle with the FCC, the station decided to launch a full-scale war with the regulatory agency's policy. Before the Supreme Court, WGCB lawyers argued that the Fairness and Rebuttal rules were an unconstitutional violation of the First Amendment guarantees of free speech. These rules interfered with the broadcasters' right to choose which programs they desired to air and, by this logic, constituted not only an attack on the First Amendment but also an attack on the cherished rights of free enterprise and free choice.

The Supreme Court refused to see it this way, ruling in Cook's favor and affirming the constitutionality of the Fairness and Rebuttal rules. The Court affirmed the concept of the "airwaves" as a public property, a scarce resource that cannot be closed to the public. And the Court went even further. Rather than being swayed by the broadcasters' claim of First Amendment protection, they turned the tables and strongly supported the First Amendment rights of viewers and listeners. In fact, the Court boldly proclaimed the supremacy of the rights of viewers and listeners.

> It is the right of viewers and listeners, not the right of the broadcasters, which is paramount. It is the purpose of the First Amendment to preserve an uninhibited marketplace of ideas in which truth will ultimately prevail, rather than to countenance monopolization of that market, whether it be by the government itself or a private licensee. . . . It is the right of the public to receive

suitable access to social, political, esthetic, moral and other ideas and experiences which is crucial here....[12]

It was a great day for those who had fought through the courts for greater access to the media. The Supreme Court's strong affirmation of the First Amendment rights of viewers and listeners was an unexpectedly firm endorsement of broader public access. While broadcasters must have been stung by the Court's strong language, they also surely realized that the case was only one battle in what was to be a long war over the public's right to gain access to the media.

Today, as then, there are those who maintain that the Fairness rule and the Court's initial strong stand on the right to free time have made broadcasters less willing to air controversial programs that might require the allocation of free time to opponents. Taking this a step further, these critics claim that the Court's position has actually undermined the purpose of the Fairness Doctrine, which is to insure that broadcasters air opposing and controversial viewpoints.[13] This line of reasoning was championed by the broadcasters themselves in the arguments in the *Red Lion* case. Justice White responded to this thinly-veiled threat in his opinion in the case, noting that such a possibility "is at best speculative" and that the "fairness doctrine in the past has had no such overall effect."[14] White went on to suggest a potential remedy for broadcasters who might put a freeze on controversial material: "If the present licensees should suddenly prove timorous, the Commission is not powerless to insist that they give adequate and fair attention to public issues."[15] While the claim that the Fairness Doctrine inhibits broadcasters' willingness to use controversial material is widely repeated, there does not seem to be any empirical evidence that demonstrates a relationship between the Court's decision and the use of controversial material.

In the same session in which the Court arrived at the *Red Lion* decision, they also refused to review a lower court decision that had added muscle to the Fairness Doctrine. The case was instigated by John W. Banzhaf III, a Manhattan lawyer and antismoking activist, who claimed that cigarette advertisements glamorized smoking; he asked for time under the Fairness Doctrine to present opposing views. Not surprisingly, the networks refused. The D.C. Circuit Court heard the case and ruled in Banzhaf's favor, ordering the networks to make time available for a response to cigarette commercials.[16] In the opinion of the Court, smoking represented an extraordinarily important public health issue, and the salience of the issue made it necessary for the networks to provide response time. No doubt horrified by the potential economic consequence of allowing opponents to respond to advertising, the networks appealed the case to the Supreme Court, which refused to hear the appeal, thereby affirming the lower court's decision.

Once again, there was cause for cheer by proponents of the FCC rules. Yet the *Banzhaf* decision did not set down guidelines for determining which issues are significant enough to warrant response time. Without guidelines, the issue of access would have to be litigated again when a broadcaster refused to give time to answer a commercial message. Celebration over the *Banzhaf* decision would have been dampened had proponents realized that the courts would never again rule favorably in cases involving access to present opposing views to commercial messages.[17] After this initial slap on the wrist, broadcasters regained total control.

By 1973, the Court had begun to change dramatically its tune about what the Fairness and Equal Time provisions required. In a case brought by the Democratic National Committee, the Court supported the rights of broadcasters to refuse paid editorial advertisements.[18] It was the broadcaster's right, according to the Court, to determine which issues are important enough to reach the public and the way these issues should be treated. Total editorial power was vested in the hands of media managers. The decision led one to wonder what had happened to the public's right to "receive suitable access to social, political, esthetic, moral and other ideas and experiences..." so heartily endorsed in the *Red Lion* decision.[19] Justices Brennan and Marshall, who dissented from the opinion, believed that the ruling would certainly limit the public's exposure to controversial views. Broadcasters who depended on mass support for their profits were unlikely to risk alienating their audience for the sake of invigorating public debate. If stations were not compelled by FCC policy to accept controversial advertisements, the dissenting Justices wondered, what could induce broadcasters to air such messages? "Angry customers are not good customers, and, in the commercial world of mass communications, it is simply 'bad business' to espouse—or even allow others to espouse—the heterodox or the controversial. As a result, even under the Fairness Doctrine, broadcasters generally tend to permit only established—or at least moderated—views to enter the broadcast worlds' 'marketplace of ideas.'"[20]

The Court's affirmation of CBS's right to refuse a paid political editorial must have concerned the political establishment. It is not comforting knowing that the networks have the power to deny political parties access to the public opinion arena. At the same time, the networks must have been emboldened by the Court's decision, because they continued to set conditions for political access.

Another major test of the networks' power to set conditions for access for political purposes began when both ABC and NBC rejected a request by President Carter's campaign committee to buy time for a thirty-minute broadcast, which was to coincide with President Carter's announcement that he would seek re-election. CBS was more generous; it offered to sell the President two five-minute spots. The networks refused to sell the commercial time because they claimed that the presidential campaign had not yet begun. Carter's campaign organization brought an action against CBS, which was eventually heard by the Supreme Court. The Supreme Court ruled in favor of Carter. The decision seems to have put some limits on the networks' discretionary power, which the Supreme Court itself had helped the networks amass. In the majority opinion, the Court ruled that the networks' blanket refusal of the Carter request had not met the requirement in Section 312 of the Communications Law, which requires television to give candidates' request for time "... reasonable and good faith attention." Broadcasters who refuse requests of candidates seeking federal office to buy time (state and local races are not covered by the decision) "... must explain their reasons and must justify the refusal by showing that compliance with the particular request would be unduly disruptive."[21]

After some heartening decisions for advocates of liberal access policies, including the *Banzhaf* and *Red Lion* cases, the Supreme Court began to take a different view of the Equal Time and Fairness Rules. With the exception of cases involving the ability of the two major parties to gain access—cases in which the political pressure to keep channels open must have been intense—the Supreme Court has generally left the media corporations free to determine how they will meet the requirements of the FCC doctrines.[22]

It now seems possible that the networks are in a position to realize their goal of eliminating both the Equal Time and Fairness requirements. The current regime at the FCC has instituted changes which have significantly diminished the scope of both rules and indicated that the agency will no longer closely monitor stations' compliance. Changes in the composition of the Supreme Court and a political climate hostile to government regulation of industry make it increasingly unlikely that the Supreme Court will act to protect the access requirements. Indeed, the concept of the airwaves as a public property, to be used as a means to provide citizens with information needed to fulfill their civic responsibilities, seem no longer to be the guiding notion in determining the rights of the public.

## Access to Print Media

While litigants continued to contest the rights given the public by the FCC's access provisions for electronic media, a similar controversy was brewing over the public's right to access to newspapers. The legal ground for access to the print media was shakier than with broadcasting, where some form of access was guaranteed by federal regulations.

Despite considerable odds, the fight for access to print media was waged. In 1974, the Supreme Court agreed to hear the case of *Miami Herald Publishing Co.* v. *Tornillo,* which concerned the right to reply to a critical newspaper editorial.[23] In 1972, the *Miami Herald* published two editorials opposing Patrick Tornillo, Jr.'s candidacy for a seat in the Florida State Legislature. The editorial branded Tornillo a bad choice for voters because of his leadership in a recent teachers' strike and his position as executive director of the teachers' union. Tornillo wrote two letters of reply and demanded that the paper print them. Management demurred.[24]

Tornillo or his lawyer managed to find a 50-year-old Florida statute which gave a candidate the right to reply to a "newspaper attack on his character or record."[25] This clever law was surely motivated by a Florida politician's fear of being without a weapon to thwart an attack by a newspaper. Tornillo and his lawyer personally delivered a copy of the statute to the management of the newspaper, which nonetheless refused to print Tornillo's reply. They contended that Tornillo did not lack access to the paper, since the campaign was being reported. Not to be outdone legally, the *Miami Herald's* lawyer produced a memorandum which alleged that the right to reply statute was a violation of the First Amendment.

Tornillo, represented by Professor Jerome Barron, a well-known and respected specialist in FCC law, won a victory in Florida's Supreme Court. In its first legal test, the Florida statute guaranteeing access to newspaper space for a reply to an attack was upheld. The decision was immediately appealed, and the stage was set for a hearing before the Supreme Court.

The case generated considerable interest among other media organizations. A number of newspapers and broadcasters instructed their legal staffs to submit *Amicus Curiae* (Friends of the Court) briefs in support of the *Miami Herald.* In the industry's estimation, the stakes were high. A victory for Tornillo would mean a substantial loss of control for the editorial staff and the possibility that newspapers might even be forced to submit to the Fairness and Equal Time provisions that governed broadcasting.

The case was argued on April 24, 1974. The key issue was whether the Florida statute violated the First Amendment guarantee of freedom of speech. Hoping that the Court could be persuaded to adopt the logic of the *Red Lion* decision, where the guarantee of speech was construed to include the right of listeners and viewers to diverse opinions, Professor Barron argued that some regulation of the press was permissible if it served an overriding public purpose. Public purpose was synonymous here with the right of the public to hear diverse opinions. Barron argued that the Florida statute did not detract from free expression but, instead, actually added to it. This argument paralleled the one made by the Solicitor General in the *Red Lion* case.

Lawyers for the *Miami Herald* argued that the statute was a frontal attack on freedom of speech and that a legislative compulsion for a newspaper to print certain materials was equivalent to government censorship of the media and repugnant to the guarantee of the First Amendment. The crucial question to be answered was, Who decides what gets into the newspaper?

The Supreme Court unanimously ruled in favor of the *Miami Herald*, holding that the Florida statute was unconstitutional. Chief Justice Burger wrote: "It has yet to be demonstrated how governmental regulations of this crucial process [the choice of material to go into a newspaper] can be exercised consistent with First Amendment guarantees of a free press."[26]

Just one year after *Tornillo*, the Supreme Court heard another case involving newspapers. In this case, a small Virginia newspaper (which had carried an advertisement for a New York abortion clinic) was convicted of a misdemeanor under a Virginia law which made it illegal to publish information which could "...encourage or prompt the procuring of abortion or miscarriage."[27] In this case, the Supreme Court struck down the Virginia law and reaffirmed the principle that commercial messages are protected by the First Amendment. Yet, as it so often does, the Court produced a decision which did not set a strong standard. Whether a commercial message was entitled to protection was to be determined, in part, by whether the information in the advertisement was "...of potential interest and value to a diverse audience."[28] Of course, it was the media themselves that would make the initial decision about the potential value of the information in the advertisement.

The Court's reluctance to apply the Fairness Doctrine to newspapers was, in part, the result of a distinction drawn between print and electronic media. Newspapers remained free from government regulation because, as was not the case with broadcast stations, there were no physical limits on the number of newspapers which could operate in any one market. Thus, it was theoretically possible for anyone seeking access to the public opinion arena to launch a newspaper. Of course, in reality, there were always financial barriers which limited access.

In recent years, the media landscape has undergone significant alterations. The initial rationale for leaving newspapers free from any obligation to provide public access, which was of dubious merit when it was first conceived, now has no pertinence. With increasing technological innovations, including cable television, there are virtually no limits on the available frequencies. As early as 1966, there were far more radio and television stations than newspapers—5881 radio stations and 721 television stations, compared to 1751 newspapers. Since that time, the number of newspapers has continued to decline, while the number of broadcast stations increases. There are now no physical limitations on either market, but the costs of opening and maintaining a newspaper are often greater than the costs of operating a radio or cable television station.

These changes have become ammunition in the arsenals of media lawyers, who have waged a fight to weaken or eliminate the Fairness Doctrine. If the rationale for regulating the electronic media no longer pertains, they argue, the government has no reason to regulate the industry. While significant changes have made the original rationale meaningless, these changes do not necessarily undermine the need for government regulation of broadcasting. There is at least as much reason to draw the opposite conclusions from this change in broadcast and print markets. The decline in the number of newspapers and the resultant rise in the power of the electronic media could make government regulation of broadcasting even more important. If the number of opportunities for citizens to gain access to the public opinion arena through the print media are declining, it makes sense to preserve or expand opportunities to participate via the electronic media. By the same token, the decline in the number of newspapers provides a reason to consider regulating the newspaper industry. If there are only finite opportunities for ownership, then the same rationale which government used to justify the regulation of broadcasting now applies to newspapers.

## FIRST AMENDMENT QUESTIONS

Aside from the challenges to FCC rulings or interpretations of the meaning of the Communications Act, the courts are the arena for the settlement of a large number of intricate issues concerning the media. Many of the cases heard in federal and state courts revolve around conflicts between the rights of the media and the rights of individual citizens and government institutions. Many of the cases reviewed in this section illustrate the delicate balance between the need to provide the avenues necessary for the media to collect and disseminate news and the rights of citizens and government to be protected trom intrusions or commercial abuse. How the courts interpret these rights and strike this balance not only affects the way the news media will operate, but also directly determines the range of rights and obligations of citizens, political actors, and the news media. In this sense, these decisions have a direct impact on the nature of a democratic society.

### Journalists' Access to Information

There are two extremely important legal questions concerning the right to information. First is the question of whether the First Amendment provides journalists with special rights to information. Do the First

Amendment protections which guarantee the dissemination of information also apply to the gathering of the information to be disseminated? News organizations have contended that these sorts of protections and rights are necessary if journalists are to carry out their responsibilities. The second legal question, which has been the subject of ongoing controversy, is whether a journalist can be forced to surrender information to legal authorities that has been gathered in the course of his or her professional duties.

On the question of special access to information, the Court has generally not recognized the claim of special privilege. In the case of *Zemel v. Rusk*, a journalist challenged the State Department's ban on travel to Cuba, contending that the ban interfered with the journalist's First Amendment right to gather information.[29] If a journalist could not travel to Cuba, contended the plaintiff, it was impossible for a journalist to gather the information needed to report accurately the news about that country. The Supreme Court was not persuaded by this argument and foreclosed the claim of special privilege. The majority ruled that "The right to speak and publish does not carry with it the *unrestrained* right to gather information."[30]

The question of special access was litigated again when journalists who were being denied access to prisons and opportunities to interview prisoners sued to gain admittance. Both cases were heard in 1974, a time when many of America's prisons were in turmoil. Journalists claimed that they needed access to prisoners to report accurately on the many riots, disturbances, and charges of administrative abuse. Both cases made it to the Supreme Court. The Court found in favor of the prison authorities, ruling that the refusal to admit journalists or permit interviews did not interfere with the First Amendment rights of either prisoners or journalists.[31] The Court took this occasion to affirm again that journalists enjoyed no special right to information.

The Supreme Court's doctrine that the media have no special right to information may have added to the ease and success with which President Reagan was able to exclude the press from covering the invasion of Grenada. News executives loudly objected to the restriction, but they were without a strong legal ground upon which to challenge the ban. The Supreme Court's rulings on the right to information significantly affected the relationship between the government and the media and, consequently, the ability of the public to receive information about the invasion. It is easy to see how the government's hand is strengthened if journalists can be systematically excluded from covering highly sensitive issues.

The principle that reporters have no unrestrained right to access has been applied to cases in which reporters seek access to government documents. Reporters' ability to examine government documents had been enhanced by the passage of the Freedom of Information Act in 1964. Amended and broadened, the act has provisions for reporters, as well as ordinary citizens, to gain access to certain government reports and proceedings. The act does not make any special provisions for the media; it gives the same rights to ordinary citizens and to journalists. Most states have followed the lead of the federal government in passing some form of disclosure legislation, now commonly referred to as "Sunshine Laws."

Neither the Freedom of Information Act or state Sunshine Laws are, according to many journalists, satisfactory means for reporters to gain access. Applying for disclosure of information under the act is a long, cumbersome process. It could be a year or more before a government agency provides the material requested. Given the premium put on "nowness" in the news, the Freedom of Information Act is not very useful. Even if reporters or citizens are willing to wait for the government to respond, there is no guarantee that they will finally receive the material they requested. There are not firm federal guidelines that specify the types of material covered by the Freedom of Information Act. While the government is required to make a copy of laws or regulations available, it is not clear whether deliberations, conferences, or minutes of hearings leading to the passage of the law are to be considered part of the "public record" and to be covered under the provisions of the act. Regulations vary considerably from state to state. Some state regulations are more liberal than those of the federal government, while others are considerably more restrictive.

### Government Access to Journalists' Information

If the journalist does not have a special right to information, does the journalist have a special right to withhold information from government authorities? Here the question is whether material compiled by the journalist is to be considered privileged information, similar to the information given to an attorney by a client (attorney-client privilege). Journalists contend that this sort of privilege is necessary if they are to discharge their responsibilities ably. They also fear that investigative reporting of government activities would become more difficult or impossible if government were able to force the disclosure of information provided by the journalists' sources. Sources would be less willing to supply vital information if they risked the possibility of being exposed.

Federal and state governments have on many occasions attempted to force journalists to disclose information and sources. Most of the attempts to compel journalists to testify have come in the course of Grand Jury investigations or trials, although House committees have, on several occasions, sought to force journalists into revealing their sources. Government authorities have claimed that such information is needed if they are to carry out investigations and prosecutions.

One of the earliest test cases involving the journalists' right to withhold information involved the actress Judy Garland. Garland, who had filed a lawsuit against CBS as a result of an article written by *New York Herald Tribune* columnist Marie Torre, brought proceedings against Torre with the aim of forcing Torre to identify the sources of information used in the article.[32] Torre refused to cooperate. The case was heard in the Circuit Court. Judge Potter Stewart, who would soon move to the Supreme Court, wrote the majority decision. While Stewart acknowledged that forced disclosure could, under certain circumstances, constitute an abridgement of the First Amendment, he held that it was necessary to balance the abridgement against the need for information. If the need for information was greater, it would take precedence over the journalist's First Amendment privilege to withhold such information.[33] In this case, Stewart ruled that the need for information was central to Miss Garland's right to sue and outweighed the abridgement.

During the 1960s and early 1970s, the confrontation between the courts and the press heightened. Subpoenas for journalists to testify before Grand Juries and reveal sources increased dramatically during the Nixon years.[34] The case of Earl Caldwell, a black reporter for the *New York Times*, illustrates a classic confrontation between Grand Juries and journalists. Caldwell had written a series of articles on the activities and beliefs of the Black Panther Party. Caldwell had managed to win the trust of members of the organization, who were suspicious of the mainstream press and constantly fearful of government prosecution. A federal Grand Jury, which, under the directions of a U.S. attorney, was conducting a very broad investigation of the activities of the Black Panther Party, called upon Caldwell to testify. Caldwell was questioned about the source of information used in the article. He refused to answer the questions. The U.S. attorney conducting the Grand Jury got a contempt citation against Caldwell, ordering him to testify or face fines and imprisonment. When Caldwell still refused to identify sources, citing the need to protect their confidentiality, he was jailed.

Caldwell, supported by the legal staff of the *New York Times*, took the case before the Federal Circuit Court. The *Times'* lawyers asked the Court to consider the question of whether a Grand Jury could force Caldwell or other journalists to reveal sources. The Circuit Court found in favor of the government's right to subpoena the testimony of journalists, including testimony concerning the names of particular individuals.[35]

The *Caldwell* case involved the *New York Times* in a long and expensive legal battle. The implicit threat was that the Justice Department could continue to subpoena journalists if the *Times* did not ease up on its criticism of Nixon. There was also a propaganda weapon for the administration when the news organization came to the defense of its employee. A news organization protecting a journalist against the government could easily be portrayed as a witting or unwitting ally of radical groups. Here was the *New York Times* protecting a black journalist who had written about a black militant organization which the government was trying to bring to justice. This was a scenario with the potential to tarnish the public image of the newspaper.

The *Caldwell* case did not provide government with "carte blanche" authority to compel journalists' testimony, nor did it establish conditions under which the government may request such testimony and the circumstances, if any, which would permit journalists to refuse to testify. In an attempt to clarify the issues, the Court accepted the case of *Branzburg* v. *Hayes* in the 1972 term.[36] In this case, a journalist had refused to supply information to a Grand Jury investigating an alleged drug offense. The journalist maintained that compelling him to testify would compromise his sources, who had provided information with the implicit understanding of confidentiality, and would make it extremely difficult for him to carry out his responsibilities in the future. The state continued to maintain, as it did in the *Caldwell* case, that it had the right and the obligation to subpoena the testimony of journalists with information concerning cases pending before a Grand Jury.

In a 5–4 decision, reflecting the difficult nature of the issue, the Court ruled in favor of the government authorities. The Court reverted to the standard developed in *Garland* v. *Torre,* saying that First Amendment rights must be weighed against other interests—in this case, the interests of the prosecutorial authorities. According to legal scholars, the most devastating part of the Court's finding for the news media was the "...refusal to afford the journalist any special status or immunity with respect to legal obligation not possessed by the ordinary citizen." Any effects on the free flow of information that might result from forcing the journalist to comply were "perceived as indirect and speculative."[37]

Those who dissented from the majority decision did not view the case as presenting a conflict between the First Amendment rights of journalists and the interests of government. It was not the First Amendment rights of the journalists that were at issue in this case, according to the dissenting opinion, but the First Amendment rights of all citizens, who depend on journalists for information. The dissenting judges in the case favored granting journalists a qualified privilege to refuse to disclose sources. By granting journalists such a privilege, the Court would assure the free flow of information, and citizens would be more knowledgeable. The minority believed that forced disclosure would have a direct impact on the ability of the journalists to collect information and report the news.

Whether a journalist can be forced to reveal information to Grand Juries at the behest of a prosecutor is a very difficult Constitutional question. There are reasonable arguments on both sides. Yet, when a Grand Jury is being used by authorities to conduct broad political investigations, which is something the Grand Jury is not empowered to do (but often does), the issues are completely different. During the Nixon years, for example, many Grand Jury investigations were motivated by a desire to stifle unfriendly political groups or to collect intelligence information.[38] Reporters called before Grand Juries were being enlisted as soldiers in a political war. There were, unfortunately, a goodly number of journalists who felt no reservations about operating as agents of government.[39] Journalists who acted in this capacity compromised their integrity and the independence of the press. But the danger to the independence of the press was even greater when government was able to force those unwilling to cooperate into submission by threatening them with jail. When government seeks to enlist journalists as intelligence agents, there seems to be a very real and pressing obligation for journalists to refuse to cooperate.

Whether journalists have a right to withhold information desired by the prosecution or defense in a criminal trial has also been the subject of considerable litigation. In most cases, it has been criminal defendants who have sought such information. A defendant's claim to such information has been premised on the Sixth Amendment's right to a fair trial, including the right to compel testimony to enable the accused to prove his or her case.[40] Again, the Court turned to a balancing standard similar to the one used in *Branzburg.*

Although the federal courts have generally upheld the right to compel journalists' testimony in criminal cases, they have made the standards for forcing testimony more stringent than those applied to Grand Jury proceedings. Considering the fact that criminal courts are directly involved in the determination of guilt or innocence and that the defendant faces imminent "injury," it is somewhat surprising that the courts would give Grand Juries somewhat more discretion in compelling testimony. In order to force a journalist to testify, the government must show that such testimony is vital to the defendant's receiving a fair trial and that there are no alternative means available, other than the journalist's testimony, to bring the information before the Court.[41] Yet, when a state court decides that the information is essential, the journalist must testify or face a possible fine or imprisonment. In a recent, highly publicized murder trial involving a New Jersey doctor, a *New York Times* reporter, Myron Farber, was ordered to jail for refusing to reveal the sources used in a series of articles that he wrote about the crime.

On occasion, courts have gone as far as sanctioning the forcible seizure of materials from a newsroom. In a case involving the Stanford University newspaper, the Supreme Court ruled that news organizations are not exempt from duly authorized searches and seizures.[42] The Supreme Court sanctioned the police seizure of pictures taken by the student paper of a protest demonstration on campus. It agreed with a municipal judge who ruled that the material was liable for seizure because it could assist the local police in identifying persons who had allegedly attacked police officers during the demonstration. Although the Supreme Court called for "scrupulous exactitude" in the application of press warrants, it reminded the press that the Fourth Amendment was applicable to all and that the framers of the Constitution did not forbid the issuance of search warrants directed at the press.[43]

News organizations and journalists desire what is called a Shield Law—a law which would shield confidential information from government authorities. Some states have shield laws, but most of these laws are not considered adequate protection by the media. In general, even where shield laws exist, the courts have narrowly defined the material protected by the law.[44]

It is unlikely that the media will be very successful in the near future in getting legislatures to pass shield laws. The nation's highest court has consistently come down on the side of prosecutorial authorities and against special privileges. Trial judges have been given considerable discretion to decide the circumstances under which the media may be excluded or limited in covering trials. There is very little sentiment in the legal community for expanding the media's rights, and the Supreme Court has consistently defended the government's position.

Despite the fact that governmental and legal authorities have been given the right to force journalists to comply, they have used this right with care. Journalists have been sent to jail for failure to comply, but none has served a long sentence, which might be considered as a deterrent to others who might refuse to comply. Media organizations have the power to defend their employees, as well as the ability to rally public opinion to their cause. Invoking the power to jail journalists brings the media and the courts into a face-to-face confrontation, which seems to be something that both sides have, until now, wanted to avoid.

### Coverage of Criminal Trials

Coverage of criminal trials, particularly those that contain a high degree of drama, are an important staple for most newspapers. Some trials receive national publicity, while some others, featuring more local folk, are actively covered by the local media. The case of Jean Harris, convicted of killing the Scarsdale diet doctor, received extensive national coverage, including substantial coverage by the networks. Klaus Von Bulow's first and second trials on charges of injecting his heiress wife with a large enough dose of insulin to put her into a perpetual coma have been given saturated coverage by all the media. The criminal trial laced with sex or violence, or featuring a look into the secret lives of the rich or famous, is considered as appealing dramatic material by both the print and electronic media.[45]

As the media have focused more attention on covering criminal trials, the concern about the effects of this coverage on the trial process has been voiced in several quarters. In the 1950s, the Supreme Court ruled on the question of whether the media coverage of certain trials had influenced the outcome of the trial. The answer was a resounding yes. In *Shepard* v. *Maxwell,* the Court went as far as reversing the murder conviction of the defendant.[46] The majority opinion registers no doubt about the strong role played by the media in influencing a verdict: "...the trial was but a legal gesture to register a verdict already dictated by the press and the public opinion [it] generated."[47]

In an important way, the Supreme Court decision calls attention to the power of the media and to their ability to influence the determination of guilt or innocence through their coverage of a trial. With the *Maxwell* decision and subsequent cases involving convictions reversed because of prejudicial coverage, the media attempted some internal controls in the form of voluntary standards. While these voluntary standards may have eliminated the most flagrant abuses, they have not solved the problem of coverage that may be prejudicial to the trial process. Many criminal trials continue to take on a circuslike atmosphere as different media fight for an inside story or do exposés of participants. Leaks of testimony or of judges' rulings on motions are not uncommon.

Trial judges have begun to use more direct methods to control press coverage of trials. Gag orders, which prohibit the press from reporting certain aspects of a trial, or prohibit coverage entirely, have been frequently used. Judges have not been required to make any showing of proof that media coverage could possibly prejudice the outcome of the trial before issuing such an order. They have the power to determine unilaterally whether to limit or prohibit coverage.

Using the gag order as a means to control the media's coverage of pretrial or trial proceedings has not always proven entirely successful. There are a number of journalists who, believing that gag orders violate a constitutional privilege, have disobeyed the judges' orders and written about proceedings. Some journalists have been willing to go to jail rather than comply with a gag order. To enforce gag orders, some judges have even prohibited journalists from sitting in the courtroom, which is considered in the public domain. But even barring journalists from the courtroom has not always eliminated media coverage. Journalists have been known to hire someone to sit in the courtroom and report back to them on what occurred.

Unable to gag the press effectively, judges, in recent years, have begun issuing gag orders to members of the court community. Prosecutors, defense attorneys, defendants, witnesses, and other court personnel have been prohibited from speaking to the press. This tactic has been a more effective means to shut down the flow of information. Court personnel are subject to the power of a judge and are, therefore, more responsive to judicial orders.

In 1976, the Supreme Court spoke on the question of the constitutionality of gag orders. In the case of *Nebraska Press Association* v. *Stuart,* the Court reversed a gag order that had been in effect for several months.[48] While the Court did not prohibit the use of such orders, it urged local judges to seek other means to curtail inadequate or prejudicial reporting. Gag laws were not to be regarded as a preferred means of control. Despite the Supreme Court's admonition, local judges continue to use gag orders, although these orders have more recently been aimed at trial participants.

Closing criminal trials to the press raises serious problems. If criminal trials are closed to the press and to the public, there will be no one to monitor the activities of the judiciary. At the local and state level, the courts are outside any system of checks and balances. The press provides the only conduit for information about activities inside the courtroom. It is a thorny problem, the weighing of the rights of the defendant against the need for uninterrupted public exposure to judicial proceedings.

There is reason to believe that the more extensive use of gag orders may be motivated by something more than a desire to protect the rights of the defendant. Many judges, particularly in large cities, are antagonistic toward the media, which have very often portrayed the court as an inefficient, ineffective, and permissive institution. Many judges believe, correctly or incorrectly, that the media do not understand how the law or the court operates. Canons on conduct prevent judges from forcefully speaking out against the press. These judges can do little to influence the way the press covers the court. Many judges refuse to speak with the press, but that does not stop the press from writing about their activities. Gag orders provide a means to control publicity in cases that are likely to be widely-covered and thus risk exposure of the conduct and the operation of the court to a wide and interested audience.

## Libel

The most important remedy available to those who believe that they have been unfairly attacked or maligned by the media is the libel suit. If persons are able to prove successfully injury resulting from information in a TV program or newspaper or magazine article, they stand to collect a significant amount of money for that damage. While libel action may protect an individual against undue harm resulting from a story in the media, it may also have a chilling effect on the media's desire to cover public issues aggressively. Fear of financial loss will likely cause a news organization to be more temperate in its coverage or to wait until there is a substantial body of evidence to support a story. Again, there is tension between a person's right to be protected against libelous or slanderous material and the media's need to bring important facts and issues before the American public. Once again, the courts have been called upon to settle the issue.

In 1964, the police chief of Montgomery, Alabama, filed a lawsuit against the *New York Times.* The police chief alleged that he was libeled by the *Times'* charge that he had mishandled a civil rights demonstration. The Supreme Court heard the case of the *New York Times v. Sullivan* and rendered a decision that broadened the protection of the media against libel suits.[49] In order to collect damages, a public official had to prove that a falsehood resulted from actual malice on the part of the news organization. To be liable, a news organization or journalist had to make the statement with intent to injure.

The *Sullivan* case established public officials as a special class, not subject to the same protections as ordinary citizens. Public officials were considered as bearers of the public trust, whose actions must be open to a greater degree of scrutiny. If the press were subject to suit by a public official for every charge of malfeasance or neglect, it would surely dampen the media's ability to monitor political activities.

*Sullivan* began a decade in which the Supreme Court's commitment to protect the media against unwarranted libel cases was firm. Even after Chief Justice Earl Warren, who had been considered one of the media's staunchest allies on the bench, left the Court, there was, according to one legal scholar, a continuing commitment to an uninhibited, robust, and wide-open debate on public issues. The principles initiated in *Sullivan* were applied to cases involving charges of criminal libel.[50] The definition of those who could be considered public figures, and thus subject to the conditions that they must prove the media had the intent to injure before being able to sue for libel, was considerably expanded.

But then, in characteristic fashion, the Supreme Court began to retreat from the strong standard of protections afforded the media. This retreat took the form of more severely limiting the definition of those persons who were considered public figures and thus were subject to the stronger burden of proof. *Time* magazine lost a case in which it sought immunity from a suit brought as a result of an article concerning the Firestone family, who owned a substantial share of the Firestone Tire and Rubber Company. Until this decision, the Firestones would have been considered public persons, who would have to prove that *Time* magazine intended to cause injury.[51] This case signaled the Burger Court's intention to accept a more restricted definition of the libel protection afforded the media by the First Amendment.

With respect to First Amendment cases before the Court, 1979 was to go down as a bad year for the media. Perhaps the most important case of that term involved a suit against the popular CBS news magazine, *60 Minutes.* Colonel Anthony Herbert, who had been a subject of one of the show's reports, brought a libel suit against the station. In pretrial proceedings, lawyers for Herbert asked Barry Lando, the producer of this segment, and Mike Wallace, the correspondent, to answer questions about their thoughts, conversations, and conclusions in preparing the show. They refused to answer, claiming that the thought processes and editorial discussions were protected by the First Amendment. The Supreme Court disagreed and ordered them to answer. The burden of proving actual malice was difficult, according to the Court, and required access to this kind of information.[52] In two other cases during this term, the Court further narrowed the definition of public figures, thereby enlarging the categories of persons who could bring suit under the lesser burden of proof.

## POLITICS AND LAW

The trend to limit some of the freedoms and protections afforded the press, which began to take shape slowly soon after the Watergate affair, has recently picked up steam. It seems surprising, and ironic, that the courts would act to limit the freedom of the press so soon after the press had been successful in exposing criminal wrongdoing in the very highest echelons of government.

Watergate set off a curious chain of reactions in the public, the press, and the political and legal establishments. It was certainly, in one sense, a testament to the effectiveness of an independent press. Had it not been for the efforts of two *Washington Post* reporters, the involvement of the President in the coverup would have probably gone undetected. This success might have been taken as a sign of the necessity of maintaining the safeguards that made this sort of investigative reporting feasible. But, rather than being a cause for celebration, the activities of the press during the Watergate affair raised the levels of anxiety in the public, in the political establishment, and in the press itself.

One of the surprising effects of Watergate was that it seemingly turned public opinion more sharply against the press. Richard Nixon's public war with the media (fully described in Chapter 7), including his campaign to convince the American people that the Eastern press was out to get him, caused many citizens, especially the large majority that voted for him in the second election, to become more cynical about the news media. In the end, the Eastern press actually did what Nixon had been saying it desired to do—attack his administration and drive him from office. His fate made his previous criticims about the abuses of the media all the more believable, cementing that hostility that Spiro Agnew's public attacks on the media helped to mobilize.

Watergate was also a very poignant demonstration of the tremendous power wielded by the major media corporations. They had managed to play the primary role in unseating a President who had recently been elected by one of the largest landslides in history. Much of the disappointment of those who felt betrayed after voting for Richard Nixon was undoubtedly vented at the press. There was a genuine fear of, and anger at, the corporate magnates who ran news organizations such as the *Washington Post* and CBS.

Watergate also caused tremors among those in the political establishment, who were forced to recognize the tremendous power of the media. If a newspaper was capable of creating the momentum to topple the President of the United States, no political official could feel particularly safe. Many elected officials probably welcomed the increased level of public suspicion toward the press in the years following Watergate.

These were some of the reactions that created the climate for a change in the Supreme Court's view of the sanctity of certain press protections and guarantees. The new attitude of the Supreme Court is most evident in its attitude toward libel law. It has slowly chipped away at the protective wall established in the *Sullivan* case. The Burger Court has never ruled in favor of the media in any of the libel cases it has heard.[53] Tyrone Brown, a former law clerk to Chief Justice Earl Warren in the late 1960s, general counsel to *Post-Newsweek* stations, and a commissioner of the FCC, attributes the changes in court decisions to public antagonism toward the press:

> All these so-called absolute principles like the First Amendment are functions of the time when they're decided. The Justices' role is a process of role-making accommodations between various power groups in the country at various times. The Warren Court balanced competing interests more in favor of the First Amendment. The Burger Court appears to be doing otherwise.[54]

One of the more important effects of the Supreme Court's more limited view of the First Amendment rights of the press has been to limit the ability and desire of news organizations to do investigative reporting. Smaller news organizations are particularly threatened by the Supreme

Court's loosening of the requirements for defendants to bring and win libel suits. One large libel judgment is enough to bankrupt many smaller newspapers and radio and television stations. One lawyer who is active in the libel field has observed a new caution in many of his clients:

> I have found that publishers who once asked me whether the subject of an article could win a lawsuit now ask simply "Will he sue?" More and more, I see unflattering adjectives removed, incisive analysis of people and events watered down, risky projects dropped.[55]

The news media are not simply the innocent victims of some giant misunderstanding or of a political conspiracy. Many of the practices and priorities of the news media have created much of this hostility. In reality, news organizations had begun to retreat from politically sensitive investigations before the most recent decisions of the Supreme Court. Fear of offending the mass audience and of losing access to sources of information in the political world has resulted in more timid reporting by major news organizations. Supreme Court decisions are accelerating this tendency. This timidity of the press increases the ability of political actors to avoid close scrutiny and adds to their control over the information disseminated by the news media. Although the media are not without the resources to hire the best legal talent, they are likely to be on the losing end of many legal actions until such time as there is a change in the public's attitude toward the press, or until there is some shift in political alignments. For the news media, Watergate has, at best, turned out to be a mixed blessing.

## NOTES

1 Doris Graber, *Mass Media and American Politics,* C.Q. Press, Washington, D.C., 1980, p. 68.
2 Quoted in Epstein, *News From Nowhere: Television and the News,* Vintage, New York, 1974, p. 49. Copyright © 1973 by Edward J. Epstein. Reprinted by permission of Random House, Inc.
3 Quoted in Epstein, *News From Nowhere,* p. 48.
4 Epstein, *News From Nowhere,* p. 40; *also see* Erwin G. Krasnow, Lawrence P. Longley, and Herbert Terry, *The Politics of Broadcast Regulation,* 3d ed., St. Martin's Press, New York, 1982.
5 Graber, *Mass Media,* p. 42.
6 David Burnham, "F.C.C. Eases Rules for Broadcast T.V.," *New York Times,* June 28, 1984, p. C18.
7 Epstein, *News From Nowhere,* p. 62.
8 Graber, *Mass Media,* p. 40.
9 *New York Times,* Nov. 9, 1983, p. A9.
10 *Red Lion Broadcasting* v. *F.C.C.,* 398 U.S. 367, 1969.
11 Quoted in Kenneth S. Devol, *The Mass Media and The Supreme Court,*

Hastings House, New York, 1976, p. 326. From *The Mass Media and The Supreme Court,* by Kenneth S. Devol. Copyright © 1971, 1976, 1982. Reprinted by permission of Hastings House, Publishers.

**12** Quoted in Devol, *The Mass Media and the Supreme Court,* p. 327.

**13** Graber, *Mass Media,* p. 95.

**14** Quoted in Thomas Emerson, *The System of Freedom of Expression,* Vintage, New York, 1970, p. 660.

**15** Quoted in Emerson, *The System of Freedom of Expression,* p. 661.

**16** *Banzhaf* v. *F.C.C.,* 405 F 2nd 1082 (D.C. Cir 1968) Cert Denier 396 U.S. 842 (1969).

**17** Graber, *Mass Media,* p. 94.

**18** *CBS* v. *Democratic National Committee,* 412 U.S. 94 (1973).

**19** Quoted in Emerson, *The System of Freedom of Expression,* p. 659.

**20** Quoted in Devol, *The Mass Media and the Supreme Court,* p. 333.

**21** *New York Times,* Nov. 9, 1983, p. A9.

**22** See Emerson, *The System of Freedom of Expression.*

**23** *Miami Herald* v. *Tornillo,* 418 U.S. 241 (1974).

**24** Fred Friendly, *The Good Guys, The Bad Guys and the First Amendment,* Random House, New York, 1975, pp. 340–344.

**25** Friendly, *The Good Guys, The Bad Guys and the First Amendment,* p. 340.

**26** Quoted in Devol, *The Mass Media and the Supreme Court,* p. 332.

**27** Quoted in Devol, *The Mass Media and the Supreme Court,* p. 332.

**28** *Bigelow* v. *Virginia,* 421 U.S. 809 (1975).

**29** *Zemel* v. *Rusk,* 381 U.S. 1 (1965).

**30** *Zemel* v. *Rusk,* quoted in Jerome A. Barron and C. Thomas Dienes, *Handbook of Free Speech and Free Press,* Little Brown, Boston, 1979, p. 413.

**31** See *Pell* v. *Procunier,* 417 U.S. 817 (1974) and *Saxbe* v. *Washington Post,* 417 U.S. 843 (1974).

**32** *Garland* v. *Torre,* 259 F 2nd 545 (1959).

**33** Barron and Dienes, *Handbook of Free Speech and Free Press,* p. 423.

**34** Barron and Dienes, *Handbook of Free Speech and Free Press,* p. 416.

**35** *Caldwell* v. *U.S.,* 434 F 2nd 1081 9th Circuit (1970).

**36** *Branzburg* v. *Hayes,* 408 U.S. 665 (1972).

**37** Barron and Dienes, *Handbook of Free Speech and Free Press,* p. 416.

**38** *Branzburg* v. *Hayes,* quoted in Barron and Dienes, *Handbook of Free Speech and Free Press,* p. 427.

**39** Some specific examples of journalists who have used their position to aid intelligence organizations or political officials are discussed in subsequent chapters. Detailed accounts of some journalistic activity can be found in Daniel Schorr, *Clearing The Air,* Houghton Mifflin, New York, 1977, and David Wise, *The Politics of Lying,* Vintage, New York, 1973.

**40** Barron and Dienes, *Handbook of Free Speech and Free Press,* p. 444.

**41** Barron and Dienes, *Handbook of Free Speech and Free Press,* p. 446.

**42** *Zurcher* v. *Stanford Daily,* 985 CT 1170 (1978).

**43** Barron and Dienes, *Handbook of Free Speech and Free Press,* p. 481.

**44** Barron and Dienes, *Handbook of Free Speech and Free Press,* pp. 419–421.

**45** This is one area where the print media may enjoy an advantage over the electronic media. Since most states prohibit television cameras in the courtroom, television does have an opportunity to get the most exciting visuals. Television news does not report trials in the detail that most people seem to enjoy. This may soon change, however, as more states follow Florida and permit television cameras in the courtroom.

46 *Sheppard v. Maxwell*, 384 U.S. 333 (1966).
47 Quoted in Graber, *Mass Media*, p. 109.
48 *Nebraska Press Association v. Stuart*, 427 U.S. 539 (1976).
49 *New York Times v. Sullivan*, 376 U.S. 254 (1964).
50 *Garrison v. Louisiana*, 379 U.S. 64 (1964).
51 *Time Inc. v. Firestone*, 424 U.S. 448, 453 (1976).
52 *Herbert v. Lando*, 99 S.Ct. 1635 (1979).
53 Martin Garbus, "New Challenges to Press Freedoms," *New York Times Magazine*, January 29, 1984, p. 34.
54 Bruce W. Sanford, "No Quarter from This Court," *Columbia Journalism Review*, Sept./Oct., 1979, p. 60.
55 Garbus, "New Challenges," p. 49.

# CHAPTER 4

# DETERMINING
# WHAT IS NEWS

For the vast majority of the population, news is the account of reality that they watch on television or read in newspapers and magazines. To the average reader or viewer, news represents a connection with the larger world, a way of finding out what is occurring in the world, a way of becoming informed. What is important about this connection is not so much the fact that news represents a way of coming to know the political and social world; rather, it is the fact that the media provide the most important, almost exclusive, channel for such information. Thus, the power of the news and the media which carry it resides in the capacity to act as a bridge between the citizen and the political world. The media must make decisions about which event ought to be covered and reported. These decisions determine what will become news and, in turn, create the cumulative political reality for the news consumer.

A variety of studies have demonstrated that there tends to be a great deal of conformity in what different media regard as newsworthy. A study by Graber, for example, presents striking evidence that the same kinds of stories and story types—though not necessarily identical stories—are reported by newspapers and local and national television.[1]

This conformity in news selection is open to several interpretations. It can be argued, as network executives often do, that the proper word to describe the frequent occurrence of certain types of stories is not "conformity," but "consensus." Certain stories appear in different media because there is a mediawide consensus of what is important. Network executives claim that this news consensus, aided by the wire services and the national dailies such as the *New York Times* and the *Washington Post,* also limits the degree to which producers or executives can tailor news coverage. So, rather than representing conformity, a sort of blind obedience to trends, the frequency of certain stories actually demonstrates a relatively independent consensus over what constitutes news.

There is, it is true, leadership exerted by national newspapers and wire services. But the news consensus does not arise as a result of ongoing professional decisions about what are important events. News consensus is a direct result of the interaction between news organizations and the political world. Essentially, all news organizations retain the same outposts and apply virtually the same criteria in deciding what is newsworthy. Rather than coming as a result of professional assessment of what is important, a daily news consensus results from the fact that the news process is repeated with numbing regularity day after day. The same criteria are applied by a group of journalists who are remarkably similar in their outlook on the world and their vocation.

What criteria are used to select what becomes news? There are two schools of thought. One group of observers emphasizes the belief that internal factors largely determine what gets selected as news. Another group of observers emphasizes external factors, such as control by political forces and by advertisers. Actually, internal and external influences on what becomes news are inseparable. It is simply easier to begin by describing them separately.

## INTERNAL INFLUENCES ON THE NEWS

The internal factors influencing the news are created by two interrelated ingredients. First, news organizations are in business to make money. Curiously, this fact is sometimes hard for Americans to fathom. The very special role afforded the press as a watchdog of the public interest has masked the fact that news is business. Lippmann noted this irony many years ago: "We expect the newspaper to serve us with truth however unprofitable the truth may be."[2] When news is no longer a profitable venture for a corporation, it will stop producing news. The recent closing of the *Washington Star* and the *Philadelphia Enquirer* are evidence that neither tradition nor public service will keep a losing venture in business. How the news is reported is, then, often the result of what makes economic sense.

Closely related to the consideration of profit is the audience. The audience is the key to profitability. Since advertising rates are based on the number of viewers or readers, it is not surprising that considerable effort goes into coming up with a product that will appeal to the public.

denotes a situation where reporters work together in large groups. The best account of pack journalism in action, or in inaction, is provided by Timothy Crouse, who was part of the press corps covering the 1972 presidential contest between Nixon and McGovern.[8] What Crouse describes about the results of pack journalism pertains to any situation in which a large number of press people cover the same events and are expected to produce a regular stream of news.

Whether on the campaign trail or covering the White House, city hall, or the state house, there are generally a large pack of reporters who face the same demands and share the same access and facilities. Each of the journalists witnesses the same events. One morning, it may be a press conference to announce a new campaign position or a recent political endorsement; in the afternoon, it may be a speech before construction workers in downtown Pittsburgh, followed by the obligatory handshakes and baby kissing; finally, in the evening, it may be a party dinner. They all receive the same briefings and press kits, describing what is to take place on a particular day, and they must fashion what they have witnessed into a story that will be of interest to editors, producers, and readers.

Given the regularity and tedium of a political campaign, the routine nature of much political news, and the requirement for daily stories, it is not surprising to find that much of the pack becomes apathetic and uninterested in breaking any new ground. The reporters discuss stories among themselves, collectively composing the sketch of the story they will all file. For some campaign events, only a small number of reporters actually cover the event and later return to "pool" the information with other reporters, who will write the story as if they had witnessed the event. A silent complicity often characterizes press on the campaign trail. The commonality of experience, vantage point, and shared vocational goals, combined with the efforts of the campaign organizations to control the information that the press will receive, quickly leads most of the press corps into following the well-worn path of least resistance. Journalists covering the campaign, says Crouse, "arrive at their answers just as independently as a class of honest seventh graders using the same geometry text. They did not have to cheat off each other to come up with the same answer."[9] Thus, the similarity of the products of pack journalism is the result of the manner in which the "occupational vision" of the reporter combines with the control exerted by the individual or organization being covered. The pack regards the same issues, events, and activities as worthy of coverage.

Pack stories seem to be quite acceptable to editorial and management personnel in the news. They may not always be the most exciting brand of journalism, but they are safe. The news organization does not run the risk of being the only organization which runs a story that may prove to be incorrect. By following the pack, the editors are assured that, if the journalist happens to be wrong about a prediction or a reading of a campaign trend, they will share the error with all the other media. Pack reporting also helps alleviate the fear that the organization might miss a story that is being covered by its competitors. When journalists are packed together, a special brand of journalistic conservatism sets in, producing a routine consensus about what is news and what is important. We will return to the issue of pack journalism in subsequent chapters.

### Pictures, Words, and Drama

Not everything generated from a news outpost will get before the public. There is only a finite amount of news space, and it is always considerably less than the amount of news that arrives from the field. With stories filed in the office, the editorial and production staff apply certain criteria to determine what to use. It is at this point that esthetic, technical, and dramatic considerations become important.

A well-written story that requires little editing has a better chance of meeting the deadline and getting into print. The heart of print journalism is the reporting of events. The technical standards demand that each story have a lead that includes the who, what, where, when, how, and why of the event. The lead is followed by more detailed information, in a descending order of importance, so that if lack of space requires it, the story can be cut from the bottom up (this form is called the "inverted pyramid"). Thus, the technical structure requires the journalist to get quickly to the facts.

In contrast to newspaper reporting, the heart of the television news is the film story. Thus, the quality of the film that has been shot for a particular story will often determine whether the story will be shown. Good film can carry a story, give it pace and energy, and keep the viewer interested. The quality of the film story has come to be considered one of the most important factors in determining whether the audience will watch a particular news show. Film is often considered as important as, or more important than, the actual news that accompanies it. This does not mean that stories without good film are totally eliminated from consideration; such stories do appear. But when the time comes to determine which stories will appear on the evening news, the stories with good visual impact are more likely to be chosen. News that cannot supply a visual, such as stories about chemicals seeping into the earth or a lake gradually becoming polluted, are unlikely to be covered until well after the fact.

Stories that contain high drama or that can be fashioned into dramatic material are given very high priority. All drama has a beginning, a middle, and an end. Television news copies this basic form, so that the viewer is presented with a neatly-packaged story. Packaging news in this way allows the viewer to join in at any stage; no prior knowledge of an issue is needed. Each story is another self-contained episode in the drama called politics. Action and conflict are central to maintaining a strong story line for the news. The object is to engage the interest of the viewer at an emotional level.

Symbols and images that are readily understandable are frequently used and repeated. When the story concerns war, for example, dramatic scenes of bombing or exchanges of rifle fire are popular. Even when a television station does not have actual footage from the war, which was the case in the war between England and Argentina in the Falklands, or the invasion of Grenada, it uses standard war footage or simulated war scenes from the archives of the Pentagon to illustrate the story. Stories on unemployment show the obligatory picture of desolate workers waiting in long unemployment lines.

Finally, news stories are stocked with leading and supporting characters. Using characters to focus the story provides something tangible for the audience, someone to cheer for or someone to despise, bad people and good people. This stock dramatic structure for news stories accounts for the apparent similarity in the ways the news is presented, no matter what the particular story happens to concern. After a while, all the stories seem to run together. It is difficult to remember the substance of the story when the form of each story is identical.

The merger of news into an entertainment format is most evident in many of the local television news shows, which devote increasing blocks of time to stories about entertainment personalities. In New York City, for example, where the evening local news runs from 5–7 p.m., the first hour is almost entirely devoted to soft news stories, features, and short interviews with several entertainment and sports figures. If present trends continue, and there is every sign that they will, it may become increasingly difficult for the average consumer to differentiate between hard news, soft news, and entertainment. The 1982 appearance of former President Gerald Ford and former Secretary of State Henry Kissinger, playing themselves on an episode of the very popular ABC soap opera, *Dynasty*, is a clear and frightening example of television's merger of politics and entertainment.

Although newspapers lack the dramatic tools of television, they have tried to spice up their copy and follow stories that have dramatic appeal. Some of the major metropolitan tabloids use exceptionally large headlines to announce increasingly dramatic and macabre happenings. Dramatic stories appear, with different wrinkles, for weeks on end. Buy the paper tomorrow for the next installment.

In keeping with the need to present the news in a dramatic fashion, the media devote most of their energy to covering the most current news. "Three-quarters of the stories out of Washington are about an event that happened yesterday, today, or is expected to happen tomorrow; the figure for television is ten percent higher."[10]

Breaking news is considered the most dramatic. There is a vicarious experience in viewing or reading about something that has just occurred. It is similar to tuning in to find out the scores of the day's ball games. Being informed becomes equated with knowing a few things that happened on a particular day. With this concentration on breaking news in newspapers and television, there is almost no space left for the more interpretive, analytic, or investigative news stories. These types of stories would require a greater degree of commitment on the part of the reader or viewer. They would take more time to read, would require more air time, and would prove generally more difficult to appreciate without some background.

These, then, are the important economic and organizational factors that determine what will become news. Some of these factors are the direct result of the bureaucratic nature of the modern news organization. Such organizations establish routines designed to insure a regular and predictable output. In news organizations, these routines or procedures give a high premium to news events that are planned well in advance and can be conveniently covered by journalists at an established beat. Many of the internal pressures discussed can also be traced to what is commonly called "the bottom line"—the need for news organizations to be profitable. Competition in television news at both the national and local level is quite fierce. Newspapers often face less direct competition but have considerable difficulty remaining profitable and, as a result, face the constant threat of extinction.

The success of some of the sensationalist tabloids, the *Star*, the *Enquirer*, and the *New York Post*, for example, have sent other newspapers scurrying to imitate this style. The *Eyewitness News* format, which presents stories in the quickest succession and gives plenty of time to the "beautiful people" and "man bites dog" stories, is a most popular news format. Not unexpectedly, it is increasingly being copied by other local news programs struggling to improve their ratings.

The need to attract and hold an audience has sent news executives rushing about for new formulas and new faces. The assumption that news watchers are really in search of entertainment—which, of course, results in a self-fulfilling prophecy and the production of entertainment —has resulted in drama, "nowness," and esthetics being elevated to premiere values in selecting news.

## EXTERNAL INFLUENCES ON THE NEWS

The internal pressures that play a role in determining what becomes news are fairly constant and identifiable. One glance at any evening news program, for example, demonstrates the value given drama, visuals, entertainment, and up-to-date happenings. In contrast, external pressures come from a variety of different sources and have an influence over the news that is sometimes difficult to measure.

External pressures are applied at the various levels of the news organizations. Journalists feel constant pressure from sources who are eager to get attention and influence the coverage they receive. Strong external pressures are laid on management by affiliate stations, advertisers, and interest groups. This patchwork of individuals, corporate advertisers, and organized political interests is probably a more significant factor than internal influences in determining what finally makes the news. The internal influences have established certain boundaries and procedures for journalists to follow. Recognizing this set of constraints established by management, these campaign organizations, political institutions, and corporate boardrooms attempt to exert influence over what is covered and how it is covered.

There are two other important external influences on the media—the legal system and the FCC. In the previous chapter, we examined the ways Supreme Court decisions have had an impact on media policy and described the role of the Federal Communication Commission, the agency charged with the regulation of the broadcast media.

**Source Pressures**

Newsmakers are in a perfect position to attempt to influence the news, since they are the actual source of the news. Sources generate pressures in a variety of ways, from presidential attempts to intimidate the media to the use of professional public relations firms to plan strategies carefully for managing the news.

Journalists usually depend heavily on their sources to identify stories for them and to provide the information necessary to write the stories. In general, journalists do not explore the political terrain for stories. They do not do outside research or probe deeply into the complexities of an issue. They depend on sources to signal them when there is a potential story.

The favored method of informing journalists about a story is the press release. The press release has been used for some time as a way of alerting journalists to upcoming events. As the use of press releases expands, they become more than a means of alerting the journalist to an event; they become a means for a skilled press agent to start the process of imposing a particular meaning on the event that the journalist is being alerted to. Lippmann was aware quite early that the nature of facts would impel individuals to attempt to cast them in a particular light for the press.

Were reporting simply the recovery of obvious facts, the press agent would be little more than a clerk. But since, in respect to most of the big topics of news, the facts are not simple, and not at all obvious, but subject to choice and opinion, it is natural that everyone should wish to make his own choice of facts for the newspapers and print. The publicity man does that. *He is a censor and propagandist, responsible only to his employers, and to the whole truth only as it accords with the employers' conception of his own interests*[11] [Our emphasis].

It is not only the employers' interest that is served by the styling of information and facts in the press release but also the reporter's. Receiving the facts and information for a story in a well-packaged press release spares reporters the need to compile the facts on their own and ɪrake judgments about what is most important.

Since there are many organizations and persons trying to get into the news, the journalist is likely to receive many press releases. Certain releases are routinely ignored, sometimes because the journalist or editor does not consider the issue, event, or personality newsworthy, sometimes on the basis of the fact that the journalist is hesitant to use new sources or report on new issues. Journalists become comfortable with their sources; often they become friends. They generally choose sources that they enjoy being with—sources that share the same socioeconomic background.

A 1976 study found that 8 percent of the press releases received from candidates running for state senate were used in the form they were received.[12] This study also found that only 31 percent of the press releases received are totally ignored. Obviously, 69 percent of the releases received are playing some role in generating news.

This relationship of mutual benefit characterizes the relationship between most journalists and sources. But this relationship is not static; it moves along a continuum. At one pole, the journalist may be a tool of a news source, shaped and manipulated with great ease. At the other end of the continuum, journalists may adopt an adversarial, critical approach to the source, questioning all that is said, even reporting attempts by the source to manipulate opinion.

The press release is only one mechanism in a large repertoire of techniques that sources use to exert influence on the news. The news conference is a clever device for attempting to exert influence. A spokesperson or a politician is in the position to feed the press a story. Questions from journalists at a news conference are either anticipated in advance, in which case standard replies are devised, or skillfully answered in a way that gives support to the position being put forth by the source. After some practice, a spokesperson can skillfully control a news conference and influence what is reported.

Another common technique used by sources is called the "back-grounder." These sessions usually involve meetings between a small number of journalists and an official. These sessions are governed by strict ground rules which a journalist agrees to before the session. The most important rule is that journalists are not permitted to identify the source of the information given and are not permitted to print certain information verbatim. The backgrounder provides an official with a mechanism to get certain issues across without having to take responsibility for a position. When information is attributed to "informed sources" or "sources close to the issue," the information has often come from a backgrounder.

Leaks are another common technique used by sources to influence the news. In most cases, just the idea of being privy to a leak is enough to get the reporter to print the leak. Leaks are a perfect way of getting the press to print certain stories that the source would rather not be associated with. It is a form of guilt by innuendo. Leaks are commonly used to discredit opponents. A leak was used to reveal the fact that Senator Thomas Eagleton had undergone electroshock therapy for emotional depression. The story hurt the presidential campaign of George McGovern (Eagleton was the vice-presidential candidate). The White House commonly uses leaks. According to former CBS Washington correspondent Daniel Schorr, "...leaking was a cottage industry in the White House. Dozens of memorandums of the Watergate period routinely advised the planting of specific stories with friendly columnists like Victor Lasky and Evans and Novak."[13]

The relationship between the source and the press may sometimes break down, which can set the stage for a power struggle—an occasion for sources to use more aggressive means to wield some influence. During the early 1970s, when the conflict between significant elements of the power structure and the media was most intense, sources sought a new means to curb the power of the media, to make it more accommodating and cooperative.* Congress has also flexed its muscles against certain elements of the news media. Congress ordered an investigation of CBS correspondent Daniel Schorr and *The Village Voice* to determine how a confidential House Committee report on the activities of American intelligence agencies was leaked to the *Voice*, which printed the report in its entirety. Schorr, who later admitted giving the report to the *Voice*, was subpoenaed by the House Ethics Committee to testify as to how he had received the report—to name his source. He refused, stating that "...to betray a confidential source would mean to dry up many

---

*Efforts by both Presidents Johnson and Nixon to intimidate the news media into a more cooperative and less adversarial posture are now well-documented.

future sources for many reporters."[14] Schorr was dismissed from CBS news.

An investigation of two CBS documentaries, *The Selling of the Pentagon* and *Hunger,* resulted in CBS's having to spend considerable time and energy defending itself. The investigation of the documentary *The Selling of the Pentagon,* which concerned propaganda efforts in support of Pentagon policy, was carried out by the House Commerce Committee at the urging of the Nixon administration. The investigation threatened to get very volatile when the Commerce Committee voted to hold Frank Stanton, president of CBS News, in contempt of Congress for refusing to turn over "unused portions of interviews and other materials connected with the production of a controversial CBS documentary."[15]

Sources rarely need to be so aggressive in their attempt to control the content of the news. In ordinary circumstances, the established procedures of the press release, the news conference, the backgrounder, and the leak will suffice to insure control by major news sources. The journalists' dependence on their sources insures that, at the heart of the relationship between the source and the journalist, there will be cooperation and continuity.

### Advertising Pressures

There is some difference of opinion about how much influence advertisers can and do exert. This sort of influence is difficult to observe and measure; it may be wielded in the inner sanctums of a station or a network and take a variety of forms. Influence may come in the form of some implied agreement between network executives and advertisers to stay away from certain subjects or to give advertisers warnings when stories that may be in conflict with their interests are to appear.

Warning advertisers is apparently common practice in the broadcasting and print media. In Gans's fieldwork at CBS, NBC, *Newsweek,* and *Time,* he found that producers or editors would check to see if there were any advertisers who might be affected by a particular story running that day.[16] The producer notifies the business department, which informs the advertising agency or the sponsor of the potential conflict. The agency is given the option to hold the commercial until the next day's broadcast or, in the case of news magazines, until the next issue. If they decide to proceed with the commercial, the producer will schedule the commercial as far from the story as possible. For example, if there were a story on the recall of Chevrolets at the beginning of the broadcast, the producer would slot a General Motors commercial at the end of the broadcast. To do otherwise would be considered as an attack on an advertiser.

Whether stations and networks do not pursue certain stories in deference to large advertising interests is difficult to establish firmly. These would largely be acts of omission. Yet there are major issues and stories with negative impact on advertisers that seem to have been studiously avoided by the networks. Remember that Edward R. Murrow's program on the dangers of cigarette smoking, when cigarette advertisers were the largest single source of advertising dollars, was considered as an act of contempt toward the network, which apparently would not have considered doing such programs. The coverage of the dangers of cigarette smoking, which were becoming apparent as early as 1936, was very thin. Most of the print media either avoided the issue or buried articles concerning the dangers in the back pages of the paper. Television news coverage of the issue was even more sparse.[17] There is good reason to believe that, at the very least, the millions of dollars of advertising revenue supplied by the tobacco companies created an incentive not to cover stories dealing with the hazards of smoking.

The media's reluctance to give visible coverage to studies documenting the hazards of smoking is matched by their coverage of the issue of automobile safety. When Ralph Nader offered a serialized version of his book, *Unsafe at Any Speed,* to the media (the book documented the design hazards of automobiles, particularly the General Motors Corvair), all 700 newspapers offered the serialization refused.[18] In his book, Nader prophetically noted how the industry's influence in the media had kept the issue of safety from the public: "... by dominating the channels of communication through which the customer receives his information about automobiles [the industry] has obscured the relation of vehicle design to life and limb and has kept quiet its technical capacity of building crash-worthy vehicles."[19]

Since the news media are dependent on the advertising dollar for survival, the advertiser's most potent weapon is the withdrawal of its advertisements. General Motors withdrew its support of an Easter program on the life of Jesus because of objection from evangelist groups. CBS was faced with a near-complete pullout of advertisers for a planned documentary on gun control and for a series of interviews with ex-President Nixon.[20]

The degree to which advertisers feel comfortable with using the advertising weapon to register their dissatisfaction with particular programs or individuals is revealed in this tale. A fan of Ed Asner, star of *The Lou Grant Show,* wrote to Kimberly Clark, a sponsor of the show, to express his support for Asner and the show. Asner had been attacked on many fronts when he formed a group of actors and sent $25,000 in medical supplies to guerrilla fighters in El Salvador. At the time, Asner was president of the Screen Actors Guild and was charged with using that office to promote the cause of the Salvadoran guerrillas. Asner received a lot of bad press, much of it insinuating that Asner was a Communist sympathizer. As a result of this bad press, Kimberly Clark must have received a large number of letters critical of Asner. The individual at the company with the task of answering the letters assumed that this letter of support for Asner must have been another critical letter and sent the writer what seemed to be the standard reply sent to those writing letters against Asner. In essence, the letter stated that Kimberly Clark was, as a result of Asner's behavior and of letters from concerned customers, withdrawing its advertising support from *The Lou Grant Show.*

A few weeks after the main furor, CBS announced that *The Lou Grant Show,* a highly-praised, Emmy Award-winning television series, was being canceled. CBS quite naturally claimed that the cancellation was caused by a drop in the show's ratings. The network was not about to say publicly that it had canceled the show because Asner had taken a controversial political position. Kimberly Clark's withdrawal of advertising demonstrates that CBS must have been feeling pressure from advertisers. Asner would have none of CBS's explanation about ratings. He is convinced that cancellation involved "a great deal of political decision making."[21] For Asner, the incident was reminiscent of the blacklisting of actors during the 1950s, caused by pressures from Senator Joseph McCarthy.

Advertisers are also in the position to apply pressure on newspapers. In a recent incident, a young business reporter was fired on his first day on the job at the *Trenton Times* for refusing to print a press release of a local advertiser verbatum—to print the release as if it were a regular news story written by the journalist. The *Trenton Times* had been purchased by newspaper tycoon Joseph Allbritten, who had dismissed a quarter of the paper's staff after taking over. Remaining staffers, who, at this time, must have been insecure about their futures, got word of the firing to the national press, which picked up the story. A *New York Times* investigation revealed that staffers had previously been instructed by management to print articles favorable to advertisers. A former business editor, who seemed to find religion after the fact, claimed that she had been instructed to print "self flattering articles" submitted by business executives. Businessmen, who were probably surprised that anyone should get excited about the revelation of cooperation between business and the newspaper's management, said quite candidly that "...they had bought space with the understanding that the paper would publish their 'news' articles about their operation."[22]

Under the strains of widespread exposure, at a time when Allbritten was negotiating to buy the *New York Daily News,* Allbritten published an editorial conceding that management had made a mistake. But actions speak louder than words in this case. No disciplinary action was taken against anyone in management, including those who had directly ordered the reporter to print the release. The reporter was not rehired.

Some of the most intense and obvious pressure has been felt by noncommercial public television. Although public television receives funding from the federal government, many of its programs are under-written by grants from large corporations. Recently, there was controversy when Mobil Oil led a campaign to cancel a public television program which allegedly exposed the escapades and intrigues of the Saudi Arabian Royal Family. The Royal Family was very unhappy about the broadcast. Mobil, which does considerable business with Saudi Arabia, lobbied to have the program canceled. Mobil's efforts included ads in the *New York Times* criticizing the objectivity of the program and rumored threats to withdraw its substantial support. Some PBS stations withdrew the program, and others carried it. Most of the stations that carried it included a panel discussion after the show, where critics were given an opportunity to respond to the program's content.

There are a number of examples of advertising pressures for program change on specific shows which have, for one reason or another, surfaced and become public. How much pressure is quietly exerted and how much self-censorship makes pressure from advertisers unnecessary is difficult to know.

## Affiliate Pressures on Television News

Since the affiliate stations are an important source of revenues, the networks must pay attention to affiliate complaints. Affiliates are not obliged to accept everything the network produces. They may refuse to "clear" certain programs produced by the networks. If a large number of affiliates refuse to carry a program, advertising revenues decline accordingly. This may make the production of a particular program unprofitable for the networks.

Many of the affiliate stations are owned and operated by businessmen who were lured into broadcasting by the romantic notion of owning a television station and by the chance to make some money. In general, the affiliate owners tend to be Republicans and conservatives, with pragmatic ideals and a preoccupation with a return on invested capital.[23]

In general, the affiliates will not show programs that they do not feel are "safe." Anything controversial, or material that might offend the sensibilities of the local audience, is avoided. Affiliates are unusually careful with network-produced documentaries, particularly since CBS ran afoul of the administration with *The Selling of the Pentagon* and *Hunger*. At NBC, the affiliates raised objections to a report on the killings at Kent State, which they termed "one-sided."[24] All the networks were subject to criticism for their coverage of the Vietnam war. Remember that affiliate stations are spread throughout the nation and that the South and the West were regions supportive of the war in Vietnam long after opinion in the East had turned against the war. Affiliates also balked at the networks, particularly CBS, for their coverage of Watergate. The Nixon administration counted on affiliate owners, many of whom were loyal Republicans, to apply pressure on CBS to alter its provocative coverage of Watergate.

Affiliates also frequently complain about the network news. While they could refuse to clear documentaries they disliked, they could not stop showing the network news during the period of the affiliate contract or edit out sections of the news that they judged undesirable. Their position of strength in being able to refuse programing, however, provided a way for them to influence the news indirectly. Constant complaints about one-sided coverage caused all the networks to become more concerned with "balance" in news reports dealing with controversial issues. They hoped that by eliminating some of the aggressive reporting about Vietnam, or Watergate, or couching this reporting in a milder form, they would quiet some of the affiliates' dissatisfaction with other programing.

How much and how often the networks are influenced by affiliate complaints is difficult to judge. Some network executives portray themselves as prisoners of affiliate wishes. Rulings of the FCC have tended to leave the affiliate the option of refusing programing—their principle weapon against the networks. The relationship between the network and the affiliate is subject to change. It is a relationship that is determined by the prevailing economic and social climate.

**Interest Group Pressures**

Many interest groups have become considerably more active in both monitoring the content of media programs and attempting to get the media to provide more and better coverage of certain of their activities, issues, or moral positions. Pressure on advertisers to withdraw sponsorship from certain programs was brought by some of these groups, who went to advertisers when the networks and the FCC were not very responsive to their suggested changes.

To date, much of the pressure from interest groups has centered on entertainment programing. The national PTA has been successful, mainly through the use of pressure on advertisers, in reducing the number of violent programs shown during early evening hours. There are, however, cases of interest group pressure applied to news programing. The American Jewish Committee, for example, applied pressure on CBS about a segment of 60 Minutes dealing with Syrian Jewry. This pressure was successful in bringing about an "amplification" of the issue in a later 60 Minutes program.[25] The recent efforts of Jesse Helms, the Republican Senator from North Carolina and leader of the conservative group called "Fairness in Media," to spark a takeover of CBS illustrates the more intense pressure now being exerted by ideological groups.

These days, the pressure being put on networks for changes in entertainment programing has a decidedly political character. Some of the most effective pressure has been applied by a group which calls itself "The Coalition for Better Television," headed by the Rev. Donald Wildman, a fundamentalist Methodist minister from Tupelo, Mississippi. "The Coalition" has close connections with the "moral majority," which is deeply involved in politics. The coalition was successful in pressuring Proctor and Gamble into withdrawing advertising from shows that they found objectionable. Rev. Wildman has also been calling for a boycott of NBC TV and its parent corporation, RCA. NBC is charged with excluding "Christian characters, Christian values and Christian culture from their programming."[26] The Coalition's efforts are aimed at forcing the networks into including programs that contain their vision of what is morally and politically correct.

### Working with Pressure

The fact that journalists and news organizations are guided by internal demands and pressured by outside forces does not mean that everything that becomes news is the result of these pressures. There are stories that are provocative and raise issues that many in the political and the corporate establishment find troubling. Certainly there are many stories which, if we apply any set of criteria, deserve to be reported. Pressures on news organizations and journalists vary; there are periods when outside forces may push hard for a desired result and other times when pressure is very limited. There are also many cases in which pressure, sometimes extreme pressure, has been gallantly resisted. Whether external pressure will be a factor in determining the news, and to what degree it will be a factor, depends on a variety of conditions which we will examine in subsequent chapters on the coverage of the political and corporate worlds.

These internal and external pressures do not affect only the form of a story or the choice of particular topics but also affect the content of the story. American journalism proclaims a commitment to objective reporting, to the presentation of facts, and to a policy of fairness and balance. It is necessary to consider how organizational policies and external pressures affect that commitment.

### FAIRNESS AND FACTS

Determining what is a fact and maintaining a commitment to objectivity and fairness are very difficult goals. There are a variety of influences which color perceptions of what is a fact, which facts to believe, and what is the meaning of a fact. Facts given or received from some sources are considered reliable and believable, while facts offered by other sources are considered fabricated and self-serving. Even if a genuine and concerted effort is made to use all available means to verify a fact, it may be markedly changed by the way it is reported and interpreted. If the mission is to present a report based on fact, a concerted commitment is required to do the hard work that is necessary before a piece of information can be given the title of "fact." To achieve objectivity and fairness also requires a sincere commitment. Journalists or editors must strip themselves of personal and ideological beliefs and report the news as dispassionate observers. They must guard against the inevitable desire of all news sources to present the facts that are favorable to their interest or to interpret facts in a kindly light. Fairness requires that news organizations and journalists present the various positions or sides of the issues. To achieve fairness, the media must present these varying positions on equal terms. Is it fair to present 20 minutes of the "establishment" position and only 2 minutes of an opposing argument? With this very simple explanation of what is required to realize the goal of objective reporting, we turn to a more detailed examination of the media's treatment of facts and their pursuit of fairness and objectivity.

Although readers or viewers may consider the news to be packed with facts, they fail to realize that "facts" may be false or may be used for purposes other than achieving objectivity and balance. Otto Friedrich, a former journalist and writer on the media, has written an interesting article, "There are 00 Trees in Russia," which reveals some of the hidden dimensions in the way that the media use "facts." Most news organizations have a sort of fetish about facts; they are often checked and rechecked, but they are often used as a means to ends other than objectivity. Friedrich shows how facts are often used simply to support a writer's point of view or highlight the dramatic elements of a particular tale. Consider this passage from a story in *Time* magazine on Henry Cabot Lodge, former Ambassador to Vietnam, once considered as a potential Republican presidential candidate.

> In the early-morning gloom of Saigon's muggy premonsoon season, an alarm clock shrills in the stillness of a second-floor bedroom at 38 Phung Khac Khoan Street. The Brahmin from Boston arises, breakfasts on mango or papaya, sticks a snub-nosed 38 cal. Smith & Wesson revolver into a shoulder holster and leaves for the office.[27]

Here is a lead packed with facts assembled by *Time* magazine reporters. What is the purpose of this presentation of minute details about the way Henry Cabot Lodge begins his day? According to Friedrich, these facts serve two purposes, neither of which is related to achieving a greater degree of objectivity. First, there is "the theory that knowledge of lesser facts implies knowledge of major facts." Cramming the first few paragraphs with these facts gives the reader the idea that "*Time* knows everything there is to know about Lodge."[28] Second, the facts are used to support the author's basic thesis and dramatic flow. The author's basic thesis in this article was that Lodge would be a good Republican presidential candidate. This is supported by the assumption that anyone who carries a gun must be tough and aggressive, two important presidential qualities, as the reporter evidently sees it. Mention of the 38 caliber Smith & Wesson is included to support the reporter's or the magazine's preconceived notion. In this representative example, the use of facts does not bring the reader closer to objective news.

There is another interesting anecdote used by Friedrich that captures another facet of the newsmagazine's use of facts. It is common for reporters working for newsmagazines to insert a double zero ("00") in front of something to indicate that they do not have an exact number. When a story containing a "00" is filed, it is the job of a researcher to find the appropriate fact. Friedrich recounts the story of a *Newsweek* researcher who received a story about the Sudanese army, described as the "00-man Sudanese army."

> No newspaper clippings could fill in the figure, and telephone calls to the Sudanese Embassy in Washington indicated that nobody there could either. The Sudanese may well have been surprised that anyone should want to know such a figure. As the weekly deadline approached, an editor finally instructed the checker to make "an educated guess" and the story appeared with a reference to something like "the 17,000 man Sudanese army." There were no complaints. The *Newsweek* story duly reached Khartoum, where the press complaisantly reprinted it and commented on it. Digests of the Khartoum press returned to Washington, and one day a Sudanese Embassy official happily telephoned the *Newsweek* researcher to report that he finally was able to tell her the exact number of men in the Sudanese army: seventeen thousand.[29]

It is not unusual for facts to be recycled, as they were in this instance. Facts can be invented, as the researcher in this story invented the figure of seventeen thousand for the size of the Sudanese army. Once in circulation, these "facts" take on a life of their own. It becomes difficult to determine the origin of the "fact" or to disprove it. If the Sudanese embassy had called the newsmagazine some weeks after the story appeared to report that a census had determined that there were twenty-five thousand soldiers in the army, there would be a competing fact. Would the public ever learn of this claim by the Sudanese, and, if so, how would the public determine which is the correct number of soldiers?

The difficulty is determining what will be considered a fact. For example, if President Reagan claims that the Soviets have nuclear superiority, is that now to be considered a fact? Suppose, the day after the President's claim, the Chairman of the Armed Services Committee claims that the United States has superiority, and, the day after that, a Pentagon general claims that there is parity between the two nations. Which is the real fact? For the press, responsibility in this area seems limited to trans-mitting the factual claims of those who are powerful enough to be able to capture the media's attention. Newsmen may use some qualifying device in reporting the story, such as writing that the President "asserts" or "claims" that the Soviets have superiority, or they may quote another powerful figure with contrasting views, but they will make little con-certed effort to do the research to establish whether the "facts" being transmitted are reasonable or unreasonable, true or false. Is it sufficient merely to present all the "facts," with some hope that the public will reject those that are not credible?

Facts are frequently used to support some preconceived notion or ideological premise, whether conscious or unconscious, about the meaning of an issue or an event. How a fact or series of facts is interpreted determines the meaning of the facts to the reader or viewer. Consider the following example of the way the basic fact of an attack on three black men was interpreted by different media. On the evening of Tuesday, June 23, 1982, three black men stopped at a delicatessen in Sheepshead Bay, Brooklyn, a predominantly white neighborhood. Subsequently, they were attacked by a large group of white teenagers. There was, of course, the question of whether the incident was racially-motivated. One television station decided to "play" or emphasize the racial character of the incident. That station's correspondent interviewed residents of the neighborhood, who swore that racial tensions in the neighborhood were high and that whites were continually attacked by blacks if they wandered into pockets of the neighborhood with a black population. One man was quite blunt in announcing that the people in the neighborhood simply do not like blacks. Another station chose to report the incident not as a racial attack but as a vicious and pointless attack by a group of troubled youths. This station's correspondent interviewed several community residents who swore that there were no racial problems in the neighborhood. One man explained that there were many black workers in the neighborhood and there had never been any trouble. Another resident said that the attack was the result of gangs of youths with nothing to do, hanging around the street corners, drinking and looking for trouble. "Something like this happens at the beginning of each summer," said one resident. What are the facts?

The account of this incident in the June 23, 1982 edition of the *New York Times* provides a different account, reporting that some community residents denied that racial tension existed, while others maintained that racial tensions were high. The *Times* account reports both groups' perceptions in the same article, rather than "playing" one group's perception, as the TV station had. Additionally, the *Times* provides a series of facts totally absent in the TV account of the incident. First, the police in the area, according to the *Times*, report that there had been several recent attacks on blacks by whites. More importantly, the *Times* reports that one of the victims (one man was killed in the attack) told police that the white youths had yelled: "Nigger, get out of here," while they pummeled him with baseball bats.[30] What facts the news consumers received was determined by the source of their news.

You can find examples like the one cited above every day of the week. One of the common exercises in journalism classes is to ask the students to do a comparative news analysis, to follow the ways a story is covered by the newspapers and TV stations. Teachers use this exercise because it always produces the same result; it is a dependable method of demonstrating the diverse use of facts and interpretations.

Although facts are regarded as icons in journalism, the journalist generally relies on only one method to collect and verify facts. Entire stories, often containing very complex factual material, are routinely composed solely on the basis of oral interviews. Washington reporters, according to Hess, rely entirely on oral interviews for three-quarters of their stories.[31] Facts received in one oral interview are verified by conducting another oral interview.

News organizations have no demonstrable commitment to research. This is evidenced by the fact that most news organizations do not even maintain research facilities in Washington. While the element of speed might be thought to inhibit the reporter from frequently using outside research sources (libraries, government documents, secondary sources, professional journals), there is little evidence to show that the journalist, given more time to do the story, would actually do more research. Hess found that when journalists have more time to complete a story, they simply do more interviews. Given the opportunity to eliminate one of the chief organizational obstacles to doing more research, the deadline, reporters continue to do what they are accustomed to doing.

Under the best of circumstances, the objective treatment of facts is very difficult, requiring reflection, analysis, and research. The organizational constraints on television and newspapers do not permit the journalist to make any sophisticated efforts at determining the facts. With the exception of the investigative reporter, who is permitted a larger block of time to prepare a story, journalists work in a business that requires a very quick assembly of facts. Organizational constraints, particularly the deadline and emphasis on "nowness," require the journalist to use what Gaye Tuchman has called "strategic rituals" in dealing with facts.[32] In essence, the journalist follows a set of well-established organizational guidelines prescribed for acquiring and using facts.

The oral interview, for example, in which a journalist interviews a source in person or, more often, calls the source on the telephone, is regarded as a legitimate method for gathering facts. Yet, in many cases, the oral interview does not yield facts. What is usually received is one individual's interpretation or representation of a fact, which may or may not be accurate. The organization does not require journalists to go any further in verifying the accuracy of the fact, and the journalists seem perfectly content to confine their inquiry to asking questions and dutifully recording the answers. With a source to back up facts appearing in a story, journalists have satisfied the organizational ritual, as well as protecting themselves from future libel suits. These rituals are not unlike going to church on Sundays or special holidays and believing that the mere attendance at a religious service is enough to make you religious and send you straight to heaven, no matter what sins you may choose to commit in your daily life. Invoking these rituals allows the journalist to *feel* "objective."

As in the case of facts, there are also strategic rituals used to satisfy the requirements of fairness. However, the journalist's conception of fairness is very narrow. Only the most obvious sides of any controversy are presented.[33] When a political issue is raised by a Democrat, the media find a Republican to respond, even if the issue is not partisan in nature. If someone is attacked, the media will usually permit a response. Rarely are more than two sides of an issue presented: this situation gives the viewer or reader the false impression that all issues and controversies are reducible to two neatly-defined positions. The most established groups are continually called upon to render judgments and opinions. The NAACP, for example, one of the most conservative black organizations, is given the role of official spokesperson for the entire black population. Routine guidelines for fairness are applied without considering the nature of the issue. With this limited definition of fairness, journalists become the natural ally of powerful, established groups and an obstacle to the expression of less powerful interests.

Certainly, one reason that journalists' attempts to achieve fairness is so perfunctory is the fault of the training the news organization provides. Journalists come to understand what is expected. They know, for example, that production and financial constraints prohibit any large-scale attempt to achieve fairness. It is easy to imagine that 30 minutes of uninterrupted airtime should be devoted to a single issue in order to treat the issue fairly. The McNeil-Lehrer Report,* a popular news show

---

*The McNeil-Lehrer Report has recently expanded to a one-hour format.

appearing on public television, does just that. Each evening, thirty minutes is devoted to a single issue in the news. Spokespersons representing different sides of an issue are questioned by the show's commentators. Commercial television is not generally willing to devote thirty minutes of prime time television to a discussion of a single issue. Newspapers have a very limited amount of news space after advertisements are inserted. They will not devote 50 or 60 percent of the daily news space to a single issue. Consequently, journalists learn early to forgo searching out and presenting the complexities of an issue in favor of following the accepted procedure of finding and using only the most obvious and established positions.

In reality, it is not very difficult to teach the news reporter the ways of the organization. The organization is careful to choose those who, they feel, will have no difficulty conforming to organizational procedures. Those candidates who demonstrate any strong feelings about particular political issues are eliminated. Television networks are known to spend time doing background checks for any trace of past political affiliations or activity.[34] Although the print media deny that they conduct background checks, management makes it apparent that those with strong ideological leanings are not welcome.[35] If correspondents with strong political interests happen to slip through, they can be eased out later. Sam Jaffee of ABC News claims that he was eased out because of his "leftist ideas." Those who make it in journalism realize that they are in a highly competitive vocation, where team play is a most valued characteristic.

While most news organizations require journalists to fulfill only "strategic rituals," it is not only the demands of the organization which prevent the journalist from making a more gallant effort to seek out opposing spokespeople and make some determination of who is telling the truth. It is the journalists' own view of the political world and their dependence on sources which limit their initiative and will.

Journalists, particularly those on television, have a very limited understanding of politics. Despite the fact that they are constantly immersed in political issues, they are essentially ignorant of the political process.[36] While Edward Epstein was researching his book on television news, *News from Nowhere*, he attempted to explore the question of how much journalists knew about politics. Assuming that those who are politically informed devote time to reading a variety of publications about politics, he asked journalists which newspapers and journals they read and how frequently they read them. Most of the correspondents not only claimed that they read the major dailies—the *New York Times*, the *Wall Street Journal*, and the *Washington Post*—but also boasted of consuming many regional newspapers and a wide variety of magazines. One NBC correspondent said he read no fewer than twelve newspapers daily and eighteen magazines a month, while other correspondents named magazines they seemed only vaguely familiar with as ones they read regularly.[37] Epstein was skeptical about this extensive list cited by journalists, probably because, during all the time that he conducted his research, he rarely observed a correspondent reading a periodical. Epstein asked correspondents to name any articles that had appeared in these publications in the last month that "...had impressed them favorable or unfavorably." The results were revealing: "Only two of the twenty correspondents he put this question to named a specific magazine article. More than half of the correspondents were not able to cite a single article in either a newspaper or magazine that they considered impressive."[38]

The journalists' lack of interest in broadening their political vision is partly a result of the fact that their organizations do not demand it. In fact, their organizations may become suspicious of a journalist who delves too deeply into conflicting views and ideological interpretations. Journalists come to regard the political world as corrupt and self-serving and politics as simply a game. Of course, if you consider politics to be nothing more than a game, it makes very little sense to risk anything to find out who might be telling the truth.

Journalists are conditioned by their organizational experience and their world view to be suspicious of those with extreme ideological beliefs. Zealots, revolutionaries, and those committed to one or another form of social change do not easily fit within an acceptable political cast of characters. Of course, what is to be considered extreme changes with time. Fifteen years ago, many of Ronald Reagan's positions would have been considered as on the extreme right. Today, Ronald Reagan is the buoy in the center of the political channel.

There is, of course, a fundamental confusion in believing that only those with strong ideological leanings find it difficult to be objective. Being in the political center does not mean that one is devoid of ideology or is uninterested in using whatever means are available to champion a point of view. What being in the center does mean is that the point of view you have is less likely to cause a majority of viewers to examine their own beliefs, to upset them with an alternative point of view, or to cause confusion. News executives want to entertain the viewer, not create anxiety or doubt. Fairness becomes defined as dealing with individuals or groups that happen to be in the political center. The view provides a very useful defense against outside political pressures, which, if they enter the news, could generate protest from parts of the audience, management, advertisers, and the government. At the same time, the journalists' definition of ideology is self-serving, if not intentionally so, for it blinds them to the fact that they also have ideologies, even if these are largely unconscious.[39]

## CONCLUSION

Neither the news media's use of facts nor their efforts to insure objectivity and fairness produce anything approaching an objective presentation of politics and reality. Some of the more sensational newspapers and news programs seem to have abandoned even a pretense of such a commitment. Yet, there are many readers and viewers who believe a large part of what they see or read and accept it as reality.

News executives do not, in general, accept the notion that what determines news is the push and pull of competing pressures. To admit the central role of these economic and organizational pressures would be tantamount, in the minds of corporate executives, to backing away from the traditional claim that the media are objective, a claim which they consider as vital to their well-being. Thus, it is not surprising that news executives vigorously reject explanations which view the news in this light.

In denying the influence of such organizational factors, news executives invoke two general explanations of the way news is determined. One explanation, usually called the "mirror model," states that the media merely reflect reality, giving emphasis to that which is objectively important to their audiences. Thus, inflation, unemployment, presidential statements, political campaigns, and the like are always newsworthy and of interest to the public. In this view, the journalist is the trained observer, the objective witness, and the recorder of events. Thus, the journalist and the news organization are absolved from all responsibility for what appears in the news. News is merely a report of what has occurred. This mirror model of the news is also useful when the media come under attack from government, business, or special interest groups. When charged with an antibusiness bias, the media respond that economic bad news merely reflects reality; when charged with emphasizing violence, they respond that America is a violent society. As Frank Stanton, president of CBS News, puts it: "...there has always been a tendency to criticize or attack the press in almost direct proportion to the fault that we find with our times—probably because the press, both print and broadcast, is so much a mirror of our times."[40] Once the mirror model is invoked, it casts those who would criticize the media as enemies of the free press. Such a model virtually ignores the role of editing and production which, as we have seen, always and necessarily involves a *selection* out of reality rather than a reflection of reality.

Closely allied with this defense of the media is the defense of journalists as professionals living up to well-defined professional expectations. In this view, professional training, in the some 500 schools of journalism across the nation, insures responsible and objective journalism. Thus, journalists, as trained observers, assure an accurate picture of events. Even if we could get media executives to concede that journalists "select" news out of a variety of events, they would maintain that this selection is guided by the informed choice of a professional. There are, of course, some journalists who initiate their own stories, get good placement, and receive little editing. However, as we have seen, news is rarely the product of one mind. Rather, it is a product of an organizational team, which includes editors, producers, and technical experts. As Gaye Tuchman has so accurately observed, "Among reporters, professionalism is knowing how to get a story that meets organizational needs and standards."[41]

## NOTES

1 Doris A. Graber, *Mass Media and American Politics*, C.Q. Press, Washington, D.C., 1980, p. 68.
2 Walter Lippmann, *Public Opinion*, Free Press, New York, 1949, p. 203.
3 Graber, *Mass Media* p. 59.
4 See Daniel Boorstin, *The Image*, Atheneum, New York, 1978.
5 Leon U. Sigal, *Reporters and Officials: The Organization and Politics of Newsmaking*, D.C. Heath, Massachusetts, 1973, pp. 69–70.
6 Joseph Dominick, "Geographical Bias in National News," *Journal of Communication*, vol. 27, Fall, 1977, pp. 95–99.
7 Stephen Hess, *The Washington Reporter*, Brookings, Washington, D.C., 1980, p. 95.
8 See Timothy Crouse, *The Boys on the Bus*, Random House, New York, 1973.
9 Crouse, *The Boys on the Bus*, p. 44.
10 Hess, *The Washington Reporter*, p. 15.
11 Lippmann, *Public Opinion*, p. 218.
12 Cited in Martin, "Government and the News Media," in Dan Nimmo and Keith Sanders, *Handbook of Political Communication*, Sage, California, 1980, p. 449.
13 Daniel Schorr, *Clearing the Air*, Houghton Mifflin Co., New York, 1977, p. 180. Copyright © 1977. Reprinted by permission of Houghton Mifflin Company.
14 Schorr, *Clearing the Air*, quoted in a caption of the picture section of the book.
15 Schorr, *Clearing the Air*, p. 47.
16 Herbert J. Gans, *Deciding What's News*, Vintage, New York, 1980.
17 Robert Cirano, *Don't Blame the People*, Vintage, New York, 1971, p. 25. From *Don't Blame the People* by Robert Cirano. Copyright © 1971 by Robert Cirano. Reprinted by permission of Random House, Inc.
18 Cirano, *Don't Blame the People*, p. 14.
19 Quoted in Cirano, *Don't Blame the People*, p. 14.
20 Graber, *Mass Media*, p. 58.
21 *New York Times*, June 22, 1982, p. C23.
22 *New York Times*, February 21, 1982, p. 39.

**23** Edward J. Epstein, *News from Nowhere: Television and the News,* Vintage, New York, 1974, p. 56. Copyright © 1973 by Edward J. Epstein. Reprinted by permission of Random House, Inc.

**24** Epstein, *News from Nowhere,* p. 59.

**25** Gans, *Deciding What's News,* p. 265.

**26** Walter Goodman, "T.V. Boycotts," *New York Times,* April 5, 1982.

**27** Otto Friedrich, "There Are 00 Trees in Russia," *Harper's,* October, 1964, p. 62.

**28** Friedrich, "There Are 00 Trees in Russia," p. 62.

**29** Friedrich, "There Are 00 Trees in Russia," p. 63.

**30** *New York Times,* June 23, 1982, p. 32.

**31** Hess, *The Washington Reporter,* p. 18.

**32** See Gaye Tuchman, "Objectivity as Strategic Ritual: An Examination of Newsmen's Notions of Objectivity," *American Journal of Sociology,* vol. 77, January, 1972.

**33** See Hess, *The Washington Reporter,* p. 115; Gans, *Deciding What's News;* and Dan Nimmo and James E. Combs, *Subliminal Politics,* Prentice-Hall, Englewood Cliffs, 1980.

**34** See Epstein, *News from Nowhere.*

**35** Gans, *Deciding What's News,* p. 195.

**36** Tests administered to students entering schools of journalism show that students are generally ignorant of politics, even to the extent of not knowing the names of the three branches of national government. Students in schools of journalism are not exposed to formal courses in politics, so they are not likely to overcome the deficiency by completing journalism school. While they may do some on-the-job political training, many studies emphasize the journalist's lack of political knowledge. See Nimmo and Combs, *Subliminal Politics,* p. 167, and Epstein, *News from Nowhere,* pp. 205–220.

**37** Epstein, *News from Nowhere,* p. 209.

**38** Epstein, *News from Nowhere,* p. 211.

**39** Gans, *Deciding What's News,* p. 192.

**40** Frank Stanton, "Violence and the News," in David J. Leroy and Christopher H. Sterline (eds.), *Mass News,* Prentice-Hall, Englewood Cliffs, 1973, pp. 126–127.

**41** Gaye Tuchman, *Making News,* Free Press, New York, 1978, p. 66.

# POLITICAL CAMPAIGNS
# AND THE MEDIA

# CHAPTER 5

# MEDIA COVERAGE

*Modern politics requires television. I think you know I've never really warmed up to television, and in fairness to television, it's never really warmed up to me. I don't believe it's possible anymore to run for president without the capacity to build confidence and communications every night. It's got to be done that way.*

Walter Mondale, after his defeat in 1984

At the 1980 Republican convention, Ronald Reagan, attempting to quiet the applause of the enthusiastic delegates, quipped, "You're using up my prime time."[1] Although clearly a jest, such a line suggests that Reagan knew where his real audience was. The political power of the media, especially television, is accepted by politicians and political journalists alike, even though exactly what this power amounts to is as yet uncertain. Of all the areas where the media may influence political life, it is the campaign for public office where the role of the media is most visible. In this chapter, we will discuss the role of media coverage in the campaign.

There are several key questions that we will examine. Within the context of the media's dual role as supplier of information *and* entertainment, how are the candidates covered? Is the relationship between the candidate and the media neutral, biased, adversarial, or symbiotic? To what degree do candidates set the agenda for the media, and, conversely, to what extent do the media set the campaign agenda for the candidates? Most importantly, how effective are the media as links between the candidates and the voters?

In many ways, the media and the political campaign are made for each other, both relying on drama, conflict, and rhetoric. The campaign has the excitement of the contest, measurable results, and, above all, winners. However, any discussion of the role of media coverage of the campaign is hampered by an imbalance in the research; presidential campaigns have been extensively researched, while local campaigns have received much less attention. Although the patterns of coverage are fairly consistent in both national and local campaigns, the impact of the media varies, depending on the office being sought. Further, political and social conditions unique to a given locality can enhance or retard the impact of media coverage. Nonetheless, since presidential campaigns do receive the greatest amount of media coverage, it is here that we get at the heart of media coverage of political campaigns.

## COVERING PRESIDENTIAL ELECTIONS

### General Patterns

On the national level, candidates rely on the news media to reach the voter and "...come to look upon the community of journalists as an alternative electorate in which they must conduct a persuasive campaign."[2] Interested voters expect to be informed about the candidates during the campaign, and nearly all of the public's political information comes through the media.

Although, as we shall see, the print media are more powerful in shaping the nature and scope of campaign coverage, the emergence of the three television networks as important sources of political news has had a profound effect on the way campaigns are run and covered. Through the broadcast media, more people are exposed to campaign information than ever before, though often "inadvertently."[3] That is, many people are exposed to television news simply as a lead-in or a lead-out to other programming. But once turning on the evening news, the viewer takes what comes. Unlike newspaper readers, television viewers cannot merely skip over news they are not interested in. As a result, more people are exposed to opposition candidates than the more natural tendency toward selective exposure would allow. Of course, the viewer can give selective attention or inattention to that information.

National network news is ideally suited to the presidential candidate. Since network news is directed at national audiences, presidential candidates have come to see the network news programs as major targets of campaign strategies. In 1960, John Kennedy stated that *Time* magazine had the greatest influence on public opinion. Less than a decade later, Robert Kennedy stated his belief that "the network evening news [is] the most influential source."[4] They both had, at their respective times, ample reason to believe that they were right.

During the campaign, the power of the news media lies in their ability to select what will be covered. Organizational needs and professional values and conventions make it inevitable that some aspects of the campaign will be highlighted and others muted. The news media tend to highlight the competition at the expense of substance, the tallies at the expense of the process, and the dramatic event at the expense of larger political issues. Douglas Lowenstein, a Washington correspondent, characterized the general patterns of coverage of the 1980 primaries by print journalists as exhibiting an "addiction to forecasting results" and "a subjugation of stories about issues by stories about pithy speeches, tactics, style, and, above all else, who was ahead."[5] Michael Robinson, who has been studying election news for years, examined CBS during the same period and concluded: "CBS coverage of the campaign has been *extensive, nonpartisan, objective* and . . . *superficial.*"[6]

One of the most striking characteristics of national election coverage is the enormous agreement about what constitutes election news. Throughout the media, we find the same stories, except that smaller newspapers and local television stations have fewer election stories. The uniformity of election news is created by many of the factors discussed in Chapter 4: a shared definition of what is newsworthy, a dependence on wire services by many local outlets, the reality of pack journalism, and the ubiquitous use of quotes from the candidates. Finally, and most importantly, the uniformity of election news, as we shall see, results from the shared interest in conflict and the almost obsessive interest in keeping score on who is winning.

When we look at Tables 5-1 and 5-2, it is clear that there existed a cross-media consensus on who was newsworthy during the 1980 primary campaigns. Three leading newspapers and the most popular network news program all deemed Kennedy, Carter, and Reagan to be the most newsworthy.

There have been changes in the way the media cover presidential campaigns. In the past, the media rarely treated candidates equally. In the 1952 presidential race between Eisenhower and Stevenson, newspapers that supported one candidate on their editorial page gave that candidate more and better coverage on their news pages. However, studies throughout the 1960s and 1970s reveal that candidates of both parties, once nominated, were given roughly equal news space and were given relatively even-handed treatment.[7]

Coupled with this trend toward uniformity is a more recent trend toward negative coverage which appears in all media and applies equally to Democrats and Republicans. The proportion of negative comments about candidates has risen from a low of 41 percent about Humphrey, in 1968, to 58 percent about Republican Ford and Democrat Carter, in 1976. Newspapers tend to be about 5 percent more negative than television.[8]

**TABLE 5-1**

PRIMARY CAMPAIGNS
(Coverage of Candidates from October 1979 to
the First Week of June 1980)*

|  | *Washington Post* | | *New York Times* | | *Chicago Tribune* | |
|---|---|---|---|---|---|---|
|  | **Number** | **Percent-age** | **Number** | **Percent-age** | **Number** | **Percent-age** |
| Kennedy | 250 | 33.8 | 161 | 29.7 | 125 | 32.7 |
| Carter | 172 | 24.2 | 122 | 22.5 | 87 | 22.8 |
| Reagan | 149 | 20.1 | 108 | 19.9 | 48 | 12.6 |
| Bush | 67 | 9.1 | 45 | 8.3 | 28 | 7.3 |
| Anderson | 40 | 5.4 | 49 | 9.1 | 59 | 15.4 |
| Connally | 23 | 3.1 | 24 | 4.4 | 7 | 1.8 |
| Brown | 16 | 2.2 | 14 | 2.6 | 15 | 3.9 |
| Baker | 14 | 1.5 | 14 | 2.6 | 7 | 1.8 |
| Dole & Crane | 9 | 1.2 | 6 | 1.1 | 6 | 1.6 |
| Total | 740 | | 543 | | 382 | |

*Taken from a study done by the *Washington Journalism Review*, Douglas Lowenstein, "Covering the Primaries," *WJR*, September, 1980, pp. 38–42.

There has been a corresponding cross-media decline in comments about qualities that a candidate *ought* to have and a slight drop in the number of positive comments about candidates.

While it is difficult to observe concerted support for one presidential candidate in the national media, this does not necessarily mean that the coverage is balanced. Imbalance can occur as a result of decisions made

**TABLE 5-2**

PRIMARY CAMPAIGNS
(CBS Network News Coverage of Candidates
from January 1 to June 4, 1980)*

|  | **Number** | **Percent-age** | **Percentage of good press** |
|---|---|---|---|
| Kennedy | 80 | 26.4 | 19 |
| Carter | 85 | 28.0 | 35 |
| Reagan | 52 | 17.1 | 36 |
| Bush | 31 | 10.2 | 6 |
| Anderson | 29 | 9.5 | 28 |
| Connally | 5 | 1.6 | 0 |
| Brown | 8 | 2.6 | 0 |
| Baker | 8 | 2.6 | 0 |
| Dole & Crane | 5 | 1.6 | 0 |
| Total | 303 | | |

*Taken from "The Media at Mid-Year: A Bad Year for McLuhanites?" by Michael Robinson, with Nancy Conover and Margaret Sheehan, in *Public Opinion*, June/July, 1980, p. 42.

by the candidates themselves. For example, if an incumbent president chooses to stay out of the campaign, and many incumbents have done so, there will subsequently be more coverage of his challenger's campaign. Nonetheless, as an incumbent, any president is guaranteed coverage, even if it is not directly campaign coverage. Further, there are inherent structural biases in campaign coverage which result from the characteristics of a given medium. Television and newspapers have a greater focus on "breaking news," while news magazines provide less coverage of timely campaign actions, like candidate tours, and more emphasis than television and newspapers on campaign issues. Newspapers give more coverage to stories that produce a follow-up the next day. For example, a candidate's attack on the opponent has a natural follow-up in the opponent's response. Naturally, television tends to provide more coverage than the other media of that which can be shown.

The overall pattern of uniformity in campaign news means that Americans across the country receive similar information. However, what the voter learns from the media will be determined by such variables as level of interest, prior knowledge, need for information, level of education, strength of party loyalty, and, of course, the impact of social, political, and economic events of the day. Nonetheless, the uniformity of election coverage shapes the perceived nature of the campaign and limits the range of discussion. Once again, the media do not determine what we think but rather what or whom we think about.

### The Media as Kingmakers: The Pre-Pre-Campaign and the Primaries

The power of the media is generally thought to be related to a decline in party loyalty in presidential campaigns. Much evidence is cited in support of this thesis, and recent studies indicate that party loyalty has taken third place to candidate personality and image and the consideration of issues in the voter's final decision.[9] Since the media are the major sources of data on image and issues, it is reasoned, media's role becomes more important. However, the single most important factor in the increased influence of the media lies in the fact that the nominating process is no longer controlled by party leaders.

After 1968, several changes in the nominating process were instituted by the Democratic Party. Under the previous rules, 70 to 80 percent of the delegates to the nominating conventions were handpicked by state and local party leaders. The potential candidate had to answer to a small group of powerful men who controlled the nominating process. Prior to 1968, only 30 percent of the convention delegates were selected by direct primary. Under the new rules, which began to take effect in the early 1970s, binding primaries began to be established around the country in which delegates were elected by direct vote of party members and were required to vote at the convention in accordance with the electorate's wishes. There were twenty-five primaries in 1972, thirty in 1975, and thirty-eight in 1980. The number of delegates selected by party leaders dropped to about 25 percent. Since the establishment of primaries is done by state law, Republicans had to live with the same system. Since about 75 percent of party delegates are now selected by direct primary, presidential candidates must seek the nomination through the primaries, and the mass media are the most effective means to reach potential voters. While the potential candidate still needs money, a good staff, and a strong organization, the way to the nomination requires the media, as the candidate goes from one key primary state to the next, seeking local and national news coverage.

Some of the power which had been taken from the political parties was returned to the Democratic party leaders through changes in the 1984 convention rules, which created a new group of "superdelegates" who did not have to be elected in primaries. Superdelegates, numbering 568 out of a total of 3933 seats, were party officials, governors, mayors, and members of the House and Senate (Gary Hart and Jesse Jackson supporters contend that, since this group gave disproportionate support to Walter Mondale, Hart's and Jackson's popular support was underrepresented, and they are asking for counterreforms in 1988).

It is generally thought that the campaign includes the preprimary period, the primaries, the nomination, and the general election. The preprimary period, theoretically, begins when the candidates officially declare. However, the period of campaign coverage has come to include the period prior to the preprimary period, when potential candidates start maneuvering toward announcing their candidacy. This period has been called "the pre-pre-campaign." The pre-pre-campaign can be almost any length the politicians or journalists deem it to be. It can begin when candidates start sounding out their support in such places as Iowa and New Hampshire. Three months after Reagan's 1980 inauguration, the press began to speculate about whether or not he would run again.[10]

At the preprimary stage, the period between the time a candidate declares and the first primary, the media play the role of the "Great Mentioner," which confers name identification and credibility (clearly, this role is particularly meaningful within a field of relative unknowns, for example, Jimmy Carter in 1976). For example, by the end of 1981, journalists had mentioned thirty Democrats and fourteen Republicans as potential candidates in 1984.[11] After mentioning comes "winnowing," separating and distinguishing possible winners. Newspapers, particularly those with reporters based in Washington, D.C., lead the pack during this stage.[12] The most enthusiastic participants in the winnowing process are members of the Washington press corps who are "election junkies" and who never really unpack from the campaign trail (on September 9, 1981,

David Broder of the *Washington Post* and James Reston of the *New York Times* both had columns on the 1984 presidential race).[13] At this stage, the field is unstructured and ambiguous, and the press enjoys a maximum of discretion in defining the situation. By the summer of 1982, the Democratic field was narrowed to seven, with Kennedy and Mondale proclaimed front runners. When Kennedy dropped out, of course, the scoreboard changed.

Most of this very early coverage is of the activities of potential candidates, so it would be inappropriate to say that the press creates their candidacy; all had either filed, or intended to file, with the Federal Elections Commission. This coverage includes the announcements of announcements: in mid-January of 1983, Senator Alan Cranston's staff let it be known that he would announce on February 2; Senator Gary Hart's staff let it be known that he would announce on February 17; former Vice President Walter Mondale's staff let it be known that he would announce on February 21.[14] Before the field of potential candidates becomes established, the coverage is rarely negative and is even more concerned with trivia at that point than in the campaign itself.

In a multicandidate preprimary campaign, the news net may be quite wide in range, covering all possibilities, but small in quantity, with only a few reporters assigned to the race as a whole. During the primaries, the news net begins to tighten and stabilize, as the print and broadcast media report the primary results and evaluate the candidates' chances of winning.

The turning point in media coverage, from the point of view of the candidate, comes when the major news media designate their "beats" and assign reporters to cover a specific candidate's campaign. For a newcomer in the national political arena, early victories constitute the most important way of becoming routinely covered by the media. Once reporters are so assigned, increased coverage is assured. Thus, Iowa and New Hampshire, followed by Massachusetts and Florida, become major markets for the candidate, despite the fact that the number of delegates involved in these early races is never sufficient for observers to predict the outcome of the convention. What they lack in quantity, however, these delegates make up for in quality, for journalists look to these early primaries for the "mood" of the nation, "momentum" or lack of it, and candidate "image."

Candidates and the press get to these markets early. In the 1980 campaign, reporters were in Iowa by early November of 1979, three months before the January 21, 1980 caucus.* For the 1984 campaign, when the

---

*A causus differs from a primary in that it is an actual meeting of party members, in a given state, who elect delegates to a convention. Obviously, the numbers are significantly smaller than in primaries, where voters go to the polls.

Iowa caucuses were tentatively scheduled for February 27, the Democratic organizers were there in the fall of 1982, more than a year and a half ahead of time. Candidates began to make appearances by February of 1983.[15] Early caucuses and primaries are the first "hard news" stories in the presidential race, and politicians, the media, and the public come to exaggerate their significance. The percentages of the votes received and the early interpretations of these percentages are widely considered to determine the candidate's ability to attract political and financial support and the amount of news coverage he or she will receive. After the Iowa caucuses, in 1976, Carter gained the status of "front runner," even though Henry Jackson actually received more votes. Within a few weeks, Carter was on the covers of *Time* and *Newsweek*. In 1976, 30 percent of the stories (television and newspaper) about the first eight primaries were devoted to New Hampshire. It has been calculated that this means that the Democratic vote in New Hampshire (82,381) received 170 times as much attention as the later Democratic vote in New York (3,764,414).[16]

Since the early primaries do not produce nearly enough delegates for a candidate to win the nomination, the significance of the early showing is open to any number of interpretations, which the media are quite eager to provide. A narrow loss can be interpreted as a demonstration of growing strength or "momentum"; a narrow win can be interpreted as weakness. For example, the media interpreted Eugene McCarthy's 42 percent of the vote in the New Hampshire primary in 1968 as a "victory"; George McGovern "tarnished" Edmond Muskie's "image as a winner," in 1972, with only 37 percent of the vote; however, in 1976, Ronald Reagan "lost" with 49 percent of the vote.[17]

The tendency to exaggerate the importance of the early presidential primaries is greatest in television. This situation can be explained in part by television's need for the spectacle. Nonetheless, early opinions about front runners tend to originate in the print media, with the *New York Times,* the *Washington Post,* the *Wall Street Journal,* and the two news-weeklies taking the lead. The *New York Times* is slightly more powerful in establishing a front runner than the others.

Although the important political reality is the final delegate count, it is really the interpretation or psychological impact of the early results that is at issue. The power of journalistic interpretations is greatest in the pre-primary and early primary period, when indications of real political support are weakest.

Jimmy Carter's 1976 campaign is a case in point. The media covered Carter more extensively and more favorably than other Democratic candidates. Carter was declared the "man to beat" after the New Hampshire primary in February of 1976, with only 30 percent of the Democratic vote. Television and newspaper front-page coverage gave Carter three and four times the attention of his major opponents, Senator Henry Jackson and Representative Morris Udall.[18]

This has led many political observers to conclude that the media "elect" candidates according to the way they cover the preprimary period and the early primaries. Since political parties have become weak and fragmented, it is reasoned, the process of singling out and anointing the candidate has shifted to the media.[19] People who vote in later primaries, and those who respond in later opinion polls, are believed to gravitate toward the candidate declared as front runner by the media.

However, this generalization may be an overstatement. In the fall of 1979, the media had given the nomination to Kennedy on the Democratic side as a result of Carter's unpopularity in the polls. The media had given the Republican nomination to George Bush, seeing Reagan as too old and/or too ideological.[20] After the Iowa caucuses, the press declared that Bush had "momentum." The media saw other potential candidates, John Connally and Howard Baker, as stronger than Reagan (*Time* gave Connally a cover).

The view of the media as "kingmakers" can overlook the fact that political parties, though clearly weakened on the national level, do still exert influence, and, in 1980, that influence was substantial. The party tradition of the incumbent's getting the nomination was upheld by the Democrats, and Reagan had a long-standing base of political support in the Republican Party. The Republicans, in 1980, showed that party finances, organization, and ideological strengths can still have an impact on election results. Republicans raised eight times the amount of money the Democrats did, had thousands of people in the streets getting out the vote, and had the kind of party unity that made it difficult for Democrats to portray Reagan as an extremist.

The initial indifference of the press may have helped Reagan win the nomination by not focusing a more critical eye on him until the primaries were almost over. The media did not take him seriously in the early stages of the 1980 campaign and, therefore, did not provide as much coverage as his ultimate victory should have warranted.[21] When they did cover him in the early months of the primary campaign, they tended to focus on the reasons that Reagan could not win. In February of 1980, age was the issue, but, by March, when Reagan began to be established as a "front runner," he was too ideologically extreme to win. Gradually, the press began to awaken to the real possibility that Reagan might actually become the fortieth president of the United States. The press might have thought Reagan too old and too extreme, but the rank and file of the Republican party did not; with each primary Reagan moved closer to the nomination. Only late into the primary campaign did the press begin to focus on Reagan's qualifications and, finally, on the issues of his campaign.

Although the view of the media as kingmakers can be exaggerated, it is important to note that such analysis is more often than not appropriate. The economic realities of double-digit inflation and unemployment and Reagan's firmly-established image as a fiscal conservative may have created special conditions. Here, "real-world" events and image may have merged to make Reagan more sellable in the electoral market of 1980 than he was in 1976. Even though journalists were wrong when the campaign began, they nonetheless designated the field of eligibles as each primary was covered and the news net tightened.

### On the Campaign Trail

As these news nets tighten throughout the primaries, and as the media assign reporters to cover specific campaigns, a new relationship is established between the candidates and the media. The discretionary power of the media to pick and choose what candidates to cover weakens as news organizations concentrate on the front runners. Establishing such news beats, or news outposts, makes the organization's journalistic tasks more manageable, but it means that candidates who have been judged not likely to win receive little coverage, insuring, in turn, that they cannot win. Primary candidates ignored in 1980 included Howard Baker, Edmund Brown, Robert Dole, and Philip Crane.[22]

However, there are exceptions to this bias against minor candidates. In 1980, the national news media were fascinated, for a time, by John Anderson and his campaign. Anderson stood the third highest in terms of positive coverage throughout the primaries, even though he never won a primary or a caucus (see Table 5-2). Anderson won a media victory when he almost won the March 4th primaries in Massachusetts and Vermont. However, as the campaign wore on, Anderson began to slip in the polls, and his press became less favorable. After the primaries were over, Anderson's press coverage actually became harshly negative.[23]

Once a reporter is assigned to a particular candidate, the traditional exchange relationship grows stronger. Journalists now have contact with high-level staff members and, as a result, become privy to policy issues and shifts in campaign strategy. Yet, at the same time, the journalists' dependence on campaign officials grows. Officials are now in the position to concentrate more effectively the journalists' attention on desirable aspects of the campaign. On the campaign trail, journalists even come to depend on the staff for transportation, meals, accommodations, and the means to communicate with the reporters' organizations.

With the reporters' attention focused squarely on the candidate, all political activity not directly on the campaign trail—advertising, grassroots organizing, direct-mail fund raising—falls outside the campaign reporter's view. The campaign comes to be defined as the particular activities of the candidate. The bulk of the coverage becomes what the candidate says or does, which is, naturally, controlled by the candidate. There is the potential loss of a comparative perspective and a tendency to see everything from the point of view of the single candidate's campaign. This does not necessarily mean that reporters come to be biased in favor of the assigned candidate, but merely that the perspective on the entire campaign can be lost. David Jones, National News Editor for the *New York Times*, states:

> ...the experience of our political reporters is that when they get on that campaign plane, they get trapped; they're in a cocoon and it distorts their perception of everything that's happening in the campaign because they don't see the broader dimensions....[24]

An example of the way reporters become so immersed in specific campaign activities and, consequently, have trouble seeing the forest for the trees is provided by Ronald Brownstein, a staff reporter for *Ralph Nader Reports*. Brownstein stayed behind after a Reagan campaign stop in Youngstown, Ohio. During this visit, Reagan had made much of a factory closing that he said had resulted from government interference and the press dutifully reported the charge. Brownstein seemed to have little difficulty establishing that Reagan had misrepresented the facts; the plant closing was not caused by government interference but was the result of corporate mismanagement.[25]

Journalists traveling with a candidate are also influenced by what their colleagues think and write. Some campaign stops are covered only by a press pool, which includes a print reporter, a still photographer, the wire services, and at least one network crew. Reporters who have not covered an event depend on the pool for copy. In 1980, Carter's campaign staff regularly provided a written pool report; Reagan's people occasionally did so. Pool reports were also used in the 1984 campaigns. These pool reports include such things as standing in the polls, the "mood of the campaign," and, in 1980, information on the possible release of the American hostages in Iran. Campaign strategists attempt to determine the lead for the day by creating the principal story: Reagan speaks on the economy, Mondale attacks a Reagan policy, and so on.

In some modern presidential campaigns, there has been an attempt to isolate the candidate from the press. This phenomenon was first noted in 1968 by Joe McGinnis, in *The Selling of the President*, where it was pointed out that Nixon appeared in public only under controlled circumstances, avoiding questions from the press. Incumbents can try to avoid the campaign trail altogether by what has been called the "Rose Garden strategy," where the incumbent appears only in his official capacities at the White House. Nixon did it in 1972, Ford did it in 1976, and Carter did it in 1980.

On the trail or in the Rose Garden, candidates do not want a continual press conference and try to avoid reporters' questions. It is in informal exchanges with the press that the slip or blunder is most likely to occur. Reporters take to shouting questions at the candidate whenever they have a chance, as when the candidate is getting in or out of a limousine (called "door-stopping").

Reporters are not isolated only from the candidate; they are also isolated from their own news organizations. With all that is provided, there are no television sets, radios, or newspapers on a regular basis. Even Tom Wicker, on the 1980 campaign trail for the New York Times, had to settle for a day-old Times. Reporters resort to frequent calls to their respective "desks."[26]

If any one factor has changed the modern campaign trail, it is the presence of the television camera. In the modern campaign, the candidate does not have to hustle from place to place, shaking hands, kissing babies, repeating the same speech over and over again. Media events can be planned and staged.

Things have changed even since Timothy Crouse's description of the 1972 campaign in The Boys on the Bus.[27] Crouse's picture of the exhausted reporter falling into bed in the wee hours of the morning, only to be awakened in a few hours to file onto the bus in pursuit of a campaign story, is no longer the case. Everybody, candidate and reporter, gets more sleep now.

> Campaigns are organized for pictures, not for words or ideas. In fact, the Boys-on-the-bus—romantic truth-tellers licensed to lurch from coast to coast with presidents and would-be presidents—have become irrelevant.[28]

Things on the campaign trail are scheduled for the convenience of the camera and the camera crew. Millions can be reached in one airport stop, rather than many. Pictures take precedence over words, and pictures lend themselves to a particular kind of manipulation. For example, Reagan's staff always positioned the camera platform close to the speaker's platform, which made the crowd look bigger. Roping off the "press area" forced the crowd to pack into the space between the candidate and the camera. A "synthetic campaign" is created when a candidate stop or a rally is not for the purpose of talking to live people who are present but for the people who will watch it on the evening local and network news. Carter, Reagan, and Anderson, in 1980, each made stops to have their pictures taken with people of the "right" demographic characteristics—factory workers, blacks, senior citizens, and members of ethnic neighborhoods.

Print journalists have come to feel like uninvited guests, as their needs become secondary to visuals. Print journalism's superstars, like David Broder of the *Washington Post,* spend less time on the campaign bus than they did in 1972, when Crouse did his study. The three networks get preferential treatment. During Reagan's 1980 campaign, 22 of the 51 press seats in the candidate's plane were reserved for the networks. Reagan's press secretary, Lyn Nofziger, often gave the networks releases and transcripts that he withheld from other reporters. Nofziger explains:

> The most effective thing we can do is put [Reagan] on television whenever we can. Each of the three networks has tremendously bigger circulation than any individual newspaper or magazine.[29]

Within the context of an increasingly orchestrated campaign, two reactions set in: boredom and the perception that the press is being manipulated. The reporters begin to look for the slip, the blunder, or anything unexpected. It has been suggested that there is a "front runner double standard," in which front runners are covered more negatively than their challengers. In 1979, for example, when Kennedy was a front runner, his coverage was more negative. In 1980, when Kennedy slipped behind, the press became relatively neutral. Between January and June of 1980, Carter and Reagan were treated more negatively than the other serious candidates.[30] These considerations go a long way to explain some of the patterns of coverage that we will examine in the rest of this chapter.

### The Interplay Between Candidates and Journalists

Although candidates and the news media have different goals—candidates want as much favorable coverage as possible, and reporters want news that is dramatic, controversial, and new—their relationship is rarely adversarial. There exists between the candidate and the media an accommodation which is, by and large, mutually beneficial: news organizations define elections as important events which must be covered; candidates use news reporting as the most inexpensive way to communicate with the public. As political scientist James Barber puts it:

> [Candidates] learn to *use* journalism, as journalism uses them. They and the journalists grapple in a reciprocal relationship of mutual exploitation, a political symbiosis. If the journalists are the new *kingmakers,* the candidates are the new *storytellers,* active plotters of dramas they hope will win for them [Emphasis ours].[31]

The press acts as a conduit for the candidate's messages by reporting the facts of prepared speeches and news releases. To that extent, the candidate controls the agenda. However, as willing as the candidate is to provide reporters access to campaign information, he cannot directly control what the reporter will say. The best the candidate can do is seek to "narrow the range of available stories and interpretations."[32] Clearly, any attempt to manipulate the press must be subtle; it would be foolhardy to alienate the press. Reporters, of course, want more than speeches and press releases; they want independent information about strategies, tactics, organization, personal character traits, controversies, and conflicts. Between the campaigner's push toward manipulation and the reporter's pull toward meeting personal and organizational goals lies mutual accommodation.

In seeking to influence news coverage, candidates must have some understanding of the way journalists work. This kind of expertise is what is expected of the candidates' press secretaries, many of whom received their training as journalists. Campaigns accommodate themselves to the media by scheduling events to take place before deadlines, by allowing time for filing stories, by providing typewriters and telephones, by providing food and transportation for reporters, by passing out schedules, advance texts, and news releases, and by arranging private interviews with influential reporters.

However, campaigners have more than this technical expertise. Candidates also accommodate themselves to journalistic values, such as the desire for the dramatic and the fascination with campaign strategies. Even more, campaign strategists know that early success captures media attention, that issues and policies sounded early are the most repeated, that news-gathering organizations focus on the same issues and events, and that media professionals tend to define news in terms of winners. Media strategists know the importance of establishing relationships early in the campaign with elite print journalists from national newspapers and magazines. They know the importance of appearing on local television as often as possible in states that hold early caucuses and primaries. They know that, early in the campaign, local coverage is easier to control and that it is wise to hold national network news until later stages of the campaign.[33]

Reporters have their agenda as well. They try to create drama by asking questions which will highlight controversy or conflict between the candidates. Reporters try to encourage candidates to challenge each other. Moreover, the very length of the presidential campaign (about 300 days) gives the press more discretion in creating its own agenda. There are a limited number of major policy statements that can be made. This encourages the reporter to seek out stories—some of which will inevitably be trivial.

When it comes to the political issues of the campaign, journalists and candidates have different interests. Although the coverage of substantive issues increases as the campaign progresses, stories concerning issues take third place behind stories on who is winning and strategies and tactics.[34] Candidates tend to offer more substance than the media report.[35] However, if the candidate suggests that the big issue is "who can you trust," as Carter did in 1976, the media cannot be expected to concentrate on substantive issues.

There is a conflict between the media and the candidates when it comes to the types of issues they prefer to discuss. When the press does cover issues, it prefers clear-cut issues, especially those that produce conflict or controversy.[36] Clear-cut issues, more often than not, mean issues without complex details, which can be stated in simple terms or, for broadcast journalists, can be stated in a thirty- to ninety-second spot. Particularly attractive are issues that have a convenient shorthand label, such as busing, detente, tax cuts, bureaucratic waste, military buildup, and abortion.

Candidates naturally prefer more diffuse issues, which have a broader base of appeal. Diffuse issues include a healthy economy, law and order, fighting inflation, and peace. Thomas Patterson's study of the 1976 campaign showed that, when the candidate controls the communication in paid advertising and convention speeches, just over 50 percent of the content is related to diffuse issues and less than 25 percent to clear-cut issues. When the news media report on the candidate, about 50 percent of the news content referred to clear-cut issues, and 25 percent to diffuse issues.[37]

The preference for clear-cut issues is true for all the media but most clearly for television. Television, even more than the other media, gravitates toward issues that can be stated briefly, do not require lengthy explanations, and provide good visuals. As Richard Kaplan, a producer for *CBS Evening News,* puts it:

> We just can't handle issues the way a newspaper can. A writer can go into all kinds of detail to explain things. We have to have something on that film. And you've got ninety seconds to tell it.[38]

The general pattern of media preference for clear-cut issues reduces the candidate's control over the agenda. The reporters' interest in clear-cut issues and the candidates' interest in the diffuse issues has created a situation in which reporters see the candidates as evasive and the candidates feel reporters do not cover all they say. From the perspective of their differing interests, they are both right.

During the conventions and the general election period that follows, issues are given more attention by the media. This is in part a result of the fact that the conflict shifts from within one party to between parties. In September of 1980, the network news media were still concentrating on campaign issues such as the debate about whether to debate, blunders, and personal attacks. By October, however, CBS news gave priority to the coverage of the economy, American military strength, social security, and U.S.-Middle Eastern relations.[39] In October, CBS News gave almost as much time to issues as it did to who was winning in the polls. This is impressive if we remember that issues remain the same unless a candidate makes a radical change in position. Polling results, on the other hand, change day by day. All three networks did specials on the candidates in October of 1980.

If candidates and journalists have different interests when it comes to issues, they seem to have similar interests when it comes to presidential qualifications. Doris Graber, in her study of the 1976 campaign, found that 61 percent of the newspaper coverage of the candidates concerned presidential qualifications. However, the discussion of qualifications is dominated by the analysis of personal capacities, as opposed to professional capacities. Personal capacities include style, image, and personality traits such as integrity and compassion. Professional capacities include the ability to conduct foreign and domestic affairs, the ability to project a political philosophy, and the ability to organize public support. Graber found that 77 percent of the media coverage was devoted to personal capacities.[40] When the candidates, themselves, talked about presidential qualifications, Graber found that they, too, talk about personal capacities approximately 75 percent of the time.[41] Thus, candidates, as well as journalists, use the same criteria in assessing presidential qualifications.

In sum, candidates and journalists depend on each other as valued resources; politicians need access to the public, and journalists need access to information to attract, inform, and entertain that public. The relationship between candidates and journalists is an exchange of information for publicity. In this exchange, candidates have a privileged access to the press, but they get to have their say through a format controlled by journalists.

## STYLES OF CAMPAIGN COVERAGE

### The Strategic Game and the Melodramatic Imperative

Reflecting the priorities of their news organizations, reporters tend to view the campaign as a strategic game, where the players calculate and pursue strategies designed to defeat competitors. Public problems and policy issues become the backdrop against which the game is played.[42] Issues are important largely in terms of the way they are used or the way they affect the candidate's "game plan." In covering the campaign, the press is drawn to game metaphors: "clash," "fight," "attack," and "take the offensive." But this is more than a linguistic style; it represents a point of view and a set of assumptions about what is news and newsworthy.

Closely allied to the strategic game perspective is what Paul Weaver calls the "Melodramatic Imperative" of campaign coverage.[43] The melodramatic imperative is essentially the need to entertain as well as to inform. It means that the focus is on the novel and the dramatic. What has been called the "triumph of junk news" is largely brought about by the dominance of television in presidential campaigning.[44] The melodramatic imperative provides the reporter and the candidate with a "dramatic scenario," within which the candidate's activity is reported and given meaning. Paul Weaver describes the process:

> Instead of participating in a long, confusing and often inchoate political process, as he does in the real world, television's politician acts out a clear and gripping melodrama. . . . It opens in the snows of New Hampshire; the plot develops, election by election, until it reaches its denouement before the national conventions, not as people who are running for elective office, but as figures deeply and totally embroiled in an all-out struggle.[45]

Thus, strategy and tactics are placed within the context of a dramatic struggle between winners and losers, in an unfolding narrative, structured to entice and sustain audience interest over a period of several months. The winner "isn't simply the candidate with the most votes," he is "a person who, by virtue of his success, has the *character* of a winner." Losers "are never merely defeated and disappointed. They are overcome by catastrophe; they become filled with 'desperation'; they start to 'scramble' for their very survival."[46]

Within the context of the strategic game and the melodramatic imperative, campaign coverage takes shape. Thomas Patterson makes the distinction between game stories and substance stories. Game stories are those that concern winning and losing, strategy, logistics, appearances, and hoopla. Substance stories are those that cover issues, policies, traits, records, and endorsements. In the 1976 campaign, Patterson found that 50 to 60 percent of the coverage was game stories; 30 to 35 percent were substantive stories.[47]

The most popular game story is the "horse race" story—who won the primary or who is winning in the latest polls. The ratio between stories on winning versus issues was roughly three to one in 1972, 1976, and 1980. During the 1976 primaries, 64 percent of all network stories were about the horse race.[48] In 1980, 67 percent of the stories on CBS news, during the primaries, were horse race stories.[49] A study of the coverage of the 1980 primaries in the *New York Times,* the *Washington Post,* and the *Chicago Tribune* showed between a three to one ratio and a two to one ratio in favor of "who is winning" stories over issue stories (see Table 5-3 below).

By focusing on winning and losing, the media overlooked or under-played other kinds of election news. The CBS coverage of the 1980 pri-maries included almost no explicit evaluations of the candidates in terms of competence, integrity, or issue consistency. Evaluation existed only in terms of success at the polls. In 99 percent of the coverage, no position was taken on competence or personal integrity; 98 percent made no comment on issue consistency.[50]

However, the combined impact of strategic game perspective and the melodramatic imperative means more than the focus on the horse race; it means that events, policy statements, and issues are defined in terms of strategy. For example, Ford's decision, in 1976, to stay in the Rose Garden was defined as his attempt to "look presidential." Speeches may not be reported in detail, but the marketing strategy behind them often is. Instead of examining the policy statement, the press prefers to examine the group to which the policy was intended to appeal; for example, "In an attempt to appeal to the black vote, Mondale announced today. . . ." This can be followed by a poll to see whether the marketing strategy worked. In seeking to explain the outcome of a given vote or poll, the press tends to focus on the strategies used to appeal to the public, rather than seeking traditional explanations, such as party loyalty or party organization.

As issues come to be seen in terms of their tactical value, their larger social and political significance fades into the background. By empha-sizing the tactical significance of campaign activities, the media give readers and viewers an "insider's" view of how the campaign is run. Even the press analysis of political commercials focuses on the way the candi-date came across, what audience he or she was trying to reach, and

**TABLE 5-3**
HORSE RACE VERSUS ISSUE
(Coverage of the 1980 Primary Campaigns for the Presidency:
from October 1979 to the First Week of June 1980)*

|  | Horse Race | Issue |
| --- | --- | --- |
| *Washington Post* | 538 | 186 |
| *New York Times* | 323 | 185 |
| *Chicago Tribune* | 224 | 127 |

*Taken from a study done by the *Washington Journalism Review*, Douglas Lowenstein, "Covering the Primaries," *WJR*, September, 1980, pp. 38–42.

*Note:* "Horse Race" stories are those concerning who is leading or who is falling behind, strategy and tactics, forecasts, and the results of polls. "Issue" stories include superficial or substantive coverage of issues, in-depth analyses of a candidate's closest advisors, and attacks on the opponent over policy.

whether the advertisement was effective in reaching the audience. Little or nothing is said about the content or substance of the message.[51] The strategic game perspective does more than affect the selection of what is to be covered; it also provides the "context for interpreting what the public sees or hears."[52] For example, if the candidate discusses unemployment, one level of interpretation can consider whether the candidate offers a viable solution. However, the strategic game perspective encourages interpreting such a statement in terms of its tactical significance for the campaign.

The presentation of issues as tactics depicts the candidate's public position as merely a strategic ploy. Frank Mankiewicz, a Carter aid, complained in 1976: "Reporters are...telling Americans no candidate takes any position except to enhance his election prospects. It's automatically assumed that nobody can do anything because he believes it."[53] As John Carey puts it:

> The "strategic frame" suggests, in effect, that to get at the real meaning of what the candidate said or did, the viewer should interpret its strategic significance in the campaign.[54]

Although newspapers do slightly better than television in presenting issues, the reader or the viewer learns from the media that politicians are strategists whose actions and statements are contrived solely to win votes. Commenting on the 1976 campaign, James McCartney, a Washington correspondent, states:

> The media simply never took "issues" seriously on their own terms. The press, in all of its branches—written and electronic—often would fail to present them straight; issues, if mentioned at all, would be buried in stories constructed around other subjects—strategy and tactics, evaluation of candidates' momentum, and all of the other kinds of political small talk that arise in any campaign.[55]

Television coverage of the 1976 primaries never showed the candidates' basic speeches. If television allowed the candidate to speak for himself, it was only after television had redefined the statement as a tactic or a ploy to get votes. Thus, when Jimmy Carter presented his complicated position on health care and abortion, ABC said: "He's deliberately outlining vague positions that allow everyone to believe he's on their side."[56]

As the media have come to focus on tactics and strategies, many candidates have come to engage in activities meant to demonstrate their strategic skills, or what Carey calls engaging in the "meta-campaign," the campaign about the campaign.[57] Candidates discuss their strategies with the press. Campaign advisors and pollsters grant interviews to the press in order to release their latest public opinion polls, announce signs of "momentum," and outline new strategies. As James Barber puts it:

> Campaign maneuver itself became the featured story; the Presidential implications of what the candidates were saying faded into the distance. Horse race imagery gave way to Parcheesi politics—war against the scoreboard—a new game of expectations and scenarios and surprises played as vigorously by the candidates as by the press reporting them. By the end of the 1970's, journalism...took to reporting how the candidates were going over with the press itself.[58]

Covering the campaign maneuvers may be the ultimate pseudo-event. It is not merely an event planned for the sole purpose of being covered by the press; the coverage of the maneuver behind the event itself becomes an event, in effect, a pseudo-event about a pseudo-event. So campaigners make their strategies news, in part by succumbing to the imperatives of press coverage, which thrives on political combat rather than political discourse.

It must be remembered that, in the day-to-day coverage of the campaign, reporters hear the same speeches over and over. How many times can the same policy statement remain news? There are rarely major policy shifts in a campaign, but there is much tactical maneuvering and an ever-increasing number of polls to report. In a campaign that lasts over 300 days, there may not be enough substance to keep substance at the top of the news.

The demand for daily campaign stories means that reporters must go even beyond covering strategies and tactics and, guided by the melodramatic imperative, "create" stories. When reporters cover a campaign beat, which only occasionally generates real news, it is almost inevitable that the slip-up, factual or verbal blunders, will become "news." Particularly after the primaries, when there are few concrete events to report, it is natural for the press to turn to the mistakes in both camps. Blunders fulfill the dramatic imperative; they are unexpected, and they are entertaining. Blunders can be seen as clues about which candidate is more skillful at playing the game. Blunders are newsworthy without necessarily being intrinsically important, like Carter's 1976 admission in a *Playboy* interview that he had "lust in his heart." Ford's blunder about the lack of Soviet domination in Eastern Europe, on the other hand, might be of greater significance, casting doubt on the candidate's ability to handle foreign affairs. The 1980 campaign saw its share of blunders. Reagan's repeated misstatements of facts were widely covered, as was the time when, asked about the age of French President Giscard d'Estaing, Reagan replied: "Who?" Carter's remark, during the debates, that the issue of nuclear war was raised by his young daughter, Amy, came under press scrutiny. The press dutifully reported Carter's reference to Edmund Muskie as a "senior citizen" rather than a "senior senator" and his remark that the hostages had been moved to "another country," when he meant to say "city." After the first debate in the 1984 campaign, the *New York Times* ran a comparative analysis, a sort of box-score, of the errors made by both candidates.

Beyond factual or verbal errors, even errors in syntax became items of news in the 1980 campaign. In the fall of 1979, an article on Edward Kennedy stated: "He spoke haltingly and sometimes fumblingly," and another: "Some of his sentences never get finished, and others, lacking verbs, are not sentences at all. Frequently, he says the wrong thing, such as 'issue of substance' or the 'rising price of inflation.'" In May of 1980, the *New York Times* said of Reagan: "However, when he has been pressed by reporters for specifics to back up statements in his speeches, his syntax tends to become jumbled...."[59]

Politicians have complained about the press obsession with blunders. Carter, in that same *Playboy* interview, complained that news media "had absolutely no interest in issues at all.... The traveling press have zero interest in any issue unless it's a matter of my making a mistake. What they're looking for is a forty-seven-second argument between me and another candidate or something like that. There's nobody in the back of this plane who would ask an issue question unless he thought he could trick me into some crazy statement."[60] Malcolm MacDougall, Ford's media advisor, observed that "to get an issue-oriented speech on the network news was almost impossible. All you get is the goofs."[61]

Arterton suggests that this obsession with blunders is not merely for their dramatic worth but is also, at least in part, a result of what he calls a "press crisis" that emerges when the press begins to react to the perceived news management by the candidate and the campaign staff.[62] Focusing on candidate errors enables the press to take control of the agenda. In an increasingly managed and staged campaign, blunders offer excitement for the reporter, as well as for the public.

Finally, the need for "news" and the dramatic imperative cause reporters to reach for stories where there are none. Lowenstein provides the following leads from some non-stories which appeared during the 1980 primary campaign.

- Seven Republican presidential candidates staged a replay of last month's Iowa debate tonight in which the only thing new was the addition of Ronald Reagan. (*Washington Post*, February 21, 1980)
- George Bush, his cliff-hanging campaign for the Republican presidential nomination pulled back from the brink once more by yesterday's victory in Pennsylvania, relaxed at his home here today and savored the taste of even momentary triumph. (*New York Times*, April 24, 1980)
- As the GOP main event moved into the final round, underdog George Bush was still on his feet after jolting Ronald Reagan in Tuesday's Michigan primary. (*Chicago Tribune*, May 22, 1980)[63]

## Television Events

The big melodramatic event for television is coverage of the national conventions, even though they no longer have the excitement of the unexpected or the possibility of a "dark horse" candidate. In the past, presidential candidates were really nominated at the national conventions. With most states now having primaries to nominate the candidate, most convention delegates rubber-stamp the voters' choice. Therefore, it is fairly certain before the convention who will win the nomination (not since 1952 has there been a multi-ballot national convention). National conventions have become ceremonial investitures. Scheduling, length of speeches, and the traditional balloons are designed and timed for the benefit of television—a combination of politics and show business.

In 1980, the news media together sent 15,000 people to Detroit to cover 1993 Republican delegates and 11,500 media people to New York to cover 3380 Democratic delegates.[64] The three networks spent $60 million on convention coverage. In 1980, to cite one example, CBS in Detroit had 700 people, fourteen cameras, five minicam units, four mobile units, five control rooms, 204 television monitors, and 750 phones.[65] In 1984, the networks alone sent 14,500 people to the Democratic convention; they outnumbered the delegates and alternates three to one.

Why all this coverage of what has become a fairly predictable ritual? Clearly, convention coverage is in keeping with the strategic game perspective and the melodramatic imperative. All the ingredients are there: rhetoric, drama, excitement, measurable results, and a winner. Moreover, from the point of view of television, live convention coverage has been one of the few substantial blocks of time that the news divisions have won from the entertainment divisions. Further, network newscasters have believed that the audience they have attracted at conventions has tended to stick with them for the news over the next four years.

However, by the summer of 1984, the networks came to recognize that gavel-to-gavel coverage of the conventions was, in the words of Jeff Gralnick, the vice president of ABC news, "a dinosaur that was dying."[66] Convention coverage now will be edited coverage, with the three networks going on the air for a few hours during prime time. As edited coverage, rather than complete coverage, convention coverage becomes a highly selective process, opening up the possibility of conscious or unconscious editorial bias. In turn, the parties are further encouraged to organize their conventions so that what they think is important will occur during prime time. This means that the parties will tailor themselves even more to the dramatic needs of television. At the 1984 Democratic convention, such things as platform challenges and reports of rules and credentials committees took place in the afternoon. Prime time was programmed for major speeches and displays of party unity.

The next big television event has come to be the debates. It will be remembered that the first presidential debates took place in 1960 between John Kennedy and Richard Nixon. It took sixteen years to have a second set of presidential debates. In 1976, Ford and Carter had three debates, and the first vice-presidential debate took place between Robert Dole and Walter Mondale. In 1980, there were, for the first time, five Republican primary debates; there were two general election debates, one between Reagan and Anderson and one between Reagan and Carter. On October 28, 1980, over one hundred million Americans watched the Reagan/Carter debate, which was the most heavily-viewed campaign event of the general election.[67] In 1984, Reagan and Mondale met in two debates, after Reagan ridiculed Mondale's suggestion to hold six debates.

At least in theory, debates offer an opportunity to overcome some of the flaws of routine campaign coverage. Here policy issues and ideological positions can be communicated. In theory, the debates are opportunities for the public to see and hear the candidates' spontaneous answers to questions put to them by political journalists of national stature. In reality, the candidates and their advisors spend weeks preparing for the debates, trying to second-guess the questions and practicing appropriate answers. When a briefing book for the debates falls into the hands of the opponent, as it did during the Reagan/Carter debates of 1980, it becomes clear how well-prepared a candidate can be. After examining both the Carter and Reagan briefing books, Henry Fairlie cites the pervasive assumption about how to prepare for the debates: "Televised political debates focus on image attributes more than issue positions" (this is actually stated in the Reagan briefing book). Thus, Reagan is counseled to display "Competence—Compassion—Reasonableness, moderation, and thoughtfulness—Strength." In turn, Carter is advised to evince "Integrity, sincerity, openness, intelligence, steadiness and common-man touch."[68] In a blatant disregard for traditional campaigning, Reagan was urged *not* to defend his own record as a conservative in order to "appeal above party to the ticket splitters and even disaffected Democrats."[69]

In the 1984 debates, Mondale was counseled: "Show strength. Demonstrate your sense of fairness and contrast it with Reagan's. Focus on the importance of this election to the future of the country.... Grant Reagan his sincerely held beliefs and persuasive abilities. Instead of attacking him, emphasize the future."[70] Reagan's briefing book included twelve pages on "big issues," a collection of previously successful one-liners, suggested answers to possible questions, and the advice "do not necessarily respond" if pressed.

While protesting the lack of substance in the debates, the press is an eager participant in the image game. The debates receive massive publicity from the time of the nominating conventions. The debates are initially promoted by the press as opportunities for the voters to learn how the candidates stand on key issues. However, as the debates approach, the discussion turns to who will win, how the candidates will perform, and how the debates will affect the election. In 1980, the public was alerted to the possibility of blunders, and the press took to second-guessing the performance: "Carter will be articulate, workmanlike, thorough. Reagan will be eloquent, slick and hard as blazes to pin down."[71] Walter Cronkite, introducing the Reagan/Carter debate, declared: "It's not inconceivable that the election could turn on the next ninety minutes."[72]

Once the debates are over, the news coverage is dominated by the question of who won. In 1976, more than half of the coverage focused on who won.[73] After the 1980 debate between Reagan and Carter, the press rushed to explain who won. The media used various techniques to arrive at such an evaluation. The most vulgar, statistically, was ABC's instant telephone polling, where viewers were invited to call in their opinions. Although ABC received severe criticism from professional pollsters and print journalists, ABC's results were widely reprinted and broadcast across the nation.

While print journalists complained that the candidates were evasive and that the debates were issueless, the candidates' delivery and appearance proved to be more important than substance. As David Broder of the *Washington Post* put it in 1980: "Substance aside, in all important areas of the contest for public confidence, Reagan has the advantage.... Reagan has the physical presence, the size, the looks and most important, the voice to dominate the proceedings. It is a supple, deep and trained voice, the more authoritative in contrast to Carter's breathy squeaks...."[74]

After the first debate in 1984, the media decided that Mondale had won. The consensus was that President Reagan defeated himself with his faltering style and his wandering closing statement which made him appear old. Most important, though, was the networks' choice of a segment of the debate which they repeated on their evening news programs the next day. Called a "sound bite," the television networks showed Reagan using his "There you go again" phrase, so winning in the 1980 debate, which Mondale turned against Reagan. Mondale reminded Reagan that he first used that phrase when Carter charged that Reagan would try to cut Medicare, which had since turned out to be true. In covering the second debate, the networks gave the "sound bite" to Reagan by showing Reagan's response to a question about his age: "and I want you to know that also I will not make age an issue of this campaign. I am not going to exploit for political purposes my opponent's youth and inexperience." Even Mondale laughed, and the age issue was effectively buried.

The final big television event is election-night coverage, where the networks use computers and sophisticated sampling techniques to predict winners. Here television shines, as print journalists, along with the public, turn to the television screen for the latest results. It is the final act in the melodramatic struggle between winners and losers. Here, at last, the horse race figures are really the news of the day, and the obsession with predicting the outcome is the focus of attention. (In 1980, NBC predicted Reagan's victory at 8:15 p.m. Eastern Time, long before the polls were closed in the West. Not surprisingly, it has been discovered that knowledge of the projected outcome decreased the likelihood of voting for those who had not yet voted.[75]

On election night, all the themes of campaign coverage come together, as commentators and outside experts analyze the entire campaign scenario that began back in Iowa. As the horse race figures come rolling in, strategies are examined, explanations for victory are put forth, and the heroes of the drama are crowned.

## COVERING LOCAL CAMPAIGNS

When we look at the coverage of local campaigns, we observe some of the same assumptions that inform the coverage of national campaigns. At every level, we see at work the strategic game perspective and the melodramatic imperative; the lack of an issue orientation is pervasive. In fact, John Carey developed his concept of the meta-campaign, the campaign about the campaign, while studying the 1974 congressional elections. However, there are some significant differences in the coverage of state and local campaigns.

The most obvious differences arise from the fact that there is substantially less coverage of local campaigns. However, the higher the office involved, the greater and more extensive the coverage will be. Senatorial races will get more coverage than House of Representative races, gubernatorial races more than mayoral races, and so on. There will also be variations in campaign coverage between rural and urban areas, large and small cities, cities and suburbs, black and white districts, and areas with many or few news outlets. Some local elections will receive national attention, and others will not. For example, New York City mayoral campaigns always get national review, and Chicago, in 1983, did because of the unique impact on national politics of a black Democratic candidate in a racially-divided city that was traditionally a Democratic stronghold.

The media's role as kingmakers may be mediated at the local level by such things as the strength of party loyalty and of party organizations. However, there is good reason to believe that the media are gaining in importance on the local level. For example, it has long been thought that the outcomes of congressional elections were determined by party affiliation, where voters knew little or nothing about the candidates. The percentage of party-line voters in congressional elections has fallen from 84 percent in 1958 to 69 percent in 1978. In 1976, more party-line votes were cast in the presidential elections than in the congressional elections.[76] As we have seen, when party loyalty ceases to be a major determinant of the vote, the power of the media and voter dependency on the media increase. In areas where party loyalty is weak, the voters may turn to editorial endorsements for advise on how to vote. By the same token, as we shall see in the next chapter, in areas where party organization is weak, the voters may be more susceptible to political advertising campaigns.

Since the impact of media coverage on a political campaign is closely related to voter knowledge about candidates at the start of the campaign, it is difficult to make generalizations about statewide and local elections. Some state officials have nationally-known reputations, like Senator Edward Kennedy. In a small town, a mayoral candidate may know his or her constituency personally. In such cases, the media coverage may not have much independent impact. Some minor campaigns may receive so little coverage that there may be little effect, because the media are not covering the campaign sufficiently. To some extent, this is a result of the act that local media often do not have the resources to provide day-by-day coverage of the often multiple local campaigns. Local media must rely on their own staffs, in contrast to national campaign coverage, where they can and do use the wire services. Local media outlets, operating with fewer resources, provide less campaign coverage, but they can also use more discretion in deciding what is newsworthy. Everything, even the most trivial item, is news in a presidential campaign, and the press is at the mercy of pseudo-events. On the local level, there is not the same pressure for continual coverage.

In a study of the local television coverage of the 1978 gubernatorial campaign in Columbus, Ohio, it was found that "TV news persons were skeptical of the news value of many campaign events."[77] Local television stations consciously tried to avoid being manipulated by staged media events. The one media event to which they did succumb was the appearance of a national newsmaker. For example, a Democratic rally featuring Rosalyn Carter and an appearance by Gerald Ford at a Republican fund raiser received the attention of all three local stations. However, the local candidates were all but ignored.[78]

We have pointed out that network news is ideally suited to presidential campaigns. In local elections, on the other hand, newspapers become the major source of information. In contrast to the cross-media consistency we have observed in presidential election coverage, there are clear print-broadcast differences in covering campaigns on the local level. Although almost half of all media coverage is given to campaign events, rather than issues, newspapers give significantly more attention to the local issues, or issues most important to voters.[79]

At all campaign levels, the ability of the media to set the political agenda depends on the voter's need for information in order to make a decision and on the lack of strong political interest or strong party affiliation. Thus, at the local level, the media's role is subject to enormous variation. We may need guidance to decide on our congressional representative to the state legislature but not for our United States Senator. We may live in a state where party organization is strong but in a town or city where it is weak.

## EFFECTS OF MEDIA COVERAGE

Some of the effects of media coverage are obvious to even the most casual observer. For example, there is no doubt that the modern political campaign, particularly on the national level, is arranged around the media and that television coverage has had an effect on the types of candidates that are most likely to be successful. Not so obvious, but more important, as we have pointed out, is the media's role as kingmakers in the campaign for the presidency. Whereas, in the past, the preliminary screening of potential presidents was accomplished by party leaders and large contributors, now such screening is increasingly performed by political reporters (it is not self-evident that either of these groups is more dedicated to the public good). Journalists' interpretations of weakness, strength, and momentum in the preprimary and early primary periods are frequently more important than the events themselves. Journalists create what Arterton calls the "perceptual environment" within which candidates compete.[80]

If the power of the media is, to a large extent, a result of the weakening of political parties, it is also true that the media have contributed to the weakening of party politics. The media, particularly television, have helped create what has been called the "candidate-centered campaign," where the major themes of the campaign focus on candidate characteristics rather than party affiliation.[81] This situation has contributed to a decline in the awareness of political parties among the electorate.[82] The media's emphasis on compaign hoopla, winning and losing, personal style, and candidate image means that party affiliation and political philosophy often recede into the background.

However, the recognition of the declining influence of political parties and the media's role as kingmakers does not tell us how media coverage of the campaign actually affects the electorate. We know that voter attitudes, at least on the national level, are not significantly changed by the campaign. In 1976, only 8 percent of the respondents in Thomas E. Patterson's study of the presidential campaign switched parties between

February and October of that year[83] (in a close race, of course, this could be significant).

In attempting to assess the impact of media coverage on the voter, we are confronted with a serious methodological problem. Knowing how a campaign is covered does not tell us how the public is affected by it. What we do know is that mere exposure does not mean influence. To be exposed to a message does not automatically mean that it will even be recalled. Patterson and McClure, for example, found that of people who said they had recently watched the evening news, two out of three could not recall accurately even one story. If people watch only network news, they do not know any more than those who are not exposed to any news media.[84] However, those exposed to even one newspaper learn substantially more.

The higher recall for newspaper readers, of course, makes sense. Newspaper stories are longer and can be read and digested at the individual's own pace. Television stories are short and flow by at a pace determined by the producers of the news. Television can be watched, and often is, while viewers are doing other things; reading is necessarily a primary activity.[85] It is important to remember that the audience for any news is a voluntary one, and political news is something the citizen can take or leave. Television, which was once thought to be the most demanding medium, is, in fact, among the least demanding of our full attention.

The ability to recall a message is also affected by the degree of interest in campaign events. Although voter interest in campaign news varies throughout the presidential campaign, peaking in the early primaries, at national conventions, and during the debates, only slightly more than 30 percent of the electorate expresses strong interest in campaign news.[86] This figure has remained stable since the Lazarsfeld and Berelson study in the 1940s.

Clearly, recall is by no means the only, or even a particularly good, way to measure the impact of the media. Merely because we do not recall specific items of information does not mean that the media have little or no effect on us. The impact of the media may be more sutble and generalized. Through extended exposure to campaign news, people may be influenced by the media to consider some issues or some personality traits to be of greater significance in evaluating candidates. Such perceptions need not be tied to specific facts or bits of information. By determining the range and limits of campaign news, the media may establish a more subtle agenda for evaluating candidates, regardless of measurable recall and learning. Further, media coverage of real-world events outside of campaign news can have an impact on the voter's sense of political priorities.[87] For example, the media coverage of the hostage crisis in Iran in 1980 may have led some voters to see foreign affairs as significantly more important in evaluating President Carter than might otherwise have been the case.

Nonetheless, some of us are able to recall specific items of campaign news. For those of us who do, the question remains: What do we learn? The answer is: Not much. The strategic game approach and the melodramatic imperative produce an enormous amount of trivial and politically-irrelevant information. Campaign news is placed in a context or in a perceptual environment which begins with identifying who is in the game and then shifts to determining who is winning.

In the name of fairness and objectivity, journalists report issues and policies but rarely evaluate them except in terms of strategy. As Doris Graber points out, there has been a steady decline in stories about what qualities candidates *ought* to have.[88] Thus, the audience is not given a context within which to evaluate the candidates. The habit of quoting without comment means that journalists rarely judge conflicting claims or weigh the merits of a given policy.

Although the public does not learn much of substance from the media, press coverage, nonetheless, signals to the public what is important. What is ignored by the press is relegated to the background (at best) or to non-existence (at worst). Not surprisingly, Patterson found, in the 1976 campaign, that what the press emphasized was what the public said was important. Thus, as the strategic game dominated the news, the game dominated people's thoughts.[89] The interest in the game is not merely the result of news coverage, to be sure. Voters tend, as well, to think of elections in terms of contests; news coverage exaggerates and highlights this concern. The acceptance of the press's version of the campaign is further enhanced by the consistency of campaign coverage by all of the media.

Although newspapers were found to be more important in creating the agenda than television, television is particularly important during the conventions and the debates. Live coverage gives television a special influence, since the viewer gets essentially an unmediated view of the actual event. However, television coverage is still not as effective as newspapers in informing the public. This is so because debates and conventions are one-shot events, and people tend to retain new information through repeated exposure. Thus, high-interest voters do not learn much from the conventions and the debates, because they already know the issues. Moderate-interest voters become somewhat better informed, as do low-interest voters.

The voter's perception of who is winning, on the other hand, is dependent, in large measure, on information received from the news media. When press accounts speak of an almost certain winner, voters tend to mirror that view. When the press is uncertain about winners and losers, voters also tend to be uncertain.[90] The impact of media information on public assessment of winners and losers is evident in the evaluation of who wins or loses in presidential debates. Debates themselves frequently do not change the voter's mind about a candidate, but media interpretations of who won or lost influence perceptions of which candidate was the better performer. For example, in the Ford/Carter debate, when Ford blundered about the question of Soviet control in Eastern Europe, the journalistic consensus was that Ford had lost. Of the public interviewed within twelve hours of the debate, 53 percent thought Ford had won; of those interviewed later, 58 percent thought Carter had won. Of those interviewed earlier, only 10 percent mentioned Ford's error; 60 percent of those interviewed later cited the blunder as the reason Ford lost. Apparently the public did not see the error or understand its significance until the press explained it.[91] The voter might still go out and vote for Ford, but he or she knew that Ford had lost that particular debate.

The ability of the news media to influence the image of a candidate depends on how well-formed the image of the candidate is before the campaign. In 1976, Ford's image was established; Carter was new to the scene. As a result of extensive media coverage, the proportion of the public who felt they knew something about Carter rose from 20 percent in February to 81 percent in June.[92] Since Graber found that 77 percent of media coverage of presidential qualifications concerned personal qualities in the 1976 campaign, it is not surprising that Patterson found that 67 percent of the voters' ideas about Carter concerned his personality, campaign performance, and personal background. When asked what they learned about the candidates, three out of four people gave answers that concerned personality traits.[93]

Although turning to the media to get political information means hunting through a mass of trivial information, voter awareness of candidates' positions does increase during the campaign. In 1976, people knew almost nothing about Carter's position before the campaign; they knew more, naturally, about President Ford's. However, by the end of the campaign, voters knew almost as much about Carter's policies as they did about Ford's policies. Nonetheless, at the conclusion of the 1976 campaign, there were more voters who did not know where Ford and Carter stood than those who did know.[94]

Although newspapers, as well as television, focus on the horse race dimensions of politics, it is television which is often blamed for the issueless campaign, because of its inability to cover issues in depth and its concerns with good visuals. However, the question remains: Did television really create the issueless campaign, or did candidates, in playing to television, intentionally avoid issues, gearing their campaigns to this medium that thrives on brief, succinct, and simple statements, where charges and countercharges shine, and where political combat rather than political discourse has dramatic impact? This is clearly a chicken and egg question. The issueless campaign developed along with expanded television coverage. In all probability, television's priorities and the candidate's recognition and acceptance of television's wide-ranging impact worked together to create a campaign filled with politically irrelevant information. Regardless of the exact source of the issueless campaign, the voter can discover the facts and the issues of a campaign only if he or she is willing to search through a mass of political minutiae. Crucial questions are muted or ignored and go unanswered. The crucial questions are: What do the candidates believe in, and how consistent have they been in demonstrating these beliefs?

Even though crucial information is largely unavailable on network news, and audience recall of program content weak, it still remains true that the cumulative impressions of the campaign may have a profound effect on voter attitudes and beliefs. The long-term impact of the media's coverage of the campaign is very difficult to assess. It may not be accidental that, as television campaign coverage expanded, voting behavior became increasingly difficult to predict. Traditional signposts, such as party ties, social class, and geographical region, are no longer accurate indicators of potential voting behavior. Since the 1960s, there has been a decline in the proportion of eligible voters going to the polls, a weakening of party affiliation, an increase in ticket splitting, and an increase in citizen distrust of politicians and political institutions. The emphasis on horse race stories and the avoidance of issues may contribute to the voter's inability to discriminate between candidates. The increase in negative coverage may contribute to cynicism and to the distrust of the political process.[95] Journalistic skepticism may filter into public consciousness. The "they're-all-crooks" attitude is pervasive among political correspondents. Richard Salant, of CBS News, puts it succinctly: "They are trying to sell us a bill of goods, so our job is to get behind the bullshit."[96] Television's blatant use of the strategic game perspective may contribute to public skepticism about politics and politicians. Television's narrow view of politics as a game, where everything is explained by the desire to win votes or defeat challengers, may have a cumulative effect on fundamental voter attitudes toward American politics. On television, even more so than in newspapers, political philosophy and commitment to substantive goals are not considered realistic explanations of a candidate's position. Where everything is defined as a ploy or a tactic, the public's confidence in political leadership could easily be undermined.

## CONCLUSION

In looking at the role of the media in the modern campaign, we have discovered three things that stand out: the emergence of the media as kingmakers during the presidential primaries, the domination of the media in planning campaign strategies, and the enormous amount of politically-irrelevant material presented to the public through the media. If the media have become an important link between the candidate and the voter, this link is a very inadequate one. Election news concentrates on drama, not evaluation; controversies, not basic issues; personality characteristics, not leadership qualities; and campaign styles, not political records. This does not mean that election news is not important but indicates instead that it is not adequate to guide political choice. Voters know less about political platforms than they do about campaign strategies.

We have noted that the power of the media emerges with the weakening of political parties and that the media, in turn, serve to further weaken party loyalty by emphasizing candidate personality rather than party identity. We have suggested that the cumulative effect of the modern media campaign, with its emphasis on strategies, tactics, and tallies, may contribute to declining political activism and to increasing public distrust of politicians and political institutions.

All phases of the campaign, particularly on the presidential level, are played out in the media, with television as the major target for the candidates and their campaigners. As we shall see in the next chapter, the realities of the media campaign have produced the perceived need for extraparty experts, media consultants, and pollsters, to reach the public more effectively.

## NOTES

1 Quoted in Dom Bonafede, "The New Political Power of the Press," *Washington Journalism Review*, Sept., 1980, p. 25.
2 James David Barber (ed.), *The American Assembly Race for the Presidency: The Media and the Nominating Process*, Prentice-Hall, Englewood Cliffs, 1978, p. 4.
3 Michael Robinson, "Television and American Politics 1956–1976," *Public Interest*, Summer, 1977, pp. 3–39.
4 Thomas E. Patterson, *The Mass Media Election*, Praeger, New York, 1980, p. 184, n. 10.
5 Douglas Lowenstein, "Covering the Primaries," *Washington Journalism Review*, Sept., 1980, p. 38.
6 Michael Robinson, with Nancy Conover and Margaret Sheehan, "The Media at Mid-Year: A Bad Year for McLuhanties," *Public Opinion*, June/July, 1980, p. 41.
7 See Robert G. Meadow, "Cross Media Comparison of Coverage of the 1972 Presidential Campaign," *Journalism Quarterly*, Autumn, 1973, pp. 482–488; J. Sean McCleneghan, "Effects of Endorsement on News in Texas Papers," *Journalism Quarterly*, Winter, 1978, pp. 792–793; Guido H. Stempel III, "The Prestige Press Meets the Third Party Challenge," *Journalism Quarterly*,

Winter, 1969, p. 701; Guido H. Stempel III, "The Prestige Press in Two Presidential Elections," *Journalism Quarterly,* Winter, 1965, p. 21.

8  Doris A. Graber, *Mass Media and American Politics,* Congressional Quarterly Press, Washington, D.C., 1980, pp. 174–175.

9  Walter DeVries and V. Lance Tarrance, *The Ticket Splitters,* Eerdmans, Grand Rapids, 1972.

10  Richard Stout, "The Pre-Pre Campaign-Campaign," *Public Opinion,* Dec./ Jan., 1983, pp. 17–20, 60.

11  Stout, "Pre-Pre Campaign-Campaign," p. 18.

12  Donald Matthews, "Winnowing: The News Media and the 1976 Presidential Nomination," in Barber (ed.), *Race for the Presidency,* 1978, p. 58.

13  Stout, "Pre-Pre Campaign-Campaign," p. 17.

14  *New York Times,* October 14, 1983. The New York *Times* Company, copyright 1983. Reprinted by permission.

15  *Time,* February 7, 1983.

16  Michael J. Robinson, "TV's Newest Program: The Presidential Nomination Game," *Public Opinion,* May/June, 1978, p. 43.

17  Leon V. Sigal, "Newsmen and Campaigners: Organization Men Make the News," *Political Science Quarterly,* vol. 93, Fall, 1978, pp. 465–470.

18  Graber, *Mass Media,* p. 159.

19  John Sears, "The Press Elects the President...," *Washington Journalism Review,* Sept., 1980, pp. 32 and 36.

20  Edwin Diamond, "The Press Elects the President...Not Really," *Washington Journalism Review,* Sept., 1980, pp. 33 and 37.

21  Edwin Diamond, "The Press Was the Last to Know," *Washington Journalism Review,* July/Aug., 1980, pp. 14–15.

22  Lowenstein, "Covering the Primaries," pp. 38–40.

23  Robinson, "Media at Mid-Year," p. 45.

24  Quoted in F. Christopher Arterton, "The Media Politics of Presidential Campaigns," in Barber (ed.), *Race for the Presidency,* 1978, p. 36.

25  Joel Swerdlow, "The Decline of the Boys on the Bus," *Washington Journalism Review,* Jan./Feb., 1981, p. 18.

26  Swerdlow, "Boys on the Bus," p. 17.

27  *See* Timothy Crouse, *The Boys on the Bus,* Random House, New York, 1973.

28  Swerdlow, "Boys on the Bus," p. 15.

29  Howell Rains, "Reporters Notebook: Ghost in Reagan Camp," *New York Times,* October 5, 1980, p. 11.

30  Robinson, with Conover and Sheehan, "Media at Mid-Year," p. 44.

31  James David Barber, *The Pulse of Politics: Electing Presidents in the Media Age,* W.W. Norton & Co., New York, 1980, p. 8.

32  Arterton, "Media Politics ," p. 27.

33  Robinson, "TV's Newest Program," p. 45.

34  Patterson, *Mass Media Election,* p. 29; Graber, *Mass Media,* p. 179.

35  Graber, *Mass Media,* pp. 181–182.

36  Patterson, *Mass Media Election,* pp. 31–42.

37  Patterson, *Mass Media Election,* p. 35.

38  Quoted in James McCartney, "The Triumph of Junk News," *Columbia Journalism Review,* Jan./Feb., 1977, p. 17.

**39** Michael Robinson and Margaret Sheehan, "How the Networks Learned to Love the Issues," *Washington Journalism Review*, Dec., 1980, p. 16.

**40** Graber, *Mass Media*, pp. 169–170.

**41** Graber, *Mass Media*, p. 172.

**42** Paul Weaver, "Is Television News Biased?" *Public Interest*, Winter, 1972, p. 69.

**43** Paul Weaver, "Captives of Melodrama," *The New York Times Magazine*, August 29, 1976, p. 57.

**44** McCartney, "Triumph of Junk News," 1977.

**45** Weaver, "Captives of Melodrama," p. 6.

**46** Weaver, "Captives of Melodrama," pp. 6 and 48.

**47** Patterson, *Mass Media Election*, p. 24.

**48** Patterson, *Mass Media Election*, p. 29.

**49** Robinson and Sheehan, "Love the Issues," p. 16; Robinson, with Conover and Sheehan, "Media at Mid-Year," p. 43.

**50** Robinson, with Conover and Sheehan, "Media at Mid-Year," p. 42.

**51** Lowenstein, "Covering the Primaries," p. 41.

**52** John Carey, "How the Media Shape Campaigns," *Journal of Communication*, vol. 26, Spring, 1976, p. 55.

**53** Quoted in David L. Swanson, "And That's the Way It Was? Television Covers the 1976 Presidential Campaign," *Quarterly Journal of Speech*, vol. 63, Oct., 1977, p. 246.

**54** Carey, "Shape Campaigns," p. 55.

**55** McCartney, "Triumph of Junk News," p. 18.

**56** Weaver, "Captives of Melodrama," p. 50.

**57** Carey, "Shape Campaigns," p. 56.

**58** Barber, *Pulse of Politics*, p. 313.

**59** Quoted in Lowenstein, "Covering the Primaries," p. 42.

**60** Quoted in McCartney, "Triumph of Junk News," p. 18.

**61** Quoted in Swanson, "Way It Was?" p. 244.

**62** Arterton, "Media Politics," pp. 48–51.

**63** Quoted in Lowenstein, "Covering the Primaries," pp. 38–40.

**64** Bernard Weintraub, "Party Delegates Outnumbered by the News Media's Delegates," *New York Times*, August 12, 1980.

**65** Tony Schwartz, "Networks Are Running Hard for the Viewer's Acclamation," *New York Times*, July 14, 1980.

**66** *New York Times*, July 5, 1984, p. C14.

**67** Goodwin F. Berquist and James L. Golden, "Media Rhetoric, Criticism and the Public Perception of the 1980 Presidential Debates," *Quarterly Journal of Speech*, vol. 67, May, 1981, p. 125.

**68** Henry Fairlie, "Scripts for the Pageant," *The New Republic*, August 8, 1983, p. 26.

**69** Fairlie, "Scripts for the Pageant," p. 28.

**70** *Newsweek* (Election Extra), Nov./Dec., 1984, p. 105.

**71** Quoted in Berquist and Golden, "Media Rhetoric," p. 128.

**72** Quoted in Berquist and Golden, "Media Rhetoric," p. 127.

**73** Patterson, *Mass Media Election*, p. 39.

**74** Quoted in Berquist and Golden, "Media Rhetoric," p. 133

**75** John Jackson, "Election Night Reporting and Voter Turnout," *American Journal of Political Science,* vol. 27, no. 4, Nov., 1983, pp. 616–635.

**76** Martin Wattenberg, "From Parties to Candidates: Examining the Role of the Media," *Public Opinion Quarterly,* Summer, 1982, p. 217.

**77** David H. Ostroff, "A Participant-Observer Study of TV Campaign Coverage," *Journalism Quarterly,* Aug., 1980, p. 415.

**78** Ostroff, "Participant-Observer Study," p. 419.

**79** Leonard Tipton, Roger D. Haney, and John R. Baseheart, "Media Agenda-Setting in City and State Election Campaigns," *Journalism Quarterly,* vol. 52, Spring, 1975, pp. 15–22.

**80** Barber (ed.), *Race for the Presidency,* 1978, pp. 3–10.

**81** Robert Agranoff, *The New Style in Election Campaigns,* 2d ed., Holbrook Press, Boston, 1976.

**82** Wattenberg reports that, when the 1958 Congressional Elections Studies respondents were asked what they liked or disliked about the Democratic and Republican parties, the mean number of responses was 3.4. By 1978, the mean number of responses was 1.9. A decline was true even among strong party-identifiers, whose mean number of responses dropped from approximately 4.2 to 3.2. P. 218.

**83** Patterson, *Mass Media Election,* p. 95.

**84** Thomas E. Patterson and Robert D. McClure, *The Unseeing Eye: The Myth of Television Power in National Politics,* Putnam's, New York, 1976, p. 53.

**85** Patterson, *Mass Media Election,* pp. 62–64.

**86** Patterson, *Mass Media Election,* pp. 68–69.

**87** See Michael B. McKuen and Steven L. Coombs, *More Than News: Media Power in Public Affairs,* Sage, Beverly Hills, 1981; *also see* Shanto Iyengar, Mark D. Peters, and Donald R. Kinder, "Experimental Demonstrations of the 'Not-So-Minimal' Consequences of Television News Programs," *American Political Science Review,* Dec., 1982, pp. 848–858.

**88** Graber, *Mass Media,* p. 174.

**89** Patterson, *Mass Media Election,* p. 98.

**90** Patterson, *Mass Media Election,* p. 119.

**91** Patterson, *Mass Media Election,* pp. 123–125.

**92** Patterson, *Mass Media Election,* p. 109.

**93** Graber, *Mass Media,* p. 184.

**94** Patterson, *Mass Media Election,* p. 156.

**95** See Michael Robinson, "Public Affairs Television and the Growth of Political Malaise: The Case of the Selling of the Pentagon," *American Political Science Review,* June, 1976, pp. 409–432.

**96** Quoted in Barber (ed.), *Race for the Presidency,* p. 159.

# CHAPTER 6

# CANDIDATES' USE OF THE MEDIA: MEDIA CONSULTANTS AND POLLSTERS

*The new technology is in its infant stage for those who practice the media arts. What we learn is what doesn't work, by trial and error. My value to a candidate right now is that after ten years of doing media, I won't try an idea that I had five years ago and I found bombed. We're becoming a little more error free. But we really don't know a great deal. If we knew more we would be dangerous [emphasis ours].*[1]

Robert Goodman, Media Consultant

In the previous chapter, we examined how the modern political campaign is covered by the media. We noted along the way how the candidate and his or her staff attempt to control the nature of that coverage in the form of such things as planned events and press releases. We also noted that control by the candidate is limited by journalistic standards of newsworthiness. We observed how the candidate's message is mediated by the journalist's interests and values. However, the media also provide the candidate with direct access to the public through the use of paid advertising, where the candidate has complete control over the message. In attempting to amass voter support through paid advertising, the modern politician has come to rely heavily on media consultants and pollsters. It is to the rise of these new consultants that we will turn our attention in this chapter.

Media consulting and polling have their roots in the private sector. Many of the technologies and crafts used by these consultants were first developed in public relations firms, advertising agencies, and market research organizations that serviced many of the nation's large corporations. In the late 1950s, when candidates began to see the advantages of paid advertising on television, a group of well-trained media professionals were there to offer their services. Pollsters try to tap public opinion, gauge the mood of the electorate, and identify those voters who might be susceptible to persuasion—the uncommitted voters. Using these data and the skills developed in product advertising, media consultants develop an advertising campaign in order to sell the candidate, bring issues to public attention, and bring voters to the polls.

There is, to be sure, a continuing struggle between those who represent these new techniques and those who would favor more traditional political tactics. There is an inevitable conflict between these new consultants and traditional political advisors, who would favor developing an organizational base through winning endorsements, courting elected officials and local political leaders, and organizing volunteers for local grassroots efforts. During the preprimary and primary stage, the need to organize on the local level makes traditional tactics all but obligatory. However, as we move toward the general election, which involves a choice between only two major candidates, publicity campaigns tend to take over, and the influence of media consultants and pollsters is more keenly felt.

Even more important, most politicians believe that media experts and pollsters are essential to winning an election. Hardly a nominee, at any level, believes that he or she can make it without a political consultant or two.* As Larry Sabato points out in his recent study:

> ...candidates have hired media and polling consultants at great cost without even a superficial comprehension of their techniques or their real worth—taking on faith what they had read and heard about these election wizards, believing all the while that consultants were essential for victory without knowing whether or why the common wisdom was true.[2]

Political consultants, naturally, foster the image that they are necessary. This aura of special expertise is enhanced by journalists, who rely on these consultants as ready sources of information and who report their latest polls, predictions, and pronouncements. However, consultants must be careful not to take too much credit for the successful campaign.

---

*In statewide campaigns in 1984, twenty-three of the twenty-four candidates for governor had media specialists and twenty-two had pollsters. Among the sixty-four candidates for the Senate, fifty-four had media consultants and forty-eight had polling experts. Source: *New York Times,* Oct. 19, 1984, p. A24.

As Sabato puts it: "Consultants can become an albatross around the candidate's neck by being too willing to take credit." In the face of too much self-promotion on the part of these new political experts, the "candidate's own leadership qualities are questioned."[3]

The rise of these new consultants has several implications, not the least of which is that their approach favors certain kinds of candidates. Political consultants are first and foremost in the business to make money; thus, they are out to win, whether it be national or local elections, referenda, primary campaigns, or convention nominations. Since fees are based on their record, consultants want candidates who have a chance to win. From the point of view of the consultant, it would be foolish to take on too many long shots. Unknowns have little chance to get a prestige consultant. Well-known consultants want incumbents (who usually win elections) or reasonable bets for open offices (representatives of major parties, already-established public figures, or candidates with winning records).

The best candidate, from the perspective of the consultant, is the one who best fits the technology of persuasion: the mass media, particularly television. The growing perception that television is the most important medium for selling a candidate favors the candidate most suited to the demands of the electronic media. From the point of view of the consultant, there is a clear advantage in being able to perform before the camera and in being attractive and articulate.

Another important consequence of the rise of the new consultants comes from the fact that good political consulting costs a lot of money, which has contributed to the rising costs of political campaigns. The costs of consultants show no clear pattern, and charging practices vary. There are generally three kinds of fees. The first is the consulting fee, which is the amount it takes to secure the service of the consultant, usually a flat fee, ranging from $20,000 to $100,000 for a "name" consultant. The second fee is the "incurred costs and personal expenses," which includes the cost of polling, television production, brochures, bumper stickers, and so on. Finally, the big money maker comes in the form of commissions. This is usually 15 percent of the cost of anything purchased for the campaign through the consultant. Thus, if the cost of the television commercial is $100,000, the candidate is billed that cost plus 15 percent for the consultant.[4] The cost of consulting is estimated to be about 20 percent of the campaign budget, which is no small amount when one realizes that campaign budgets run into the millions.

Political consultants are no longer behind-the-scenes advisors. They regularly appear in the press and become, themselves, media personalities. Thus, it becomes important in national elections for the candidate to get a "name" consultant. To gain access to political action committees, where the money for the modern campaign lies, a candidate needs a survey from a big-name pollster.[5] Consultants become status symbols; the "name" consultant insures legitimacy for the campaign and favorable treatment by the press. Candidates often schedule press conferences to announce their consultants. Nationally-known name consultants interview and screen candidates; they become, in effect, "preselectors," with a profit motive attached to their selection.[6]

Perhaps the most important consequence of media consultants and pollsters is the fact that they have changed the nature of the modern campaign for public office, and, in so doing, they have had a profound effect on modern government. Whereas traditional political tactics rely, to a large extent, on mobilizing party faithfuls, these modern consultants focus their attention on the uncommitted voters.[7] Even though most people still vote based on party loyalties or have made up their minds before the campaign, as much as one third of the electorate is uncommitted. A growing number of people think of themselves as independents, and a growing number of people are ticket splitters. In 1984, Republicans represented only 30 percent, and Democrats only 43 percent, of the electorate.[8] It is the uncommitted who are the real target audience for these political consultants.

On the national level and in areas where party affiliation is weak, the candidate must appeal to the uncommitted in order to get elected. The techniques of the media consultants and the pollsters are well suited to that end. However, once elected by having appealed to the uncommitted, politicians find that their support is, by definition, weak. Creating a winning coalition among those who are not bound to the candidate by party loyalty means that the alliance needs to be continually maintained. Politicians are forced to continue to use the techniques that brought victory. Some consultants become official advisers. Gerald Rafshoon, President Carter's media consultant, was the first consultant to join the White House staff. Richard S. Beal, a pollster, analyzed the Harris, Gallup, and other public polls and until 1985 reported directly to Edwin Meese, then Counsel to President Reagan. This has led Sidney Blumenthal to conclude that modern governing has become a "permanent campaign." Once elected, politicians must continually seek public approval for support of their policies. Techniques used to get the vote are now necessary to maintain public approval. As we shall see in Chapter 7, techniques used to win the election increasingly become techniques of governing.

## THE POLLSTERS

Polling has become a fundamental tool of the modern campaign. Political polling has become as essential to the campaign as market research is to modern product marketing and advertising. Through polling, the consultant tries to discover what issues will reach the un-committed voters or what issues will weaken the commitment of voters who are weakly aligned to a party. Given the nature of the shifting population, the candidate and the strategy must be geared to quick changes. As Blumenthal points out, "In order to win over the un-committed, it helps if the politician is uncommitted as well."[9] Issues emerge in response to what a pollster says is on the public mind. Taking a position on an issue is often a matter of strategy, not principle.

Polling was first used by Franklin Roosevelt to gauge his popularity. Themes for Dwight Eisenhower commercials were designed in consulta-tion with George Gallup, the most famous pollster in the post-World War II era.[10] Polling was not used extensively until the 1960 presidential campaign. Louis Harris, advisor to John F. Kennedy, analyzed public opinion in the most important primary states. Within two years, two-thirds of U.S. Senate candidates used surveys. By 1966, 85 percent of Senate winners, almost all candidates for governor, and about half of the winners in the House used surveys.[11] Lyndon Johnson put a pollster, Albert H. Cantril, on his staff to interpret the polls and analyze public opinion.[12] Patrick Caddell, Jimmy Carter's pollster, was the first pollster to become part of a president's inner circle of advisors and directly influence major decisions.[13]

In general, polls measure the concerns of the electorate by selecting a random sample of the population. In order for a sample to be considered random, every person in the population must theoretically have an equal chance of appearing in the sample. In order to generalize from the data, the sample must be large enough to insure that those being surveyed represent a spectrum of national opinion. No polling organization comes even close to realizing a pure random sample. However, using various forms of modified random procedures, polling organizations attempt to select representative samples of the population.[14]

The electorate is broken down into all major subgroups of the population, which permits the refinement and targeting of appeals. Thus, if a candidate is perceived as ineffective by middle-aged, college-educated white men, the candidate image can be adjusted. Polls can indicate potential difficulties or shifts in mood. The most important use to which the polls are put is the allocation of resources, in deciding which audience to target for television and radio commercials, or where the politician should make a personal appearance.

Polling techniques, over the years, have become more sophisticated. The use of the computer and census tracts, which provide important demographic data, has made sampling more reliable, although there is still a margin for error. A random sample of 1000 has a margin of error of 3 percent; a sample of 400 (the usual size of a subgroup sample) has a margin of error of 5 percent.[15] This means that the survey results are representative of the electorate within three or five percentage points in either direction.

The traditional errors in polling, like asking how the respondent feels about taxes (most people, naturally, feel that taxes are too high) and *not* asking how they feel about the reduction of governmental services, are a thing of the past. Great care is taken in constructing a survey; many questions are standard and used often; wording is tested over time to insure objectivity.

Of the hundreds of polling organizations, only a few take private political clients. The field is dominated by three Republican firms (V. Lance Tarrance and Associates, Market Opinion Research, Inc., and Richard Wirthlin's Decision Making Information) and three Democratic ones (Patrick Caddell's Cambridge Survey Research, William R. Hamilton and Staff, Inc., and Peter D. Hart Research Associates, Inc.)[16] Since pollsters provide the data on public opinion, they may become involved in all major campaign decisions. As Patrick Caddell put it: "In the 1976 Carter campaign I basically had input into the schedule for all the people in the campaign, the media buys, the kind of media messages, the organizational efforts, the dollar priorities. In the primaries I helped to make decisions about which states we went into, which states we did not."[17]

Patrick Caddell has been described as the "premier pollster of the new generation.... He has forged the era of the antipolitician, the outsider candidate who can inflict piercing wounds on an incumbent, but whose platform is thematic rather than programmatic."[18] Caddell's approach is unique; he does not merely ask: "What is your opinion of _____?" He attempts to tap what he calls "voter alienation," or the degree to which the voter lacks confidence in government and politicians. Caddell looks for voter discontents and capitalizes on them. For example, he used the public antipathy toward Washington politicians in a 1972 senatorial race in Delaware, and he used it again for Jimmy Carter in 1976.[19] Caddell's analysis of the country's mood ("crisis of confidence") continued to have influence throughout the Carter administration.*

### The Polls

Regardless of a given pollster's approach, there are basically five kinds of polls.[20] The *benchmark poll* is an early, precampaign poll which attempts to assess the national mood and the public's attitude toward the contenders or potential contenders. Benchmark polls may include up to sixty or seventy questions and may take more than an hour to answer.

---

*Patrick Caddell remained involved in Democratic politics after Carter's defeat in 1980. In the 1984 Democratic primaries, he was Gary Hart's pollster; after the convention, he joined Walter Mondale's staff.

They may be conducted by personal interview, but, more recently, the telephone has been used to cut costs. The size of the sample for a benchmark poll is usually large, from 1500 to 4000.

*Follow-up surveys* are based on the analysis of the benchmark poll and are attempts to probe the most important issues or themes. Such surveys attempt to gauge the effects of campaign efforts, and specific segments of the population may be singled out. This is where the targeting process begins. Follow-up survey polls are shorter in length, and the sample is smaller (500 to 600) than in benchmark polls. Two or more survey polls may be done during the campaign.

*Panel surveys* are follow-up polls which reinterview as many as half of the respondents of a previous poll in order to measure any shift in opinion. Since these surveys use a small sample (250 to 300), the margin of error is considered to be large. Reinterviewing is problematic, because it has been discerned that having once been a respondent in a poll increases the individual's political awareness.

In order to pick up shifts in mood or attitude, *tracking polls* are taken throughout the campaign. Fifty to one hundred people are called each night and are asked specific questions about issues, political advertisements, and perceptions of the candidate. A system of "moving averages" is used. Five nights of consecutive interviews are considered to be the total sample. For example, five nights of 100 interviews means a sample of 500. The average shifts as the sixth night's results are added and the first night is dropped, and so on.

The *focus group*, which is not really a poll at all, is a small group of people, usually ten or so, who are selected based on age, sex, race, or social class and who are brought together under a trained leader to discuss campaign issues in depth. The respondents are observed through a two-way mirror, and extensive notes are taken. The results are not quantifiable in the way that the results of the other surveys are, but the quality of the respondent's thinking can be observed. The major problem with the focus group is that it can be dominated by a strong personality.

However, the power of the modern national pollsters does not lie in the mere collection of data but in their interpretation of that data. As interpreters, they become strategists and tacticians. Richard Wirthlin, Reagan's pollster since 1971, advised candidate Reagan, in 1970, that moderates had difficulty visualizing Reagan as president. In a memo to Reagan, Wirthlin wrote: "Focus campaign resources to reinforce the Governor's image strengths that embody the presidential values a majority of Americans think are important...."[21] Reagan's television commercials began to stress what Wirthlin called "leadership perceptions." In 1982, surveys by Robert Teeter and Richard Wirthlin showed that public opinion was focusing on Reagan's economic policies and that Reagan's leadership image depended on whether voters would lose patience with Reagan's promises of an economic recovery. In order to buy more time for Reagan, his media advisors fashioned a political advertisement in which an elderly mail carrier speaks into the camera and says: "For gosh sakes, let's give the guy a chance."[22]

Polls tell the politician how his or her constituents feel about issues or positions. This does not necessarily mean that the candidate's positions will change in the face of public opinion; it means a probable change in emphasis. In a sense, the polls provide the script for the politician by indicating which issues to emphasize or "low key" and which positions or themes are most likely to provide a majority coalition.

The pollster's interpretation of the data can lead to specific campaign strategies that may ultimately have an effect on the governing process. For example, in 1982, polls indicated that social issues such as abortion, school prayer, and crime would have little effect on the electorate concerned with recession. Thus, a policy shift was in the making; if the abortion issue, for example, was hurting Republicans, the issue would not be geared to nationwide audiences. Rather, such appeals would be funneled to specific groups expected to help Republicans in certain districts, such as Roman Catholics in urban areas and religious fundamentalists in the South. In this way, Republicans hoped to maintain the support of their conservative base while declining to make their causes national issues.[23]

In the 1982 campaign, pollsters also reported the existence of a "gender gap." Women, they concluded, were giving more support to Democrats, while Republicans were getting more support from men. The *New York Times* reported, in October of 1982, that the latest polls showed that women were producing a lead for Democratic gubernatorial candidates in New York, Arkansas, and California. The support of men, on the other hand, had given the lead to Republicans in Senate races in California and New Mexico and in the gubernatorial race in Iowa. Since women vote in greater numbers than men, both parties began to focus on women. For the Democrats the issue was to get out the women's vote. A billboard in Bladensburg, Maryland, proclaimed: "It's a man's world, *unless women vote!*"[24] Republicans tried to counter their negative image among women by pointing to the administration's record of appointing women and by emphasizing education, equal pay, and benefits for the elderly.

Polls also tell the politician what will not work. During 1982, Democratic strategists were hoping that voters would resent federal budget cuts because the cuts would mean higher local taxes. However, the polls told them that the public had not yet made that connection.[25] Democratic strategy for 1984 was to attack Reagan on policy but not on personal grounds, because the polls indicated that many voters still thought Reagan was a "nice guy."

With the increased number of self-defined independents and ticket splitters, modern pollsters are very interested in finding out the respondent's political leanings, if any. One technique that several pollsters have used is to set up a hypothetical situation in which Republicans and Democrats no longer exist. The respondent is then asked which party he or she would favor if all he or she could go on were the following names: Labor, Progressive, Conservative, Free Enterprise, Taxpayers, Consumers, and so on.[26]

Peter Hart uses a ten-point scale to get at feelings about his candidates. Patrick Caddell has "trust indices" and "ladders of confidence" to measure voter alienation. He also uses profiles of his candidate and the opponent, asking the respondents the same questions about each one.[27]

Benchmark polls include a section on television viewing, radio listening, and newspaper reading patterns, as well as a section on demographic characteristics, such as age, education, religion, ethnic group, race, and income. This approach, of course, makes targeting possible, but it also enables the pollster to know, for example, how 30-year-old, college-educated white women with children feel about a specific issue

### Reliability of the Polls

With all the new techniques and technologies, there are still some problems with polling that are difficult, if not impossible, to overcome. On the most basic level, respondents may not tell the truth out of a desire to please, an unwillingness to admit prejudices, or ignorance.

Polls can create public opinion by merely asking the question. On the most basic level, simply asking about a given issue calls attention to it. Widely reported polling results "inform" the public of the key issues in a campaign and signal those issues about which one ought to have an opinion. On another level, people tend to want to be good respondents and will often produce an opinion whether or not they have ever seriously thought about the issue. Opinions can even be created out of nothing. A third of the respondents in one survey indicated strong opinions about the Public Affairs Act of 1975, which was a nonexistent piece of legislation.[28]

Respondents are typically asked about their past voting records, which people are surprisingly willing to talk about. However, memory is often selective. By 1964, 64 percent of the electorate claimed to have voted for John F. Kennedy, who had won one of the closest races in American history in 1960.[29]

Sophisticated random sampling still cannot overcome the problem of potential respondents who either are unavailable or refuse to be interviewed. For at-home interviews, 40 to 55 percent are either not home or refuse to participate. For telephone interviews, the figure is between 25 and 35 percent. Approximately 20 percent of respondents are "reluctant" respondents who evade, object to, or refuse to answer one or more questions.[30] It is difficult to know whether these figures reflect voter apathy, disaffection, or hostility toward the political process.

Of course, the polls or the pollsters may be biased. There is no doubt that results can be a function of the way a question is asked. Results can be deliberately or inadvertently influenced by the predispositions of the pollster or his client. Pollsters themselves can be tactical weapons when they predict victory for their own clients. Interpretation of data may be subject to great variation. Caddell's interpretation of the polls which led to his "crisis of confidence" analysis has been contested by political scientist Warren E. Miller.[31]

However, the most fundamental problem of most polls is that the opinion of the misinformed, uninformed, and uninterested is given the same weight as the opinion of those who are informed, involved, and interested. While such things as a respondent's voting record are usually taken into account in weighing his or her opinion (that is, regular voters are distinguished from infrequent voters), the informed are rarely distinguished from the uninformed. Polling encourages candidates to give in to the pressures of current trends and to evaluate their positions in terms of popularity. This problem is further exacerbated by the news media's use of the polling data.

On the most basic level, the news media give greater attention and coverage to those candidates who have the highest standing in the polls. In the beginning of a campaign, most polls are merely name identification contests which inevitably favor incumbents or political stars. The news media tend to report polling data as hard news and then make their decisions as to what is newsworthy based on those data. The pollsters and the media define the front runners, and the front runners dominate political news.*

The news media rarely tell the viewer or the reader exactly who the respondents are in a given survey: all eligible voters, likely voters, or the entire population? The media rarely give the exact wording of the question. We rarely know if the interview was done personally, by telephone, or by mail. The data are simply presented. In fact, the news media pay for their own surveys: CBS and the *New York Times* jointly conduct polls; NBC polls in conjunction with the Associated Press; ABC has commissioned Louis Harris polls and now conducts polls with the *Washington Post.* Thus, the news media become vested interests in the "numbers game," "horse race," and "boxscore" politics.

*Secret Service protection is provided to presidential candidates based on their showing in the polls.

Journalists often misuse polls and set up unrealistic expectations for the candidate. If a candidate does less well than the polls predicted, the press often defines the results as a "measured defeat." For example, in 1972 an early poll in the New Hampshire primary race gave Muskie a 65 to 18 percent lead over McGovern. When Muskie actually received a 46 to 37 percent lead, the press saw it as a win for McGovern, because Muskie had "lost" his 65 percent lead.[32] In 1976, Jimmy Carter did better in the New Hampshire primary than the polls had predicted, so, even with just his 28.4 percent plurality, the press made him a "winner."

One of the major concerns about the public's exposure to the polls is the possibility of a "bandwagon effect": swaying voters to go along with the apparent winner. However, the evidence is contradictory; some observers cite evidence that the "bandwagon" tendency has some effect, others that it has little effect, and still others that it has the effect of leading the voter to support the underdog[33] (however, the "bandwagon effect" attracts campaign contributions and bolsters the morale of campaign volunteers).

Another concern about the public's exposure to the polls has been the "complacency effect," where early poll results make the supporters of the apparent winner complacent and the supporters of the opponent firmer in their resolution. However, this view is not open to empirical verification and remains conjecture. The "bandwagon effect" and the "complacency effect" are clearly at odds. If popularity in the polls encourages voters to vote for the winner and also creates complacency among initial supporters, such trends might just cancel each other out. In effect, both hypotheses may be correct but irrelevant, which might explain, in part, the difficulty in verification.

With all the problems inherent in polling, polling is still the most reliable way to gauge public opinion. Polling data and pollsters' interpretations provide the framework for the political campaign and, increasingly, the framework for governing. The pollsters locate the uncommitted voters—the swing voters, the ticketsplitters, and the independents; the media consultants mount the campaign, target audiences, emphasize or "low key" issues, and create the appropriate image in hopes of achieving a winning consensus among the electorate.

Political polling increasingly comes to determine the issues and strategies of the campaign. Polling public opinion assures that issues and attitudes that gain political attention will typically be those that are already virtually universal in the population. Minority views or controversial positions stand little chance of recognition. There is an inevitable conservative bias in public opinion; opinion changes more slowly than events, and by the time the public changes its opinion, it may be dealing with a situation that no longer exists or with an issue that is no longer relevant. For the candidate, it is safer to keep in step with public opinion than it is to keep up with the sweep of events.

## MEDIA CONSULTANTS

The media consultant develops campaign themes and strategies and uses packaging and marketing techniques in order to sell the candidate to the public. We have already observed that one of the most important aspects of the consultant's media package is the attention and coverage the consultant can command for the candidate from the unpaid media—print and broadcast journalism. Most of all, the candidate wants to make news and to be picked up by network news programs. We have already observed how important this is during the preprimary and primary periods. Consultants create media events by arranging speeches, rallies, and press conferences. The press is given access to the candidate, and events are scheduled around deadlines. Consultants try to arrange good visuals: the candidate goes on location, making personal appearances; family members are trotted in or trotted out on the campaign trail; the candidate seeks and accepts invitations to talk shows. As we have pointed out, the unpaid media, particularly television news, add little of substance to the campaign; however, they do confer credibility.

In mounting the media campaign, media consultants tend to see themselves as independent of political parties. Indeed, media consultants see themselves as replacements for obsolete political parties. Consider the following quotations from two well-known and influential media consultants:

> The successful political consultant has become an independent operation. He has a life of his own. He is a seperate power center. It's a replacement party for the decline of the parties. The day of the political party boss is over.[34]
>
> John Deardourff, Media Consultant, Republican; moderate

> Here [in the United States] consultants are extra-party. The parties are obsolete here. Before television, in order to get your message across, you had to filter it through the party. Now you don't need the party. I work in lots of campaigns in lots of states where I don't even know who the Democratic party chairmen are. It doesn't matter to me or my candidates. I was early in my perception that the party was on the decline. The party didn't do much, it didn't mean much, it never had much money. And it was often staffed by guys who couldn't find real jobs. I didn't need them.[35]
>
> Joseph Napolitan, General Consultant, Democrat; moderate

While these statements may reflect the views or wishes of certain consultants, the reality is that media consultants cannot operate independently of political parties. They cannot ignore traditional political advisers. The media consultant's desire to place the candidate before the public as much as possible often conflicts with the need to build a strong organizational base. Decisions have to be made about how to allocate campaign resources. Shifts in strategy throughout a campaign often reflect the struggle between the media consultant's publicity offensive and what has been called the "nuts and bolts" of political organizing.* Nonetheless, the role of the media consultant can be seen in every major campaign.

Media consultants are treated with deference and respect by politicians and journalists. Some of this is a function of the aura of special expertise surrounding the consultants, but a good deal of the deference comes from the variety of things they do in slickly-packaged fashion. Besides developing themes and strategies, media consultants write, produce, and edit advertisements. They buy spots on television and radio and space in newspapers and magazines. With the help of polling services, they target audiences; that is, they place a spot to attract an audience with particular demographic characteristics. They design graphics for billboards and brochures and write press releases. Finally, they monitor and critique the candidate's and his or her staff's performances. It is easy to see how a politician could come to see the media consultant as indispensible, even while the public might see the consultant as an unsavory hustler.

Table 6-1 gives profiles of some of the major political consultants in the nation, including the names of politicians that they helped install in office.

## Political Commercials

Although media consultants do a variety of things, the television advertising campaign is the most significant, since here the candidate and his or her staff have complete control over the content of the message.* The first step in planning the media ad campaign is to look at the polls to determine the "climate of opinion," to ascertain the "mood of the nation," or, more simply put, to find out what the electorate is worrying about. Next, the media consultant must find out how the candidate and the opponent are perceived by the public. The knowledge of weaknesses and strengths permits the media consultant to stress or "low key" issues or images most favorable to the candidate and unfavorable to the opponent.[36]

*It is interesting to note that Walter Mondale's primary campaign in 1984 has been criticized for giving in to "special interests." Forming a coalition of special interests is a traditional political technique. However, in media-age politics, it somehow becomes suspicious.

*The cost of the television campaign has been steadily escalating. In 1984, it has been estimated that about $150 million was spent on television advertisements alone. A thirty-second commercial on ABC-TV's "Monday Night Football" cost about $50,000 in 1980. By 1984, the cost was about $125,000.

In the old days, perhaps, good politicians relied on their instincts, but the sophistication and proliferation of modern survey research has made instinct either unnecessary or untrustworthy in the face of what are seen as "hard data." The consultants select issues and images suitable to the mood of the nation *and* to the candidate. The well-known incumbent and the unknown candidate require different strategies. Next, the consultant selects the "visually oriented" issues and attempts to match them with the candidate's "image." For example, if the candidate has scored high in the "help-the-people" category, the consultant might consider using the picture of laid-off steelworkers in downtown Pittsburgh, against a background of smokeless factory stacks, and the candidate showing "concern" by talking to them.

In the production of television spots, the filming is usually done first, and the appropriate script is written later. As media consultant Tony Schwartz puts it: "A 'message' is not the starting point for communicating....Only at the final stage do we consider the content of a message, and this will be determined by the effect we want to achieve and the environment where our content will take on meaning."[37] Here the relationship between the form of the message and the content is nicely illustrated. The visuals are the engine of the appeal; the words are just along for the ride. The final stage is the scheduling of airing time and the targeting of carefully-selected segments of the population.

Political ads can serve several purposes. A major goal of all political ads is to develop the image of the candidate. After tapping public opinion, ads can be used to develop issues favorable to the candidate. Ads are often used to link the candidate with a political party, with other groups, or with particular individuals. Finally, political ads may be used to attack the opponent.

The art of the political commercial has been steadily advancing. Early political commercials often showed the candidate delivering a speech. They merely picked up and developed the image that most people had of what politicians do.[38] The "talking head" commercial, in which the candidate talks directly to the viewers, gradually replaced the older format. Although such ads are considered uncreative by media professionals, there is a high degree of recall of the information delivered by the candidate speaking directly into the camera.[39] Apparently, conservatives respond particularly well to the "talking head" and its straight, nononsense style.[40] Since the "talking head" supposedly projects an image of honesty, many more such spots were to be found in media campaigns after Watergate.

Another format, used as far back as 1950, the "man-in-the-street" interview, is still used and is considered to be very effective, particularly with liberals.[41] The man-in-the-street format is especially effective in

**TABLE 6-1**
SELECTED "NAME" CONSULTANTS

| Consultant | Party/Ideology* | Background/Experience | Sample of Clients |
|---|---|---|---|
| Douglas Bailey and John Deardourff Bailey/Deardourff and Associates, Inc. McLean, Virginia | Republican; Moderate | Bailey: Ph.D. in international relations; Henry Kissinger's assistant at Harvard; 1964 Rockefeller presidential campaign official. Deardourff: domestic policy research in Rockefeller 1964 presidential campaign; worked for John Lindsay in 1965 New York City mayoralty election. Considered the most prominent Republican media firm. | George Romney presidential (1968); Gerald Ford presidential (1976); Sen. Charles Percy (R-Ill.); Sen. Richard Schweiker (R-Penn.) |
| Walter DeVries DeVries and Associates Wrightsville Beach, N.C. | Democratic (formerly Republican); Moderate | Academic consultant; Ph.D. in Political Science and Social Psychology; Executive assistant to Gov. George Romney (R-Mich.); teaches at Duke; former Vice President of American Association of Political Consultants. | Romney presidential (1967); Pat McCullough gubernatorial primary (D-Mich., 1978); heads N.C. Opinion Research; conducts polls Raleigh News and Observer. |
| David Garth Garth Associates, Inc. New York City | Independent; Liberal | Volunteer in politics, New York State; co-chairman of Draft Adlai Stevenson presidential committee, 1960; first major media campaign was for John Lindsay mayoralty, 1965. One of the most widely publicized firms. | Gov. Hugh Carey (D-N.Y.); Gov. Brendan Byrne (D-N.J.); Mayor Ed Koch (D-N.Y.); Mayor Tom Bradley (D-L.A.); Joffrey Ballet; New York Jets; three presidential campaigns: Eugene McCarthy (1968); John Lindsay (1972); John Anderson (1980) |
| Robert Goodman Robert Goodman Agency Brooklandville, Maryland | Republican; Liberal | Degree in philosophy, Harvard; apprenticed in advertising; managed Spiro Agnew's Md. gubernatorial campaign, 1966; consultant to Republican National Committee for four years. | George Bush presidential (1980); Sen. John Tower (R-Texas); Gov. Arch Moore (R-W.Va.) |

| | | | |
|---|---|---|---|
| Charles Guggenheim<br>Guggenheim Productions, Inc. Washington, D.C. | Democrat; Liberal | Documentary film producer; winner of Peabody television and Cannes film awards; Adlai Stevenson presidential campaign 1956. | Robert Kennedy presidential (1968); George McGovern presidential (1972); Edward Kennedy presidential (1980) |
| Joseph Napolitan<br>Joseph Napolitan Associates, Inc. New York City | Democrat; Moderate | College English literature major; sportswriter; political reporter; prominent early consultant; founder of American Association of Political Consultants; co-founder of International Association of Political Consultants. | Humphrey presidential (1968); Sen. Mike Gravel |
| Gerald Rafshoon<br>Rafshoon Communications Washington, D.C. | Democrat; Moderate | Advertising agency executive; joined White House staff in July 1978 for a year. | Carter's Georgia gubernatorial races (1966, 1970); Carter presidential (1976, 1980); Mario Cuomo mayoralty (N.Y.C., 1977) |
| Tony Schwartz<br>New York City | Democrat; Liberal | Author of *The Responsive Chord*; won two Academy awards; independent television & radio ad producer; worked closely with Joseph Napolitan. | LBJ presidential (1964); Humphrey presidential (1968); McGovern presidential (1972); Carter presidential (1976); Sen. Patrick Moynihan (D-N.Y.) |
| Stuart Spencer<br>Spencer-Roberts and Associates, Newport Beach, CA | Republican; Moderate | One of President Ford's closest advisors in 1976 campaign; senior counselor in Ronald Reagan's 1980 campaign. | Ronald Reagan presidential (1980); Ford presidential (1976); Nelson Rockefeller presidential (1964); Reagan gubernatorial (R-CA, 1966) |

\*Party affiliation and ideological leaning is that of the individual and most of the firm's clients.

*Source:* Taken from Larry J. Sabato, *The Rise of Political Consultants: New Ways of Winning Elections.* © 1981 by Larry J. Sabato. Reprinted by permission of Basic Books, Inc., Publishers.

reaching subgroups in the society by giving the viewer someone with whom to identify. In the 1982 congressional elections, the issues of inflation and unemployment had Republicans, as well as Democrats, using man-in-the-street advertisements in an attempt to reach such subgroups. More recent formats, attempting to increase credibility, often present the candidate at a press conference, looking like a television anchorman or anchorwoman.

The format of a political commercial may be determined by the special needs of a given campaign or candidate. In multicandidate primary races, name identification is crucial at the first stage. A candidate's name may be mentioned as often as nine times in thirty seconds.[42] A political commercial for a black or a female candidate has to attempt to overcome stereotypes. Incumbents who have made unpopular decisions require special treatment. David Garth has made a reputation using the "apology" strategy. ("I've made my share of mistakes..."), which he used successfully wih New York Mayor John Lindsay in 1969, New Jersey Governor Brendan Byrne in 1977, and New York Governor Hugh Carey in 1978.[43] Occasionally, press coverage of a candidate can undermine the effect of political ads. It has been suggested, for example, that the 1984 primary campaign ads for John Glenn, which stressed his image as the heroic American astronaut, conflicted with the press's coverage of Glenn's dry discussions of issues and that this damaged his campaign by making him appear "inauthentic."[44]

There are some techniques that are uniformly included in the media campaign. For example, there is generally an attempt to associate the candidate with youth—on the beach, at a baseball game, or (in the case of Reagan) on horseback. The candidate must appear intelligent; a background of bookcases is often seen. Power and patriotism are conveyed by the American flag, scenes from Capitol Hill, or any number of identifiable national monuments.

Campaign slogans are also common, and they are usually nonideological and not issue oriented. Richard Nixon's slogan in 1970 was "Four More Years"; Lyndon Johnson's "All the Way with LBJ" is typical. Dwight Eisenhower's "Crime, Communism, and Korea" was atypical. Very common are such slogans as "He thinks like us," "He hears you," or "You know where he stands." The wrong slogan may have an unfortunate effect. According to political scientist Dan Nimmo, Barry Goldwater's "In Your Heart You Know He's Right" was a mistake, since it called attention to his extremism.[45]

One of the things that is rarely used in a political commercial is humor, since consultants feel that it hurts the candidate's credibility. Yet when a candidate appears on a talk show, humor is encouraged as a means of making the candidate appear more down-to-earth.

Negative advertisements, or ads which attack the opponent rather than support the candidate's positions, are approached cautiously by consultants. The medium of television, with the immediacy of its visual and auditory stimuli, makes attacks seem stronger than the written word or even the spoken word. For this reason, some consultants use only radio for negative advertising.[46] Negative advertising calls attention to one's rival and may backfire and produce sympathy for the person attacked. Above all, the candidate must appear to be fair. On the other hand, a negative ad could bring forth an angry response from the opponent, which, if emotional and in his or her own words, might be politically dangerous.

Negative advertising is a major trend, and it has been estimated that a third of all spot commercials in recent campaigns have been negative[47] (this trend is also observable in product advertisements, where the name of the competitor is mentioned). While many consultants used to say that negative advertisements were ineffective, these same consultants tended to use such ads when the situation warranted. Negative ads usually are used when the candidate appears to be losing. Carter's tough, anti-Reagan spots came relatively late in the 1980 campaign.

The 1982 Congressional campaign revealed some interesting trends in the use of negative advertising. Campaign strategists recognized the "necessity" of the personal attack.[48] However, despite the vast television audience, direct-mail advertising was the preferred weapon of attack. A letter denouncing a candidate can be sent to a targeted audience, and, if it is sent late in the campaign, it is difficult for the opposing organization to answer the charges before election day.

The 1984 Democratic primary campaign was particularly negative. Walter Mondale's staff created an advertisement where a red telephone was seen blinking in the Oval Office while a voice warned of the dangers of having an "unsure...unsteady...untested" hand on the receiver. Gary Hart's staff responded with an ad focusing on the U.S. presence in Central America which suggested that Mondale would risk another Vietnam by leaving some of the troops in Nicaragua "as bargaining chips."

The most famous negative advertisement was shown only once in 1964, during the Johnson-Goldwater presidential race, which was, in general, a very negative campaign. The "Daisy Spot," as this ad came to be called, was designed by Tony Schwartz. The ad depicted a little girl counting as she picked petals from a daisy. As her count reached ten, the frame froze on her face and the viewer heard a countdown followed by an explosion and a mushroom cloud. Johnson's voice was heard off camera saying: "These are the stakes, to make a world in which all God's children can live, or go into darkness. Either we must love each other or we must die." Without even mentioning Goldwater's name or his position on nuclear weapons, the ad directly played to the fear that Goldwater might actually use nuclear weapons.[49]

A more recent and standard negative device is called the "weather-vane" ad, which attempts to highlight the opponent's contradictory and changing political record. An anti-Nixon spot in 1968 showed Nixon pointing east and west at the same time, while his nose shifted from north to south.[50]

Some ads incorporate a negative commentary by suggestion. In the 1980 race for Democratic presidential nomination, one of Carter's spots included an attack on Kennedy's honesty and indirectly alluded to Chappaquiddick:

> You may not always agree with President Carter. But you'll never wonder whether he's telling the truth. It's hard to think of a more useful quality in a president than telling the simple truth. President Carter—for the truth.[51]

Outright or blatant deception in political advertising has become rare. Campaigns waged on the media are open to nationwide review, and the political consultant's, as well as the candidate's, reputation is on the line. Of course, there are mild forms of deception in the general image-making process. The political commercial can make a candidate appear to be cool, aggressive, thoughtful, or whatever is believed to be appropriate, necessary, or expedient. Camera angles can create illusion. Robert Goodman made his tall candidate (6'8" Senator Alan Simpson of Wyoming) appear shorter by having him lean against fences or rails. He made his short candidate (5'6" Senator John Tower of Texas) look taller by putting him next to undersized desks.[52] Although this may not appear to be serious, the potential for deception is very real in an age of instantaneous, repetitious dissemination of political information. Political attacks are difficult to respond to, and false information repeated over and over again is difficult to counter. Packaging campaigns has become more sophisticated, and , no doubt, forms of deception have become more subtle. Quoting out of context is still a common technique. Cleverly-edited film clips can show a cheering audience for any statement a candidate makes. Political commercials can also distort through innuendo. A 1968 commercial against Hubert Humphrey juxtaposed shots of rioters at the Democratic convention, wounded soldiers in Vietnam, and hungry farmers. The implication was clear that Hubert Humphrey was responsible for riots, war, and poverty, which, if stated explicitly, would have sounded absurd even to the most naive voter.[53]

In order to alert consumers to the fact they are watching a commercial message, all political commercials require a so-called disclaimer at the end, stating who paid for the message. The intent of the governmental requirement is to make it clear that the message is both paid for and partisan. However, a clever media consultant, like Tony Schwartz, figured out a way to minimize the negative effect of "Paid for by the Committee to Elect..." by renaming the committee "A Lot of People Who Want to See... Elected." This legal title then can be integrated into the spot by a phrase such as "And that's why this message was brought to you by...."[54] This "disclaimer" notwithstanding, it must be remembered that most political commercials come to us uninvited. By simply watching our favorite programs, we are exposed to these spots over and over again. Many people will turn off a thirty-minute political documentary, but a thirty- or sixty-second spot in the midst of *Dallas* is, in effect, forced upon us.

There are many techniques that are standard in both political and product ads, such as the use of jingles and celebrity endorsements. Very often the same announcers are hired for both kinds of ads. Both types of ads surround the product or the candidate with symbols, images, and values with which the viewer or reader can identify, like "youth," "patriotism," and the "good life." However, there are differences between product ads and political ads. Name identification, for example, is central for product ads; for the candidate, name identification is important only at the beginning of the campaign. Product ads seek only a percentage of the market (10 percent of the detergent market would be highly lucrative); the candidate needs to win the majority of the market. Advertising schedules for product campaigns are drawn up years in advance, and more time and money are spent on producing and pretesting the ads themselves. Political ad campaigns, which can seem interminable, are actually short, when compared to the length of a product advertising campaign.[55] Despite these differences, the techniques of persuasion through media packaging are fundamentally the same, and the tactics employed are based on skills developed in product advertising in a consumer-oriented society.

Nonetheless, as Patterson and McClure point out, in one of the few systematic studies of the impact of political advertising (*The Unseeing Eye: The Myth of Television Power in National Elections*), consumers make a clear distinction between the two kinds of ads and pay more attention to political advertisements. While few people remember a product ad, 79 percent of the viewers of presidential television ads remember them, and 56 percent have almost total recall of the message.[56] People, it appears, also look at presidential advertising differently from product advertising. In contrast to the viewer of product ads, the viewer of political ads seeks, and expects to find, information contained in the advertisement and attempts to evaluate its truth. This situation has led Patterson and McClure to conclude that political ads, at least presidential ones, actually educate the electorate. However, this means, as we shall see, that the electorate is "educated" on the issues only as they are defined in the media campaign. Whether this "education" is adequate to a democratic society remains to be seen.

### Scheduling and Targeting

The most important limit put on media consultants in developing television spots is the fact that these spots must be designed to fit the time made available by the networks and their affiliates. Spots come in ten-second, thirty-second, sixty-second, and four-and-one-half or five-minute time frames. Thirty- and sixty-second slots account for from 75 to 90 percent of political commercials. Although the FCC has ruled that stations cannot predetermine the length of political broadcasts, networks resist giving longer blocks of time. Networks lose from 5 to 10 percent of their viewing audience during a five-minute political commercial and they lose up to a third during and after a thirty-minute political documentary.[57]

Networks and their affiliates must grant reasonable access for candidates. However, the networks have been allowed to define the meaning of "reasonable access." There are several problems involved here. On the most basic level, there is a limited amount of commercial time available. Stations cannot just add advertising time the way a newspaper or a magazine can add a page to their publications.

In 1972, the FCC ruled that stations cannot charge candidates more than the lowest rates they charge their best commercial customers—"lowest unit rate" (l.u.r.)—for forty-five days before a primary race and sixty days before a general election (in January, 1980, the l.u.r. was extended to all political contests). The l.u.r., by itself, makes political advertisements less competitive than product advertisement. On the other hand, l.u.r. may be applied only to Saturday or Sunday morning viewing time, which would make political advertising almost useless. A l.u.r. spot may be played whenever there is an available time slot. Most political campaigns end up paying higher rates in order to be in control of when the spots are aired. Each year they pay more; television spots increased 64 percent between 1972 and 1976. One minute of network primetime was $42,000 to $68,000 in 1976; by 1980, it was about $100,000.[58]

The "Equal Time" law requires that stations make available comparable spots to each major candidate in a campaign. For every political spot a station airs, it is conceivable that it could be required to air another one or two. This can further reduce the amount of time the station is willing to sell and, thereby, limit the range of political debate and discourse.

Time buying—reserving television and radio commercial slots—is one of the consultant's most important activities. Once the political commercial is created and pretested, the next important decision is where and when to broadcast it. Media consultants can buy the time themselves, but they often subcontract with local advertising agencies, whose time buyers are more familiar with the local demographics and viewing patterns. The local agency's time buyer is often better at getting choice spots as a result of buying time on a continued basis for the agency's other clients.[59]

Time buyers need to know which slots are available, the estimated audience size, the makeup of the audience at any given time, and the geographic region reached by the station. The theory here is that political commercials must be *targeted*, that is, carefully placed to reach specific groups of voters. Tony Schwartz calls this "narrow-casting." For example, middle-class, undecided voters tend to cluster around the late news; middle-aged housewives cluster around afternoon soap operas; working women cluster around the evening news.[60] Tony Schwartz has made "narrow-casting" into a fine art, creating radio spots specifically for "car listening" and "beach listening."[61] For example, afternoon light music radio programs get an audience of older people; hence, it is a good time for a spot on Social Security issues. In fact, radio, which experienced a decline after the arrival of television, has recently become a very good tool for targeting audiences. Whereas prime time television audiences are relatively undifferentiated, radio audiences tend to be more distinctive. Radio stations have become more specialized—all-news, black, classical, religious, country, rock-and-roll—and their audiences more specific. Nonetheless, it is the television political spot that reaches the largest audience.

Sophisticated targeting techniques notwithstanding, placing political advertisements on television is an uncertain business. Clearly, the scramble is over prime time spots, where availability is severely limited because product advertisements are more lucrative for the station. However, there are other factors as well. Local stations generally have only sixty-two slots that border on network programs. During election years, networks give up some of their ad time and increase the number of local slots to be used for candidates or public service announcements.[62] The general pattern is two to four network prime-time slots per week for each presidential candidate, one or two for each U.S. Senate and House candidate, and one for each of all the other candidates for public office.[63] Even though the candidate gets relatively little time, this pattern may use up from a third to a half of a station's prime-time commercial space.

Once the advertisement is created, the audience is targeted, and spot availability is taken into account, the next concern is the airing schedule. Even though new technologies, such as videotaping, permit overnight changes in advertising strategies, there is an attempt to have an overall "game plan." There are four types of schedules: the *slow build-up* to an "orchestrated finish," where the number of advertisements gradually increases as election day nears; the *saturation* campaign, or "blitz," where every available spot is used as often as possible for about three weeks before the election; the *events schedule*, where time is bought around key events in the campaign (often pseudo-events); the *stop-start* campaign, which includes an early saturation to build name identification, then a stop, followed by soft-sell advertising, building finally to hard-sell, including negative advertisements.[64]

The media campaign includes more than political advertisements on television and radio. It also includes bumper stickers, T-shirts, billboards, buttons, posters, and anything else that can hold the candidate's name and/or slogan. Media consultants create an abundance of campaign literature, from pamphlets outlining the platform to biographical sheets. Recently, magazine political advertising has become popular as a result of zip-code targeting, where advertisements can be placed and printed in those editions that are sent to subscribers with a particular zip code (for example, a specific state or congressional district). Specialized magazines enable the consultant to target special audiences with messages suited to their interests.

### Image versus Issue in Advertising

The primacy of the image-making role of the media consultant is taken as an article of faith by consultants, candidates, and many political observers. In fact, it has often been said that consultants have created image politics, where the voter is confronted with political personalities rather than political issues. Many factors have contributed to this so-called cult of personality. However, there is little doubt that consultants use the public's interest in personal style and, in so doing, further enhance the significance of the candidate's image.

According to Patterson and McClure, however, this image making is a wasted effort in presidential elections. They concede that, in primaries and in state and local elections, television advertising may have an impact on the voter's image of the candidate.[65] This is so because the voter knows less about the candidates in primary, local, and state elections and is, therefore, not fully protected against the impact of political propaganda. On the national level, conversely, Patterson and McClure believe that the voter is better informed, is not as easily manipulated, and is more likely to be influenced by party affiliation. They take as their test case George McGovern's 1972 presidential campaign, when the little-known candidate was heavily dependent on political advertising. As they see it, if the image-making power of political advertisements really existed, McGovern's image should have been affected for better or worse. However, the results of their study showed that McGovern's image became better *and* worse, depending on the voters' politics: Democrats thought his image improved, Republicans thought it declined.[66] Although McGovern's image improved slightly among the undecided, advertising was not the reason; his image improved among people with both light and heavy advertising exposure.[67] As one would expect, after the uncommitted voters made their choices, the images of the candidates changed; the chosen candidate's image improved, and the opponent's image became worse.

All of this calls into question the consultant's assumption about the importance of the candidate's "image." Jeff Greenfield, a media commentator for CBS news and former media consultant with Garth Associates, Inc., points out that image may not be an independent variable in determining the success or failure of a candidacy:

> The gaffe and blunder are, in a mass-media age, supposed to be fatal to a candidate's chances. But Ronald Reagan demonstrated in 1980 that a candidate with a firm political base can commit at least as many disastrous gaffes and blunders as any other candidate, with no ill effects at all. ...Reagan proved himself as inept in the television give-and-take as any other candidate. But as a conservative folk hero for almost twenty years, he had a loyal constituency.[68]

If the image-making ability of media consultants is overrated in presidential campaigns, their ability to define strategic issues seems to be quite powerful. Even though Patterson and McClure see the political power of television as essentially mythical, they readily admit that television viewers learn the campaign issues from political advertisements; in fact, they go so far as to say that the American voter is educated by political advertisements: "...the contribution of advertising campaigns to voter knowledge is truly impressive."[69] They further say: "...presidential advertising contributes to an informed electorate."[70] However, by their own admission, material contained in television advertisements is "incomplete" and "oversimplified." Patterson and McClure insist that "simplicity" and "repetition" successfully transmit the major issues of the campaign, especially to the less-interested and less-informed members of the electorate.[71] The less-interested and the less-informed ("women, the poorly educated, the economically disadvantaged, the young and the elderly")[72] are, thus, "educated" by political advertisements on issues which are made simple, are repeated over and over again, and are packaged in thirty-second, colorful, sight-and-sound spots. Naturally, it is precisely these groups that the media consultant wants to reach. The interested have typically made their political choice before the campaign begins, and the informed are, by definition, less susceptible to media techniques of persuasion. Since the informed have access to other types of political information—newspapers, magazines, and political discussions—they are not dependent on the electronic media, and political advertisements function merely to reinforce or activate predispositions.

The estimated one-third of the electorate who are politically uncommitted, it must be remembered, are not necessarily uninformed or uninterested. The uncommitted include the ticket splitter, the politically independent voter, and the single-issue voter, who may, indeed, be very well informed and very interested. It is likely that such people will look beyond political advertisements for political information in making their final decisions. Nonetheless, counted among the uncommitted will be a goodly number who fall into the category of "uninformed and uninterested," which Patterson and McClure estimate to be about one quarter of the electorate.[73] These people generally make no effort to acquire political information; political information intrudes on them, so to speak, as they sit before their television sets. And what they learn, in hit-or-miss fashion, are the issues that can be stated in a thirty- or sixty-second spot and lend themselves to the certainty implied by a thirty- or sixty-second statement.

If modern political advertisements have little substance, it must be remembered that old party bosses rarely lifted the level of political discourse, either. The party boss's power resided in bringing in a bloc of votes, acquired through patronage and favor, regardless of issues and/or candidates.[74] If political issues are highly selective, it must be remembered that it is quite natural for the consultant to choose those issues that will help the candidate. Joseph Napolitan, an early media advisor, counsels: "I tell the candidate never to lie about his real position on an issue if asked, but if it is one that's going to cost him votes, he just shouldn't publicize it."[75]

If image making seems to be more important to the consultant than the issues are, it must be remembered that much of this image making is done to attract the press for "free" or "unpaid" advertising. If personality seems to overwhelm the campaign, it must be remembered that candidates believe, rightly or wrongly, that voters vote based on personality rather than issues. If political advertising makes stars out of politicians, it must be remembered that stars have become politicians (Reagan, of course, is the most well-known. Others include George Murphy, who was elected to the United States Senate in 1964). A few political families have become the equals of Hollywood stars (the Kennedys, the Roosevelts, and the Rockefellers on the national level; the Byrds of Virginia, the Browns of California, and the Longs of Louisiana on the state level).

## CONCLUSION

In the summer of 1984, Bill Moyers, on a program about political commercials aptly entitled "The 30-Second President," interviewed media consultant Tony Schwartz, who stated with some degree of satisfaction that "All the important things in our life have been restructured by television. We find that the political parties are no longer the major communications force in politics; the networks are. You might say the three parties are ABC, NBC and CBS."[76] Although clearly an overstatement of the facts, in general direction and tone, this statement has an uncomfortable ring of truth.

The media have become the arena for the modern political campaign, and media consultants and pollsters have become essential to winning an election. These modern political persuaders use market research and advertising techniques to sell the candidate for public office. As professional campaign consultants have perfected their techniques, such techniques have become more and more objective procedures, which can be used or applied to any candidate, in any election, to serve any ideological bent.[77]

Not only do these consultants contribute to the high cost of campaigning, their techniques also favor those candidates most suited to the media, particularly television. Their influence goes even further, as media and polling techniques come to determine the key issues around which a campaign is fought. Political issues become strategies packaged in thirty- to sixty-second commercials, and political qualifications give way to political image.

Media and polling techniques have become links between the candidate and the voters. Once elected, the political official needs the same techniques to maintain public approval. As we shall see, the techniques required to win elections have increasingly become techniques of governing. As such, media consultants and pollsters become officially, or unofficially, part of the political apparatus. Their essentially bipartisan techniques of persuasion become techniques of government.

## NOTES

**1** Quoted in Larry J. Sabato, *The Rise of Political Consultants: New Ways of Winning Elections* Basic Books, New York, 1981, p. 17. Copyright © 1981 by Larry J. Sabato. Reprinted by permission of Basic Books, Inc., Publishers.

**2** Sabato, *Rise*, p. 4.

**3** Quoted in Ron Suskind, "The Power of Political Consultants," *New York Times Magazine*, August 12, 1984, p. 35.

**4** Sabato, *Rise*, p. 51.

**5** *New York Times*, November 9, 1982.

**6** Robert Agranoff (ed.), *The New Style of Election Campaigns*, 2d. ed., Holbrook, Boston, 1976, pp. 68-69.

**7** Sidney Blumenthal, *The Permanent Campaign*, Beacon Press, Boston, 1980, pp. 1-10.

**8** *Time*, November 14, 1984, p. 64.

**9** Blumenthal, *The Permanent Campaign*, p. 6.

**10** Stanley Kelley, Jr., *Professional Public Relations and Political Power*, Johns Hopkins, Baltimore, 1956, p. 189.

**11** Dan Nimmo, *The Political Persuaders: The Techniques of Modern Election Campaigns,* Prentice-Hall, Englewood Cliffs, 1970, p. 85.

**12** Sabato, *Rise,* p. 70.

**13** Blumenthal, *The Permanent Campaign,* p. 29; Sabato, *Rise,* p. 70.

**14** For further discussion of random sampling and its problems, see Charles W. Roll, Jr. and Albert H. Cantril, *Polls: Their Use and Misuse in Politics,* Basic Books, New York, 1972; David Gergen and William Schambra, "Pollsters and Polling," *The Wilson Quarterly,* vol. 3, no. 3, Spring, 1979; and Earl R. Babbie, *Survey Research Methods,* Wadsworth, Belmont, California, 1973.

**15** Sabato, *Rise,* p. 97.

**16** Sabato, *Rise,* p. 72.

**17** Quoted in Sabato, *Rise,* p. 74.

**18** Blumenthal, *The Permanent Campaign,* p. 29.

**19** Blumenthal, *The Permanent Campaign,* p. 33.

**20** Sabato, *Rise,* pp. 75-77.

**21** Sidney Blumenthal, "Marketing the President," *New York Times Magazine,* September 13, 1981.

**22** *New York Times,* September 3, 1982.

**23** *New York Times,* September 24, 1982.

**24** *New York Times,* October 27, 1982.

**25** *New York Times,* September 4, 1982.

**26** Sabato, *Rise,* p. 88.

**27** Blumenthal, *The Permanent Campaign,* pp. 29-30.

**28** Alan Baron, "The Slippery Art of the Polls," *Politics Today,* vol. 6, no. 5, Jan./Feb.,1980, p. 25.

**29** Gergen and Schambra, "Pollsters," p. 70.

**30** Sabato, *Rise,* p. 98.

**31** Warren E. Miller, *Public Opinion,* vol. 2, no. 5, Oct./Nov., 1979.

**32** Sabato, *Rise,* p. 84.

**33** Agranoff, *New Style,* p. 363.

**34** Quoted in Blumenthal, *The Permanent Campaign,* p. 186.

**35** Quoted in Blumenthal, *The Permanent Campaign,* p. 141.

**36** Suskind, "Political Consultants," p. 55.

**37** Tony Schwartz, *The Responsive Chord,* Anchor/Doubleday, New York, 1972, pp. 26-27. Copyright © 1973 by Anthony Schwartz. Reprinted by permission of Doubleday & Co., Inc.

**38** Kelley, *Professional Relations,* p. 13.

**39** National Republican Congressional Committee (NRCC), "Political Advertising on Television: A Review," Washington, D.C., October, 1979, pp. 11, 19.

**40** Sabato, *Rise,* p. 207, n. 41.

**41** Sabato, *Rise,* pp. 123, 207, n. 42.

**42** Sabato, *Rise,* p. 127.

**43** Sabato, *Rise,* p. 129.

**44** Suskind, "Political Consultants," p. 55.

**45** Nimmo, *Political Persuaders,* p. 55.

**46** *National Journal,* March 1, 1980, p. 346.

**47** Sabato, *Rise,* p. 166.

**48** *New York Times,* November 9, 1982.

**49** Schwartz, *Responsive Chord,* p. 93.

**50** Sabato, *Rise,* p. 172.

**51** Quoted in Sabato, *Rise,* p. 173.

**52** Sabato, *Rise,* p. 162.

**53** Cited in Ronald Steel, "The Vanishing Campaign Biography," referring to Kathleen Hall Jamieson's forthcoming study, "Packaging the Presidency," *New York Times Book Review,* August 5, 1984, p. 25.

**54** Schwartz, *Responsive Chord,* pp. 90-91.

**55** Sabato, *Rise,* p. 77.

**56** Thomas E. Patterson and Robert D. McClure, *The Unseeing Eye: The Myth of Television Power in National Politics,* Putnam's, New York, 1976, p. 110.

**57** George H. White, *A Study of Access to Television by Political Candidates,* Institute of Politics, JFK School of Government, Harvard, Cambridge, Mass., May, 1978, pp. 14, 113; NRCC, p. 27.

**58** Sabato, *Rise,* pp. 181, 213, n. 198; *National Journal,* February 23, 1980, p. 313.

**59** Sabato, *Rise,* p. 182.

**60** *New York Times,* September 27, 1982.

**61** Schwartz, *Responsive Chord,* p. 104.

**62** White, *Study of Access,* pp. 49-57.

**63** Sabato, *Rise,* p. 187.

**64** Sabato, *Rise,* p. 184.

**65** Patterson and McClure, *Unseeing Eye,* p. 165, n. 8.

**66** Patterson and McClure, *Unseeing Eye,* p. 113.

**67** Patterson and McClure, *Unseeing Eye,* p. 164, n. 11.

**68** Jeff Greenfield, "The Myth of Media's Political Power," *Channels,* June/July, 1982, p.18.

**69** Patterson and McClure, *Unseeing Eye,* p. 116.

**70** Patterson and McClure, *Unseeing Eye,* p. 117.

**71** Patterson and McClure, *Unseeing Eye,* pp. 125-126.

**72** Patterson and McClure, *Unseeing Eye,* p. 128.

**73** Patterson and McClure, *Unseeing Eye,* p. 123.

**74** Kelley, *Professional Public Relations,* p. 217.

**75** Quoted in Sabato, *Rise,* p. 144.

**76** "The 30-Second President," on *A Walk Through the 20th Century with Bill Moyers,* August 8, 1984, PBS; also cited in the *New York Times,* August 5, 1984, p. H21.

**77** In 1983, The Political Campaign Institute of San Francisco produced a two-and-one-half-hour videotaped course on how to win a political campaign, taught by a bipartisan faculty of professional campaign consultants (including Matt Reese, a Democrat, and Stuart Spencer, a Republican). The course sold for $975. *New York Times,* September 21, 1983.

# THREE

# THE MEDIA AND PUBLIC AND PRIVATE INSTITUTIONS

# CHAPTER 7

# THE PRESIDENCY

## DIFFERENT PRESIDENTS/DIFFERENT POSTURES

By the late nineteenth and early twentieth century, the present system of covering the presidency began taking shape. News organizations were coming to define themselves as independent and nonpartisan observers of the political scene. As news organizations expanded their systematic coverage of Washington, the presidency inevitably became a major focus of attention. Regular coverage meant that an enduring and systematic relationship between the news media and the White House was essential. The media's interest in the presidency created the need for press secretaries and other press specialists to provide a steady flow of information. As the range of presidential activities grew, and the amount and diversity of presidential information multiplied, it became necessary over the years to increase the number of specialized assistants with knowledge of the press and with publicity skills.[1] The president's press people and the press eventually formed a symbiotic and mutually advantageous bond.

Franklin Roosevelt is generally considered to be the first president to use the press and the radio skillfully for political ends. Roosevelt was indeed a good communicator and well understood the craft of journalism. His effectiveness was due, in part, to his estimable personal skills, including the ability to be charming, to be cunning, and to use intimidation when it was called for. His success was also the result of the historical period in which he served. It is entirely likely that Roosevelt might not be nearly so successful in using the available modes of communication if he were president today.

Roosevelt was able to generate more news about himself and his administration than any of his predecessors. This ability to generate news was largely the result of the overwhelming degree of exposure to the press. In Roosevelt's first term, he held 337 news conferences. This astonishing number of personal appearances before the press was actually surpassed in his second term, when he held 374 news conferences. Although the number of conferences dropped to 279 in his third term, he increasingly took to the airwaves to communicate directly with the public. No other president has even come close to holding this number of press conferences. Roosevelt's policy of frequently, perhaps compulsively, communicating with the press can be better appreciated when compared to that of his immediate predecessor, Herbert Hoover, who held only twenty-three press conferences in his first term in office and twelve in his last term.[2]

Roosevelt early mastered some of the principles and techniques for dealing with the news media, techniques which successive presidents would also adopt. He was sensitive to the constraints on the media, the need to meet deadlines and to hold stories to a particular size, and he would structure his news agenda to meet these needs. He clearly felt he could only benefit from efforts to help the journalists do their job. He understood the relationship between information and control; he knew that an official with the most information could dominate the story. Perhaps most important was his understanding that news stories are essentially mosaics, which can be designed and packaged in a number of different ways, and his ability to shape stories so that they reflected well on him and his policies.[3] When the "carrot" was not an effective means to accomplish his ends, he was not averse to using the "stick." Marshaling the store of good feelings that he had established with the press corps, he was able to get members of the press to pressure colleagues who asked too many difficult questions or had trouble conforming to the rules established by Roosevelt.

This new marriage between the president and the press elevated the importance of the press. Having regular access to the president was sure to raise one's political stock. Apart from the natural dividends that accrued to the press, Roosevelt consciously pursued a strategy of elevating the importance of the press. There were cases where Roosevelt went to the press with information before giving that information to Congress. In essence, Roosevelt tried, with considerable success, to transform the press into a political institution. The benefits of creating a new political institution which could be largely controlled by the president are evident. Under Roosevelt, the press was truly elevated to the position of the "Fourth Estate." This development resulted in a significant shift in the balance of the political power at the federal level and changed the nature of the presidency. It was to be, from that point on, a considerably more "personalized office."[4]

Roosevelt was also an effective mass communicator, who quickly understood the power of radio and adopted it as a personal political weapon. He used the radio to make personal appeals to the population and to sooth the fears and uncertainties so rampant during the Depression. While his manner on the radio was relaxed and informal, his speeches were carefully conceived and crafted with the knowledge that they would be read aloud over the airwaves. When aides suggested that he was spending too much time working on these speeches, he said that he believed that the speeches were the most important thing he would ever do.[5]

His success in communicating on radio was partly because of the novelty of this technique. No president prior to Roosevelt had been able to use radio to reach such a large audience, and no president had made this form of direct and intimate communication a priority. People who heard these broadcasts undoubtedly thought that they were the recipients of a new and special gift. After all, the President of the United States was taking time to speak directly to them. Of course, as time went on, and this form of communication became more commonplace, it was no longer possible to reap benefits from simply appearing on radio and television.

Novelty was also an important factor in explaining Roosevelt's success with the press. Journalists were unaccustomed to meeting frequently with the president, and they had never before been treated to the quantity and quality of information delivered by Roosevelt. Because of these factors, they were, no doubt, rather easily seduced and manipulated. As a result of the uniqueness of Roosevelt's relationship with the press and his talent as a communicator, he was able to use the existence of persistent crisis, a situation which today is fraught with great risk, to his own political advantage.

By the time that Dwight D. Eisenhower parlayed his military career into a run for the presidency, television was fast becoming the most powerful means of direct communication with the public. Eisenhower distrusted and disliked TV and was wary about the possibilities of its being used as a tool by demogogues. Despite these objections, he became the first presidential candidate to use a variety of modern television techniques in his campaign and later in his administration. He was the first candidate to announce his candidacy on live TV and the first to use advertising experts to design an image to be presented on spot commercials. He was able to use television to project an image of independence, which helped him wrest the nomination away from his opponent, Robert Taft, the archetypical Republican party man.[6]

Once in office, Eisenhower was very ably represented by his press secretary, James Hagerty, who seemed to have an instinctive feel about how Eisenhower could best use the media, particularly television. Hagerty had correctly counseled Eisenhower to advocate a televised political convention, believing that he projected a more suitable television image than Taft. Hagerty arranged the first televised presidential news conference and even convinced Eisenhower to allow television to sit in on some cabinet meetings.

John F. Kennedy is now commonly referred to as the first television president. It is widely assumed that he could have never got the nomination or won the election without the skillful use of television. Marshall McLuhan, one of the most important investigators of television, believed that Kennedy had the face and manner ideally suited to the new medium. Indeed, the Kennedy image has left such an enduring mark on the American public that a variety of politicians (such as, most recently, Gary Hart) regularly attempt to imitate it. Kennedy, like Eisenhower, used television to assist in taking the nomination away from the designated candidate of the party. After Kennedy's campaign, there should have been little doubt about the power of television to sway the political emotions of the population.

Kennedy used the media masterfully during his years in office. He was effective in every way. He developed close relationships with many of the reporters who covered the White House and was careful to pay close attention to their needs. At total ease in a press conference or in delivering a speech, he seemed to savor and truly enjoy his frequent television appearances. His immense personal appeal and charm, now commonly referred to as the "Kennedy mystique," were awesome weapons that won him popular admiration and respect from the press.

Lyndon B. Johnson had neither the personal charisma nor media skills of John F. Kennedy. Johnson had an abiding antagonism toward the press, partly as a result of his perception, which was accurate, that the press, especially television, had robbed the party of political control and partly as a result of his feeling that the press had treated him shabbily. Johnson's bitterness toward the press was his worst-kept political secret. In an interview with Hugh Sidey, he lambasted the media. "They warp everything I do, they lie about me and about what I do, they don't know the meaning of truth. They are liars and cheats. They behave vulgarly."[7] While Kennedy had relied on the cooperation of individual reporters, Johnson tried his hand at coercion. He tried on several occasions to get news executives to reassign or control reporters who he felt were hostile. Kennedy had, on occasion, done something similar, but it was not perceived in the same light as Johnson's attempts, because of Kennedy's overall relationship with the news media.

Johnson's troubles were also magnified by the fact that he was the first president to be in charge of a "television war," in Vietnam, which was to become increasingly unpopular with the majority of the country. The antagonism between Johnson and the press continually flared, as the news media brought more and more attention to bear on the war effort and the policies of Johnson. The era of peaceful coexistence between the press and the White House seemed to be coming to an end.

The quiet war between Lyndon Johnson and the press became a public war with the election of Richard Nixon. The Nixon years were truly a turning point in the relationship between the president and the press and have left an enduring legacy for both the press and subsequent presidents.

Richard Nixon's attitude toward television and the press was an amalgam of admiration and suspicion. He was fascinated by television and well understood the raw political power of the medium. He attributed both his greatest successes and failures to television. In his book *Six Crises,* he credits his "Checkers Speech," in which he defended himself on national television against charges of campaign irregularities, as saving his political career. "If it hadn't been for that broadcast, I would never have been around to run for the Presidency."[8] Television is also blamed for his defeat by John Kennedy in 1960.

> I paid too much attention to what I was going to say and too little to how I would look. Again, what must be recognized is that television has increasingly become the medium through which the great majority of the voters get their news and develop their impressions of the candidate.[9]

Coupled with this recognition of the political power of television was a deep and abiding hostility toward the press. Nixon's legendary hostility toward television news was undoubtedly connected to his belief in the power of that medium. Patrick Buchanan, a former Nixon speechwriter and now Director of Communications in the Reagan White House, says that Nixon frequently used to tell his aides: "Boys, the press is the enemy."[10] Within six months of his taking office, the White House became headquarters for Nixon's campaign against the media. Almost all senior White House aides were to play a role.

Nixon's first major salvo was aimed at the networks' practice of following presidential speeches with analysis by news commentators. Nixon ordered his staff to prepare a speech attacking the practice of "instant analysis." The speech was also to contain a broad-based attack on the power of the news media. Patrick Buchanan, who had a reputation as the most strident speechwriter in Nixon's stable, was asked to prepare the address. Nixon himself reviewed the first draft and sent it back with suggestions about how to make it tougher. Vice President Spiro Agnew,

Nixon's first vice president (who would later be forced to resign because of a kickback scandal) was well known for his fiery attacks on other administration foes, and it was he who delivered the speech to a Republican gathering in Des Moines in November, 1969. The networks were described as ". . . a tiny and closed fraternity of privileged men, elected by no one, and enjoying a monopoly sanctioned and licensed by government."[11] In a less-than-veiled reference to the network practice of analyzing presidential speeches, Agnew asserted that the president had a right to communicate directly with the people who elected him ". . . without passing through the prejudice of hostile critics."[12] He attacked the press for editorializing and for representing the views of two unrepresentative American cities—New York and Washington, D.C.[13]

The first attack was quickly followed by other speeches by Agnew. Many of the same themes were sounded. Agnew's speeches were dutifully covered by the media. The public response to Agnew's attacks was better than anyone in the administration might have hoped. In the days following the first speech, the networks received 150,000 communications, two-thirds supporting Agnew. Agnew's speech had tapped a very deep current among Americans, ". . . a fear of the ability of television to manipulate them."[14]

Despite the fact that Agnew's speech had seemed to put the networks on the defensive, Nixon saw his overwhelming victory in 1972 as an opportunity to enlarge his campaign against the networks. Charles Colson, a senior aide to the President, was given responsibility for designing a battle plan. Daniel Schorr, who was one of the CBS Washington correspondents in those years, reports that Colson phoned Frank Stanton, president of CBS News, to spell out the administration's strategy. Colson described the administration's five-point plan:

1 Government to promote cable TV.
2 Strict limitations on network reruns.
3 Renewal troubles for network-owned stations.
4 Proposal for licensing networks.
5 Divest company-owned stations from networks.[15]

Colson claimed that he was responsible for altering the networks' coverage of Nixon. Among his major triumphs, he cites his success in convincing William Paley, the powerful chairman of the board at CBS, to intervene and limit the broadcast time of a CBS news segment devoted to the breaking Watergate scandal.

What is significant is the fact that the Nixon administration introduced several innovations in presidential-press relations and significantly changed some prevailing practices. The well-orchestrated and coordinated attack on the media and the sophisticated efforts to use the power of the Executive Office to punish the media were unprecedented. The staff and resources devoted to the media effort surpassed those of previous administrations. Nixon was also considerably more insulated from the press than any of his modern predecessors, and his press office operation was noted for its lack of cooperation with White House reporters.

The Johnson and Nixon years had a considerable impact on the relationship between the president and the press. The discord and antagonism altered the public's perception of both the press and the President. Nixon's charges against the press had the effect of reawakening a lingering suspicion about the press's motives and power. The campaign against the news media succeeded in damaging their credibility. He painted an image of news organizations as commercial ventures, owned by a powerful Eastern elite, served by reporters interested only in furthering their own careers, out of step with the beliefs of the average American, "the silent majority."

Yet, at the same time that Nixon was successful in transmitting a negative and self-serving image of the press, the public's perception of the President had also been transformed. A long series of deceptions about Vietnam in both the Johnson and Nixon administrations, and Nixon's intimate involvement in the Watergate affair, severely damaged the image of the President as an honest public servant.

Both the press and the presidency had been wounded in the battle that had begun in the early years of the Johnson administration and had ended with Richard Nixon's boarding a helicopter after surrendering the presidency. This hostility was to continue, albeit in a different form, despite Gerald Ford's and Jimmy Carter's promise that their administrations would be more open and cooperative.

Jimmy Carter's route to the presidency followed the already established path of Eisenhower and Kennedy. However, Carter's dramatic rise is even more astonishing than those of his predecessors when one considers the fact that Carter was more of an unknown and not well connected to any substantial party circle. Indeed, much of Carter's success resulted from the fact that he was able to turn this supposed liability into a virtue, running as an independent, anti-Washington type. While he was without the verbal skills and charm of John Kennedy, his looks and manner suggested certain qualities perceived by some as Kennedy's and well suited to television. These attributes and his popular appeal were surely enhanced by the fact that he arrived in a period of deep disillusionment and despair.

Ronald Reagan's election and reelection were the fulfillment of a phophecy by Roger Ailes, Nixon's media advisor, who is quoted by George McGinnis, in the *Selling of the President 1968,* as predicting that if things continue as they have been, with politicians putting increasing emphasis on the media, only a performer will be able to be President of the United States.[16]

There is no doubt that Ronald Reagan's considerable skills and ease before the camera, as well as his genial personality, have served him well since coming to office. These assets are, however, often overestimated as the source of Reagan's considerable success in getting across his message and in receiving desirable coverage. The success to date is also the result of a carefully-planned campaign, which draws heavily upon the successful techniques of earlier presidents, while carefully avoiding some of the pitfalls. He has, for example, openly criticized the press when he was troubled by the form or substance of a story. He has even telephoned Dan Rather, the CBS News anchorman, in the middle of a broadcast to complain about a particular story. While he has used the technique of attacking the press, often used by Nixon and tried by Carter, he has learned that the style of the attack is at least as important as the substance. As Jack Nelson, Bureau Chief of *The Los Angeles Times*, remarks: "... one way that Mr. Reagan gets by with it, is that he doesn't bare his fangs the way Mr. Nixon did. He does everything with a smile and he does it with a joke and a one liner."[17] Reagan's success in mobilizing and using public opinion and the press to his advantage are also the result of the fact that political and economic conditions have been generally favorable, particularly in the last two years of his first term. Any president's ability to manage communications is always determined by a combination of the policies pursued and the political circumstances.

From this very brief review, it is evident that the relationship between the president and the press is a changing one, characterized by periods of hostility and cooperation and tempered by a variety of institutional, personal, and idiosyncratic factors. Yet, according to the authors of a recent, exhaustive examination of this relationship, both reporters and officials follow routines established by the enduring needs of their organizations.[18] These institutional requirements provide stability and continuity and unite the press and the president in a search for means to cooperate: "... the cooperative elements in the relationship are at least as strong as those that are antagonistic, for a fundamental reason: Presidents and news people depend on each other in their efforts to do the job for which they are responsible."[19]

Jody Powell, who was President Carter's press secretary, sees these institutional requirements as the most important factor in determining the relationship between the president and the press. In his view, what gets reported as news

... has much more to do with the impersonal institutional pressures that work upon both the people in the White House and the people who are trying to cover the people in the White House, than it does the personalities or any intent to deceive on the part of the people in the White House or to mislead on the part of the people who are covering it.[20]

### Goals

There is a historical responsibility for presidents to provide information for the news media. However, when presidents communicate with the news media, they are doing so not only to fulfill this obligation but also to satisfy some political goal. Of course, the overall objective is to try to get the media to provide favorable reports on presidents and their programs. This is the essence of the endeavor. The media are considered to be the most important tool for building public support for presidents' legislative initiatives and foreign policies. There is a strong faith, sometimes bordering on a blind faith, that policies are good or bad, or rise or fall, on the basis of how they play in the media. "It generally is believed at the White House that the manner in which a policy is presented to the press is as important as the substance in determining how the public will ultimately view what the president is trying to do."[21] Since it is the media that will present most policy to the public, the president's goal is to get the most favorable display.

The president and senior advisors often use the press to influence other political actors. Presidents have frequently authorized tactical release of information or used the media to criticize Congress or regulatory agencies. President Reagan, for example, has consistently used the media to apply pressure on Congress. Sometimes this is done with the idea of breaking through some of the inertia that characterizes the work of Congress and segments of the bureaucracy. Often the tactic is used to build political capital by making an opponent look bad.

The option to use the media in this manner is also open to presidential advisors and cabinet members, many of whom have independent relationships with members of the press. These senior members of the administration may, on occasion, use the media to force the president to take certain actions. At times when the president must choose among options offered by advisors, one or another of these advisors may turn to the press with information intended to influence the president's decision. In early 1984, when President Reagan was trying to decide whether to follow the advice of Secretary of State George Schultz, who advocated keeping American troops in Beirut, or the advice of Secretary of Defense Casper Weinberger, who wanted to withdraw the troops, the quantity and quality of information being released at the State Department and at the Pentagon dramatically increased.

The President has also used the media to signal dissatisfaction with the activities of executive departments or to force an individual to resign by not sending out the customary signal of support. Such was the case when James Watt, who made a number of derogatory remarks about various groups, again found himself the object of the media's attention when he referred to an advisory panel as being composed of two blacks, a Jew, a woman, and a cripple. When Watt watched the television news and read the newspapers that week and found no words of support from the President, he must have realized that his days in the job were numbered. Indeed, he left the Department of Interior soon thereafter.

The primary goal of the president is to use the media to influence public opinion. If a president is able to marshall a strong show of public support for presidential policies, there is a good chance of overcoming any political resistance. A president's ability to influence public opinion seems most importantly related to his popularity. Unpopular presidents are not able to turn public opinion on particular issues to their favor. There is even evidence that attempts by unpopular presidents to change public opinion may actually have a negative impact, leaving the presidents with fewer supporters than when they began the campaign to alter public thinking.[22]

The picture is quite different for the popular president. Page and Shapiro, who have done some fascinating work in this field, have found that presidents who enjoy high marks in the public opinion polls were able to alter public opinion significantly. One of the nation's most popular presidents, Franklin D. Roosevelt, was able to change public thinking on the question of whether the United States ought to aid England in the war effort by seven percentage points over a two-month period. While this appears to be an unusually dramatic change, it demonstrates the potential power of the president. On the average, Page and Shapiro found that popular presidents could produce changes of five to ten percent in public opinion on an issue over a 4½-month period.[23]

When the president is riding a crest of popularity, there is no political actor able to compete in the public opinion arena. In such periods, the public has a greater psychological identification with the president, which further enhances the presidential exercise of policy leadership.[24] Interest groups, or even critics inside the administration, appear to have no impact on the popular president's control of the public opinion arena. Even changes in objective conditions do not quickly change policy preferences. Such changes must, according to Page and Shapiro, go through a process of interpretation by other political figures before they can have an impact.[25]

The only competitors in the public opinion sweepstakes are the media. When the New York Times, the newspaper used to measure the coverage received by various presidents in the Page and Shapiro study, ran a front-page story that took a strong editorial stand on an issue, the change in public thinking on that issue was dramatic—an average of 15 percentage points. The authors correctly call this "...media power with a vengance."[26]

These findings seem to confirm something that presidents have always assumed—that the media constitute a formidable political power that affects the realization of most personal and political goals. If a president is to survive and prosper politically, he must find a way to harness this power, neutralize it, or control the adverse effects that it can produce.

## THE MEDIA APPARATUS

In order to accomplish the difficult objectives and to manage the relationship with the press, the president depends on a large cadre of publicity staffers. As the power of the media has grown, and the complexity of managing the flow of information has increased, the number of people who have some responsibility for communications has soared. Today, it is estimated that one-third of the high level White House staff are directly involved in media relations. Even those with no direct role are cognizant of the need to protect the president's image. This section describes the various functions of the White House offices that handle communications.

Most of the regular, day-to-day functions of getting out the news and answering the inquiries of the White House press corps are handled by the press office. While the press office has, through various administrations, continued to handle a considerable portion of the monumental tasks associated with portraying the president, different presidents have experimented with restructuring the press operation. In many cases, these organizational changes were occasioned by the ever-increasing demands of the news media and by the desire of the president to get out the desired messages more effectively.

Although the various organizational changes have altered some of the responsibilities and created a variety of new tasks and jobs, most of the daily work still falls to the press office. It is the engine of the press operation. The press office is responsible for the preparation of the daily news summary, which provides capsulized versions of how the media reported the previous day's activities. According to Sam Donaldson, ABC's White House correspondent, verbatim transcripts from all network news shows are part of the summary prepared for President Reagan.[27] This summary provides a means for the President and advisors to monitor coverage. The press office also provides a variety of services for the press. All requests for interviews with the President are processed through the press office. The press office makes all the arrangements and provides all the necessary facilities, including hotel accommodations, typewriters, and telephones for all the reporters traveling with the President. "You arrive at your hotel room and your bags are in your room," according to Ann Devroy, the

Gannett Chain's correspondent at the White House.[28] These services are not provided with the idea of seducing or bribing the press, although they may, on occasion, have such an effect, but simply as a means to make certain that everything is in place for the press to cover the activities that the President and advisors want covered.

"The commander in chief" of the press office is the press secretary, who is the liaison between the Washington press corps and the president. The press secretary meets with the Washington press corps at least twice daily. These briefings are designed to alert the press to the president's schedule and provide information about issues or personalities connected with these activities. Briefings provide one of the official forums for the president to transmit information to the press.

By its very nature, the job of press secretary is difficult. At the root of the complexity is the need for the press secretary to satisfy two distinct constituencies: the president and his closest senior advisors and the reporters who will cover the White House and the news organizations who employ them. Because the White House and the press have a certain continuity of interests, the task of satisfying both constituencies is possible. When interests coincide, the task of the press secretary is considerably easier. When the interests of the press and the president are divergent, the job can be next to impossible.

Despite the fact that the press secretary serves these two constituencies, it is important to remember that his or her primary allegiance is, in almost all cases, to the president. The press secretary is interested in satisfying the press because that is what is necessary to represent the president more effectively. A president expects total loyalty from this spokesperson.

The press secretary must maintain a precarious balance between representing the interests of the president and providing information, assuring access, and maintaining sensitivity to the needs of the press. His or her task is to get the very best possible coverage for the president, which cannot be accomplished without the continued cooperation of the Washington press corps.

The ability of the press secretary to be successful is determined by three important factors. First, the press must believe that the press secretary is truly expressing the opinion of the president. The second factor that determines effectiveness is the press secretary's ability to maintain a cooperative and amiable relationship with members of the press corps. A press secretary who is liked enjoys an advantage over those who are considered arrogant and totally self-serving. Finally, the ability of the press secretary to represent the president successfully is affected by prevailing social and economic conditions.

The press secretary can accurately represent the views of the president only if he or she has good access to the president. Evidence shows that press secretaries in most recent administrations have seen the president at least once a day.[29] Reporters put a high value on access, partially because it is such a valued commodity in their own trade. In the reporter's mind, access is highly correlated with credibility. George Skelton, the White House correspondent for the *Los Angeles Times,* compared two recent press secretaries: "You knew when Jody [Powell] told you something he had some credibility, because he knew what Carter was thinking...whereas, you don't have it from Speakes."[30] While access certainly increases the possibility that the press secretary will be up to date on what the president may be thinking about particular issues, it certainly doesn't insure that the press secretary will completely and accurately present these views.

A press secretary's access to the president, what he or she is told by the president, and what latitude he or she is given to represent the views of the administration vary. Some presidents count the press secretary as part of their inner circle of advisors and provide opportunities for the press secretary to determine what should be released and how it should be fashioned. Operating from the inner circle, these press secretaries are also in a position to exercise influence over the formulation of policy. Roosevelt, Eisenhower, Kennedy, and Carter carved out this sort of role for their press secretaries. Jody Powell, for example, was certainly one of the three most powerful people in the Carter White House and was privy to all discussions of major policy initiatives. Presidents Johnson, Nixon, and Ford severely curtailed the role of their press secretaries. These secretaries were given a very short rein, and their activities were carefully monitored. President Reagan has chosen this latter role for his press secretary. According to Dom Bonafede, a reporter for the *National Journal* and a lifelong student of presidential-press relations, the press secretary in the Reagan administration is not to be an insider. He is to act essentially as a "mouthpiece" and to avoid commenting on policy issues.[31] In general, the press secretary's role is determined by the overall strategic approach to dealing with the press. Since Jimmy Carter put a high premium on having an "open administration," he chose one of his closest advisors as press secretary and gave him maximum latitude and responsibility. President Reagan's overall approach has been to concentrate more attention on direct appeals to the public and give a relatively low priority to maintaining close contacts with the Washington press corps. This accounts for the very limited power of his press secretary.

The second factor which determines effectiveness is the relationship that the press secretary is able to establish with the press. It is somewhat difficult to assess the importance of this factor, but there is no doubt that it plays a role. All the White House correspondents that we spoke with agreed that the press secretary's personality and rapport were important. In much the same way that the force of Ronald Reagan's personality has been an important asset in relationships with the press and others in

Washington, a press secretary with a genial, open, and cooperative approach can reap dividends. What made Jody Powell so different from Ron Nessen was not the quantity or even necessarily the quality of information he supplied to the press. The difference was the atmosphere through which that information was filtered.

> The residue of good feeling he [Powell] had acquired ran out after the administration's fortunes began to slump in 1977, but it did provide benefits to him for several months and may even have softened the impact on the White House of a particular crisis.[32]

Finally, the effectiveness of the press secretary is determined by political and economic conditions and the needs of the media. If the press judges the nation to be in an economic crisis, for example, there is very little that a press secretary can do to alter that perception. In periods of crisis or conflict, where the press turns concentrated attention on an issue, the press secretary's ability to convey the administration's interpretation is constrained. Jody Powell explains this phenomenon: "Once a story takes off and becomes a rolling story, your ability to do anything about it is very limited. As it begins to slow down a little bit, then you have a greater ability to ameliorate the situation."[33] The press secretary's influence is also constrained by the enduring needs of the media and the White House establishment. For example, if the press discovers a story which corresponds to the established news priorities, a story about possible corruption or a loss of political support, there is very little chance of the press secretary's holding off with the story or being effective in putting it in some better light.

These are some of the factors which account for a press secretary's effectiveness as a spokesperson. Yet, the ability of the press secretary and the president to get good coverage and deliver political messages derives from the ability to manage information. Here lies one of the great mine fields in presidential-press relations. In an effort to maintain control, presidents revert to a number of strategies that often have the effect of distorting or bending reality to suit their needs.

## INFORMATION CONTROL

### Agenda Setting

The key to good publicity lies in getting the press to cover the issues the president wants covered. It is therefore necessary to control information in a manner that maximizes the chances of keeping undesirable items off the agenda and keeping a bright luster on those being covered. It is not so much controlling what is said that is crucial as it is determining which issues are going to be discussed.

Of course, the president's ability to control what gets reported is importantly constrained by the roulette of world events. The bombing of the Marine compound in Beirut thrust the issue of the American presence in Lebanon back into the headlines at a time when the administration would have been delighted to watch the issue recede into the background. There was very little that Jimmy Carter was able to do to deflect attention to other policies while Americans were held captive in Iran.

There are other political actors who compete with the president to exercise some influence over the agenda. Congress, for example, can have a significant role in determining which issues get onto the agenda. Political opponents may also penetrate the agenda under certain circumstances. When Speaker of the House O'Neill accused President Reagan of being insensitive to the needs of the poor, the issue of the President's domestic policy was thrust onto the agenda.

But the most significant constraint on the president's ability to control the agenda is the press itself. An issue which is melodramatic or meets the other organizational criteria for news will, in most cases, get onto the agenda despite the resistance of other political actors. The media have displayed an ability to keep such issues on the agenda despite efforts by the president to reinterpret or erase them.

Although the competition to set the agenda is sometimes intense, modern presidents have enjoyed considerable success in setting the terms of public debate. Control of the agenda is simply not a matter of getting certain issues reported. To control the agenda is also to control the manner in which issues are reported, particularly the issues that can be politically damaging. Control of the agenda brings the power to determine how issues will be defined and, consequently, received. The struggle to control the agenda is the struggle to control political reality. According to pollster Richard S. Beal, running the presidency *"boils down to the question of who is in control of the agenda"* [emphasis ours].[34]

This ability to define an issue on one's own terms can be illustrated by comparing definitions of the conflict in El Salvador offered by President Carter during his reign with those offered during President Reagan's term. The existence of political revolution in Central America is an issue that is impossible for a president to avoid. Since it will inevitably be part of the agenda, the president must seek to define the issue in a way that is consistent with his world view and with the policies which he has advocated. Jimmy Carter chose to define the problem of El Salvador as essentially an internal conflict; Don Hallin characterized Carter's analysis this way:

> El Salvador was a struggle between extremists of the Left and Right, with a moderate government caught in the center (though the emphasis, clearly, was

on violence from the Left). More important than the political interpretation of the conflict, though, is the cumulative impression of "senseless" violence. Cold War imagery was rarely invoked; to the extent that journalists bothered to explain the conflict they did so in terms of domestic causes.[35]

This overall definition of the conflict found its way into the reporting of the war. Here is an example of an NBC news report laden with Carter's imagery of the war:

David Brinkley: In the tortured country of El Salvador the violence and killing continues every day, and it is random and senseless. It doesn't even have the cold clarity of one side killing those on the other, as Phil Bremen reports from El Salvador.

Bremen [wrapping up]: Before the violence, tourists came to see the ruins of an ancient civilization. In the face of modern ruins, the United States is urging Salvadorians to put a little civilization into their politics.[36]

Early in his administration, President Reagan sought to change the definition of the conflict from an internal struggle to one that was being orchestrated by Cuba and the Soviet Union as a means to extend their domination. An administration White Paper, conveniently leaked to the *New York Times* before its official release, contained charges of a Soviet and Cuban plan to funnel tons of arms to "Marxist led guerillas in El Salvador." The conflict was defined in traditional Cold War terms. NBC's Ike Seamans explained the potency of this new explanation: "Anybody who'd been to Salvador as much as the people who normally cover it knew it was a pretty simplified view of the situation. But if the leader of the Western world makes a statement, it's policy almost."[37]

After planting the seed, Reagan officials saw the story take off in a surprising direction. While all the major media dutifully reported the story of the Cuban-Soviet plot in the most lurid terms, it soon began to fuel speculation that Ronald Reagan was preparing the American public for another Vietnam. There was initially strong editorial opposition throughout the country. "We did not appreciate how rapidly El Salvador would take off in the minds of the press as a Vietnam," said one White House aide.[38] Memories of the war in Vietnam had lingered in America's collective political consciousness, causing widespread apprehension about anything resembling a sequel. Reagan's strategists had also failed to consider the pervasive fears among the press and the public (which had been fueled in the first campaign) that Reagan would lead the country into another war. Administration strategists, showing a sensitivity about the President's image that had been lacking in the Carter administration, decided to deemphasize or, in the vocabulary of agenda setting, "low key" the issue. Information about El Salvador suddenly dried up. Figure 7-1 shows the astonishing degree to which the

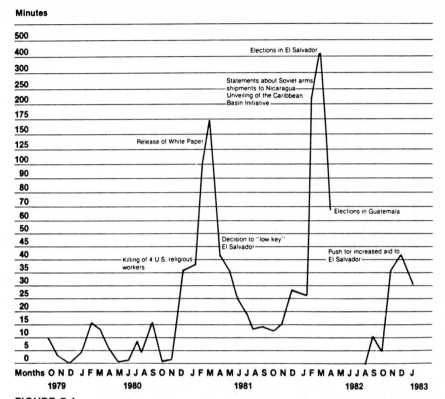

**FIGURE 7-1**
Network news timetable for coverage of Central America issues October 1979 to
January 1983

*Source:* Compiled by Dan Hallin from videotapes of news coverage by ABC, CBS, and
NBC. Adjusted for deletions.

administration was successful in diminishing the amount of coverage
devoted to the war in El Salvador.[39]

The retreat from actively pushing the Central American issue turned
out to be only temporary. About a year after the release of the White
Paper, the Reagan administration began slowly to reintroduce the issue
of El Salvador and again push it onto the national agenda. At this point,
the administration also began to introduce the Nicaraguan connection,
charging that Nicaragua was receiving mass shipments of Soviet arms and
funneling them to the Salvadorian guerillas. At the same time that the
administration was introducing the Nicaragua threat, the CIA was
involved in a massive effort to supply, train, and aid rebels who were bent
on overthrowing the Sandinista government.

As the issue made its way back into the headlines, substantial pockets of resistance to defining the conflict in traditional Cold War terms persisted among segments of the press. But the resistance and criticism had abated since the time that this explanation of the conflict had first been presented. The fallout resulting from the use of this Cold War imagery was evidently judged to be of little danger to the standing of Ronald Reagan, because the administration made no effort to withdraw the issue from the agenda or modify its explanation of the conflict. After a tactical and clever withdrawal, Reagan was largely successful in imposing his definition of the conflict.

> In a sense, what is really remarkable is not the degree of skepticism one sees in the press or the public or congress, but the fact that the administration has succeeded as well as it has at keeping the spotlight on "Soviet expansionism" in Central America, despite the objective weakness of its case.[40]

Once a president has successfully imposed a definition on an issue, it is extremely difficult to alter the terms of the debate. Hodding Carter, former spokesman at the State Department, believes "...that big government sets the terms of the public discussion about major issues far more often than the press likes to admit or the public understands."[41]

The president's control of the agenda results from his control of information and the ability to get virtually whatever he says reported. Random voices that carry a different message are not much competition for a well-orchestrated chorus performing in the news capital of the world.

> [A] Split between what is released in Washington and what is attributed to either dissatisfied, or simply more knowledgable, sources in a field is common in foreign affairs reporting. The problem is that these are one shot affairs, appearing for a day in one or at most a handful of newspapers, while the official Washington line is reported day in and day out in all the major media.[42]

The president's ability to control the agenda is much greater when it comes to international news. Even President Reagan, who has shown an unusually high degree of mastery in setting the terms of foreign policy debates, has not always been so successful when it has come to domestic issues. In the first two years of his administration, he had great difficulty in redirecting the focus of the press away from negative developments in the economy. It is easier to dominate the debate in foreign policy matters because the administration can exert considerably more control over the available information. There are few alternative sources to depend on for information. Ann Devroy, the Gannett correspondent at the White House, observed that the key to control of the agenda is controlling information and access.[43]

During his first term, Ronald Reagan successfully used secretiveness and careful control, management, and manipulation of information to control the agenda. The administration introduced a small, select number of issues that it wanted on the agenda and then literally refused to talk about anything else. Members of the Washington press corps were well aware of the administration's control. Of course, efforts to control the agenda did not originate in the Reagan era. What is unique about the Reagan administration's policy is the extraordinary success it has achieved. George Skelton, White House correspondent for the *Los Angeles Times*, has said that the Reagan White House establishes the agenda to a very large degree. Ann Devroy has echoed these sentiments: "They've been extraordinarily successful in controlling the agenda, far more than Jimmy Carter was."[44]

Maintaining control of the agenda involves an unremitting struggle to control and use information properly. The president or the president's communications people cannot simply add and delete from the agenda at will. Control of the agenda cannot be maintained without measures to limit and filter the information that goes to the press, as well as strategies for allowing the president most effectively to use media opportunities.

The basic commodity in this equation is information. If one cannot maintain some control over who gives information and the type of information which is offered, it is very difficult to maintain the upper hand. Stamping out or stemming the flow of "unauthorized" information to the press must be coupled with a plan for using opportunities, whether it be a press conference, group interview, or press release, to reinforce the administration's interpretation of events and information. It is also essential to provide the president with a number of well-planned events through which he can directly appeal to the public for support.

### Controlling the Sources

The prevailing wisdom on how to be successful at managing communication is to limit severely the number of people authorized to speak with the press. It has become increasingly commonplace for the President to place limits on senior advisors, as well as high- and middle-ranking officials throughout the Executive branch of government. The rationale for limiting the number of senior advisors is fairly simple: it is far easier to monitor and direct what is said by a small number of spokespeople.

This tendency to curtail the number of people authorized to speak with the press is not new. Richard Nixon followed this course, particularly when the press began to get aggressive about the conduct of the Vietnam war and about the White House's involvement in Watergate. After being severely hurt by ignoring the received wisdom on how to deal with the press, Jimmy Carter withdrew his open invitation for members of the Cabinet and staff to talk with members of the Fourth Estate. The Reagan administration is, if anything, more tight-lipped and secretive than the

Nixon administration. Access to senior officials is rare. George Skelton of the *Los Angeles Times*, who is regarded by his colleagues as having the best entree to the White House, did not talk at all like a "front runner" in the competition for access. "...there are fewer people to talk to because they [the administration] don't like to talk to you."[45] Several journalists, including Norman Sandler of UPI, characterized the administration as having a disregard that at times borders on contempt or resentment toward the press.[46] The exceptions to this policy of limited access are select members of small news organizations. White House efforts to promote meetings between this group and senior members of the administration or the President are discussed in the next section.

There is surely justification for a president to attempt to control who in the administration speaks to the press, particularly at times when there are deliberations about sensitive policy issues. It is not at all uncommon for Cabinet and senior officials to use the press to further some personal or political goal, sometimes at the expense of the administration's goals. The fear that permitting senior officials to speak openly would result in the media's using this material to headline conflict and discord is, to a large degree, justifiable when the history of the news media's commercial exploitation of these circumstances is considered. That a president will attempt to exert influence over who speaks with the press is taken for granted. What is important is the degree to which control is exercised and the measures that are chosen to gain it. Recent efforts to limit contacts between the press and the White House and Executive branch officials, and to stamp out leaks, go far beyond the commonly-accepted measures used by previous presidents and other public officials.

Despite efforts to channel communications through only authorized spokespeople, there have always been leaks. All modern presidents have been concerned about these unauthorized releases of information. In almost all cases, individuals leaking information to the press are not revealing classified or secret material. In general, leaks are either statements by a person who is not authorized to speak about a policy issue or some information about the position of important individuals in the policy-making process. Leaks are considered by the news media to be part of the rules of the game, and the media consistently search out leaks, as a means of finding out what is occurring inside the corridors of power. Although all presidents have complained about the evils of leaks, none has been adverse to using the leaks as a calculated political maneuver.

There is disagreement over the extent of leaks at the Reagan White House. Lyn Nofziger, a former aide to the President, claims that the Reagan White House has been the leakiest he has ever seen.[47] Others feel that there are, by comparison, very few leaks in the present White House. Whatever the case may be, the administration has taken very stringent steps to eliminate any drainage of information. Jack Nelson, bureau chief of the *Los Angeles Times* and a mainstay in Washington journalism, provided his view on a recent *Viewpoint* show on ABC television:

> This administration is obsessed, absolutely obsessed with leaks. They have given lie detector tests to the very highest officials in the administration. I was told by somebody in the White House...that Secretary of State George Schultz walked in on a meeting with President Reagan and William Clark—at the time national security director—and Ed Meese was there, and George Schultz says:"The minute you try to give me a polygraph test, I'll walk out."[48]

Many of the measures supported by the Reagan administration to stop leaks would also have the effect of making it considerably more difficult for the public and the press (who have no more formal right to material than the general public has) to gather information. The Reporters Committee for Freedom of the Press, an organization which monitors activities threatening press freedom, has recently published a comprehensive report on actions taken by the Reagan administration to restrict access to government information. An example of some of the thirty-eight actions documented in the report are listed below:

- *Lie detector tests for news leaks.* President Reagan announced that all government employees having access to moderately classified information (SCI—Special Compartmentalized Information), which is leaked to press, must take lie detector tests or face punitive job actions. After adverse publicity, White House agrees to suspend program until end of 1984. Date: 03/83.
- *Government budget cuts back on government reports.* The 1982 budget cuts way back on a variety of government reports in a number of agencies. Particularly seems to affect education, health, urban affairs, labor and agriculture. See *New York Times,* 11-16-82 at p. A1; Date: 04/82.
- *Jan. 1982 preclearance for national security interviews with news media.* White House sets up new rule that all interviews with "national media" involving national security (i.e., foreign affairs and defense) must be pre-cleared by White House. Backed down after confrontation with White House press corps. Date: 01/82.
- *Jan. 1983 preclearance of all interviews with White House staff on all topics.* In effort to protect national security and to avoid embarrassment to President ("keister" statement), President orders through James Baker memo that all interviews, except for those with a few officials, be cleared by White House Communications Office. Date: 01/83.
- *Exempt Secret Service from FOI.* Currently supports effort to exempt, in interests of national security, the Secret Service from FOI Act. Note that Secret Service provides clearance for reporters to obtain White House press credentials. Date: 03/83.

• *Exempt CIA from FOI.* Supports a total exemption for the CIA from the FOI Act. Would allow for suppression of information even if it showed that agency violated law or policy directives. Date: 08/82. (Senate Action) Senate passed total exemption for "operational files" of agency. Date: 11/83.

• *New FOI guidelines encourage information suppression.* Atty. Gen. William French Smith issues new guidelines stating that any information technically covered by the FOI Act should be suppressed even if its release would pose no danger to the government or any third party. This reverses Carter Administration guidelines which said that information technically covered by Act should be released unless it posed a danger to government or a third party. Date: 04/81.

• *Privacy Act can be used as bar to FOI Act.* Justice Department appeals case to Supreme Court urging that Privacy Act can be used to bar access to FOI Act requests. *(Provenzano v. DOJ).* Date: 03/84.

• *CBS reporter threatened with Espionage Act because of Iranian books.* FBI seized books of CBS News stringer William Worthy. The books, bought in Iran, contained secret documents obtained when militant Iranians took over U.S. embassy in 1979. The books had been published in Europe and were on sale to the public in Teheran. The FBI threatened Worthy with prosecution, but the charges were finally dropped and the government paid Worthy $16,000. Date: 08/81.

• *Reporters required to sign secrecy pledge.* Defense Department asked reporters to sign a secrecy pledge before receiving a briefing on Soviet Union's military build-up. Date: 12/82.

• *Canadian films registration.* Required film distributed by film board of Canada to carry notice of "political propaganda" when shown in this country. Films were on pollution and nuclear disarmament. Done under Foreign Agents Registration Act, which has exemption for info not primarily benefiting foreign government. Justice also invoked Act to require that film board provide names of all American groups who seek to obtain film. Date: 02/83.

• *Prepublication agreement extended to all persons having access to classified information.* Announced that all government employees with access to classified information, including those in Depts. of Defense, State, Justice, Treasury, etc., must sign prepublication agreements. After much adverse publicity, White House agreed to suspend program until end of 1984. Date: 03/83.

• *Excludes American news media from covering U.S. invasion of Grenada.* During the invasion of Grenada, the Administration:

• Excluded American reporters from covering the invasion while allowing foreign reporters to remain;

• Brought in their own Dept. of Defense news service to provide favorable coverage of the invasion;

- Detained three American reporters who were already on the island during the invasion;
- Threatened to shoot at any reporters who attempted to reach the island on their own.

Later, Secretary of Defense Casper Weinberger, and White House Chief of Staff, James E. Baker, tell reporters that the Administration has the right to exclude the news media from future military operations should it wish to do so again. Date: 10/83.[49]

As in the case of restricting the press's access to members of the administration, there is nothing intrinsically wrong about a president's seeking to stop leaks. Unauthorized releases of information can, at times, make the policy-making process more difficult and, conceivably, rob the President of various policy-making options. The other danger which leaks pose is that they loosen the administration's control and open it up to questions that it might wish to avoid.

A boundary separates efforts to stamp out leaks that may be damaging to the policy-making process of the president and staff from efforts to eliminate dissident voices or unmanicured pieces of information. Most recent presidents have crossed this boundary, seeking to eliminate leaks in the hope of wiping out information not consistent with the president's view. It is not easy to say whether these measures adopted by the Reagan administration are anomalous, the product of one administration's conception about how to frighten the troops into compliance, or simply the next step in a continuing campaign by presidents to exercise a monopoly over the information that gets to the American public.

Leaks have sometimes been the only method by which journalists can obtain information that is purposely withheld from the public. Presidents have traditionally sought to hide damaging and embarrassing information from the press. Richard Nixon withheld a variety of information about American activities in Vietnam and Southeast Asia, including the incursion into Cambodia. John Kennedy ordered U.S. military commanders in Vietnam to try to prevent reporters from learning that Americans were directly involved in combat missions.[50] While campaigning for election in 1964, Lyndon Johnson was publicly advocating restraint, while directing plans for the bombing of North Vietnam. President Reagan withheld information about America's invasion of Grenada, even as the invasion was taking place, and subsequently barred reporters from covering the activities in Grenada.

Controlling leaks is only one method for limiting the flow of information to the press. Information that could prove troublesome and might be difficult to hide is often ordered classified as secret. Damaging information is routinely deemphasized to minimize its impact. When there is a danger that the collection of certain information might prove potentially embarrassing, a president may simply order that the data not be collected. Lyndon Johnson, who attempted to keep his Great Society programs intact and fight the Vietnam War without seeking a tax increase, asked his economic advisors to avoid collecting and reporting certain costs of fighting the war.[51]

Sometimes maintaining control requires the White House to stage a tactical discovery of information. A journalist is allowed to find some information which he or she assumes that the White House did not want found but which was actually put there by the White House. Journalists who believe that they have discovered some buried treasure of information will be far more likely to use that information in its original form than they would if that same information were provided by White House officials.

If it is absolutely necessary to release politically dangerous information, there are a number of strategies to minimize the hazards. When, for example, the Reagan administration decided to support a tax exemption for schools that racially discriminate, it released the information at the Justice Department late on a Friday afternoon.

When all else fails, information can be presented in a way that obfuscates its meaning, or a president may simply lie. This is precisely what Dwight D. Eisenhower did when he denied the U.S. role in a 1954 coup in Guatemala. Further, Eisenhower may have been the first President to lie on network TV, when he swore that the U2 spy plane shot down over Russia was there by accident. John F. Kennedy was guilty of lying about the role that the United States played in the Bay of Pigs invasion in Cuba. Despite extensive evidence to the contrary, Ronald Reagan continues to maintain that the CIA's mission in Nicaragua is not aimed at overthrowing the present government. Lying, or obfuscating information to a point where it is perilously close to a lie, is a common technique in controlling communication.

## MEETING THE PRESS

More than thirty news organizations cover the White House on a daily basis, and hundreds more show up when there is something special going on. White House regulars include reporters, camera crews, and photographers who work for daily newspapers, newsweeklies, the wire services, television and radio networks, and the foreign press. White House reporters are a diverse group of fifty to sixty journalists who operate within a heady atmosphere of power as they rub shoulders with the White House staff. Being assigned to the White House confers a kind of celebrity states, and it often represents the achievement of a major career goal.[52] Since White House stories, which are typically stories about the president, almost always get printed or aired, the reporter gets high visibility with the public. Given the prestige of the White House assignment, it is interesting to note that few reporters recognize any need for special preparation on White House operations or on the presidency.[53]

Coverage of the White House and of the presidency takes place within a context of established routines. Press releases, briefings, and press conferences mean that reporters are essentially given the same information in highly-controlled situations. Reporters with hourly deadlines (radio and the wire services) or daily deadlines (daily newspapers and the networks) are often little more than conduits for the White House message. Columnists with weekly columns and news magazines have a different relationship to the information provided by the White House and have more opportunity to analyze it.

Aside from the constant flow of press releases, the most institutionalized White House routine is the daily briefing, when the press secretary appears before the press to make announcements and to answer questions. Both sides express dissatisfaction with this particular ritual: press secretaries complain that there is not enough news to warrant daily briefings, and journalists complain about news management and assert that most information is so routine that simple releases would do just as well. However, fear of missing something keeps most reporters in regular attendance.

## Press Conferences

The president has a historical obligation to meet with the press. Meetings may take the form of personal interviews for journalists or groups of journalists or of answering questions posed by journalists at formal news conferences or impromptu occasions. Since the Kennedy administration, most major news conferences have been nationally televised by all the networks. This has vastly increased the potential audience watching and listening to the president and the press, and the political danger which could occur from a serious mistake has grown much more real. Televised news conferences also provide a forum in which the president can seek to strengthen his image as a strong, decisive, and compassionate leader. Television has been an important factor in turning the press conference into a blend of image montage and ideological proclamation. The difficulty, however, is knowing where one ends and the other begins.

Except for rare opportunities for personal interviews with the president, the press conference is the only opportunity for journalists covering the White House to question the president. Not only does the press conference provide a forum for questions, it also provides an opportunity to get the president to speak on the record. His responses at televised news conferences are heard by millions of viewers and listeners and are collectively documented by all the major news organizations in the United States. Press conferences may also provide an opportunity to engage the president in a dialogue, removing some of the protective covers that generally blanket the president when he is delivering a speech or officiating at a public ceremony. At best, the press conference can be an important means to achieve a degree of presidential account- ability, as the president is forced to defend and explain his actions.

There is no obligation for the president to hold regular news confer- ences. Without any agreement to meet the press on some preordained schedule, the president and his staff are free to decide when to hold a news conference. This freedom means that the president may hold news conferences at times that are considered advantageous and avoid exposure when it might be damaging. Many presidents have entered office with a promise to hold regular and frequent news conferences, only to break this vow when they have found that these conferences robbed them of the ability to control the flow of information and opened up the President to potentially embarrassing and difficult questions.

Presidents use the press conferences as a strategic weapon. There is no consistency or pattern in the use of press conferences by modern presidents.[54] Each president has attempted to use the press conference when he feels he can benefit from it or, at times, when it is necessary to repair some damage. Some presidents have more regular press confer- ences during periods of crisis, and some have fewer. Much depends on the overall strategic approach to the press and the ease of the president in appearing at press conferences. Increasingly, the press conference has come to be regarded as a necessary evil. Although some presidents would probably have been happier if they never had to hold a press conference, it is impossible for presidents to isolate themselves totally from meeting the press in televised news conferences. The increased friction between the press and the president that has, in varying degrees, existed since the Johnson years has made presidents even more cautious about opening themselves up to questions on national television. This combination of fear and antagonism has caused many presidents to take measures to minimize the dangers of appearing live before the press. The danger can be lessened by planning and orchestrating the news conference as much as possible.

From the president's point of view, the best scenario is to know in advance the precise questions that the press is going to ask. There is no better way to know what will be asked than to plant questions with the press. The fact that success at planting questions has been very limited does not detract from the frightening fact that presidents and their media people have tried this strategy. Delighted by a question planted by a member of his staff, Lyndon Johnson encouraged his aides to plant all the questions for the next news conference. He was disappointed to learn that there were not enough journalists willing to play along.[55] Ron Ziegler, President Nixon's press secretary, suggested to a "friendly" reporter that a question about Nixon's efforts to bring government to people would be very welcome at the next news conference. The reporter asked the following:

> Mr. President, this press conference is sort of a climax to a series of activities that you have described as bringing government to the people, such as your recent meeting in Louisville, Fargo, Salt Lake City and your work at the Western White House at San Clemente. What benefit do you see to you and the country from such activities?[56]

Although planting questions removes all uncertainty, the president's media people, particularly the press secretary, can generally anticipate what questions the press is going to ask. Daily contact between the press corps and the press secretary puts the press secretary in an ideal position to recognize what the press is interested in learning. When David Gergen was Director of Communications in the Reagan administration, he would, according to Ann Devroy, "...send people from the press office to troll the press room to find out what reporters are saying..."[57] The ability to anticipate questions is maximized when the administration is exercising influence over the news agenda. Keeping the press focused on a clearly-defined set of issues, issues which the people in the White House press operation have themselves conceived, limits the risk that the president will be pulled into uncharted water.

Once the questions can be anticipated, the rest is fairly simple, if the president can stick to the script. A briefing book, with all possible questions and the responses of the president, is prepared weeks prior to the news conference. The president studies the book and meets with his advisors to clarify the responses and to rehearse. Even if members of the press ask a question with an unexpected angle, a rare occurrence, a skillful president can steer the question directly into one of these prepared responses. It is not unusual to witness the president offering an answer which seems to have only a passing resemblance to the question he was asked. In general, reporters are very aware that press conferences have become another staged event and that they are nothing more than props for the performance. Despite this knowledge, they continue to participate, because that is what they are expected to do. There are some journalists who persist in asking provocative questions, in the hope that they can nudge the president away from the prearranged script and get him to provide a more candid or spontaneous answer. These journalists consider such actions as part of their professional responsibilities. But these journalists are the exception. In general, the press corps provides a lot of "fat pitches" for the president to swing at. "A study of press conferences between 1961 and 1975 found only two occasions in fifteen years when the number of hostile questions asked by reporters at any press conference exceeded three."[58]

Careful preparation and good intelligence work, coupled with well-timed appearances, not only limit the potential for negative fallout as a result of a news conference but also give the president an opportunity to influence public opinion. Yet, no matter how well all is planned, there is a chance that a president can make a significant error and suffer political damage. Ronald Reagan frequently encountered trouble at press conferences in his early years as president. He would become flustered, make repeated verbal errors, stumble, and misstate a variety of facts. Richard Nixon got angry at several press conferences and became unusually aggressive. The possibility of making a mistake in a world where the press is considered eager to exploit any error is more of a risk than most presidents desire to take.

Another way of eliminating this risk is to reduce the number of formal news conferences and use different forums with different characters. One alternative forum is the backgrounder. Backgrounders are a common means for the administration to put something out without taking responsibility. In an administration that favors limited public contact and limited dealings with journalists, the backgrounder is a perfect means to get desirable information out to the public. Of course, the problem with backgrounders is no different at the White House than at other branches of government. "You have to judge whether they're telling the truth or whether they're bullshitting," said George Skelton, "because what they say can't be traced back to them."[59] Despite the significant potential for manipulation, almost all journalists who cover the White House will participate in backgrounders.

### Journalists' Access

While the White House press corps continues to be troubled by the decreasing number of news conferences and opportunities to interview the president, there exists a small cadre of elite journalists that the White House cannot generally afford to ignore or avoid. In fact, Presidents often seek them out. This elite is made up of bureau chiefs, syndicated columnists, anchorpersons for the networks' news, reporters for major news organizations who, as Grossman and Kumar have put it, "command their own audiences," and television figures who run political discussion programs and the journalists who regularly appear on them.[60] These journalists have access; they usually get to see the people they want to see, and their phone calls are typically returned.

From the point of view of the White House, these elite print and broadcast journalists are part of the opinion-making apparatus of American society. As stars within their own profession, they can set the tone of coverage and highlight key issues for other journalists. It is not at all surprising that presidents have often blamed failures on the unfavorable attention of these media elites. Taken together, they are a formidable group, almost a special constituency, with which the president must deal. Having allies among them is a major goal of any administration.

Another group of journalists who have recently enjoyed much greater access to the White House are the reporters, editors, and executives who represent the local and regional print and broadcast media. The policy of greeting, meeting, and wooing local and regional editors, broadcasters, and reporters began in earnest with John F. Kennedy, who inaugurated a policy of regular meetings with non-Washington-based media people. This practice was quickly adopted by successive presidents. It is, no doubt, an idea that is motivated by a desire to break the perceived monopoly over the dissemination of information enjoyed by the news giants. For Republican presidents, it is a means of bypassing the Eastern press, which is perceived as being more liberal and critical. Many local executives are ideological allies of the Republicans. Of course, this policy also allows the president to limit contact with the national press, which is viewed as being more aggressive, while at the same time claiming to fulfill the responsibility of meeting with members of the news media.

In and of itself, there is nothing objectionable about the president's meeting with local media, if the purpose of the meeting is to provide them with more access to decision makers at the White House. Unfortunately, this is not the case. These meetings are not for the purpose of making more information available or allowing local media to question high-level officials directly; they are "sales sessions" designed to provide a forum for the administration to merchandise its policy and ideological wares. Like all sales presentations, the information that is employed in this effort is selective and tailored to make the policies look good. Often less familiar with the officials' previous statements and with relevant policy information, and naturally more awed by meeting high-level officials than those who commonly meet with them, local media people are prime candidates for the quick sell.

Funneling information through the local press, which is now standard practice at the White House, is not limited to these meetings with the President and presidential advisors. These get-togethers are simply frosting on the cake. The White House press operation devotes considerable time and energy to the task of providing local media with policy information. With the advances made possible by technology, the White House operation is reaching toward a high degree of sophistication in identifying and targeting potential allies through whom information can be channeled. The operation is similar to the one described in Chapter Eight but considerably better staffed and funded and more experienced.

The Nixon White House, for example, maintained an active file on

150,000 media contacts and policy groups. The file was indexed by various categories, providing the ability to identify useful individuals and groups. Here is an example of one of Nixon's efforts to target information:

> In a two week period during April, 1971, the White House prepared sixteen mailings and sent materials to one hundred and forty-six thousand groups, publications or individuals. The materials included 1) Booklets on environmental policy and government regulation to one thousand one hundred reporters and news organizations. 2) Statements opposing abortion to one hundred ninety-eight Catholic media organizations, labor policy information to one thousand three hundred and sixty-four labor and finance writers, a senior citizen proclamation to one hundred thousand concerned with the aging, and a copy of James Kilpatrick's column to nine thousand two hundred and seventy-three academics and Republicans.[61]

Jimmy Carter further expanded the practice of funneling information to the local media. In much the same way that candidates identify and target segments of the electorate, the White House has divided the community of journalists, editors, publishers, and other opinion leaders into strategic categories. Since there is no obligation to provide the same information to all news organizations, information is selectively distributed to members of this community who are likely to be sympathetic to particular policy initiatives. The White House has come to realize that friendly factions can be cultivated and can provide some of the strongest political support available to a president. Increasingly, the media are not considered as a group of objective professionals but as simply another political group containing friendly and hostile factions.

### Presidential Image

A president's ability to project an effective image has to be every bit as important as the ability to manage information. It is difficult to do one successfully without the other. Considered among the most important qualities a president should demonstrate are decisiveness, strength, competence, and leadership ability. The president must also be perceived as an advocate of the people who interacts with ordinary citizens and is a good family person. While it is arguable whether all these qualities are the ones that make a good president, these are the qualities that are considered to be important to project, qualities that will endear the president to the voters. Television is the medium through which these qualities can be most effectively displayed.

Much of the routine coverage of the president is perfectly suited to this aim. With the knowledge that the press will dutifully cover and, in most cases, will report everything that the president does, it is fairly simple to engineer situations for the president to enforce the desired image. Appearing at a vast number of ceremonial functions allows the Chief Executive to be shown "being presidential." Greeting dignitaries visiting the White House highlights the president as a leader. Trips across the country, visiting factories, schools, daycare centers, rodeos, and so on allows the president to be shown mingling with the masses. First Ladies have frequently accompanied the president, which projects an image of family unity. Perhaps the best opportunity for showcasing these presidential qualities is foreign travel. It is not surprising that many presidents choose to travel abroad as election time draws closer. Travel abroad and meetings with foreign leaders vastly increase the already-abundant coverage of the president and pushes other issues off the news agenda. Except when a president receives an overtly hostile reception, the coverage of foreign travel is highly favorable.

The degree of effort and concern that goes into preparing the visual stage for coverage during trips abroad suggests that the possibility for fortifying the president's image is a stronger motivation for many trips than any attempt to work out an agreement or consult on important issues. Former Vice President Mondale, certainly in a position to know the anatomy of foreign travel, said that almost no time is generally spent in discussing real issues on these trips.[62]

When Richard Nixon traveled abroad for an important meeting with French President Georges Pompidou, a foreign service specialist who had been sent to work on policy issue with the president was startled to learn that neither leader seemed much interested in policy.

> All they cared about was how things would look on television. White House aides fussed about the lighting, about who would stand where, what the background would be. The entire time I was assigned to the detail, no one asked me one substantive question. I'm sure they didn't care. All they seemed to care about was television.[63]

Stories abound in Washington about the Herculean efforts made to set up good picture opportunities for the president. When President Reagan visited South Korea, a considerable block of time was spent deciding the best vantage point for the President to be photographed at the Demilitarized Zone. Various positions and poses were rehearsed in advance. To make certain that all this work would not be undercut by a spontaneous error by the President, the staff painted footprints inside the military bunker where Ronald Reagan was to stand. He was to walk into the bunker (stage left), plant his feet inside the footprints, and look out over the horizon. David Gergen, who directed these activities, commented on the importance of these visuals:

> The picture says as much as anything could say. Audiences will listen to you more if they see the president in an interesting setting. Their memory will be more vivid. We've spent a fair amount of time thinking about that.[64]

In the case of visuals, the needs of the White House completely correspond with the needs of those media personnel responsible for visuals. A good picture for the White House is a good picture for print photographers and television cameras.

The family life of the president has always been of great interest to the media. Even the president's relationship with pets provokes intense interest. After all, a president who loves his dog can't be all bad. Portraits of the president's family life provide ample opportunities to project the president as compassionate and caring. In this age of fascination with personalities, this sort of story is of even greater interest to the media. Heavy with the sentimental symbols so valued in the news, family portraits provide a potential bonanza of good images, words, and pictures.

> News organizations usually are willing partners in the White House effort to publicize the personal life of the President and members of his family. Because his personal qualities are easier to portray than the complex policy developments of his administration, editors have a larger appetite for family stories than for articles about government reorganization or natural gas regulation.[65]

A chain reporter in the Carter White House said: "It's a lot easier for me to get into several newspapers in the chain with a story about Amy than with an important policy development."[66]

The use of image events which provide the president with an unfiltered channel to the public has been steadily rising. Not only have modern presidents used the traditional image opportunities, they have also expanded the repertoire. Jimmy Carter reached back into the treasure chest of props and devised a series of fireside chats. Wearing a cardigan sweater to emphasize the informality and hominess of the occasion, sitting before a roaring fireplace, Carter addressed the nation on such issues as energy.

Of course, Ronald Reagan's experience before the camera makes him perfectly suited to this type of performance. He has used television with more frequency and effectiveness than any other president. Television has become a means to marshall public support for administration policies. "Every time a key vote was coming up he'd go to the tube with a little chart and graph and magic numbers."[67] Although Reagan has appeared frequently on television, his media advisors are keenly aware of the potential dangers as well as the advantages. David Gergen has counseled against overexposure. "You simply cannot go on national television at night, every three or four weeks, on some issue. I think neither the public nor the networks nor the President would welcome such a thing."[68] According to Gergen, a president must marshall support carefully and avoid commenting on everything, every day: "I think Carter made a mistake in that regard."[69]

Advisors are now always on the alert to find new ways to advertise the virtues of the President. A *New York Times* article reveals some of the fascinating stagecraft which is fast becoming a staple of White House operations. After President Reagan interrupted a staff meeting to give members a pep talk, word of the interruption made its way to the press and resulted in some very favorable stories. This led aides to wonder whether the President might not interrupt a meeting on arms control to stress his concern about the issue.

> The idea, according to one official, was that the press office could then disclose another supposedly surprising incident as a slice of reality at the White House. Another aide questioned whether such a fascinating device, using White House routine as a kind of theatre backdrop for dramatic Presidential gestures, was at best a one time move *and risked having form triumph too obviously over substance* [Our emphasis].[70]

Reagan did interrupt a meeting on arms control, and word was leaked out quietly.

This high premium on image has spawned a new and highly influential group of presidential advisors. All the recent presidents have heavily depended on advisors with considerable experience in advertising, public relations, or media consulting. It has become increasingly difficult to find a line that separates image and policy. Policy is often used as simply a means to create opportunities to reinforce a particular image. More disturbing is the relationship that has developed between the President and his image merchants. After studying the briefing books of the candidates for the Carter/Reagan debate, *The New Republic* provided this poignant analysis of their significance:

> What the books show is not only a profound malignant contempt for politics, for democracy, for the electors, but a deep condescension toward and disrespect for the candidates themselves. No opponent or critic of either man could think them to be such fools as their advisors take them to be. They do not have to suspend disbelief to put their candidates on the screen. They do not believe that their men ever exist outside their manipulation of them.[71]

It is, of course, understandable for a president to opt to present his policies and conduct in a favorable light. The problem is the degree to which these practices influence the conduct of politics. Most of these preconceived television and public appearances add nothing to the information needed by the public to exercise reasonable political choices. As most journalists recognize, they are simply a means for the president to build political capital for his programs without subjecting them to the possible scrutiny of the news media.

George Skelton of the *Los Angeles Times* describes the practice in the Reagan administration:

> They don't even bother to try to influence the press, they simply [pause] where's the camera, turn it on, that's it. That's what they want. They have nice backdrops and pictures, colorful frames for the president. A lot of human interests stuff. Most presidents don't have the entertainment skills that [Reagan's] developed.[72]

Norman Sandler of UPI offered a strikingly similar picture. "They're not interested in the needs of the media. Once you decide to put the president in public, the overriding concern is how he will look and how he will project on the tube."[73]

## A THEORY OF PRESIDENTIAL-PRESS RELATIONS

Walter Mondale may have proclaimed an end of an era when he declared, shortly after his loss to Ronald Reagan, that it appears that it will never be possible for someone without good media skills to succeed in becoming president. But it is not simply good looks or ease before the camera that will be required for victory; it will be an ability to manage communications. While Ronald Reagan's skill on television was an important factor in his victory, it was not the only factor. Ronald Reagan's second presidential campaign was simply an extension of the tactics that had been successfully used throughout his first term in office. The message was designed for the medium of television and perfectly executed. Debates on substantive policy issues were scrupulously avoided. It all worked as well as it did because of a generally favorable set of economic and political circumstances, which allowed the administration, somewhere toward the middle of the first term, to gain control of the news agenda and to determine the interpretation of political reality.

Ronald Reagan's victory calls into question some of the generalizations about the way television coverage affects the power of a president. Since no incumbent president after Richard Nixon was able to win reelection, observers were led to speculate that the media had diluted the power of the president to a degree that it was virtually impossible for an incumbent to win reelection. Television was thought to create a number of difficult, if not impossible, dilemmas for a president. The concentrated coverage of all activities was thought to produce a more educated audience. Pressure created by television's desire to have instantaneous responses and decisions would, at the same time, create pressure on the administration to act quickly. A modern president would be confronted by a public that knows more and expects more and by a news establishment hungry for action:

> ...television's most obvious and important effect is that it has significantly compressed the time American governments have in which to institute programs and achieve the results needed to sustain these programs for as long as may be necessary for politicians, and the rest of us, to get their full benefits.[74]

In addition to decreasing the time that a politician has to get his programs recognized or labeled as a success, television was thought to rob the political leader of some of the traditional means for exercising power. There are higher expectations, less time to meet them, and few resources to call upon. This creates, according to critics, a sort of triple bind. Thomas Cronin, a student of presidential politics, observes: "Television is a leveling medium; it diminishes the mystique and authority a leader might be able to develop. The aura of leadership is so dissected by overexposure on television, it wears down the legitimacy of institutions."[75]

Other observers believe that it is not the intense coverage but the emphasis on personality in that coverage which has made it more difficult for the president to innovate. In essence, the concentration on personalities puts additional responsibility on the president while diminishing his institutional power. Since the media cannot or chooses not to handle the structural and political complexities involved in the bringing about reform—the stalemate that often results from attempts to move vested interests is characterized in personal terms—as a "conflict between the political will, influence and savvy of the president and his opponents. If the innovation fails...the media's framework allows but one explanation: a personal failure of the president."[76]

Ronald Reagan's term in office demonstrates the frailty of some of these generalizations. The way television will affect the power of particular presidents depends on a number of factors that cannot always be anticipated or calculated in advance. During the Reagan term, television did not, for example, act to "level" the office of President and strip it of its authority. Reagan demonstrated that this effect is controllable and depends on the manner in which the President chooses to portray the office through the medium of television. Carter wanted the President to be pictured as simply a man of the people and consciously sought to devalue the trappings of the office. Ronald Reagan has done just the opposite; he has skillfully manipulated the entire tableau of national and psychological symbols to elevate the office and its holder to a loftier plane. In this case, the power of television to affect a president's power is largely determined by the way the president uses the medium.

Reagan has also seemed to be immune to the danger of television's depicting failures resulting from institutional impediments as personal failures of the president, thereby undermining the public's confidence in the president's abilities. In fact, Ronald Reagan has seemed particularly resourceful in using television to accomplish just the opposite result, turning what might have justifiably been considered to be personal failures into institutional failures of other branches of government, particularly of Congress.

The claim that television has shrunk political time and put additional pressure on the president to produce results seems more plausible. Pressures for action are created by the incessant drive of the media to get the administration to respond quickly to fast-breaking events and to make decisions in time for the media to meet the deadlines. But, again, Ronald Reagan has seemed to overcome this institutionalized tendency. When, for example, the media created intense pressure for the President to do something about the rapidly-deteriorating situation in Lebanon in 1984, he eventually withdrew American troops, effectively pulling the rug from under the media. This may be one of the clearer examples of the way considerations of agenda management push policy considerations in a particular direction. At other times, Reagan has seemed to be able to resist the strong clamor for results generated by the media. In the first two years of his administration, when the clamor was the strongest, he would use television to deliver impassioned appeals for public support, creating a sort of public counterweight to the pressure of the media.

All this is not to imply that Ronald Reagan possesses any magical powers. He is, no doubt, the best at using television as a personal tool since John F. Kennedy. Yet, various presidents, including John F. Kennedy and Richard Nixon (during his first term), have had similar success in avoiding some of the untoward consequences of being president in the media age. How a president's power is affected by the media is, in large part, determined by two related factors. In essence, a president able to retain control of the news agenda can use the media to enhance his power. If the president loses control, the media can drain some of the president's power. Whether a president can control the news media is, in turn, determined by two factors—the overall public perception of the political and economic health of the country and the public's attitude toward the press and the president.

The example of the Reagan administration's attempts to introduce El Salvador into the news agenda illustrates this relationship. Toward the end of 1980, when the Reagan administration first made a concerted effort to get the issue on the agenda, the economic picture was still bleak, and the President was not particularly popular. These were the reasons for his failure to gain control of the agenda and to define the conflict in his terms. The administration was successful in getting coverage, but it could not control the way the issue was being covered. Realizing that no coverage of the issue was far better than coverage that could not be controlled, the administration cleverly decided to retreat.

When the issue began to emerge again at the beginning of 1982, public perceptions about the health of the economy and about the ability of the President had changed. This change allowed the administration to succeed where it had previously failed. The explanation of the conflict as an attempt by the Soviets and the Cubans to use El Salvador and Nicaragua as bases to spread their influence was generally accepted as an appropriate definition. Certain news organizations resisted this simplistic explanation, but that resistance was not great enough to challenge the administration's increasing grip on the terms of the debate. Incrementally, the administration's "line" on the conflict infiltrated all news from the area.

The other important variable in this equation is public attitudes toward the media. Strong public support for the media, or for the media's interpretation of political reality, will increase the media's immunity to presidential control. In the absence of strong public support, or in the face of public hostility, the media's relative position and power are weakened. As Reagan entered office, the pendulum of public opinion toward the media was swinging in the "right" direction; there was a good deal of hostility and bitterness.

Struggle for control of the agenda, which was firmly in the hands of the media during most of the Carter years, was protracted, and forces were set in motion that fueled public resentment of the media. As control began to shift, many of the journalists working for major media organizations continued to resist the administration's attempts to control the agenda. This resistance was increasingly perceived by the public as capricious attacks on the President, who had built up considerable public support in frequent television speeches. The President was on the offensive, and the pressure on journalists to accept White House control intensified.

Several White House correspondents said that editors had signaled dissatisfaction with hostile questions asked at news conferences and persistent stories detailing the administration's distortions. In these journalists' estimation, editors were reacting to strong public displeasure with these kinds of stories. Much of this public reaction was being orchestrated by well-organized, grass-roots conservative organizations, but much of it was hostility toward the press that was suddenly surfacing. This public response caused news executives to worry about the way a continued struggle with the President would affect their competitive positions.

When a president controls the agenda, he is going to receive more favorable coverage. Yet, a study of presidential coverage reveals that even presidents who do not exert strong control over the agenda have been able to use the resources of the office to engineer favorable news. When President Johnson was complaining about his treatment during his first year in office, stories in the *New York Times* were favorable at a ratio of six to one; in *Time* the ratio was ten to one.[77] Vietnam and Watergate produced expanded coverage of the White House and increased the percentage of negative stories. However, a study of twenty-five years (1953–1978) of *Time* and the *New York Times* and ten years (1968–1978) of CBS News shows the balance of coverage to be favorable, with an overall ratio of two to one.[78] While these findings demonstrate the strong role of the president in influencing the news, it would probably not satisfy most presidents and their advisors, who have shown an intolerance of any negative reporting.

Research seems to indicate that presidents have had reason to be wary of negative coverage. Page and Shapiro have found that the media are the only institutional or organizational forces that are able to compete with the president's power to set the terms of the public debate. Congress, interest groups, or even dissidents in the president's own administration are incapable of countering a presidential message. Only the media are able to change public opinion to a degree equal to, and, in many cases, greater than, the change which can be produced by the concerted efforts of a president.

The struggle between the president and the news media is perhaps the most significant political fight in the nation. If the president triumphs, he has a relatively free hand to dispense his version of political reality, no matter how distorted that view might be. If the news media prevail, they will establish an agenda of issues which conform to their news values and commercial interests. Considering the potential scenario if one or the other side were to gain total control, the existence of struggle is perhaps the only encouraging sign.

## NOTES

1 For a thorough treatment of this evolution see Michael Baruch Grossman and Martha Joynt Kumar, *Portraying the President: The White House and the News Media*, Johns Hopkins University Press, Baltimore, 1981.

2 David Halberstam, *The Powers That Be*, Dell, New York, 1979, p. 19. Copyright © 1980 by David Halberstam. Reprinted by permission of Alfred A. Knopf, Inc.

3 Halberstam, *Powers That Be*, p. 20.

4 Halberstam, *Powers That Be*, p. 30.

5 Halberstam, *Powers That Be*, p. 29.

6 Halberstam, *Powers That Be*, p. 330.

7 Lyndon Johnson quoted in Hugh Sidey, *A Very Personal Presidency: Lyndon Johnson in the White House*, Atheneum, New York, 1968, p. 163.

8 Richard Nixon quoted in Daniel Schorr, *Clearing the Air*, Houghton Mifflin Co., New York, 1979, p. 37. Copyright © 1977 by Danial Schorr. Reprinted by permission of Houghton Mifflin Company.

9 Schorr, *Clearing the Air*, p. 37.

10 Patrick Buchanon on "Viewpoint," ABC News, Jan. 19, 1984, show no. 704.

11 Schorr, *Clearing the Air*, p. 39.

12 Schorr, *Clearing the Air*, p. 39.

13 Halberstam, *Powers That Be*, p. 32.

14 Schorr, *Clearing the Air*, p. 40.

15 Schorr, *Clearing the Air*, p. 57.

16 George McGinnis, *The Selling of the President 1969*, Pocket Books, New York, 1969, p. 160.

**17** Jack Nelson on *Viewpoint,* ABC News, Jan. 19, 1984, show no. 704.

**18** Grossman and Kumar, *Portraying the President,* p. 14.

**19** Grossman and Kumar, *Portraying the President,* p. 14.

**20** "Jody Powell on the Press and The Presidency," *Washington Journalism Review,* April, 1981, p. 34.

**21** Grossman and Kumar, *Portraying the President,* p. 169.

**22** Benjamin I. Page and Robert Y. Shapiro, "Presidents as Opinion Leaders: Some New Evidence," *Policy Studies Journal,* vol. 12, no. 4, June, 1984, p. 637.

**23** Page and Shapiro, "Presidents as Opinion Leaders," p. 659.

**24** See Dan Thomas and Lee Sigelman, "Presidential Identification and Policy Leadership: Experimental Evidence on the Reagan Case," *Policy Studies Journal,* vol. 12, no. 4, June, 1984, pp. 663–675.

**25** Page and Shapiro, "Presidents as Opinion Leaders," p. 653.

**26** Page and Shapiro, "Presidents as Opinion Leaders," p. 656.

**27** Personal Interview with Sam Donaldson of ABC.

**28** Personal Interview with Ann Devroy of the Gannett organization.

**29** Grossman and Kumar, *Portraying the President,* p. 151.

**30** Personal Interview with George Skelton of the *Los Angeles Times.*

**31** Dom Bonafede, "The Press and the Hollywood Presidency," *Washington Journalism Review,* Jan./Feb., 1981, p. 48.

**32** Grossman and Kumar, *Portraying the President,* pp. 154–155.

**33** "Jody Powell on the Press and The Presidency," *Washington Journalism Review,* April, 1981, p. 35.

**34** Quoted in Dan Hallin, "White Paper, Red Scare," *NACLA Report on the Americas,* North American Congress on Latin America, New York, vol. 17, no. 4, 1983, p. 5.

**35** Dan Hallin, "When World-Views View The World," *NACLA Report on the Americas,* vol. 17, no. 4, 1983, p. 30.

**36** NBC News, April 1, 1980. Quoted in Hallin, "When World-Views View The World," p. 30.

**37** Ike Seamans, quoted in Hallin, "White Paper, Red Scare," p. 3.

**38** Quoted in Sydney Blumenthal, "Marketing the President," *New York Times Magazine,* Sept. 13, 1981, p. 43.

**39** "Network News Timetable for Coverage of Central America Issue," Oct., 1979 to Jan., 1983, in Hallin, "White Paper, Red Scare," p. 17.

**40** Hallin, "White Paper, Red Scare," p. 6.

**41** Hodding Carter quoted in Hallin, "White Paper, Red Scare," p. 4.

**42** Hallin, "White Paper, Red Scare," p. 8.

**43** Personal Interview with Ann Devroy.

**44** Personal Interview with Ann Devroy.

**45** Personal Interview with George Skelton.

**46** Personal Interview with Norman Sandler of UPI.

**47** "Lyn Nofziger on Ronald Reagan and the Press," *Washington Journalism Review,* March, 1982.

**48** Jack Nelson on *Viewpoint,* ABC News, Jan. 19, 1984, show no. 704. Courtesy ABC News, Copyright © 1984, American Broadcasting Companies, Inc.

**49** "Action Taken by the Reagan Administration to Restrict Public Access to Government Information," The Reporters Committee for Freedom of the

Press, Washington, D.C., April 1, 1984.
50  George C. Edwards III, *The Public Presidency*, St. Martin's Press, New York, 1983, p. 41.
51  Edwards, *Public Presidency*, p. 56.
52  Dom Bonafede, "...The Press," *Washington Journalism Review*, May, 1980, p. 48.
53  Grossman and Kumar, *Portraying the President*, pp. 33–34.
54  Grossman and Kumar, *Portraying the President*, p. 245.
55  Grossman and Kumar, *Portraying the President*, p. 249.
56  Edwards, *Public Presidency*, p. 117.
57  Personal Interview with Ann Devroy.
58  Edward Morgan, Max Ways, Clark Mollenholf, Peter Lisager, Herbert Klein, *The Presidency and the Press Conference*, American Enterprise Institute, Washington, D.C., 1971, p. 5.
59  Personal Interview with George Skelton.
60  Grossman and Kumar, *Portraying the President*, p. 206.
61  Edwards, *Public Presidency*, p. 127.
62  Democratic Presidential Primary Debate, NBC, Sunday, June 3, 1984.
63  Quoted in Edwards, *Public Presidency*, p. 75.
64  "Key Presidential Buffer Looks Back," *New York Times*, Jan. 10, 1984. The New York Times Company copyright © 1976, 1983, 1984. Reprinted by permission.
65  Grossman and Kumar, *Portraying the President*, p. 231.
66  Quoted in Grossman and Kumar, *Portraying the President*, p. 231.
67  Personal Interview with Ann Devroy.
68  "A Talk with David Gergen," *Washington Journalism Review*, April, 1982, p. 43.
69  "A Talk with David Gergen," p. 44.
70  Francis X. Clines, "Interruption Ploy: No Rerun," *New York Times*, July 23, 1983. The New York Times Company copyright © 1976, 1983, 1984. Reprinted by permission.
71  Henry Fairlie, "Scripts for the Pageant," *The New Republic*, August 8, 1983, p. 27.
72  Personal Interview with George Skelton.
73  Personal Interview with Norman Sandler.
74  Austin Ranney, *Channels of Power*, Basic Books, New York, 1983, p. 124.
75  Quoted in Dom Bonafede, "The New Political Power of the Press," *Washington Journalism Review*, Sept., 1980, p. 27.
76  David L. Paletz and Robert M. Entman, *Media Power Politics*, Free Press, New York, 1981, p. 76.
77  Grossman and Kumar, *Portraying the President*, p. 253.
78  Grossman and Kumar, *Portraying the President*, pp. 254–255. Stories were read by two coders and rated on a continuum. Stores were defined as favorable if both coders agreed that they were favorable; stories were defined as negative if both agreed that they were negative. In between were the stories one coder said were favorable and the other coder rated as neutral, or both agreed were neutral, or one said were negative and the other rated as neutral. In making tabulations, the researchers cited only stories on which both coders agreed as favorable, neutral, or negative.

# CHAPTER 8

# CONGRESS

## COVERING CONGRESS

Congress has had no shortage of dilemmas in these last three decades. It has, for example, been faced with the task of trying to control the actions of several presidents conducting the war in Vietnam and then with the awesome responsibility of judging whether Richard Nixon should be impeached. Recently, both the House and the Senate have been forced to expel some of their own members caught in the act of using their positions to enrich their bank accounts. Public esteem for Congress is very low, and the president has found Congress an easy target for blame when things are not going according to plan.

On top of these difficulties, Congress is faced with a new and complex dilemma: how to respond to the demands created by the media's important role in the political process. Congress has had great difficulty in learning how to adapt to the new political drama. Despite a growing recognition by the congressional leadership that the institutional power of Congress depends upon how well it uses the organs of communication, the *institution* has been slow to respond and to initiate change. This problem of adapting to the new political landscape is not shared by *individual* members of the House and Senate, who have become increasingly sophisticated and comfortable with the techniques of political communication through the media. The congresspersons' knowledge of using the media is the result of the experience gained in political campaigns. Since most members of Congress share an interest in being reelected or in attaining higher office, and since the media are considered the prime instruments for the satisfaction of that interest, it is not surprising that the individual members are more in tune with ways to use the media than are the leadership and the leadership's staff.

As an institution, Congress has been affected by the growing powers of the media to define political reality. Television's concentration on presidential activities has increased the perceived importance of the president and, in conjunction with other factors, has bolstered the power of the executive over the legislative branch. This was the opinion of former Senator William Fulbright of Arkansas, the powerful former chairman of the Senate Foreign Relations Committee, who told Congress in 1970: "Television has done as much to expand the powers of the president as would a constitutional amendment formally abolishing the co-equality of the three branches of government."[1] Decades earlier, Walter Lippmann had identified information as an important source of institutional power: "Nothing affects more the balance of power between Congress and the president than whether the one or the other is the principal source of news and explanation and opinion."[2]

In total coverage, roughly the same amount of space is given to the president and the Congress in both print and electronic media.[3] Rather than demonstrating the equality of coverage, these findings reveal the powerful advantage enjoyed by the president. Coverage of Congress is diffuse; it includes reports on the activities of many individual members, committee work, investigations, and pronouncements by the many leadership factions in the House and Senate. Coverage of the president is focused on the activities of one individual or on the actions of members of the executive branch whom the president controls. This gives the coverage of the president a natural focus and consistency that is lacking in the coverage of Congress. For this reason, equal coverage amounts to more and better coverage of the executive.

Added to this lack of focus is the fact that the media tend to treat Congress more harshly than they do other political institutions. There is more negative coverage of Congress, portraying Congress as slow, ineffectual, petty, stupid, all of the above, or some of the above. One study of comparative coverage shows that only political parties exceeded Congress in the amount of negative coverage received in print media.[4] A study of network coverage came to similar conclusions.[5] Not only does Congress receive less coverage than the president, the coverage that it does receive tends to be less favorable than that afforded other branches of government.

As an institution, Congress is particularly vulnerable to negative coverage. Sam Rayburn, who served for sixteen years as the Speaker of the House, seemed to sense the vulnerability of Congress to the media. At a time when President Eisenhower was opening up the presidency to television, Rayburn was unalterably opposed to making any concession to television. Excluded from the House, television concentrated on the presidency. Rayburn knew that Congress was a cumbersome and fragile institution, one that might not look so good when exposed to the public eye. It is an institution built on compromise, the necessity to get members from different parties and regions to agree to the inevitable give and take of passing legislation. Rayburn, even suspicious that the print media might be undermining the leadership's ability to control the institution, was convinced that the electronic media would lead the House to sensationalism and paralysis. Rayburn believed that the work of the House required a certain degree of discipline and secrecy. House members, thought Rayburn, would use the media to further their own political ambitions, without considering the needs of the institution. Across Capitol Hill, the Senate had opened the hearing rooms to television. Television quickly warmed to covering the senate hearings. Rayburn watched what was happening in the Senate with consternation. "All they do there is preen and comb their hair and run for president," he said.[6]

Congress is also vulnerable to negative criticism for other reasons. Because it moves very slowly and deliberately, it is out of step with the prevailing news rhythm—the fast, staccato beat that often characterizes news emanating from the president, the Supreme Court, or state and local officials. In an age of fast-breaking action, a congressional waltz appears out of step with the prevailing political tempo.

Because Congress is composed of so many members, it lacks a personal identity and is often treated as an institution. Other institutions are not attacked in the way that Congress is attacked in the media. Negative stories about other branches of government tend to focus on individuals within that branch and not on the institution itself. Critical reporting on the president, for example, rarely gives the impression that there is something wrong with the institution of the presidency. Much of the negative reporting on Congress conveys the impression that the institution is in some advanced state of disrepair. It is often, implicitly or explicitly, pictured as an archaic monument, populated by scoundrels who would do anything to feed their egos and ambitions.

Congress thus is hampered by a lack of personal rapport with the press corps. Relationships between particular members of Congress and the press may be very good, but there is nothing on an institutional level that rivals the president's relationship with the White House press corps. Journalists are less dependent on individual members of Congress for stories. If one congressperson is not willing to cooperate, another will. There is more than one main news source. The press's personal relationship with the president, and its dependence on the president to supply news, puts the chief executive in a stronger position to influence the agenda of the media and to get issues into the press.

Presidents of the media age must also bear some responsibility for the decline of congressional power. As the prime newsmaker, with media focusing on all that he says and does, the president is in a perfect position to use the media as vehicles to criticize Congress. Each attack on Congress is dutifully carried by the media. By shifting attention to the "inaction" or "irresponsibility" of Congress, the president helps to get the media's critical juices flowing. They turn toward the Congress, eager to uncover the story of congressional ineptitude. President Reagan has used the tactic quite successfully during his presidency. It has been so successful that it has contributed to his ability to break congressional opposition to certain programs and to cause defection among many members of the opposition, who have dreaded the thought of being pictured as part of a "do-nothing" Congress, as big spenders or prisoners of special interests.

The president is in a position to "command" free air time. Presidential news conferences and addresses are almost always covered by all three commercial networks. This gives the president access to free air time, which may be used for any purpose except to deliver explicit, partisan campaign messages. This restriction does not mean that the president is forbidden to use the time to attack Congress or even opposition members of Congress.[7] President Reagan has used the presidential address format to launch several broadside attacks on Congress.

Congress does not have this ability to command air time. One study showed that, during a 10-year period, Presidents Johnson, Nixon, and Ford "sought simultaneous coverage of presidential addresses on 45 different occasions, and it was granted 44 of those times."[8] In contrast, the congressional leadership was not nearly as successful. Out of eleven requests for air time over a 7-year period, Congress was granted access on only three occasions.[9] Congress must depend on the networks to provide time to respond to presidential messages. Even if congresspersons consistently received this reply time, they would have to overcome a number of important advantages which accrue to the president, not the least of which is the ability to influence the political agenda and thus set the terms of political discourse.

The studies that indicate that Congress receives more negative coverage should not lead to the conclusion that the media are out there punishing Congress with critical reporting. The fact is that most of the stories concerning Congress either are neutral, contain no easily-discernible position, or are stories that treat Congress favorably. Two researchers found that 86 percent of all stories on Congress studied over a period of months could be categorized as either neutral or noncritical.[10] So, at most, 14 percent of all stories concerning Congress are critical, which does not amount to any assault on the institution. The fact that the negative coverage of Congress is treated as an issue by observers in the field says more about the sad state of critical reporting on other branches of government than about the fine job being done by journalists covering Congress.

Congress is not without weapons that can be used to influence the media. Its most powerful weapon is the FCC. Congress controls the agency's budget and has the power to pass regulatory legislation. The Senate confirms the President's nominations to the commission. Congress also has the power to investigate the media. It has exercised this power on several occasions, including its investigation of the CBS documentary "The Selling of the Pentagon" and the Kerner Commission's inquiry into the conduct of the press during the riots of the 1960's. In each case, Congress made its potential power felt but eventually backed off from any head-on confrontation with the media. In general, Congress has not exerted any strong control over the industry; this failure has left a political vacuum which the industry has generally filled. Yet, Congress does have the power to help or hurt the industry, which may explain why the media are cautious about poking the "sleeping tiger" too sharply.

The institutional relationship between Congress and the media is very different from the relationship between individual members of Congress and the media. We begin to appreciate better these differences by focusing on the routine activities of the journalists who cover Capitol Hill.

## THE CONGRESSIONAL REPORTER

Congress is a major beat on the Washington press path. Virtually all the news organizations that cover the activities of the president also have correspondents who cover Congress. Often the staff covering Congress is as large or larger than the number of journalists assigned to the president. Two thousand correspondents are accredited to the press galleries in the House and the Senate. Four hundred correspondents exclusively cover Congress.[11]

The media covering Congress can be divided into three groups. There are the large, prestigious organizations, including wire services, news magazines, national newspapers, and television networks. Just below this group are a number of medium-sized dailies, serving many of the nation's major cities, and chain bureaus, which distribute Congressional news to their many affiliated newspapers. By far the largest group of media covering Congress is composed of smaller daily newspapers, local television and radio stations, independent news bureaus (stringers), and specialty publications.

The number of Washington correspondents has been steadily rising over the last two decades. This overall increase is reflected in an increase in the number of media covering Congress. Washington has been at the center of the news explosion, an explosion caused by the tremendous growth in the electronic media. Between 1960 and 1975, there was a 175 percent increase in accredited TV and radio journalists and a 37 percent increase in the number of print journalists.[12] Cable television has entered the news business in earnest. Three cable news networks are producing round-the-clock news programs that are aired on channels that exclusively cover news in local cable markets across the country. Local and regional media, particularly television, have an increased presence in the congressional press corps. Congress has reacted to this growth in the media in Washington with delight, realizing that such growth provides additional opportunities for media coverage.

Washington reporters covering Congress live in a sea of information. Information is churned out of congressional offices at a pace that would rival that of any highly developed mass production line. A phenomenal amount of time, money, and energy is spent on spinning out these reams of information, much of it obscure, useless, or self-serving.

If you are a national reporter covering Congress, you can be a potential target of 535 members of Congress, who may at any one time feel that they are doing something deserving national coverage. If you are a regional reporter for a chain, Gannett or Newhouse, for example, the number of members of Congress that you report on is smaller but is still, in most cases, a sizable contingent of public officials. A reporter for a major chain bureau in Washington who covers the New York area follows the activities of the entire New York and Connecticut congressional delegation. Another chain reporter covers Congress for newspapers in Iowa, Missouri, Nebraska, and Kansas. Many small, daily newspapers have one- or two-person bureaus in Washington. Reporters in these bureaus have smaller congressional delegations to follow, but they must generally cover other Washington beats. Since there is no conceivable way for the reporter to cover a sizable percentage of the daily congressional process, a choice is inevitable. There are stories which an editor directs a reporter to cover. At the chain bureaus, some of these are assignments referred to by reporters as "fools' errands"—requests from one of the local papers in the chain to cover the visit of a small-town mayor to Washington, D.C., or coverage of the Cherry Blossom Princess visit to Washington for her hometown local in Stuart, Florida. However, the majority of the stories written by congressional correspondents are initiated by the correspondents themselves. What influences their decision? There are four interrelated criteria used by journalists to determine what stories to cover. They are personal interest, national news consensus, salability, and the availability of sources.

Much of what the reporter covers and writes about is simply the result of what he or she finds most interesting. Stephen Hess believes that "Boredom—or the absence of excitement—is the most uninvestigated explanation of media resource allocation."[13] Journalists' interests can be divided into two categories. There are particular topics which are more interesting than others to the journalists. Most journalists would find doing a story on unemployment more interesting than a story on the congressional archives. There are also certain varieties of stories that are inherently interesting. Anything involving congressional scandal or corruption seems interesting to a journalist. A favorite is the story of the congressional junket, where a congressman uses official funds to finance trips that turn out to have more to do with getting a vacation than discharging official business. But the number of cases of corruption or scandal uncovered by one means or another will not fill much copy. In the absence of these sorts of stories, many journalists will gravitate toward stories that feature political drama.

Luckily for the reporters, there is ample political intrigue in the House and Senate, where one or another political deal or rumor is often the subject of speculation. One reporter has called these sorts of stories "politics as spectator sports." Many reporters are political junkies who thirst for political speculation and intrigue. The spectator stories they write will generally emphasize the process of legislating rather than the product. They may describe anything from the last-minute attempts to round up support for a bill to speculation about who will be invited to the next state dinner at the White House. While these stories are interesting to Washington insiders who enjoy following the various moves, they are of questionable value to the general public. On this subject, a reporter concedes: "A lot of the stuff we have to follow is not worth very much." These sorts of stories highlight the reporters' perception of politics as a game.

The tendency to write these sorts of stories is reinforced by the fact that reporters have virtually no contact with their readers. Many chain reporters, for example, have never visited the town where a chain paper that they write for is located. Even local reporters with roots in their local communities rarely return home or maintain networks of contacts once they are stationed in Washington. Often, their understanding of problems of citizens in the local communities is obscure, and their efforts to keep these citizens informed of the voting records of their representative meager. That is mundane material. Since congressional reporters are writing for themselves, their peers, and members of the House and Senate, who will ultimately evaluate their performances, they are eager to write stories that are interesting and provocative by Washington insider standards.

Local and regional reporters use the major media, particularly the wire services and national newspapers, for story ideas. Wire services provide a steady stream of news about every aspect of congressional activity. National newspapers determine which issues are to be given national exposure. Many of the topics and types of stories appearing in the national newspapers appeal to the journalists' interests. A story that appears in the national media also carries a certain amount of legitimacy that can be used as a selling tool with editors. But local editors are beginning to place increasing emphasis on stories that are relevant to local interests, particularly stories on Congress. This means that the journalist must often find a local angle for many of the stories adopted from the national media.

This poses a dilemma of sorts for the working journalist. All journalists enjoy seeing their stories printed or broadcast, so they must consider whether a particular story is likely to sell. Stories with a solid local angle are easier to sell, but they are less interesting to the journalist than the big "spectator" stories. Lou Peck, a congressional reporter for the Gannett chain, summed up his dilemma when he said that he feels that the impact of the stories that he writes is inversely proportional to the interest that he has in the subject. A story that concerns a local issue, with a genuine connection in Washington, has the most impact on readers. As an example, Peck cited a story that he did on pending congressional legislation that would affect the levels of pollutants dumped into local rivers. This was very important to local readers, but it was, at least for this reporter, a very time-consuming and boring story. Stories about the "state of Congress" were the most interesting for this reporter but had the least impact on the local readers. Many reporters solve the problem by writing a number of largely perfunctory local stories and devoting their major efforts to more personally interesting issues.

A final criterion that helps determine a reporter's choice is the relationship between sources who are close to the story and the reporter. If reporters have a good relationship with sources who are attached to the story or have good access to sources who can provide information about the story, they are more likely to become interested in writing a story. With a deadline to meet, reporters will tend toward stories where they have prior knowledge of the issue or where there is a source whom they trust to supply reliable information.

Journalists differ in selecting the criteria that they emphasize in choosing stories. There are some journalists, for example, who will pursue a story simply on the basis of a feeling that it is an important story that needs to be written. There are certain journalists who will tackle a story even when there is limited access to good sources. Some depend on the national news consensus more than others; some are really inclined to dig for a genuine local angle, while others are willing to impose a local angle on a story in order to get it into print. Despite the individual differences, which are important, story selection is guided by these four factors.

In general, the stories on Congress appearing in the national media usually concern the power struggle between the legislative and executive branches, committee hearings, large legislative proposals, potential or real scandals, or personalities. What is commonly referred to as the "nuts and bolts" of the legislative process, the shepherding of legislation through the House and Senate, is, for the most part, ignored. The national press, particularly television, chooses news that is dramatic, timely, and predictable. In essence, the national press covers stories that often deal with the operation of Congress. The choices of the local press, which are discussed in a subsequent section, are quite different. Among the choices available to the national reporters, committee hearings emerge as the most frequently-covered legislative activity.

## HEARINGS: THE MAIN EVENT

There are a very large number of committees and subcommittees in the House and the Senate. Almost all of the committees hold hearings at one time or another. There are several types of hearings. There are often hearings when a committee is considering a piece of legislation that has been proposed by a member. In these hearings, the committee will often invite "experts" to testify on the merits or demerits of the proposed legislation. Hearings are also held for what are called "markups," a process by which the committee considers various aspects of a proposed bill. Finally, there are hearings that are held for the express purpose of investigation. Probably the most familiar investigative hearing in recent years is the Watergate hearing, which paved the way for the hearings to impeach President Nixon. Investigative hearings are held on a variety of matters, ranging from investigations of official misconduct to probes into the pacemaker industry. The list of potential areas of investigation is endless, and the number of congressional probes in some stage of progress is very long.

The media may be lured into covering a hearing on proposed legislation, particularly if the hearing deals with a matter that generates public concern, such as economic policy, taxes, foreign policy, or crime, or if there are prominent individuals testifying before the committee. The most widely-covered type of hearing, however, is the investigative hearing. National coverage of Congress is primarily coverage of the investigative hearing.[14] A study of network news indicated that stories concerning committee action made up the largest category of stories about Congress, constituting 45 percent of all stories dealing with Congress. Film was frequently used in preparing committee stories; three-quarters of the stories on investigative committees contained film segments.[15] The high premium that television puts on "dramatic" news makes the investigative hearing a prime topic for coverage.

The newsmaking potential of the investigative hearing has been no secret in Washington. As early as 1943, when the Hill was the province of print and radio journalists exclusively, committees were formulating strategies to get the best possible coverage for their work. One committee, which was investigating the Federal Communications Commission, decided to seek the advice of a journalist and hired an international wire service reporter to instruct its members on the best methods for influencing coverage. Below are the seven recommendations given to the committee.

1 Decide what you want the newspapers to hit hardest, then shape each hearing so that the main point becomes the vortex of the testimony. Once that vortex is reached, adjourn.

2 In handling press releases, first put a release date on them, reading something like this: "For release at 10:00 A.M. EST July 6," etc. If you do this, you can give releases out as much as 24 hours in advance, thus enabling reporters to study them and write better stories.

3 Limit the number of people authorized to speak for the committee, to give out press releases, or to provide the press with information to the fewest possible. It plugs leaks and helps preserve the concentration of purpose.

4 Do not permit distractions to occur, such as extraneous fusses with would-be witnesses, which might provide news that would bury the testimony which you want featured.

5 Do not space hearings more than 24 or 48 hours apart when on a controversial subject. This gives the opposition too much opportunity to make all kinds of countercharges and replies by issuing statements to the newspapers.

6 Don't ever be afraid to recess a hearing, even for five minutes, so that you keep the proceedings completely in control so far as creating news is concerned.

7 And this is the most important: don't let the hearing or the evidence ever descend to the plane of a personal fight between the committee chairman and the head of the agency being investigated. The high plane of a duly authorized committee of the House of Representatives examining the operations of an agency of the Executive Branch for constructive purposes should be maintained at all costs.[16]

Congress does all it can to make journalists comfortable and make their jobs easier. The congressional press gallery has wires which carry the stories generated by the press services. A congressperson may give a speech one minute and read about it over the wire the next. There are typewriters, lounges, and a large cadre of aides paid for by Congress who are put at the disposal of the media. A messenger service carries press releases from Capitol Hill to the National Press Building downtown. Congress does what it can to share some of the prerogatives of power with the media. These services provided by Congress for the journalist certainly bring the journalist closer to the congressional fraternity, giving him or her a greater sense of being part of the club. One senate press secretary most aptly referred to the relationship as "incestuous."

While most members of the House, as distinguished from senators, are more interested in the way the local media are reporting their activities than in getting the attention of the national media, this does not mean that these members of the House are not delighted to receive national coverage. They realize that national coverage has a way of reverberating in big stories back home as well as exposing their names to the masses. Yet only a choice few in the House have the ability to engineer national coverage for themselves, so most press secretaries for House members concentrate on relationships with journalists from the larger outlets in the district.

More senators, particularly those regarded as presidential hopefuls or those with powerful committee assignments, are in a better position to engineer national coverage for themselves. Press secretaries for these members are more familiar with the workings of the networks, the news magazines, the wire services, the *Washington Post,* and the *New York Times.* While some senators are successful in getting themselves national coverage, this type of coverage produces certain dangers. It is much more difficult to control than coverage in the local media, and it is very difficult to counter an image of the senator used by the media—an image that may be reinforced by additional exposure. This difficulty with the national media may be starting a movement in the Senate toward giving more attention to the local press. There is some evidence that this may be the next wrinkle in senatorial-press relations.

### Producing Your Own Words and Images

Working with the press is now being coupled with a practice which can be called "working through the press." This strategy involves the production of broadcast or print materials which are ready for immediate and diversified use by the media. The obvious advantage of this approach is that it eliminates the journalist and provides a means for the member to communicate directly with constituents through the media. All fear of unflattering coverage is eliminated if the media use materials that have been exclusively prepared by the member's staff.

A traditional practice in working through the press is the preparation and distribution of newspaper columns written by the member. Almost all members of Congress produce such a column. In most cases, these columns are actually written by the press secretary. Some congress-persons choose to use a weekly column, while others are satisfied with distributing something biweekly or monthly. In essence, these columns are either reports on the member's activities or comments about pending legislation or national issues. The purpose of these columns is not simply to give members a chance to praise themselves, although some of that is done, but mainly to serve as vehicles for keeping the member's name before the constituents. These columns are meant to convey the impression that the member is aware and involved in the important issues of the day. Some press secretaries are experimenting with different types of columns. One senatorial office, for example, sends out a column that contains comments on several different issues and can be easily edited. This is meant to reduce the number of columns that are not used in weeks when the amount of available copy makes it impossible for the newspaper to use the column in its entirety. Another Senate press secretary is toying with the idea of producing columns targeted to particular areas, rather than using one column distributed statewide.

All the press secretaries that we spoke with claimed that their weekly columns were a smashing success in the small papers. Senator Moynihan's column is sent to 490 weekly newspapers around the state. His press secretary claims that figures from his clipping service show that 40 percent, or between 190 to 200 papers, regularly print the column. With a certain contempt, he characterized the operation of these small papers: "Small dailies and weeklies are desperate for coverage and will take anything." Not a very comforting thought.

The newspaper column will probably remain a permanent part of the media operation. It is not very difficult to produce, it can be widely distributed, and it keeps the member's name in front of the readers. This operation may become more sophisticated. Ideally, these columns could be targeted to certain areas. A different column could be prepared for distinct areas of the state. Each column would then discuss a more local issue, creating the desirable impression that a representative in Washington was actually working on local problems. For now, however, the newspaper column is taking a back seat to the production of radio and television spots featuring the member.

It is now very common for members of the House and Senate to have either a radio or television program. Senator Alfonse D'Amato, a Republican from New York, has a 15-minute radio show which goes to 100 stations around the state. Congressman Daub, who represents the second Congressional District in Nebraska, does a cable TV show that is broadcast on all four cable outlets in his district. These are just two examples of a wide variety of shows produced by most members of Congress. The production of most television and radio programs is done in the studios located in the House and Senate office buildings. Each studio contains technology for making broadcast-ready television and radio shows and a staff to assist or supervise production. Studio time is paid for by the member, but the charge is nominal. The difference is paid for by the taxpayer, who is, in essence, subsidizing programs designed to improve the member's image. Studio use indicates the special popularity of these programs on the Hill. In 1967, 200 members took advantage of the facilities. In 1978, 352 members produced programs in these studios.[31] Today, the studios are so busy that members, particularly those who wish to use even more sophisticated production technology, are repairing to private broadcast studios to tape their shows.

There are a variety of formats used for these congressional shows. Some shows consist of a monologue by the member, who talks about issues and policy. This format is often spiced up with prerecorded statements of the member during a committee hearing or with pieces from interviews given to other media. An increasingly popular format has the member acting as a host and interviewing one or more guests. Usually a member of Congress will interview another member of Congress; most often it is a member from the same party with the same views on issues. This format is popular on both television and radio. These shows become a convenient way for members of Congress to reach constituents directly and to advertise each other.

Smaller radio and television stations can use the programs in a variety of ways. Many of the programs are run as they are produced, but others are edited and used in different spots on the station. If, for example, a tape contains a representative's remarks on an important farm bill, a radio or TV station in Kansas may choose to excerpt that part of the tape and use it with a news story on the subject. From the member's and the station's point of view, this is highly desirable. The station's news story is spiced up with a statement by a House member or senator. It is edited into the story in such a way that it appears to a listener or viewer that the station has specifically interviewed the politician for this news story. No one realizes that the statement has been cut from a "canned" message from the member. Listeners and viewers get the impression that their little station has a direct line to the Capitol. For the politician, there are at least two advantages. First, his or her name and statement appear in the news. Second, the statement is transmitted during a news broadcast and not used to fill time devoted to "public affairs," which is usually the air time when the audience is smallest. The station gets free programming, and the official gets free air time. The public either gets deceived or spoon-fed a self-serving declaration.

Many press secretaries find it profitable to "work" the radio stations. Congresspersons feed radio stations prepared statements on a regular basis. Many congressional offices have "actuality" systems. Those that do not have them have access to them. These systems take messages recorded on cassette tape and feed them through phone lines, so they can be taped by a radio station in the home state. Almost all of the stations accept these "actualities," and many of the stations use them. Often they are used on news programs in "drive-time" periods, when commuters in cars are likely to be listening to the radio. Members also frequently speak to radio stations over the phone, giving live interviews or commentary.

The House of Representatives has taken a further step into the media age with the introduction of television into the House chambers. A satellite cable network called C-SPAN now broadcasts continous live coverage of House and committee hearings to 895 cable TV systems across the country. Television production of House proceedings is controlled by the Speaker of the House, who has cleverly structured the coverage in a way that avoids potential embarrassment to members. Only the congressperson addressing the House may be filmed, so the audience will not see a chamber sparsely occupied or see members sleeping, reading, or chatting away while their colleagues are addressing them on matters of national urgency. Audiences cannot see how members vote on legislation, an obvious measure to conceal legislators' voting records. Members are permitted to purchase tapes of speeches before the House for use on their own programs or by local commercial and cable television stations.

The results of the televising of House proceedings are still quite tentative, but there are some interesting signs. Network news has not often used television film of House proceedings. This may be because television resents that the Speaker of the House is in control of production. Members have not often availed themselves of the option to purchase their taped appearances for broadcast back home. Some claim that the televised sessions have kept members more informed of proceedings on the floor. They can remain in their offices and keep track of what is occurring on the floor.[32] It is still too early to predict whether television, as it is presently constituted, will raise the House's profile in the media.

The Senate, by all indications, will soon follow the House into the era of televised government. There is pressure on the Senate from certain members and from the broadcasting industry to give control of televising the proceedings over to the industry. This may help in getting more film of the proceedings on the news than the meager amount taken from

House television. For senators who are seeking increased national exposure, this prospect bodes quite well. For other senators, particularly some *leaders* in the Senate, the potential for losing more control over the troops must be frightening.

The increased use of the media favors the new brand of politician in Congress. Younger members of Congress are aggressive in their approach to the media. These are the "hard-driving" members who have been groomed in the media age. As candidates, they employed all the modern arsenal of media weapons—television advertising, media consultants, public opinion surveys, and direct mail. They are accustomed to blending policy to fit with an image projected over the media. As members of Congress, they continue to utilize many of the same techniques. Robinson reports that "... the class of 1978 was three times more likely to make heavy use of congressional recording studio, three times more likely to regard the House TV system as very useful, three times more likely to have relied a lot on TV in the last election."[33]

## INDIVIDUAL MEMBERS AND THE MEDIA: CONCLUSIONS

The substantially different treatment received by the institution of Congress and the individual members helps explain one of the puzzling trends in congressional elections: namely, the fall in public esteem of Congress and the rise in the number of incumbents elected in the House. In part, the negativity about Congress as an institution, which shows up on all public opinion polls, is the result of the way that Congress is portrayed in the national media. Although the coverage is not consistently adversarial or probing, Congress comes in for a greater degree of negative institutional coverage than the other branches of the federal government. Yet, the impact of this negative institutional coverage is blunted by the very favorable portraits of individual members painted in the local media. Voters receive the vast majority of their news about local representatives from local sources. There is no doubt that this pattern of coverage contributes to the national disdain for Congress and the local love of its members. Incumbents enjoy the tremendous advantage of years of favorable coverage in the local press, much of it designed and composed by the members themselves. This is surely not the only factor that accounts for incumbents' success. They enjoy the traditional advantage of being able to attract more campaign money; they have a political office from which to launch a campaign. Yet, the virtual control over the dissemination of news at the local level and the ability to disassociate themselves from the negative coverage of Congress play large roles in the incumbents' increasing ability to hold on to political office.

There are indications that Congress will continue to benefit from this relationship and may be in the position to strengthen its control over the way it is portrayed by the media. Robinson reports that the national media, which have often been considered more aggressive in their reporting of Congress, have actually become more temporate in their coverage. At the same time, Robinson believes that the local media have become even softer, easier for the members of Congress to control. The increased production and dissemination of "in-house" media materials further adds to the incumbents' ability to control their image. The 1982 congressional elections indicate that the trend toward electing incumbents is holding. Only 29 of 383 incumbents, 26 of them members of the party holding the presidency, which traditionally loses seats in by-year elections, were defeated. In the Senate, where a large number of incumbents were defeated in the 1980 elections, things have markedly improved for incumbents. Only two incumbents were defeated in the 1982 elections.[34]

The relationship between Congress and the press makes it difficult to give much credence to the assumption that the press is acting as a watchdog for the public interest, a "fourth estate" of government. Many members of the press, particularly print journalists, who have prided themselves on tough, adversarial reporting, are pessimistic about their ability to have an impact on the public's perceptions of local representatives. They feel impotent in the face of cable, radio, television, and print programs that are now a part of the members' overall public relations efforts. They ask whether even consistently critical coverage of a member's activities could overcome the tremendous well of good feelings created by the member's public relations programs and the close relationship with the local press. There is a sense of defeatism, a feeling that it is impossible to reach the reader. As a result, even the more aggressive reporters take refuge in writing spectator stories.

The production and use of media programs generated by members of Congress are, in essence, writing the reporter out of the script. Most of these programs are designed so that they can be printed or put on the air without additional costs or preparation. Because they are cost-efficient, they are attractive to management. Why employ a reporter when you can receive a statement or an article free of charge? These programs are sold to editors and to management, who make the programming and copy decisions at the smaller media outlets. Although most congresspersons can profitably coexist with reporters, they can also nicely prosper by getting the media to use materials that have been written and produced by their own staff. Eliminating the reporter removes one of the last remaining buffers or mediators of political information fed to the population.

There is another consequence of the members' use of "in-house" materials and their leverage over the press which is rarely discussed. The reading and viewing public is being systematically deceived about the origins of the materials which are presented as news. The knowledge and acceptance of this deception is so great in Washington that press people actually pride themselves on their ability to get "in-house" materials presented as objective news.

It is no wonder that both members of the House and the Senate express satisfaction with the way they are treated by the media. Robinson found that only 3 percent of the legislators whom he polled felt that they had been treated badly.[35] They may carp about the media's control of the national agenda or about how impossible it is to get the media to pay attention to issues which they regard as important, but the vast majority are satisfied, even with a press that has a reputation for frank, critical reporting. Members may not like some aspects of the media's performance, but they are not complaining, because the system works for them. The sacrifices that must be made, like abandoning certain issues that are likely to be ignored by the press or issues that might rebound in bad coverage, are considered routine. Efforts to prod the media into more thorough and intensive coverage of Congress will not emanate from the houses on the Hill.

## A CASE STUDY: THE REPUBLICAN CONFERENCE

The Republican Senate Conference Committee was formed during the Lincoln administration. By 1874, both parties had conference committees, which assisted "... in formulating and executing their legislative agenda."[36] Over the years, the activities of the conference committees evolved, and both the Democratic and Republican committees functioned as research arms for their respective parties. In 1979, under the direction of Senator Robert Packwood, a Republican from Oregon, the Republican Conference assumed direct responsibility for increased and improved communications with the public.[37] In order to accomplish this task, the Republican Conference Committee has developed strategies and programs for using the mass media to disseminate information. Communication with the public has also become a major concern of the Democratic Conference, but it has not developed the sophistication of the opposition party. Almost all of the modern techniques of political communication are used by the Republican Conference Committee. It is, in many ways, an organization that represents the wave of the future. This is the reason that the Republican Conference was chosen as the subject for this brief case study.

The director of the communications division of the Republican

Conference (hereafter referred to as the Conference) is Carter Clews, a young, aggressive, and articulate political operative. His background is in public relations. Before joining the Conference, Clews worked for the Right to Work Committee, a well-known conservative lobbying organization opposed to many programs of organized labor. The prime functions of the Conference, according to Clews, are to disseminate news nationally about the activities of Republican senators and to act as an in-house production shop for senators who need help in producing their own programs. This involves the Conference in the two areas of prime importance: working through existing media outlets to get favorable coverage and producing independent media materials. In this sense, their activities are similar to those of the press secretaries in the Senate.

Although the Conference's emphasis is on getting material about Republican senators printed and broadcast around the country, as opposed to the press secretaries' concern with local coverage, there is a potential for conflict. To minimize potential conflict, each secretary is given a "sign off" privilege, an opportunity to see the material going out about his or her boss. The Conference endeavors to keep senate press secretaries informed about the various programs. The Conference needs to reinforce its credibility with press secretaries and senators because it needs their continual participation. The Conference is, in many cases, asking senators to devote time to work on media projects that are not aimed at their local constituencies. It is asking senators to devote time to the production of programs to promote the greater good of the party.

Clews justifies this activity by citing a theory that depicts senators as representatives of all the people, not just the citizens of their state. "Every Senator has two constituencies—a primary and a secondary. There are only 100 Senators to serve 200 million people. In a very real sense every Senator is my Senator and every Senator is your Senator." From this perspective, it is vital that we receive views from every member of the Senate. Clews gives an example of the way citizens could employ this information. "If the senator from Kansas is sponsoring legislation that I support, I should know about it, so that I may write the senator to express my support or to tell him to support the legislation proposed by the senator from Kansas."

Clews is very careful to put the mission and activities of the Conference in the proper context. He consistently emphasizes that the Conference is not an organization that presents a partisan view. "We're not here to put out a view," says Clews; "we're here to put out information." Since the Conference is funded by taxpayers' dollars (with a $461 thousand budget), Clews's reticence about describing the organization as partisan is understandable. Yet it is difficult to take seriously the position that the Conference is not partisan. All the information distributed by the

Conference is generated by Republican senators or is supportive of policies and programs favored by Republicans.

Perhaps the single most important asset possessed by the Conference is its mailing list, containing the names of journalists, editors, publishers, commentators, and broadcasters across the country. According to Clews, the master list contains 25,000 names. This may well represent the most comprehensive list of media contacts in Washington. A full-time employee is assigned to the task of keeping the list current. Names are constantly added and deleted as personnel change assignments. This data base is maintained on a computer in the Conference's offices.

This master file on the computer is divided, subdivided, and cross-referenced, so that mailings of material can targeted at particular groups. There is a "list of lists," which contains the various categories of media people. There is a list that contains only the names of editorial page editors; there is another that lists education editors, foreign policy correspondents, farm journal editors, and a variety of others. Publications are also indexed. There are lists of small dailies (3000-50,000 circulation), small weeklies, the satellite press, Jewish publications, black publications, and so on. To do a mailing, one simply goes down the list and indicates the type of publications or the category of personnel that one wants to have material dispatched to, and the computer does the rest.

## Programs

One of the many Conference programs is called Op/Ed. This program sends opinion columns under the name of Republican senators to chosen newspapers. These types of columns generally appear on the page opposite the paper's editorial page. The Op/Ed list, which is a combination of several smaller lists, contains 4000 to 6000 names. Out of the thousands of potential editors on the list, about 130 are targeted for each Op/Ed mailing. Several criteria are used to select appropriate editors. There is a sophisticated distribution system, which insures that a certain number of newspapers in the same section of the country will receive the Op/Ed piece. No two newspapers in the same commercial market receive the same editorial, which guarantees exclusive rights to the paper that prints it. As the official description of the program notes: "The distribution of the editorial is designed to achieve a balance in both population density and geographic location."[38]

Packaging is an important part of the communications effort. Along with each Op/Ed piece, which is sent in a print-ready format, goes a cover letter, a biography of the author, and a 4" by 5" velox photograph. The Conference employs a full-time graphic artist, who designs accompanying graphics and cartoons. The idea is to provide the potential user with a product that is attractive and easy to include in the newspaper, a product which meets organizational needs.

Among the other programs aimed at the print media is one called "Issue Update." This provides newspapers with selected excerpts from several of the Op/Ed pieces distributed that month. Newspapers may use these excerpts on the Op/Ed page or include them in news articles. If a newspaper is doing a story on the economy, for example, and it receives an excerpt from an Op/Ed on the subject written by, say, Senator Howard Baker, the paper may choose to take a quote from the Op/Ed piece and use it in the news story. In this way, these opinion pieces regularly find their way into news articles. "Issue Update" is a monthly publication mailed to 13,000 newspapers and broadcast editors across the country.

"Conference Reports" is another Conference publication. It is similar to the regular newspaper columns produced by almost all members of the Senate, except that this column is syndicated nationwide. Like the Op/Ed program, this operation provides an opportunity for senators to reach a national audience. "Conference Reports," unlike the other print programs described, is distributed on a subscription basis. It is free of charge, but newspapers and broadcasters desiring the publication must complete a subscription card. Since the production and distribution of these materials is expensive, limiting distribution to subscribers is a means to cut costs. Restricting the publication to subscribers is also a natural way to target those who are more likely to print the material. According to Conference literature, the program has over 1000 subscribers, including some of the largest newspapers and radio and television stations in the country.

### Broadcast Programs

A division of the Conference has responsibility for the conception, production, and distribution of programs specifically aimed at radio and television. This is the area of the Conference that has experienced the most dramatic expansion over the last year. If the funds are available, it is likely to continue to grow. This operation is guided by a young woman who got her training as a public relations representative for the hot tub industry and as a press secretary to a liberal Democratic representative. This gives some idea of how interchangeable skills and political affiliations are in the nation's capital.

"Operation Airwaves" is the radio equivalent of the "Issue Update" program, except for the fact that it is a subscription program. (By now, you may have noticed the quasi-military code names given to these programs.) In "Operation Airwaves," anywhere from six to twelve GOP senators offer one minute of commentary on the same subject. One program, for example, features ten senators commenting about unemployment. These short tapes are designed for use on radio news programs. A radio station may excerpt any part of any statement and use it on a news program. If a radio program is reporting on unemployment, the program may use the remarks of several senators on the tape. These remarks are often preceded by a question or narrative by a local newscaster, so that the listener believes that the local news station has interviewed the senator specifically for the story. Listeners must be impressed with their local station's ability to interview these political notables. There are, according to the program director, 800 stations that subscribe to this program. The director claims that the program is widely and regularly used by subscribers and shows data to support the claim. The reported results of a recent poll of subscribers showed that 73 percent regularly use excerpts from the program. This is an impressive number and is probably not far off the mark. There are very good reasons for a local station to use these programs. Perhaps the reported success of the program makes it easy for senators to pay the 100 dollars that they contribute to cover some of the costs of the show.

There is also a television version of the "Issue Update" and "Operation Airwaves" program that goes by the name "Operation Uplink." "Operation Uplink" was born out of the discovery by someone at the Conference that there is a relatively inexpensive and efficient way to transmit television programs to stations around the country. The answer is to purchase satellite time and beam the programs to all the stations with satellite. Receiving disks provide a means to send programs to almost all of the cable and many of the commercial stations in the country. Satellite time can be purchased at a cost of $600 for thirty minutes. This is a fraction of the cost of mailing videotapes of the program around the country.

The first "Uplink" show took place on the night of President Reagan's State of the Union address. The idea was to provide time for Republican senators to comment on the President's address. These responses were satellcast to the senators' home states. Judging by the fact that twenty-six senators chose to participate, the idea appeared to be an instant success. Twenty minutes were set aside for each senator to produce a one-minute response. This provided time for senators to do a number of takes until they were satisfied with their performance. The White House cooperated by releasing advance copies of the President's speech. Since the speech was delivered late in the evening, it would have been impossible without advance copies of the speech to tape all the responses and send them off to stations around the country in time for the evening news. These taped comments about the speech were used by many local television stations. "Operation Uplink" was in orbit. It is now a regular feature of the Conference, providing time for thirteen senators to tape five minutes of comments to be used on local news programs.

"Conference Roundtable" is another of the shows produced by the

Conference. This program is also sent by satellite to 575 cable and 25 commercial stations that subscribe to the program. "Roundtable" is patterned after the TV news discussion program. Each show features three lawmakers (two senators and one representative) and two journalists in a question-and-answer format. According to the show's producer, the journalists are chosen at random from Hudson's Directory, which lists the names of the Washington press corps. However, when we reviewed the list of journalists who participated in shows between March 1982 and August 1983, there was a predominance of conservative journalists or journalists representing conservative publications. Journalists' willingness to participate in a show produced by a partisan political group and designed to disseminate the Republican point of view raises serious questions about the relationship between the press and political party organizations bent on influencing public opinion.

### Issues and Trends

The Conference is leading the way in bringing greater sophistication to many of the techniques used by individual members, as well as pointing the way to new paths in the effort to influence public opinion through the media. The Conference has chosen to make a concerted effort to work with small and medium-sized newspapers, radio stations, and cable and commercial stations around the country. Clews recognizes the error in regarding the press as monolithic or in concentrating on getting coverage on the networks and big outlets. The press is made up of thousands of journalists around the country, says Clews, "each of whom has different interests." Clews maintains that "being in the *Arizona Republic* is almost as important to us as being in the *New York Times.*"

The coming of cable television is received with great enthusiasm at the Conference. The proliferation of local cable stations provides a new, unique market for Conference programs. The Conference has been involved with cable since its inception and understands the medium as well as, if not better than, any other organization in Washington. Cable is particularly desirable because it provides a means to break the hold of the networks. The tremendous power of the networks always poses a danger. Cable television, according to Clews, is the leading edge of a movement that he labels "the dissolution of the mass." If the concentration of the media has led to the creation of undifferentiated mass, cable television is breaking society down into local groups with identifiable characteristics. Of course, the advantage for a group like this lies in the ability to target particular populations or citizens interested in single issues.

Cable's effects are already evident, according to Clews, who believes that the networks are "not as important as they once were and they'll be even less important in the future." Alternative networks, such as Cable News or The Christian Broadcasting Network, have already, in Clews's estimate, undermined the power of the networks. Clews maintains that The Christian Broadcasting Network, which carries many of the Conference's programs, is capable of delivering an audience of 30 million. Enthusiasm for independent networks is matched by the affection Clews has for the local press. There is almost a folkloric attachment to these country artisans. Clews describes the local press as easier to work with, as less rushed, as ready to sit down and listen to what you have to say. Local journalists are less cynical than the press from the big city papers, and it is easy to develop a close relationship with this group of journalists and managers. In practical terms, this means that the local press is far more receptive to printing and broadcasting materials produced by the Conference.

The Conference is also pointing the way to the more sophisticated use of independent programming. It has produced a variety of materials that can be employed by the media in ways that best suit their needs. In general, this material is professionally packaged and produced, in contrast to some of the material produced by legislative staffs, which is often rudimentary and bland. The Conference is particularly far-advanced in television production. It makes continual use of video equipment which is owned by Senator Ted Stevens, the Senate Majority Whip. Senators can be whisked off the floor into Stevens's chambers for quick television interviews. A new member of the staff is developing plans for producing a variety of new cable shows featuring members of the Senate. Content control is the name of the game. Whether all or part of these programs is used, there is no way to go wrong if the entire content of the show is controlled.

Where possible, Conference programs are designed to appeal directly to editors or management. There are only a few programs directed at the working journalist. The reason for this is simple, according to Clews: editors decide what will become news. This tendency to work through management will likely become more popular in individual Senate and House press operations.

## NOTES

1 Quoted in Robert O. Blanchard (ed.), *Congress and the News Media,* Hastings House, New York, 1974, p. 105.

2 Quoted in Douglas Cater, *The Fourth Branch of Government,* Houghton Mifflin Co., Boston, 1959, p. 47. From *The Fourth Branch of Government* by Douglas Cater. Copyright © 1959 by Douglas Cater, Jr. Reprinted by permission of Houghton Mifflin Company.

3 Doris Graber, *Mass Media and American Politics,* C.Q. Press, Washington, D.C., 1980, p. 209.

**4** Arthur H. Miller, Edie N. Goldenberg and Lutz Erbring, "Type-Set Politics: Impact of Newspapers on Public Confidence," *American Political Science Review*, vol. 73, March, 1979.

**5** Michael J. Robinson and Kevin R. Appel, "Network News Coverage of Congress," *Political Science Quarterly*, vol. 94, no. 3, Fall 1979, p. 412.

**6** David Halberstam, *The Powers That Be*, Dell, New York, 1980, p. 346. From *The Powers That Be* by David Halberstam. Copyright © 1980 by David Halberstam. Reprinted by permission of Alfred A. Knopf, Inc.

**7** Under provisions of the Fairness and Equal Time provision, networks may be required to provide time for Democrats to respond to a presidential message. The initial decision about whether to permit a response is made by the networks themselves. See Chapter 3 for a discussion of these provisions.

**8** "A Report on Simultaneous Television Network Coverage of Presidential Addresses to the Nation," *Congressional Record*, Jan. 20, 1976, p. 105.

**9** Les Brown, "Albert Says T.V. Favors Presidents," *New York Times*, Jan. 18, 1976.

**10** Robinson and Appel, "Network News Coverage," p. 417.

**11** Graber, *Mass Media*, p. 211.

**12** Michael J. Robinson, "Three Faces of Congressional Media," in *The New Congress*, Thomas E. Mann and Norman J. Ornstein (eds.), American Enterprise Institute, Washington, D.C., 1981, p. 83.

**13** Stephen Hess, *The Washington Reporter*, Brookings, Washington, D.C., 1980, p. 122.

**14** Susan Miller, "News Coverage of Congress: The Search for the Ultimate Spokesman," *Journalism Quarterly*, vol. 54, 1977, pp. 459-465.

**15** Robinson and Appel, "Network News Coverage," p. 412.

**16** Quoted in Cater, *Fourth Branch*, pp. 58-59.

**17** Halberstam, *Powers That Be*, pp. 201-202.

**18** Halberstam, *Powers That Be*, p. 285.

**19** Charles P. Sohner & Helen Martin, *American Government & Politics Today*, 3d ed., Glenview, Illinois, Scott-Foresman, 1980, p. 321

**20** There are at least two other factors which account for the increase in the number of committees. The increased complexity of the tasks facing Congress has led to more specialization and to a greater division of labor. Committees also multiplied as a result of the 1964 Legislative Reorganization Act, which, among other things, increased the funds for legislative staffs.

**21** The study followed coverage in the *Washington Post, Chicago Tribune, Los Angeles Times*, and *New Orleans Times-Picayune*. See Susan H. Miller, "News Coverage of Congress: the Search for the Ultimate Spokesman," *Journalism Quarterly*, vol. 54, 1977, pp. 459-465.

**22** Miller, "News Coverage of Congress," p. 463.

**23** Quoted in Susan H. Miller, "Congressional Committee Hearings and the Media: Rules of the Game," *Journalism Quarterly*, Winter 1978, p. 659.

**24** David L. Paletz and Robert M. Entman, *Media Power Politics*, Free Press, New York, 1980, p. 87.

**25** Robinson and Appel, "Network News Coverage," p. 417.

**26** Miller, "Congressional Committee Hearings," pp. 657-663.

27 Robinson, "Three Faces of Congressional Media," p. 83.
28 Ben H. Bagdikian, "Congress and the Media: Partners in Propaganda," *Columbia Journalism Review*, Jan./Feb., 1974. pp. 3-19.
29 Lee Polk, John Eddy, and Ann Andre, "Use of Congressional Publicity in Wisconsin District," *Journalism Quarterly*, vol. 52. Autumn 1978, p. 545.
30 Robinson, "Three Faces of Congressional Media," p. 80.
31 Robinson, "Three Faces of Congressional Media," p. 63.
32 Robinson, "Three Faces of Congressional Media," p. 68, and Graber, *Mass Media*, p. 210.
33 Robinson, "Three Faces of Congressional Media," p. 93.
34 *U.S. News and World Report*, Nov. 15, 1982, pp. 20-21.
35 Robinson, "Three Faces of Congressional Media," p. 82.
36 White Paper, *Senate Republican Conference: Past and Present*, p. 2.
37 White Paper, p. 2.
38 Senate Republican Conference, Communication in Brief.

# CHAPTER 9

# THE SUPREME COURT

## WHAT WE LEARN FROM THE MEDIA

The Supreme Court is a distinct branch of the federal government. It is ostensibly a legal rather than a political body. It does not pass legislation or decide foreign policy. Its mandate is to settle certain types of legal disputes and to decide the constitutionality of legislation or of acts of other branches of government.

The general public knows very little about what the Supreme Court does. This is partly the result of the Court's practice of operating in almost total secrecy. The conferences in which justices deliberate cases are closed not only to journalists but to virtually all Court personnel as well. Virtually every aspect of the decision-making process is carried out in strict secrecy. The public's lack of knowledge is also the result of the electronic and print media's lack of interest in what the Court does. Even if a citizen desired to learn more about the operation and output of the Court, this information could not be obtained by relying on the coverage in the mass media.

Despite the widespread ignorance about what the Court decides each term and about the implications of those decisions, there is a general sense that the Court makes very important decisions. In the 1984 presidential election, the issue of the future composition of the Court seemed to spark genuine concern among the electorate.

## Press Coverage Problem

No one, with the possible exception of the media corporations, seems satisfied with the way the Court is reported. Five members of the recent Courts have spoken or written about the problems:

> Chief Justice Warren's view has been that the Court is inadequately covered by the media. Three justices—Tom C. Clark, John M. Harlan, and William O. Douglas—have been specific in their criticism of press coverage. Justice William I. Brennan, Jr. has included the press in his general expressions of concern about misunderstandings of the Court. Perhaps the most involved critic of all was Felix Frankfurter, who played several significant, behind-the-scenes roles in calling attention to press coverage problems and in urging others to do something about them.[1]

One of the major complaints about the way the media cover the Court is the almost total lack of media stories about anything other than particular Court decisions. While the decisions are certainly a vital part of the Court's activity, it is by no means the only activity which has political importance. Critics claim that the reporting on decisions is narrow and ignores both the important political factors in Supreme Court decision-making and the public policy implications of particular decisions. In addition, the problem of covering only actual decisions is magnified by the fact that newspapers and electronic media report only a small number of decisions. A study of the 1974 term, which seems to be one of the few content analysis studies available, shows that the *New York Times,* considered the newspaper which best covers the Court, reported 112 of the 145 decisions of the term. Some of the large metropolitan dailies carried significantly fewer stories. The *Detroit News,* for example, covered only 44 of 145 decisions, while the Ann Arbor paper carried the wire service roundup (a feature on decisions), which provided news of fifty-three decisions.[2] A study of a Chicago newspaper found that 5 percent of all news stories were devoted to stories on the judiciary, primarily the Supreme Court.[3] Television coverage of the Supreme Court is even more meager. Only 3 percent of the stories on the TV news involves coverage of the courts, including the Supreme Court.[4] Many decisions of the Court, which often have very significant social, economic, and political consequences for the public, are given scant attention. The average decision, according to one researcher, "was either covered by no article or by articles of such short length that on the face the quality of coverage was poor."[5]

Aside from the complaints about the amount of coverage received by the Court, there are a variety of complaints about the quality of the coverage. Coverage is often focused on what is considered to be the most important decision of the day, while other decisions go unreported.[6] The news media focus on cases that they deem important. Although it is difficult to identify a set of hard-and-fast criteria which determine which cases are considered the most important, the standard commercial and organizational values play a determining role. The unusual cases, or those involving big names (such as Richard Nixon), are given high priority. Decisions about an issue of deep social and emotional importance, one laden with controversy, such as bussing or abortion, are likely to receive coverage.[7]

There are some other criteria which determine whether a decision is likely to get reported. Cases where the Court is sharply divided, where the vote is 5–4, are considered more newsworthy because of the conflict.[8] One area of Supreme Court activity that does not want for coverage involves freedom of press cases. On these matters, the media seem vigilant in bringing the decisions of the Court to the attention of the American public.[9]

Dissatisfaction with the practice of identifying and reporting decisions that are commercially viable is matched by disquiet over the way these decisions are presented. One study found that the coverage directly preceding the release of a decision does not necessarily imply coverage of the actual decision. Most coverage, according to this study, "... virtually ignored what the Supreme Court had said, and generally even what it had decided, and reported instead on national, state and local reactions and conjecture."[10]

Actual coverage of decisions tells how the Supreme Court decided a case but generally ignores reporting what the Court decided. It is comparable to learning the score of a sporting event but nothing about how the game was played or how the result affects the standings of the various participants. If, for example, the Supreme Court decides that schools which discriminate on the basis of race, sex, or other issues cannot be denied federal funds, the news media will generally report that decision. What the reader will not learn from coverage of the decision is the fact that the Court was unwilling to extend the guarantees of the Equal Protection clause to cases involving discrimination by private organizations, as opposed to discrimination by state institutions. While the task of translating the legal vocabulary into language that can be understood by the general public is not simple, it could certainly be done if there were an organizational commitment. If citizens are to have some basic understanding of the way the Court is interpreting the Constitution and of the impact of that interpretation on individual and collective rights, detailed explanations and analysis of Court decisions are a prerequisite.

There seems to be little disagreement with the sentiments of one student of Court-press relations who believes that the "Supreme Court is the worst reported and worst judged institution in the American system of government."[11] While some of the causes of the superficial reporting can be traced to the news organizations' definition of what is usable news, other problems result from the journalists' training and the way they define their tasks as Supreme Court reporters. What is especially significant and interesting is that many of the problems with coverage seem to be caused by the policies and procedures of the Supreme Court itself. In contrast to the president, and in even sharper contrast to Congress, the Supreme Court seems to follow a policy that makes it difficult for journalists to cover its activities accurately and comprehensively. In an epoch of budding political stars, the Court players have been content to wait in the wings.

## WHY WE LEARN WHAT WE LEARN

### Time

Only the wire services, the *New York Times,* the *Washington Post,* and the *Wall Street Journal* regularly cover the Supreme Court. Other media dispatch correspondents when a major news event is brewing. Generally, a major news event involves either the presentation of a controversial issue to the Court, such as the issue of whether the government could prohibit the *New York Times* from publishing the Pentagon Papers, or the Court's rendering of a decision in such a case.

AP and UPI provide most of the stories on the Court. Wire service stories are picked up by newspapers and radio and television stations across the country. This means that coverage of the Court is far more centralized than coverage of the Congress or the President, where the press pool is far larger. With the exception of regular readers of the major eastern newspapers (the *New York Times,* the *Wall Street Journal,* the *Washington Post),* the remainder of the nation learns about the Court through the words of the wire service staff.

The hottest news days at the Supreme Court are opinion days, when the Court's decisions are made public. Opinion day procedures have, until recently, followed a traditional script. A justice on the bench will either read the entire decision of the Court or summarize the decision. As soon as the justice begins to read the decision, copies of the opinion are given to reporters from the wire services, the *Times,* the *Post,* and the *Wall Street Journal,* all of whom have desks inside the Court. Word of the decision being read is sent from the Court to the press room, which is located on the ground floor of the building. Upon receiving notice of the decision being read in the majestic hall above, the press officer for the Court unlocks a steel cabinet containing the decisions that will be announced that day and distributes the appropriate decision to the journalists gathered in the press room. Now the task is to read the decision as quickly as possible, determine if it is potentially newsworthy, and, if it is, begin to construct the outlines of a story. When the justice finishes the reading of the opinion, the Court begins a reading of the next decision, and the procedure is repeated.

For the journalists, there are several problems with this system, but the most pressing is the time constraints. With decisions being delivered one after another, it is very difficult actually to read and digest the often complex logic and language of Supreme Court decisions. Yet the news organizations, particularly the wire services, demand that stories on important decisions go over the wires soon after they are released. The inherent time problem was compounded by the fact that, until 1965, the Court would issue decisions only on Mondays. Since there were only a finite number of Mondays in each term, this procedure required that a large number of cases be read each Monday. To add an even further obstacle, the Court would not convene until noon, soon before the afternoon deadlines.

The need to transmit the news as it occurs puts a very heavy burden on the journalists, particularly wire service reporters. They have no advance notice of which cases are to be announced that day, so they have no way of preparing themselves to write a story on the decision. While many members of the premanent press corps have knowledge of the important pending decisions, the large volume of cases puts limits on how much time they can devote to understanding each case. Wire service reporters prepare some stories in advance, leaving space to fill in information about the decision when it is delivered. Preparing the outline of a story may help in speeding it to wire service subscribers, but it does not overcome the problem of having to read and write quickly about the decision. The high premium placed on speedy coverage prohibits journalists from fully reading and digesting decisions and then translating the decisions into stories which can be understood by the general public. As long as the prime value is the speed with which the story can be dispatched, rather than the clarity and educational value of the report, the public is bound to remain abysmally ignorant about the impact of Court decisions. One well-known writer on the subject sums up the conflict this way: "The competition to be first with the story has been the chief obstacle to a better understanding of the Court and our liberties and laws."[12]

Time pressures have been somewhat lessened by a series of reforms instituted by the Court (discussed in later sections of the chapter). Despite these changes, the Supreme Court reporter is faced with institutional procedures which are not at all convenient. Supreme Court procedures remain out of step with the many measures taken by other branches of government to distribute news in ways that reflect concern for the constraints on reporters covering that branch of government.

## Secrecy

While the president and Congress strive for more media coverage, the Court seems content to labor in relative obscurity. There are no formal press conferences at the Court, and none of the justices employs a press secretary. In general, justices do not speak with journalists for the record and almost never submit to interviews. They are sequestered inside the Court, where armed guards patrol the entrances to the judges' chambers.

Secrecy has always characterized the work of the Court and is justified as a means of protecting the independence of the judiciary and the integrity of the legal process.[13] The secrecy and insulation of the Court are means of limiting political pressures that could affect the decision-making process. Secrecy is also designed to prevent insiders from taking economic or political advantage of upcoming decisions. The secrecy that surrounds the decision-making process does not end when a Court decision becomes public. Justices will not generally comment on a decision or editorialize about what considerations influenced their reasoning. Once the decision is released, it becomes part of the public record, and it is left to the legal scholars and policy analysts to dissect the decision and pass judgment. Justices maintain a public posture of studied aloofness.

The Court has been relatively successful in maintaining a high degree of secrecy. In comparison to other branches of federal government, it is a very small and very cohesive institution, which, no doubt, accounts for its success in keeping its enterprising staff from funneling material to journalists.

Because of the premium put on secrecy, the journalist is not able to use sources in the accustomed fashion. As a matter of fact, the journalist covering the Court has very few traditional sources. There is really nothing for journalists and their sources to exchange, and, consequently, there is no basis for a relationship.

The Supreme Court does have a press office and a press officer, who is an official liaison between the Court and the media. But the press officer at the Court, unlike the press secretary in the legislative and executive branches, is not a source for the journalist. In the chapter on Congress, we saw that the press secretary is the journalist's most natural source. At the Court, the press officer's tasks are essentially administrative. He or she acts, as one observer noted, as "primarily a feeder of information, not a source."[14] The press secretary at the Court merely facilitates the delivery of information that is available to all journalists. A good source, on the other hand, provides a journalist with exclusive information.

Despite all the elaborate security measures, there have been leaks. Many of the leaks involved some of the most controversial cases before the Court. *Time* reported that the Court would find that abortion was legal by a 7–2 vote a week before that decision was made public. National Public Radio was, on the basis of a leak, able to predict the Supreme Court's 1977 5–3 decision against reviewing the convictions of the Watergate defendants.[15] And, in 1979, ABC-TV correctly reported a Supreme Court decision regarding the rights of federal courts to question journalists about thoughts they had had and conclusions they had come to while preparing a story.[16] It is reasonable to assume that these leaks resulted, in part, from journalists' appetite for information— that the journalists either encouraged a leak or let it be known that they were prepared to print certain information that might happen to find its way onto their desks. Their appetite for information was, no doubt, enhanced by their editors' interest in getting a scoop on one of these big stories. So, despite the extraordinary security measures, which were reinforced and expanded with each of the major breaches in secrecy, journalists have, on more than one occasion, been able to break into the inner sanctums, if editors encourage such an invasion.

In 1979, Bob Woodward (who, with Carl Bernstein, had broken the Watergate story at the *Washington Post)* and Scott Armstrong published *The Brethren,* which provided a detailed account of many of the secret deliberations of the Court between 1969 and 1976, the first seven years of the tenure of Chief Justice Warren E. Burger. What is amazing about the book is the very detailed descriptions of the highly secretive judicial conferences, including repeated references to statements made by the justices during the conference. This sort of material had never before reached the public. Equally intriguing is the fact that the authors seemed to have a relatively easy time locating sources who were willing, if not eager, to discuss what they knew about the Court's most sensitive operations and to provide the authors with confidential documents to support their claims. Woodward and Armstrong claim to have conducted "interviews with 200 people, including several justices, more than 170 former law clerks, and several dozen employees of the Court."[17]

If, despite the elaborate secrecy, journalists are capable of discovering important aspects of the decision-making process, why do they seldom make the effort to acquire and report this information? One of the factors that inhibit their desire to pierce the wall of secrecy is the abiding respect they have for the institution of the Supreme Court. In general, journalists show an inordinately high degree of respect for the work and the legitimacy of the Court.[18] The simple fact that justices do not openly engage in electoral politicking or bureaucratic intrigues gives them a special character in Washington. Another factor which explains the journalists' timidity is the editors' lack of interest in detailed stories about the work of the Court. Even if one were to work hard to discover interesting elements of the justices' deliberations, a news organization would probably show little interest or enthusiasm, unless the public had an awareness of the case or it involved a well-known figure or dramatic scenario. Consequently, there is no incentive for the journalist to provide anything more than the routine, superficial coverage. These two tendencies reinforce the pattern of reporting and, as we shall see, add to the Court's ability to influence the way it is covered.

## Skills

Even given a desire by news organizations to cover the Court adequately, the skills required are so distinct from those practiced by journalists that they would not be equipped for the task. Take, for example, the skill of interviewing, which is probably the most developed and valued journalistic skill and the one that yields the journalist most information. Interviewing is of little use at the Court. There is virtually no one to interview who is willing or able to provide the journalist with usable information.

The same holds true for aggressiveness, which is a prized trait in the journalist but is not highly valued or particularly useful if one's organization simply desires stories on decisions. Reporters do not even cover the Court in the sense that they cover other institutions. They almost never attend any of the Court's sessions where arguments are heard. Covering the Court is equivalent to gathering in the press room and waiting for the press officer to pass out copies of decisions. Journalists never have occasion to interview participants, to develop sources, and to provide their readers with an inside view of the personalities, procedures, and policies of the institution.

The skills that are most important to the journalist covering the Court are analytic skills. A good Court journalist is simply one who can read a complex court decision, understand the legal reasoning, and write a short story that can be understood by the general public.[19] This requires some familiarity with the language employed in decisions and some understanding of the way legal arguments are structured and analyzed. If the journalists covering the Court do not possess these skills in sufficient quantities, there is a good chance that the reporting will, on occasion, be misrepresentative, inaccurate, or even completely false. Such is often the case. Several studies have found a high proportion of inaccurate reporting in stories concerning the Court.[20] It would almost be unreasonable, considering the procedures followed by the Court and the background of journalists, to expect it to be otherwise. Reporters are not trained in analytic skills. In the course of their careers, they almost never do the sort of detailed analysis of documents or primary sources that is required to understand the operation of the Court and the significance of its decisions. They rely almost entirely on the oral interviews to acquire data for a story. At best, journalists are skilled craftsmen who can take data and turn them into a story that can inform. Only a very few have the ability independently to analyze the significance of primary data, which is what must be done to understand the implications of many of the Court's decisions.

After years of complaints about the journalists' inability to understand the work of the Court, and with the urging and intervention of Justice Frankfurter, who was particularly disturbed by the lack of clarity and precision that characterized the news media coverage of the Court, the *New York Times* agreed to send its Supreme Court correspondent back to school. Anthony Lewis was sent off to the Harvard Law School for a year of intensive study. According to observers, Lewis's reporting was of a different caliber as a result of his year at Harvard; "...his reporting extends to detailed coverage of the Court as an institution rather than to stories of isolated decisions alone."[21]

Today, some of the reporters covering the Supreme Court are lawyers, and others have some training in the field. There are, however, many who have come to the Court directly from another beat. A 1974 survey found that most journalists covering the Court had general assignment backgrounds.[22] Few reporters seem to spend enough time on the Supreme Court beat to acquire and master the requisite skills. In the same 1974 survey, reporters covering the Court in 1974 had an average tenure of 2.5 years.[23] The relatively short tenure of Supreme Court reporters may be because journalists are generally not very happy languishing in the basement pressroom of the Supreme Court buildings, far from the excitement of the more glamorous political beats.

The nature of the institution and of the work gives these journalists considerably less power than other members of the Washington press corps. At the Supreme Court, as David L. Grey notes: "Newsmen are accepted but not courted."[24] From the news organization's point of view, there is little sense in wasting a good, experienced reporter at the Supreme Court, where the coverage is regarded more as an obligation than an opportunity. So the lot of Supreme Court reporters is apparently not a happy one. They do not often get to use the tools of the trade, they are locked out of the inner sanctums, and they have few sources and very little power in relation to their colleagues. This seemingly unhappy situation results, in large part, from the policies adopted by the Court.

This total disregard for the needs of the press would seem to indicate that the Court has very little interest in the amount or type of coverage it receives. Is this the truth?

### Does the Supreme Court Need the Media?

One of the main reasons that politicians are so keenly concerned about the coverage they receive is that they believe that the media's portrayal of their activities will significantly influence their chances for reelection, and, of course, most politicians are concerned about keeping their jobs. Supreme Court justices do not need to be concerned about being reelected. Appointed for life, they can be unconcerned about the vicissitudes of electoral politics. It is unnecessary for Supreme Court justices to keep their names before the public and maintain a good electoral profile. Nor has it been necessary, except on a few occasions, to protect the institution from outside political pressures. There does not seem to be the same compelling need to use the media—a need which creates the political establishment's dependence on the media and, of course, gives the media their power.

While the needs of the Court may not be the same as those of other institutions, this does not mean that the Court is impervious to the way the media report its activities or that the Court does not attempt to exercise influence over the press. Justices follow the coverage they receive in the media, particularly in the eastern press, which dominates Court coverage. They are sensitive to press reports of the reaction of other political elites and of the public to their decisions. Justices use the press as a barometer to measure public pressure and to determine the effect of their work. Since justices have virtually no contact with the public or with party or political figures who may have readings on public attitudes, the media are their most important source for this type of information.

Aside from depending on the media for readings of the prevailing political climate, justices also realize that the media are the sole means for the public to learn about the activities of the Court. The public's attitude toward the Court, which is almost entirely formed by the media's coverage of its activities, is vital to the Court. Since the Court has limited power to enforce its decisions, it must, to a large degree, depend on the voluntary compliance of the population.[25] Whether the public chooses to comply, resist, or defy Supreme Court decisions depends on the attitudes of the public toward the Court. If the public believes that the Court is exercising legitimate authority in a ruling, people are more likely to comply than if a decision appears to be beyond the bounds of what people believe the Court has a right to decide. As one scholar notes:

"... respect for the Supreme Court and law in general depends increasingly upon popular appreciation of the inherent merits of the Court's work."[26] The Court depends on the press to show its "inherent merits" to the population at large.

When the Court is portrayed as crossing the boundaries of legitimacy, the public is likely to react, particularly if the issue in question is perceived as having some impact on people's lives or is a moral or political question that they regard as important. Massive resentment of and resistance to *Brown* v. *Board of Education*, the landmark decision that found the "separate but equal" doctrine unconstitutional, was fueled by the belief that the Supreme Court did not have the legitimate authority to tell people where they could send their children to school. Public attitudes were shaped by the more intensive and critical reporting of the case. Although the media were certainly not the only forces creating public disquiet about the decision, the failure to treat the decision with the customary blend of deference and indifference left the Court without the bedrock of legitimacy routinely provided for its decisions.

The Court's interest in the coverage it receives varies and depends on a variety of factors. Some justices might be particularly interested in the way the news media cover an important case in which they wrote a majority or dissenting opinion. In order for the justices to take an interest in the media's coverage of their activities, there must be coverage to be interested in. The routine coverage, consisting of minimal attention to the decisions in what are considered to be important cases and to the reaction to these decisions, does not provide much of a basis for attracting the justices' attention. When the amount of coverage increases, the justices' interest in that coverage also increases. The key to more coverage is the existence of cases with dramatic, legal, or political conflict.

One of the fiercest conflicts between the Court and the president took place in the early days of Franklin Roosevelt's New Deal legislative program. The Supreme Court ruled one after another of Roosevelt's New Deal programs unconstitutional. Frustrated by the Court's actions, Roosevelt threatened to seek legislation to enlarge the number of justices, thereby limiting the power of those sitting on the Court. This conflict appealed to the media, which focused a great deal of attention on the Court. All of a sudden, the slowest beat in Washington was now the center of excitement. According to one media analyst, the continuous attention "... turned Supreme Court reporters into combat correspondents."[27] With the Court's future at stake, there can be little doubt that the justices followed the media's coverage carefully, hoping to learn how other political elites were reacting to the crisis and to see what was being reported to the public and how public opinion was shaping up on the issue.

Conflict between the Supreme Court and other political institutions will almost always attract media attention. These are also conflicts in which the political stakes may be very high. The stage for this type of drama was again set during the Watergate period, when then President Nixon refused to surrender tape recordings secretly made in the Oval Office to a Senate and House investigating committee. Nixon claimed that he was protected from disclosure by executive privilege. Congress challenged this claim and turned to the Supreme Court to settle the impasse. The Court found in favor of Congress's right to have the tapes.

Because these cases generate a lot of news about the Court and affect people's attitudes toward the Court, it is logical for the justices to be interested in the way they are being reported. If, for example, all the justices whom Nixon appointed had voted in favor of Nixon, the public would quickly learn of those votes, and the question of whether they cast their votes out of political loyalty would inevitably have been raised. The justices are also interested in the way these cases are reported, because they realize that the media will play the paramount role in interpreting the conflict and its resolution to the American people. These cases also illustrate another important principle; if the coverage of the Court is more systematic, the justices and the Court itself will likely be held more accountable. There is more discussion on this later in the chapter.

The Supreme Court will also get considerable attention when it decides cases that produce wide public backlash. The Warren Court was dedicated to a policy of "judicial activism"—a position which advocated a strong social role for the courts. This activist posture drew much public wrath. From early in the Warren term, when the Court decided *Brown* v. *Board of Education*, the Warren Court was faced with hostility and conflict. This was the most heavily-covered period in Supreme Court history.[28] Thus, it is not suprising that Warren was acutely interested in how the Court was faring in the press; he was very much the politician, aware of the importance of public appearances.[29]

An example of a more recent case which has created a continuing social tremor is *Roe* v. *Wade,* in which the Supreme Court ruled in favor of legalized abortion. In a recent and unprecedented interview with Justice Blackmun (discussed in some detail below), the Associate Justice describes how the public has lashed out at him (Blackmun wrote the majority decision in the case). He has received 45,000 letters about the decision: "Think of any name," he says, "I've been called it in these letters: Butcher of Dachau, murderer, Pontius Pilate, Adolf Hitler."[30] More than ten years after the decision, Justice Blackmun is still sometimes picketed by antiabortion groups when he speaks at law schools. Recently, the FBI announced that it was investigating a death threat to Justice Blackmun by a group calling itself The Army of God. The continual turmoil over abortion was probably one of the reasons that the justice agreed to comment publicly on the case.

Despite its veneer of disinterest, there is much to suggest that the Court realizes the power of the media and looks to the media for a variety of purposes. News media make the population aware of the Court's decisions and play a pivotal role in giving the Court and its decisions the legitimacy necessary to foster voluntary compliance. In an age where the legitimacy of all government is subject to increased scrutiny, supportive treatment by the news media is no small blessing.

In general, Supreme Court reporters have been very cooperative in helping the Court maintain a desirable image. Some observers suggest that Supreme Court reporters understand the Court's needs and are motivated by a desire to help the Court: "[Journalists] sense, if they do not fully comprehend, the vulnerability of the Court's legitimacy."[31] Awed by the majesty of the Court and respectful of its traditions and its supposed political neutrality, journalists come to identify with the institution and to protect it. The reporting is deferential. They are rarely critical of the justices' opinions.[32] The Supreme Court escapes much of the cynicism and suspicion which other political elites regard as part and parcel of much of the reporting of the national media. Because the Court holds an "anointed" place in the eyes of the media, it does not need to make the same effort to influence the news media.

### Strategies for Influencing the Media

Whether the Court is trying to limit the media's exposure to its activities or is concerned about the way certain issues are being covered, there are various methods available to aid the Court in influencing the coverage it receives. Carrying out its functions in secret sessions has a justifiable role in guarding the integrity of the legal system, but it may also be used as a mechanism to control the information the media receive. Since the media's coverage of the Court depends on the information that the Court makes available, this ability to function out of the sight of the press and to control the information being released puts the Court in a powerful position:

> By not trying to manipulate public opinion, the Court paradoxically is manipulating public opinion. The Court controls the flow of news by releasing only what it wants to say and by often leaving vague what it does not want to say.[33]

This ability to operate in secrecy gives the Supreme Court a tool which other branches of government covet in the media age. It provides a natural and justifiable means to centralize and control the flow of information getting to the press. A number of recent presidents have tried very hard to plug the flow of information from the executive branch of government to the media, but none has come close to being as firmly in control as the Court.

Secrecy provides a rationale for controlling the news and gives the Court a unique informational character. According to one Court scholar, it has put the Court in the enviable position of being able to get regularly what it wants from the media. "Perhaps the court's standards of news judgment are imposed upon newsmen to a greater extent than those in any other field of governmental activity."[34]

Yet, as the media grow in political importance, the pressure on the Supreme Court to loosen its iron grip on the dissemination of news has mounted. And there are signs that the Court is slowly altering some time-honored practices. In the last two decades, the Court has altered its decision-day practices and has been slightly more willing to communicate with and through the media. Chief Justice Warren was sympathetic to the idea that the Court should take a more active role in the opinion arena. Justices Frankfurter, Goldberg, and Douglas frequently departed from the practice of making only very limited public appearances. These judges had a relatively high public profile, gave frequent speeches, and wrote extensively on Court matters. Media executives lobbied for procedural changes. They argued that some of the problems that the legal community found in the media's coverage of the Court were the result of the Byzantine procedures used by the Court. If the Court desired better or more extensive coverage, it would be necessary to eliminate the procedural obstacles.

Even with the mounting pressures and the growing realization of the media's importance, there was significant resistance to change. Supreme Court traditions are firmer and more resistant than many political traditions. Some members of the Court feared that procedural changes might lead to a breach of secrecy. Others felt that it would be inappropriate for the Court to appear to be giving in to the demands of the news media.[35]

Eventually, the Court agreed to modify the decision-day proceedings. Mondays were still reserved as decision days, but the Court also used other weekdays to deliver opinions. This would mean more opinion days and fewer opinions per day. Under the Mondays-only system, there might be only fifteen to twenty opinion days in the entire October-to-June term. Under the new scheme, the number of opinion days per term has doubled.

Additional concessions were forthcoming. Starting time was moved back to 10 a.m. from noon, leaving the journalists with more time to read opinions and write stories before their deadlines. Readings of the opinions were somewhat spaced out, so that one reading did not immediately follow another. The Association of American Law Schools chipped in by funding a project that prepares legal memoranda for the media on important cases that have been argued before the Court.[36] None of these changes was very sweeping or had major impact on the way the Court was covered. What the changes did was make the job of the reporter easier.

At the time that these changes were made, there were, according to John MacKenzie, who covered the Court for the *Washington Post,* a variety of other ideas for change that were rejected. A suggestion that the Court issue opinions to journalists a few hours before they were made public, to give journalists adequate time to study them, was rejected. Justice Abe Fortas, at his confirmation, urged the Court to consider adopting new policies to facilitate radio and television coverage. But the Court was evidently satisfied with the very limited coverage it received on television. It was quite evident that there would not be any significant additional TV coverage unless the Court was prepared to allow further opportunities for television pictures.

Decision making in the Supreme Court is still carried out in secrecy, but there have been recent signs that some change may be in the offing. Despite the fact that few justices were willing to speak to Woodward and Armstrong while they were writing *The Brethren,* the authors were able to provide readers with a detailed inside view of the workings of the Court. In recent years, Justices William O. Douglas and Hugo Black have granted television interviews, departing from the protocol of refusing interviews. Perhaps the most outspoken justice is Associate Justice Harry Blackmun, who seems willing, even eager, to talk to the press.

In 1982, Justice Blackmun participated in a 50-minute program on the Cable News Network, which has a significant viewing audience across the country. Just a few months after this appearance, Justice Blackmun agreed to talk to a *New York Times* reporter at length about his views on the work of the Court. The interviews led to a long feature article in the *New York Times Magazine.* Blackmun was well aware of the fact that he was breaking with Supreme Court protocol. "We shouldn't talk out of school," he said. "The rule around here is no interviews at all."[37]

Not only did Blackmun violate the unwritten rule against interviews, he also spoke candidly about some of the innermost workings and conflicts of the Court. He openly criticized the Chief Justice and charged that the Court's decisions were influenced by ideological factors. Justices Burger, Rehnquist, and O'Connor were singled out as a group that was particularly motivated by political ends. Blackmun used the interview to expound his own theory on the political balance of the Court: "I know I would be happier if the Court didn't plunge back and forth from left to right, just by the addition of a new Justice."[38]

Why would Justice Blackmun risk the censure of his colleagues by breaking the vow of silence so publicly? There is little in the interview itself that suggests an answer. According to the interviewer, Blackmun was motivated to speak because of political and personal concerns. "I have a little anger underneath it all," Blackmun said. "Anger from being categorized over the 12 years I've been here in a way that I think never fit."[39] Blackmun's political intention is to alert the public to danger of the "rightward" shift in the composition of the Court and to endorse publicly the idea of keeping the Court in the political center.

There is a significance in the Blackmun interview that is not expressed by the justice himself or the interviewer. If Blackmun was motivated by a desire to set the record straight about his performance on the Court—and there is every reason to believe that this was one impelling reason for the interview—it is fascinating to note that Blackmun should choose to do this by communicating through the electronic and print media. Who is going to write the history that Blackmun is interested in altering? Choosing to go public through the media signals, at the very least, a recognition that histories, even those of Supreme Court justices, are partially the result of the way the media record their activities. Blackmun has done something unique by attempting to use the media as a means to alter public opinion, as well as attempting to influence the way his portrait has been painted by the media. Of course, for most political actors, this is routine. But Supreme Court justices have never publicly behaved like other political actors.

Is Blackmun's interview a harbinger of things to come? Soon after the Blackmun interview, Justice Stevens delivered a ringing public denunciation of Supreme Court conservatives.[40] It was recently reported that Chief Justice Burger had been doing his own behind-the-scenes press work, carrying on off-the-record briefings with journalists covering the Court. These examples represent some significant changes in the relationship between the justices and the press. This doesn't mean that the justices of the Court will soon be hosting their own television shows, like their colleagues in the Senate and White House. But it does show that there is growing recognition of the power of the media not only to define reality but also, in the course of doing so, to influence history.

It would be surprising, although not impossible, to envision a situation where the Court would quickly and dramatically alter its approach toward the media. Such a revolution could come about only if the Court felt an extreme political threat from another branch of government or from a movement of irate citizens. Since this sort of institutional threat does not seem likely in the near future, the changes in the relationship between the media and the Court will be slow but steady. Change will occur because the Court recognizes that the media now play a crucial role in informing the public about the Court's work and in promoting the Court's legitimacy.

While there is a realization that politics change, there is also a reluctance to tamper with practices that have kept the Court removed from the daily, sordid commerce which takes place between Washington's political establishment and the media. To date, the media have treated the Supreme Court well, and this treatment stems largely from the Court's ability to retain secrecy and to control the flow of information. If the Court changes these policies, there will be no returning to old procedures. Once the press is admitted into the inner sanctum, it will be very hard to justify expelling it. This is the gamble, and there is every reason to believe that the justices are aware of the stakes.

## CONCLUSION

After this analysis of the impact of the media's coverage of Congress and of the executive, it is legitimate to ask whether the media's general lack of interest in the Court (and the justices' reticence to communicate with the press) has helped the institution avoid some of the pitfalls of politics in the media age. Does the institution function more effectively in secret?

One of the potential effects of more and better coverage of the Court might be an increase in the justices' accountability to the public at large. Virtually the entire population is ignorant of who sits on the Court and of the direction that their votes traditionally take. If the votes of the justices were held up to continual analysis and public scrutiny, justices might be more concerned about the way the public perceives their performance. Of course, justices do not need to be reelected and are, theoretically, immune from public pressures. Yet there is much evidence to indicate that justices are concerned about the way they are perceived by the public.

While more intensive coverage and analysis of Supreme Court decisions might produce this sort of accountability, it is not at all evident that this exposure would make the Supreme Court a better institution. One could argue that it is important for the justices to interpret the Constitution in relative isolation, without being influenced by considerations of the way their decisions will be received by the public. Of course, this argument presumes that justices now make decisions devoid of political considerations. To dispel this myth, one need look no further than the statements of Justices Blackmun and Stevens, who criticize their colleagues for deciding cases according to political rather than strictly legal criteria. Political ideology plays a key role in determining voting patterns. This being the case, there is a strong argument to be made for the idea that the work of the Court should receive greater public exposure.

There is an even more serious reason why the prevailing coverage of the Court is inadequate and politically disturbing. Many of the decisions of the Supreme Court have an enduring legal and political impact on citizens. The present coverage of the Court leaves citizens without a basis on which to understand the legal and political consequences of Supreme Court decisions. If democratic society is built on a Constitutional foundation of rights and liberties, a foundation which is often altered by decisions of the Court, citizens must know the nature and scope of their rights.

Secrecy is an important part of the judicial process and needs to be guarded. Even within the present strictures, there is much more the media could do to create some public awareness about the decisions of the Court. There is also good reason to consider lessening the secrecy attached to some Court activities. Opening the Supreme Court chambers to all of the press and televising some proceedings from the Court are ideas worthy of consideration.

Yet, if the Supreme Court were to open up its proceedings tomorrow, it wouldn't make much difference in the future coverage of the Court unless news organizations were willing to commit many more resources to covering, explaining, and interpreting the activities of the Court. Unless the issues before the Court were dramatic and fit within the prevailing values determining the news, there is no reason to believe that the news media would provide the coverage needed to inform and educate the public.

## NOTES

1 David L. Grey, *The Supreme Court and the Mass Media*, Evanston, Northwestern Univ. Press, 1968, p. 50.
2 David Ericson, "Newspaper Coverage of the Supreme Court: A Case Study," *Journalism Quarterly*, vol. 54., Autumn, 1977, p. 605.
3 Doris Graber, *Mass Media and American Politics*, Washington, CQ Press, 1980, p. 194.
4 Graber, *Mass Media*, p. 194.
5 Ericson, "Newspaper Coverage," p. 607.
6 Ericson, "Newspaper Coverage," p. 605.
7 Grey, *Supreme Court and the Mass Media*, p. 77.
8 David W. Leslie, "The Supreme Court in the Media: A Content Analysis." Quoted in David L. Paletz and Robert M. Entman, *Media Power Politics*, New York, Free Press, 1981, p. 104.

9 Hale V. Dennis, "A Comparison of Coverage of Speech and Press Verdicts of the Supreme Court," *Journalism Quarterly*, no. 56, 1979, pp. 43-47.

10 Chester A. Newland, "Press Coverage of U.S. Supreme Court," *Western Political Quarterly*, no. 17, March 1964, p. 27.

11 Ericson, "Newspaper Coverage," p. 605.

12 John P. MacKenzie, "The Supreme Court and the Press," in Kenneth S. Devol, *Mass Media and the Supreme Court*, 2d ed., New York, Hastings House, 1976, p. 353.

13 There is some question as to whether the procedures to insure secrecy actually ferret out political influence and permit the Court to make judgments based strictly on the facts and legal issues. Most observers are convinced that the Court is subject to a variety of political pressures, including the influence of public opinion. See, for example, Harold Spaeth, *An Introduction to Supreme Court Decision Making*, San Francisco, Chandler Press, 1972.

14 Grey, *Supreme Court and the Mass Media*, p. 46.

15 William Rivers, *The Other Government: Power and The Washington Media*, New York, Universe Books, 1982, p. 88.

16 Rivers, *The Other Government*, p. 88.

17 Carl Woodward and Scott Armstrong, *The Brethren*, New York, Simon and Schuster, 1979.

18 See Paletz and Entman, *Media Power Politics*, p. 103, and Grey, *Supreme Court and the Mass Media*, p. 58.

19 Grey, *Supreme Court and the Mass Media*, p. 43.

20 See, for example, Newland, "Press Coverage," and Grey, *Supreme Court and the Mass Media*.

21 Newland, "Press Coverage," p. 21.

22 Larry Berkson, *The Supreme Court and Its Publics*, Lexington, Massachusetts, Lexington Books, 1978, p. 58.

23 Berkson, *Supreme Court and Its Publics*, p. 58.

24 Grey, *Supreme Court and the Mass Media*, p. 47.

25 There are rare cases in which the President may act to enforce Supreme Court rulings. Eisenhower, for example, sent troops to Little Rock, Arkansas, to enforce the Court's order to integrate the public schools.

26 Newland, "Press Coverage," p. 15.

27 Rivers, *The Other Government*, p. 92.

28 Grey, *Supreme Court and the Mass Media*, p. 18.

29 Grey, *Supreme Court and the Mass Media*, p. 18.

30 John A. Jenkins, "A Candid Talk With Justice Blackmun," *New York Times Magazine*, Feb. 20, 1983. The New York *Times* Company. Copyright © 1983. Reprinted by permission.

31 Paletz and Entman, *Media Power Politics*, p. 103.

32 Grey, *Supreme Court and the Mass Media*, p. 55.

33 Grey, *Supreme Court and the Mass Media*, p. 22.

34 Grey, *Supreme Court and the Mass Media*, p. 79.

35 Grey, *Supreme Court and the Mass Media*, p. 36.

36 MacKenzie, "The Supreme Court and The Press," in Devol, *Mass Media and the Supreme Court*, p. 359. Copyright © 1971, 1976, 1982. Reprinted by

permission of Hastings House, Publishers.

**37** Jenkins, "A Candid Talk," p. 22.

**38** Jenkins, "A Candid Talk," p. 23.

**39** Jenkins, "A Candid Talk," p. 23.

**40** Stuart Taylor, Jr., "Justice Stevens Is Sharply Critical of Supreme Court Conservatives," *New York Times,* Aug. 5, 1984, p. 1.

# CHAPTER 10

# THE CORPORATION

The history of the relationship between the media and big business has been a history of easy accommodation; the corporation has used the media to sell its products, and the media, except for instances of business scandals, have left the assumptions underlying the corporate structure untouched. During the 1970s, this relationship changed, with both participants, the media and big business, reassessing their relationship to each other.

We have seen the emergence of the media as a political force. We have described how candidates for political office and political officials vie for favorable media coverage and how they use the media to mold opinion. As the media have become the most prominent arena for political activity, it is not surprising that interest groups have begun to use the media to push political policy. The American corporate structure, as an interest group, is particularly well-prepared to use the media to expand its political influence. Not only does big business have the money to wage media campaigns, it also has the expertise of the media professionals— advertisers, public relations agents, and market researchers—who grew up and developed their skills in the service of corporate America, in order to sell both its products and its ideology.

Although we would suggest that corporate America would have eventually recognized the media as a political force, events of the 1970s made it absolutely essential for some companies and industries to reach many different audiences and influence public opinion directly. During the 1970s, corporate America came under attack from a variety of citizens' groups, such as consumerists, environmentalists, woman's liberation advocates, the civil rights movement, and anti-nuclear plant advocates. Such groups began to generate news that exposed policies of corporate abuse and neglect to which big business had to respond. In responding to these citizens' groups, corporate America has a clear advantage. Business interests have both financial superiority and media expertise at their command. Business interests also have the advantage of clearly-defined goals. For example, attacks on the auto industry come from relatively amorphous and broadly-based consumer groups, who want a variety of different things. Some want auto safety, some better gas mileage, some cleaner motors, and so on. In contrast, the auto industry, a clearly definable and identifiable entity, wants to sell cars and make a profit.

Government regulation of business also grew during the 1970s, particularly in health, safety, and environmental areas. For example, the creation of the Occupational Safety and Health Administration (OSHA) and the Environmental Protection Agency (EPA) meant that government was intervening directly in business affairs. Government regulation means increased scrutiny of corporate operations. Regulation requires corporations to divulge certain aspects of their operation that they have previously been able to keep secret. With increased disclosure, journalists have a new and independent source of information about corporations.

At the same time, the economic uncertainties of the 1970s and a variety of business scandals have made big business news. As the media's coverage of business news has expanded, corporate America has responded by expanding its public relations efforts in order to counteract the adverse publicity and to begin to lobby against government regulation. Corporations have stepped up their use of the media to create a more favorable and benevolent image and to convince the public that government is treating the corporation unfairly. Corporations also have used the media to wage war against citizens sponsoring ballot initiatives that have conflicted with corporate interests.

## CORPORATE NEWS MANAGEMENT

The American corporation has several distinct advantages when it comes to media news coverage, not the least of which is the fact that the media depend upon the corporate advertising dollar for survival. Corporations can punish any media enterprise by withdrawing or withholding advertising. However, such instances have become rare in recent years. Corporations' real advantage lies in the fact that, as private institutions, they are not accountable to the public and can deny reporters access to corporate information. Private executives, unlike elected officials, do not have to answer to the press. How many corporate presidents can any of us name? Who is the president of IBM, Mobil, AT&T, or General Motors? Corporations must make financial statements public, including the names of their principal stockholders, and they may have to answer questions asked by government regulatory agencies, but they do not have to say anything to the news media. Thus, in the day-to-day routine coverage of business news, the corporation has the upper hand.

Covering business is, in large measure, the processing of stock and bond tables, investment advice, wire service stories from New York and Washington, futures prices, foreign exchange rates, and, overwhelmingly, corporate press releases. Since reporters do not have access to corporate information, they come to rely on corporate press releases and the public relations departments which produce them. Public relations departments answer routine questions, provide background information, and protect executives from unwanted attention.

The corporate press release is the most straightforward attempt at news management. Through it, information favorable to the corporation is distributed to the media, in the hope that the release will be printed or broadcast without further investigation. Routine press releases include such things as the announcement of new policies or procedures, the opening of a new plant or office, new research findings, and quarterly profits. It must be pointed out that most business activity is not particularly newsworthy. Except for the recent spate of corporate takeovers, business news is not often controversial, glamorous, or dramatic. Further, financial maneuvering, speculations, interest rates, and mergers are complicated and difficult to simplify. To be able to cover the corporation requires, therefore, not only access but also an expertise that few journalists have. In the face of routine information, on the one hand, and complexity, on the other, the ordinary reporter often merely reprints the corporate press release verbatim.

Even the *Wall Street Journal,* the largest circulation daily in America, which prides itself on in-depth business coverage, is dependent on news releases. In 1979, Joanne Ambrosio, of the *Columbia Journalism Review,* studied a typical issue of the *Journal.* Of the day's 188 news items, 111 were short items about specific companies. Ambrosio wrote to these companies and asked for the press releases they had sent to the *Journal.* Seventy companies responded. In fifty-five cases, the news stories were based solely on the press release and were reprinted almost verbatim or contained "only the most perfunctory" additional reporting. Of these stories, twenty carried the by-line "By a *Wall Street Journal* Staff Reporter." Ambrosio projects that, on a typical day, 45 percent of the

*Journal's* news items are based on press releases. She quotes the *Journal's* executive editor, Frederick Taylor: "Ninety percent of daily coverage is started by the company making an announcement for the record. We're relaying this information to our readers."[1]

Reporters, in general, are less likely to investigate corporate press releases than they are government press releases, both because of the lack of access and the lack of the technical expertise to do so. Further, business reporters are fewer in number than political reporters, and, after they process the routine business data of the day, there is little time for research. Finally, the business reporter, unlike the political reporter, cannot rely on the opposition to supply information. Organized opposition to the corporation is a relatively recent phenomenon. Only recently have consumer groups and environmentalist groups become vocal opponents of some corporations.

Most corporate press releases are, naturally, good news messages. If, however, bad news cannot be buried, it can be released at inconvenient times, for example just before a deadline, so that the reporter has no time for research, or on Friday, because Saturday's readership is lower than a weekday's. For instance, in the summer of 1973, seven American corporations were forced to admit that they had illegally donated money to President Nixon's reelection campaign. Almost invariably, each company issued its public statement late on Friday afternoon. The result was a short article in Saturday's newspaper and a brief broadcast. By Monday, it was old news.[2]

Although business initiates most business news through the press release, there are other tactics that the corporation can use to influence media coverage. Corporations and industry associations pay Business Wire, a privately-owned, San Francisco-based public relations wire service, to carry their press releases. Business Wire rewrites the releases to look like AP and UPI wire stories. They go out to teletypewriters installed, without charge, in newsrooms of subscribing newspapers, magazines, and broadcast stations. In 1980, Business Wire had 2000 customers and over 200 outlets across the country. Some Business Wire stories are picked up by AP and UPI.[3]

Companies like the U.S. Press Association and North American Precis Syndicate write feature stories and editorials for their corporate clients, which are then mailed out to news outlets. Large corporations or industries may write their own "canned" material, as these stories have come to be called. Big metropolitan dailies usually refuse this canned material, but smaller newspapers, in need of well-written, well-researched, and free articles, often accept the material. A canned piece is picked up by roughly 200 papers. If the corporation placed ads in all 200 papers, it would cost twice as much and would probably be less effective.

Part of the effectiveness comes from the fact such canned material appears as straight news or editorial comment.[4]

Many papers publish commentary written by industry representatives. For example, Armand L. Fontaine, an official of the American Building Contractors Association, contributes a weekly column to the Los Angeles Times, "Tips to Homeowners," which includes advice to homeowners to use licensed contractors whom Fontaine's group represents.[5]

Another tool of the corporation is pseudo events, created for the express purpose of being covered. These include press conferences and interviews, conventions, dedications, and any number of publicity stunts. For example, in the late 1970s, when New York City was debating whether or not the supersonic Concorde should land at Kennedy Airport, Richard Aurelio, a public relations agent, created a pseudo event that apparently won over the previously neutral business community to the pro-Concorde side. He convinced French President Valery Giscard d'Estaing to fly the Concorde to Houston, Texas. There the French President was met by the mayor of Houston, who said, with the landing of the Concorde, that Houston was the new New York. The New York Times carried a front page story: "Mayor of Houston Twits New York."[6]

Corporations can also provide trips for reporters to see the site for a story. Throughout the 1970s, for example, the nuclear industry provided journalists with tours of nuclear plants in order to dazzle them with the new technology and to assure them that nuclear reactors were safe. The Atomic Industrial Forum sponsored six such press tours.[7] Although the public records of the Nuclear Regulatory Commission included reports of equipment failures and careless operating procedures, few journalists were motivated to dig them out. Government and industry scientists reassured the journalists, and few newsmen had the technological background to dispute the experts.

In 1978, the Atomic Industrial Forum, lobbying for the expanded use of nuclear power, organized a tour of nuclear facilities in the Soviet Union for seventeen American journalists. The Atomic Industrial Forum must have been delighted when Time magazine reported: "While perfervid demonstrators, dallying bureaucrats and well-paid lawyers are holding back the development of U.S. atomic power, the USSR is moving ahead rapidly with its own nuclear programs."[8] The accident at Three Mile Island, in March of 1979, was to end this journalistic romance with the nuclear industry.

When business news is confined to the business pages, corporations retain the upper hand. However, when big business becomes big news, moves to the front page, and becomes the lead story on network news, corporate news management techniques are severely weakened. This is what happened to some corporations during the 1970s. The 1970s was a period of economic bad news: inflation, energy shortages, volatile interest rates, unemployment, plant closings, product recalls, and reduced earnings. The 1970s also witnessed a number of scandals and accidents which broke down the routine patterns of business news. During the 1970s, *Fortune* magazine reports that 117 of the largest and most prestigious corporations were convicted of federal offenses or made settlements. A. Kent MacDougall, a *Los Angeles Times* reporter, comments: "And the *Fortune* survey was limited to just five domestic offenses—criminal antitrust violations, bribery and kickbacks, illegal political contributions, criminal fraud, and tax evasion. *Fortune* said the list would have been longer had it included foreign bribes and kickbacks."[9] There were environmental scandals as well: toxic waste dumping at Love Canal, hazards in uranium mining, aerial spraying of herbicide 2,4,5-T, a cancer scare at General Motors, oil spills, and the shock of the Three Mile Island affair.

It is little wonder that public confidence in the heads of large corporations fell from 55 to 15 percent between 1968 and 1977 and that the number of people who agreed that business strikes a fair balance between profit and public interest dropped from 40 to 15 percent. A Gallup poll measuring levels of confidence in American institutions placed business at the bottom.[10]

It is also not surprising that the coverage of business news began to expand by the late 1970s. Economic uncertainty and such events as those mentioned demand coverage. The expansion of news coverage, however, occurred largely in big-city newspapers, in news magazines, and on the television networks. In 1978, the *New York Times* began publishing a separate business section every weekday, with an enlarged staff of seventy. The *Chicago Tribune's* staff grew from eight in 1977 to twenty-six in 1980 for its once-a-week business section.[11] In 1980, the *Los Angeles Times*, the *Boston Globe,* and the *Washington Post* all added business sections.[12] *Time* magazine doubled its coverage of business and economics in 1979.[13] All three networks hired business correspondents. However, on the local level, patterns of business coverage showed little change. A 1979 survey of 186 daily newspapers revealed that 71 percent did not employ a single full-time business financial reporter.[14]

In the wake of the bad publicity and the expanded coverage of business news, it was predictable that the affected corporations and industries would charge the media with an anti-business bias. Business had long felt mistreated by journalists, whom it believed to be ignorant and naive about the financial and economic realities. Business had long believed that journalists give a bad name to profits and exaggerate workplace and environmental hazards. However, in the 1970s, this discord grew. Louis Banks, a former managing editor of *Fortune* magazine and teacher at Harvard Business School, speaks for business in an *Atlantic Monthly* article, entitled "Memo to the Press: They Hate You Out There":

> [Business reporters are] kids with loaded pistols prowling through the forests of corporate complexity to play games of cowboys and Indians or good guys and bad guys. Their only interest in business is to find a negative story that will get them promoted out of business into Woodward and Bernstein.[15]

Louis Banks exaggerates the journalist's role. The business news of the 1970s was mainly negative: plant closings, product recalls, reduced earnings, nuclear accidents. These stories were not the result of investigative journalism. However, such stories were easily perceived as attacks by a corporate America that had never really been attacked before.

The unfavorable impression of business is linked to unfavorable news, not investigative journalism or misrepresentation. When a corporation or an industry calls attention to itself by generating unfavorable news, the media feel obliged to scrutinize it. For that matter, the most extensive attacks on business have come not from the news media but from books like Ralph Nader's *Unsafe at Any Speed*, about automobile hazards, and *Silent Spring*, by Rachel Carson, about the dangers of pesticides. However, books that attack business reach only about 20,000 buyers, who are usually convinced of corporate malpractice before they read the books. More worrisome is negative business news that reaches 50 million viewers of network news.

Representatives of business have been particularly vocal in criticizing network news. James Ring Adams, writing in the *Wall Street Journal*, states: "Three of the most profitable companies in America, the commercial networks, produce a steady stream of news reports and documentaries...in which businessmen play the heavies."[16] The chairman of the American Association of Advertising Agencies asserts: "There seems to be an unwritten rule among some of the TV newscasters that no week should go by without some denunciation of business."[17] However, business stories that appear on network news are more often than not initiated in Washington through White House statements, Congressional hearings, and regulatory agency investigations which have exposed windfall profits, dangerous products, pollution, rigged prices, and the like.

## ISSUE ADVOCACY

To combat the perceived liberal bias of the eastern press and of the networks, the stiffening of governmental regulations, and the rise of public distrust, a growing number of corporations and industries have fought to tell their own stories. They have turned to issue advocacy to bring their messages directly to the public. The two most important media techniques used by the corporation are "image" and "issue" advocacy advertisements. These advertisements are totally distinct from the familiar product advertisements that we have all come to know only too well.

Product ads are, obviously, designed to sell specific products, while image ads are designed to create a favorable public attitude toward a company and to sell the idea that a company is a well-run, public-spirited organization. Image advertising is particularly useful for monopolies that are subject to government regulation, like American Telephone and Telegraph (AT&T), Con Edison in New York, and Pacific Power and Light in the west. Where there are no competitors and the consumer must buy the company's product at the price set by government, it becomes essential to promote public confidence in the corporation. Lack of confidence could produce grassroots pressures to lower rates or, even more alarming to the corporate interest, a movement to break up the monopoly.

Companies that deal in products sold to other companies use product ads in trade journals and image ads in the mass press, such as Dupont's "Better Things for Better Living" campaign. Image advertising is also useful for corporations with a temporary image problem. In 1979, an American Airlines DC-10 crashed at Chicago's O'Hare Airport. For a while, all DC-10s were grounded. When the ban was lifted, McDonnell Douglas Corporation began a media campaign to reassure the public that DC-10s were safe. Its "Cleared for Takeoff" campaign was directed to the public, who, of course, do not buy planes. However, airlines are not going to buy planes that the public thinks are unsafe.[18]

In contrast to product ads and image ads, advocacy advertising champions particular positions on public policy. Advocacy advertisements defend corporate interests in two ways. Advocacy ads can attempt to sustain or change public opinion on the fundamental values that underlie the corporate structure, such as free enterprise, the profit motive, and private property. These ads may also be used to sustain or change public opinion on specific policy positions and to attack opponents. The leader in advocacy ads has been the oil industry, which spent millions of dollars in the 1970s to argue for the easing of environmental regulations, for the defeat of the windfall profit tax, for the granting of federal subsidies for shale oil development, and for the defense of rising prices and profits.

Product ads and image ads are considered a legitimate business expense and are, therefore, tax-deductible. Advocacy ads, however, are not tax-deductible, and most companies do not run the risk of an Internal Revenue Service challenge. Companies typically do not take a tax deduction for any ad where there is even the slightest doubt. Mobil Oil, for example, does not take a deduction for from 60 to 70 percent of all its ads.[19]

Advocacy ad campaigns are not new. In order to counter negative public opinion, AT&T, in 1908, launched a national campaign to persuade the public that AT&T provided excellent service, that its rates were fair, and, above all, that the telephone industry could serve the public best if it *remained* a monopoly.[20] In order to promote legislation favorable to business, the United States Chamber of Commerce and other organizations sponsored a "What Helps Business Helps You" campaign during the Great Depression in the 1930s.[21] In the 1940s, the American Medical Association defeated President Truman's National Health Insurance program, in large measure, by successfully redefining it as "socialized" medicine, an especially pejorative word at the time.

Warner and Swasey, a Cleveland-based manufacturer of machine tools, textiles, and construction machinery, has been using advocacy ads since 1936 to champion individualism, hard work, and America itself. Most of its ads have fewer than 150 words, and one ad, in 1979, made its point in fourteen words: WHEN SOME PEOPLE LOOK AT THE LIBERTY BELL, ALL THEY SEE IS THE CRACK. Warner and Swasey ads ran in *Business Week, Newsweek, U.S. News & World Report, Forbes,* and *Industry Week.* Although these ads are simplistic and unsophisticated by recent advertising standards, the headlines read like a capitalist manifesto:

> WHO WOULD SIGN THE DECLARATION OF INDEPENDENCE TODAY? THE MOST SUCCESSFUL FREEDOM MARCH WAS THE ONE IN COVERED WAGONS. IF YOU OWN A HAMMER, YOU'RE A CAPITALIST. HOW MUCH FEDERAL AID DID THE PILGRIMS GET? THE ALARM IS RINGING. IT'S TIME TO GET UP AND GET TO WORK. THE GREATEST WAR ON POVERTY IS A SUCCESSFUL CORPORATION.[22]

These Warner and Swasey ads have different objectives from the more recent advocacy advertising campaigns. They are not pushing for particular legislation or policy; the recent advocacy ads are responding to a crisis. The economic bad news of the 1970s created the need for some corporations and industries to use public relations and advertising as tools for problem solving. "A PR problem today does not simply mean loss of goodwill," says John J. Bell, a senior vice president for communications at Bank of America. "It threatens a corporation's ability to achieve its business goals."[23] The main public relations job used to be to get a company's name in the news, to get publicity for a new product, or to build a corporate reputation. Now, as Loet A. Velmans, president of Hill & Knowlton, the country's largest public relations agency, puts it: "The corporation is being politicized and has assumed another dimension in our society that it did not have as recently as 10 years ago."[24] The role of public relations changed from mere publicity and image making to strategy: an active attempt to gain public support for business values. The American corporate structure, although not monolithic, is responding to what it believes is a threat to the free enterprise system and a threat to corporate autonomy. The nuclear industry mounted a campaign to argue that nuclear power is safe; the oil industry mounted a campaign to defend soaring prices and profits; the chemical industry mounted a campaign to counter public perception that it is contaminating the country with toxic pollutants.

There is little difficulty in placing advocacy ads in newspapers and magazines. Network-owned stations, however, tend to reject them. Although networks might fear that public issue commercials might bore or antagonize some viewers, network reluctance to show advocacy ads stems from the Federal Communications Commission's interpretation of the Fairness Doctrine:

> Editorial advertisements may be difficult to identify if they are sponsored by groups which are not normally considered to be engaged in debate on controversial issues. This problem is most likely to arise in the context of promotional or institutional advertising; that is, advertising designed to present a favorable public image of a particular corporation or industry rather than to sell a product. Such advertising is, of course, a legitimate commercial practice and ordinarily does not involve debate on public issues.... In some cases, however, the advertiser may seek to play an obvious and meaningful role in public debate. In such instances, *the fairness doctrine—including the obligation to provide free time...applies* [italics ours].[25]

The distinction between image ads and advocacy ads is not airtight. For example, an advertisement presenting a "favorable public image" of the nuclear industry is also taking a position on a "public debate." All ads which picture corporations as public-spirited are designed to support the view that corporations are socially, economically, and politically benefi-cial. Nevertheless, network-owned stations resist those ads, which are clearly advocacy advertisements. On the other hand, affiliate and independent stations are much more willing to air advocacy ads. A poll of nearly 400 stations, in 1980, found 89 percent willing to accept advocacy ads.[26]

### The Mobil Campaign Sets the Tone

In the late 1970s, vice president Herbert Schmertz of Mobil Oil mounted a campaign in newspapers to get the networks to relent on their policy of refusing advocacy advertising. The networks stood firm. In order to circumvent the networks policy and to reach the largest possible audience, Mobil bought a six-part series, "Edward and Mrs. Simpson," early in 1980. Mobil then bought prime time on fifty individual stations to air the broadcasts and inserted its advocacy ads. Fairness doctrine complaints came in, and most stations granted free air time to reply.[27]

It is, in fact, the oil industry, led by Mobil with Herbert Schmertz at the helm, which has led other corporations in pursuing issue advocacy. Like most recent advocacy campaigns, Mobil's was conceived in crisis. As early as 1969, Mobil concluded that an energy crisis was coming and that Mobil was unlikely to get "fair and balanced" coverage. In order to reach the public directly, Mobil turned to Herbert Schmertz and launched a many-faceted advocacy campaign that has become a model of corporate advocacy.

Herbert Schmertz would, at first glance, seem an unlikely candidate for his role. A lawyer, who served as general counsel for the Federal Mediation and Conciliation Service, Schmertz was originally hired by Mobil, in 1966, to handle labor relations. Schmertz had worked in the John F. Kennedy presidential campaign; he worked for Robert Kennedy in 1964 and 1968; in 1972, he supported liberal Democrat George McGovern.[28] However, it was precisely Schmertz's acquaintance with liberal Democrats which made him attractive to Mobil's chairman and chief executive, Rawleigh Warner, Jr.

Schmertz's first foray into the use of the media took the form of image advertising, through the sponsorship of a variety of cultural projects, including support for art exhibits and the publication of art books and an illustrated cultural magazine, *Pegasus*, for distribution abroad. One of the most visible aspects of Mobil's image campaign, for American audiences, was Mobil's support, beginning in 1970, of "Masterpiece Theatre," the Sunday evening presentation of British imports on Public Television. Although Mobil received only brief mention on the air, in its newspaper advertisements Mobil regularly reminded the public of its generosity. Mobil's cultural activities aimed to create a "goodwill umbrella," which would build acceptance and later allow Mobil to speak out on policy issues and be heard.[29]

Also, in 1970, the *New York Times* decided to sell advertising space on its op-ed page. Since surveys showed that the op-ed page is read by Washington politicians, commentators, and editors, Mobil signed up quickly for some space. Used initially to advertise "Masterpiece Theatre" (see Figure 10-1) and herald Mobil's support, the op-ed page ads later became the first forum for Mobil's advocacy ad campaigns. Schmertz explains why Mobil initiated its advocacy campaign in 1970:

> ...enormous external forces were already buffeting our company and our industry. We believed those forces would do enormous and irreparable damage unless we recognized their existence and attempted to counter them. What were these forces? A powerful environmental lobby had emerged, and

**Example 10-1**

Reprinted with permission of Mobil Corporation.

politicians and the press could not leap on that bandwagon fast enough. Nor did they pay attention to the costs of near-pristine air and water. Coupled with this was the emergence of consumerism dramatized by the anointment of Ralph Nader as its patron saint. *As never before business institutions were under critical review, scrutiny and attack. The very social utility of the private economic system was being questioned in many unexpected quarters.* [Italics ours].[30]

The Arab oil embargo of 1973 and 1974 and the oil and gas shortage caused Mobil to expand its advocacy campaign even further. A Gallup poll showed that eight out of ten Americans believed that the oil companies had created the shortage in order to raise prices. Rumors appeared in the press which suggested that a fleet of oil tankers were anchored in Delaware Bay in the midst of the oil crisis. Schmertz believed that the nature of the press coverage (particularly that of television) made the oil industry a target for politicians.[31] In the spring of 1977, President Carter spoke at press conferences and on nationwide television of "rip-offs" by the oil companies and of "70 billion dollars" windfall profits. In Schmertz's view, the threat to the oil industry and private enterprise was widespread and dangerous.[32] By July of 1979, Carter said that the crisis was real. Nonetheless, a *Times*/CBS poll showed that 65 percent of the public still believed that the energy crisis was a hoax. Schmertz accused the press of gossip and sensationalism. Like other businessmen, Schmertz saw the press as distorting reality and undermining the values of the free enterprise system: "We have seen the emergence...of an almost ludicrous western-movie type of struggle between the 'good guys' and the 'bad guys.' Anyone whose role is directed toward profit making is suspect....The good guys are assumed to be pure because they are not profit-motivated."[33] As Schmertz saw it, the press refused to raise the question of whether it was really Big Oil that was being attacked or the "whole American economic system." Within this atmosphere and from this ideological stance, Mobil fought back.

Mobil broke all the rules of traditional public relations. Its campaign was more visible, more controversial, and more intense than any that had been attempted before. With a budget of $21 million by 1978, an estimated $30 million budget by 1981,[34] and a staff of 110 for "Public Affairs" (as Mobil and other corporations now prefer to call it), Mobil entered into the "battle of ideas" with a distinct advantage. Donald Stroetzel, Mobil's Manager of Communications Programs, estimates that 6 to 8 million dollars go to print advertising and 3 million to television commercials.[35] Mobil continues to intertwine its support for the free enterprise system with support for educational and cultural institutions; approximately $7 million is used to support public broadcasting programs.[36]

Mobil's first target was opinion leaders—politicians, journalists, educators, and the business community—through the use of Mobil's op-ed messages. Since January 13, 1972, Mobil's op-ed advertisements have appeared every Thursday in the *New York Times* and in eight other newspapers, including the *Wall Street Journal,* the *Washington Post,* the *Los Angeles Times,* the *Chicago Tribune,* and the *Boston Globe.* (During the crisis year of 1974, op-eds appeared in 103 papers around the country.)[37] Op-eds are still occasionally used to advertise "Masterpiece Theatre" and to promote good causes such as the United Negro College Fund and the Urban Coalition (these ads are tax deductible). However, op-eds, written in newspaper editorial style, are overwhelmingly used to support Mobil's political and economic positions.

The op-ed message rarely exceeds 600 words and has a boldface headline with a characteristic light touch: MORE POWER TO THE PEOPLE (referring to energy, not politics), GROWTH IS NOT A FOUR-LETTER WORD, STAGNATION IS STILL THE WORST FORM OF POLLUTION, NO NUKES IS BAD NEWS. Many op-ed "editorials" are not related directly to oil or energy. A six-part series, "Toward a Healthier Economic Climate," which appeared in the spring of 1975, argued the need for increased profits and more capital formation. However, the series also included an endorsement of more social welfare measures and a national health insurance program. In this deliberate appeal to liberals, the message hastened to add that such programs had to be predicated on economic growth. Following Mobil's lead, Allied Chemical, Union Carbide, Gannett newspapers, Amway, and the chemical industry, to name but a few, have used the op-ed format.

While op-eds are aimed at opinion leaders, "Observations," a Mobil-produced column, is aimed at a popular audience. It appears in Sunday supplements every other week. "Observations" goes to 500 newspapers, and Mobil estimates that it reaches 40 million households and 80 million adults.[38] "Observations" uses bold-type headlines, cartoons, a gossip column style, and human interest stories. Schmertz is convinced of the effectiveness of "Observations." He cites surveys that show that people exposed to "Observations" have a greater affinity for the free-market economy and domestic energy development than those with similar demographic characteristics who are not exposed to "Observations."[39]

During the 1970s, the op-ed and the "Observations" advocacy ads played on the fear of "unnecessary" and "damaging" dependence on foreign oil sources. In both instances, Mobil continued to urge public policy that would allow the United States to develop its own energy sources through decontrol of natural gas prices, opening up of offshore drilling opportunities, support for nuclear power, and easing of restrictive environmental regulations. This print advertising was also useful in attacking what Mobil thought to be unfair practices of the media. Figure 10-2 shows Mobil's op-ed attack on television; in it, Mobil asserts that network television distorted Mobil's earnings and then refused to sell Mobil air time to respond. Mobil accuses network television of denying the freedom of speech. Figure 10-3 shows an op-ed attack on newspapers, in which Mobil accuses most American newspapers of prominently displaying stories about oil company abuses but failing to publish news when the oil industry is in the right.

Mobil also produces television commercials that are shown on fifty to eighty independent stations, often during the local evening news program. Some of them feature the "Mobil Information Center," with an "anchorman" and field "reporters." These commercials are crafted specifically to look like newscasts. Mobil's television commercials are 60-second or two-minute spots on taxation, government regulation, and energy policy. Among the most controversial ads was a series of "fables" entitled "A Fable for Now...by Mobil." These were cartoon fantasies that amounted to clever sugar-coated statements of Mobil's philosophy. Figure 10-4 is an op-ed which offers the flavor of the television commercials without the visuals. As in the television "fable," the op-ed fable ends with a moral—in this case a justification for the energy industry's high profits.

Between 1976 and 1981, Mobil produced eleven television special reports on such topics as oil exploration, gasoline prices, and government policy. Each "special" is one half-hour in length and features a television journalist interviewing Mobil executives and energy experts who support Mobil's policies. These "specials" are sent out free to television stations and are usually aired late at night or on weekends. They acknowledge Mobil only with a credit line at the end. The half-hour special can be broken up into interview segments and can be inserted into newscasts. Mobil estimates that 110 stations have used individual segments of its "Energy at the Crossroads" special.[40]

"Energy at the Crossroads" is a typical example of Mobil's specials. Reporter Roger Sharp, of ABC-TV, interviews Mobil executives, politicians, and an economist who support more government incentives for oil exploration, believe that energy regulations and taxes are excessive, blame the federal government and the greedy consumer for the energy shortage, and call for easing restrictions on nuclear, coal, and oil development. There are no interviews with environmentalists or others who might disagree with Mobil's position. Sixty-two stations have shown "Energy at the Crossroads."[41] It is aired as news, with no hint that Roger Sharp was employed by Mobil. Mobil's role is revealed only at the end, with "Produced for Mobil Oil by DWJ Associates."

Hiring journalists to lend credibility to the corporate version of the facts has become a fairly common practice. The Fertilizer Institute hired

**Example 10-2**

# The impossible freedom

In the world of network television, even the news departments lean on the tired crutch of the rerun—their answer is always "no" whenever we attempt to purchase air time to rebut attacks or misrepresentations. The loser is the viewing public.

The latest case in point involves the reporting of our third-quarter earnings, which we felt left the viewer with false and misleading impressions. We sought to purchase air time to respond, and, as usual, we were turned down. So we ran two full-page messages in newspapers to attempt to set the record straight—a record that had been distorted on the air. We would have much preferred to have it corrected on the air. But the issue is really much broader than this latest incident. The real issue is access to the airwaves—access that has been denied to us and to others many times in the past.

In its news account of the current incident, *The New York Times* quoted one network spokesperson as saying: "We don't sell time to any special-interest groups of any shape or color." The stated reason: unfairness to groups unable to afford to buy time. But what about unfairness to individuals or institutions, rich or poor, who suffer unjust attacks or are otherwise misrepresented on the air? They simply have no recourse. In the name of freedom of the press, network TV has succeeded in whittling away at freedom of speech. And in the name of the poor, nobody has access to television. If poverty is the real problem, it would be far better to devise a way to provide access for everybody.

The *Times* also quoted the network spokesperson as saying, "It's not easy for anyone to plow through the thicket of an oil company's accounting." Inadvertently, she put her finger on one of the major problems of TV news, namely, the structure of the medium.

Time is a major constraint on television, and in half an hour, the news shows have to cover 10 or 12 major stories, "headlines" of other stories, and an essay by the network commentator—and still leave time for commercials. No less an authority than Walter Cronkite has conceded that this "hyper-compression" leads to "distortion." At the same time, the networks usually employ generalists able to cover any story with seeming coherence, rather than specialists who really understand complex subjects. And, since the networks are basically in the entertainment business rather than the news business, even the news shows compete for ratings. As the result of all these factors, TV news simply cannot cover complex issues thoroughly enough to help the American people make crucial decisions on vital issues.

One network told us it was their "general policy... to sell time only for the promotion of goods and services, and not for the presentation of points of view on controversial issues of public importance." They added their belief that "the public will best be served if important public issues are presented in formats generally determined by broadcast journalists." Theirs, of course.

How is this consistent with freedom of speech? It isn't, not when the accused or the criticized has no access for a response. We repeatedly have offered to pay twice the going rate for air time, and to let the networks select anybody they chose to present an opposing view. Again, no takers.

We even offered to restrict our comments solely to the correction of errors made by broadcast journalists, so as not to interfere with the network control of their news format. Once more, rejection.

In our view, the time for remedy is long overdue. Television's absolute control of the news is an impossible freedom, in the sense that it leaves too many Americans either uninformed or misinformed, and those attacked with no means of defense on television. Some way must be found to open the airwaves to all shades of comment and yes, even to controversy. Television broadcasters are, after all, are licensed to operate the public's airwaves, so in a sense they work for all of us. They should, therefore, have an even greater obligation than newspapers or magazines, which are unlicensed, to permit all shades of opinion to be heard.

The print media permit access through various means—letters to the editor, guest columns, free-lance journalists, and even advocacy advertising. What's needed on television is a process of innovation and reform that will permit this same flow of ideas.

The reform process should arise from television itself, to head off the danger of reform by government edict. Moreover, such reform should come quickly, because a free flow of ideas is essential to a free society. Without access to the airwaves, the flow of ideas becomes sharply reduced, and all Americans are the losers.

**Mobil**

Reprinted with permission of Mobil Corporation.

**Example 10-3**

# The news story you never got to see

**(unless you read the Wall Street Journal, Los Angeles Times, or the fine print in a few other papers)**

## Mobil Wins $200 Million Suit

### Federal Court Finds Energy Department Action On Refining Costs 'Arbitrary and Capricious'

NEW YORK, DECEMBER 4—The Temporary Emergency Court of Appeals has upheld a lower court ruling that the Department of Energy had improperly refused to allow Mobil Oil Corporation to include in its prices more than $200 million in costs since 1974, the company announced today. A Mobil executive said he did not expect the DOE to hold a press conference to announce the disposition of the case, as it so often does when it institutes actions.

Allen E. Murray, president of Mobil's Marketing and Refining Division, said: "It's interesting. The DOE is quick to publicize its charges against oil companies and spread grossly inflated dollar figures around. But when the courts tell them they are wrong, as is often the case, they are strangely silent."

The case had to do with the amount of cost increases the DOE, via its complex price regulations, required Mobil to assign to petroleum coke, a low-value by-product of the refinery process. "Although coke was exempted from price controls in April 1974," Mr. Murray said, "the federal energy agency then passed a regulation forcing us to assign an unrealistic

percentage of any increased crude costs to coke, rather than other products. The regulation was passed without benefit of a hearing or notification, or any valid regulatory proceeding, which clearly violated federal law."

The appeals court agreed with the U.S. District Court for the Eastern District of Texas, Beaumont Division, that the FEA'S action had been "arbitrary and capricious and beyond the agency's authority," and failed to comply with federal law.

In recounting the steps leading to the suit, Mr. Murray explained: "Our major problem was that petroleum coke is the bottom of the barrel and, as such, is not a money-maker. Market conditions did not permit us to collect even one-third of the costs the FEA forced us to assign to this product. We appealed to the FEA for an exception to the rule, and they turned us down."

In 1975, however, the FEA granted Getty Oil substantially the same kind of relief Mobil had requested. "Once the FEA approved the Getty application, we again asked for an exception, assuming it would be only fair for Mobil to be treated the same way," Mr. Murray continued. "The FEA turned us down again, and we decided to sue."

News stories such as the one above should have appeared in many of the nation's newspapers. But unless you read the *Wall Street Journal* or the *Los Angeles Times*, which ran similar stories, you never saw this article in print. A handful of other papers mentioned it—as a short appendage to a longer article about another oil company signing a consent agreement in a price violation case.

Strange how most of America's newspapers

display prominently any stories in which oil companies are accused of overcharging, but fail to publish the news when the oil industry is proven right and the government wrong.

The story above is the text of a news release we distributed, detailing a court decision vindicating our accounting and pricing practices. We hope you read it. And wonder, as we do, why a valid news item finally had to appear as a paid message.

## Mobil

Reprinted with permission of Mobil Corporation.

## Example 10-4

*A Fable For Now:*

# Why Elephants Can't Live on Peanuts

The Elephant is a remarkable animal...huge, yet able to move quickly...stronger than any person, yet willing to work hard if properly treated.

One day, an Elephant was ambling through the forest. To her surprise, she found her path to the water hole blocked by a huge pile of sticks, vines, and brambles.

"Hello?" she called out over the barricade. "What gives?"

From behind the pile popped the Monkey. "Buzz off, snake-snoot," the Monkey shouted. "It's an outrage to little folk how much you take in, so the rest of us animals have seized the water hole and the food supply. You're gross, and we're revolting!"

"You certainly give that appearance," the Elephant noted quietly. "What's eating you?"

"It's *you* that's doing too much eating," the Monkey replied, "but we're going to change all that. Strict rations for you, fat friend. No more of your obscene profiteering at the feed trough." Overhead, a Parrot screamed: "From each according to your ability. To each according to our need. Gimme your crackers, gimme *all* your crackers!"

The Elephant was upset at this enormous misunderstanding. Yet, though her heart pounded, between the ears she was quite unflappable. "A moment, please," she said. "Though it may seem that I consume a great deal, it's no more than my share. Because I am large—not fat—it just takes more to keep me going. How can I work hard if you won't let me have the proper nourishment?"

The Monkey sneered. "Knock off that mumbo-jumbo, Dumbo," he said. "You already net more than a million Spiders. You take in more than a thousand Pack Rats. You profit more from the jungle's abundance than a hundred Monkeys!"

"But I also can haul tree trunks too heavy for any other creature," the Elephant said. "I can explore for new food supplies and water holes, and clear paths through the jungle with my strong legs. My feet can crush, my shoulders can pull, my trunk can lift. I am full of energy. I even give rides to the little ones. But I can't survive on peanuts."

Hours passed. The Elephant, denied access to her eating and drinking grounds, felt hungrier and hungrier, thirstier and thirstier. But soon, so did the other animals. For the sticks and vines that the animals had dragged together and woven into a barricade had become a solid dam, diverting the stream that fed the watering hole. "Help, help," the animals shouted, "crisis, crisis!"

The Elephant surveyed the scene. "Friends," she said, "see what a fix we're all in. Thank goodness I still have the energy to help. And, with your permission, I will." They quickly consented, and she set to work on the dam, pushing earth and pulling plants until the water hole again began to fill. "That's nice," the animals cried, greeting her undamming with faint praise.

"You see," the Elephant said, "you need a big beast for a big job, and a big beast has big needs. Not just to stay alive and growing, but to put a bit aside for tomorrow. And to have a bit extra for working especially hard, or for sharing with have-not animals."

She noticed that everybody had resumed drinking thirstily. Well, that tickled her old ivories, for all she really wanted was to be allowed to go on doing her customary work without any new wrinkles. No need for hurt feelings. After all, who ever heard of a thin-skinned Elephant?

Moral: Meeting America's energy needs is a big job and it takes big companies. If an energy company doesn't earn a profit proportionate to its size, it won't be able to seek and produce more energy. And that's no fable.

**Mobil**

©1979 Mobil Corporation

Reprinted with permission of Mobil Corporation.

Martin Agronsky to anchor a special report on the fertilizer industry: "And One to Grow On." Agronsky has been a correspondent for each of the three networks and moderates a nationally-distributed talk show, "Agronsky and Company." In the 18-minute "And One to Grow On," Agronsky sits in a fake television newsroom with a fake desk and fake television monitor. The "reporter" in the field, doing the actual coverage, is an actress. She sums up her report: "If we didn't supplement our soil with nitrogen-bearing compounds, millions of the world's cupboards would be bare, and food prices would skyrocket. Fertilization is not merely desirable; it is essential. This is Joan Levetter reporting. Martin?"[42] A spokesman from the Institute explains the choice of a newscaster and the TV newsroom format: "An actor doesn't have the authority or credibility that a newsman has. The public presumes actors can be paid to say anything, whereas newsmen say what they believe to be the facts."[43]

As part of its public affairs activities, Mobil carefully monitors the media; news programs are recorded on videotape, computer terminals can quickly display a pertinent newspaper article, and the major wire services are scrutinized. This news-monitoring and information-retrieval operation is called the "Secretariat." The Secretariat enables Mobil regularly to tape replies to radio and television editorials and quickly to respond to adverse newspaper coverage. To Schmertz, nothing, apparently, is minor. In 1974, Schmertz came across an episode in a cartoon strip, "Kelly," in the New York Daily News. In it, a talking dog speculates that he might get away with stealing chickens by explaining that his mind "had been took over by th' forces of darkness an' evil." Kelly asks the dog: "What would the oil companies want with your mind?" Schmertz wrote a letter to the publisher, deploring this "bias against oil companies" and asking whether the News would have published it if Kelly had asked: "What would newspapers want with your mind?"[44]

Also in 1974, Mobil responded to a WNBC-TV in New York special feature called "The Great Gasoline War." It appeared as a nightly feature on the six o'clock news for one week, Monday through Friday. Mobil monitored each segment, looking for errors and distortions, and, according to the company, found "every nasty rumor about the oil industry has been included." Mobil responded one week, and a good deal of research, later with a full-page ad in the New York Times (March 5, 1976), the Daily News, and the eastern edition of the Wall Street Journal entitled "What ever happened to fair play?" The subtitle stated: "WNBC-TV's recent series on gasoline prices was inaccurate, unfair, and a disservice to the people." The ad cited seventeen "hatchet jobs," each "job" illustrated with a little hatchet and followed by a quote from the program and Mobil's fact-filled response. The particular Mobil ad created quite a stir, and news stories followed that gave Mobil even more coverage of its views.

Other corporations and industries have followed suit and have become more active in directly responding to media criticism. In 1980, ABC's 20/20 accused Kaiser Aluminum and Chemical Corporation of knowingly marketing unsafe aluminum house wiring. Kaiser took out a full-page ad accusing ABC of "Trial by Television" and demanding the right to an unedited reply. ABC eventually agreed to air a four-minute rebuttal but insisted that it appear on "Nightline" rather than on 20/20. In 1979, Illinois Power Company produced a 42-minute rebuttal to CBS's "60 Minutes," which had charged that Illinois Power had mismanaged the construction of a nuclear plant. The rebuttal was called "60 Minutes: Our Reply," and over 2000 copies were distributed to corporations, trade associations, journalism schools, community organizations, and some members of Congress. Illinois Power got "60 Minutes" to correct two factual errors on the air. "CBS Morning News" showed two brief excerpts from the film. Supporters of the uranium industry produced "Uranium: Fact or Fiction?" as a rebuttal to ABC's 1980 documentary, "The Uranium Factor," which portrayed the uranium industry and federal and New Mexican authorities as lax in protecting miners, mill workers, and the environment from radiation. Robert Goralski, an NBC White House correspondent, conducted the interviews for "Fact or Fiction" but was never identified as an employee of Gulf Oil, which owns a large uranium mine. (Goralski went on to become an information director for Gulf Oil.)[45]

In contrast to more traditional public relations policy, many corporations have taken to making their executives available for television appearances. Mobil promotes "media blitzes." Mobil once sent out twenty-one executives to twenty-one target cities, where they appeared in more than 100 talk shows, news broadcasts, and radio call-in programs, as well as meeting with local editors. The aim was to beat back congressional moves to break up the giant oil companies.[46] Schmertz reports that, in 1978, twenty-three senior Mobil managers visited twenty-nine cities in twenty-one states, called on thirty newspapers, and appeared on sixty-nine television shows and sixty-eight radio programs. The theme of this campaign was "Is America running out of oil and gas?"[47] Most of these executive participants go through a two-day training course in Chicago, using videotape playbacks of their performances and receiving instruction on how to handle themselves. Later, a two-hour refresher course is provided.

It is still more common, outside of Mobil, to send out a single company representative on the talk show circuit. John Swearingen, chairman of Standard Oil, appeared on network shows to urge gasoline conservation and to defend the oil industry against "excessive" taxation.[48] Shell Chemical Company sent Kathy Sommer, a toxicologist, on a one-week tour of six television stations, nine radio stations, and two newspapers, to spread the word that there was no need for more federal regulations to protect workers from carcinogens.[49]

While almost all of Mobil's Public Affairs products are created in-house, most corporations and industries continue to use the canned feature services previously mentioned and independent advertising agencies. However, Mobil's approach may well be the wave of the future. In 1979, Atlantic Richfield Company (ARCO) developed a televison news magazine called "Energy Update," a half-hour program with three energy-related stories. The producer, writer, and host of "Energy Update" is Anthony Hatch, manager of media relations for ARCO and a 16-year veteran of CBS in New York. The half-hour cassettes are sent monthly to more than 115 commercial television stations and to more than twenty-five cable systems.[50] Hatch estimates that at least twenty-four stations have used all or part of these programs and may or may not have indicated the source of the material.[51]

For those corporations and industries that do not have the in-house facilities, Modern Satellite Network produces a program called "Viewpoint," which interviews business advocates for a fee ($6000 for five minutes) and beams it to 451 cable systems for six days.[52] "Viewpoint" is hosted by Suzanne Leamer, an actress in television commercials. The corporation or industry provides Leamer with the questions to ask. Corporations which have availed themselves of this service include Ford Motor Company, Swanson Frozen Food, and Dow Chemical Company.

The traditional voice of the business community, the U.S. Chamber of Commerce, stepped up its media efforts by the end of the 1970s. The U.S. Chamber of Commerce (with a $70 million budget)[53] is a Washington-based association of businesses organized to promote the private enterprise system. The Chamber had already published *Nation's Business,* the most widely distributed business magazine (1.3 million circulation). The Chamber regularly generates canned editorials to help defeat unwanted legislation such as labor-law reform and legislation to establish a federal Consumer Protection Agency. The Chamber gathers editorials from newspapers, including Chamber-originated editorials, and distributes them to legislators to prove the widespread support for its positions. However, in 1979, it added *Washington Report,** a weekly newsmagazine, a weekly radio panel discussion, "What's the issue?" and a weekly television panel discussion, "It's Your Business." "It's Your Business" is

---

*On September 26, 1983, the *Washington Report* was renamed *The Business Advocate* (*New York Times,* 9/26/82).

carried by 155 stations, generates a revenue of $950,000 a year, and makes a profit.[54] In October of 1982, the Chamber began an hour-long daily television news program, "BizNet News Today." The cable signal is sent by Modern Satellite Network to its 451 cable distributors, and the Chamber itself beams a signal by satellite to fifteen broadcasters, creating a potential audience of 20 million households. The program is given without charge, and the Chamber keeps six of the 12 minutes of commercials for itself and gives six to the distributors. The Chamber has also created an hour-long phone-in program called "Ask Washington," where the viewer can phone in questions to Washington personalities. At this writing, it is presented at 9 a.m. on Monday mornings, with Senator Orrin G. Hatch, Republican of Utah, who is chairman of the Senate Labor and Human Resources Committee. The program will go on five days a week. The Chamber's $4 million television studio has also been used for political fund raising in support of Chamber-backed candidates for Congress and for "teleconferences" in which President Reagan and other officials have talked to business groups around the nation and answered questions. In effect, the Chamber has created the first television network dedicated to American business and the private enterprise system.

### Public Service Announcements

One of the cheapest uses of the media by the corporation is the Public Service Announcement. PSAs are supposed to be noncommercial messages which provide vital information to the public. PSAs are produced by the Advertising Council, a corporate-funded organization. They are printed or broadcast free. PSAs include health and safety announcements, such as one urging the reader or viewer to get a checkup for cancer or contribute to medical research; environmental messages, such as the Keep America Beautiful campaign; and community welfare messages, such as support for the United Negro College Fund.[55] However, they also include messages that are thinly-disguised corporate advocacy. For example, the following was presented as in the public service by Mobil:

> Scene: a small boy and girl on a nature hunt.
> Voice: Today, the research efforts of U.S. industry are actually lagging because of costly government regulations and discouraging taxation.... So let's not hobble American research with regulations and taxation that stifle creative minds. Let's give Tommy and Sue and anybody else the chance they deserve to make America a better place to live.[56]

In 1976, the Advertising Council started a campaign, "You Are the American Economic System," which the council believes helped turn the public against government regulation. The campaign included a thirty-two page booklet that attempts to convince the public that the individual is the decisive factor in corporate America. It includes such statements as "You determine utility rates," "You govern controls on pesticides," and "You govern advertising claims."[57]

Even the apparently innocent "Keep America Beautiful" campaign depicts pollution as a problem of people's littering rather than corporate abuse of the environment. Fighting pollution is equated with anti-litter and community clean-up projects, not auto emissions controls, smokestack filters, and prohibitions on disposable bottles and cans. As a matter of fact, Keep America Beautiful, Inc. is a privately-funded organization, with Pepsi Cola as one of its major contributors.[58] The "Don't be Fuelish" campaign implies that individuals can ease the energy shortage, even though individuals use only 25 percent of the energy, compared to industry's 75 percent. The advertising agency of Young and Rubicam handles the General Foods account but is also responsible for food, nutrition, and health PSAs. It is hardly likely that Young and Rubicam would produce a PSA warning against nonnutritional General Foods products.

Another way that corporations can defend their positions is through giving money to underwrite public television programs that support business causes. Corporations have become more active in funding programs that explicitly support free enterprise values. Conservative commentator William F. Buckley, Jr.'s "Firing Line" has been on public television since 1971. However, starting in 1980, "Firing Line" has received substantial corporate support. Corporations funded conservative economist Milton Friedman's ten-part series, "Free to Choose," which advocated, among other things, dismantling the welfare system and most government regulation. Corporations also funded "In Search of Real America," a thirteen-part series by Ben J. Wattenberg, a senior fellow at the conservative American Enterprise Institute for Public Policy Research. This series included a segment called "There's No Business Like Big Business," which argued that most corporations are sensitive to consumer needs and to societal conditions. "Ben Wattenberg's 1980" series also received corporate funding. In it, Wattenberg argued that the government has gone far enough in taxing and regulating the private economy.[59]

It is interesting to note that public television initially rejected any labor union funding for the "Made in U.S.A." series on labor history because, it was claimed, unions had a direct self-interest. (PBS eventually set a limit of one-third union funding.) An argument to reject or limit corporate funding of business-oriented programs, such as Friedman's and Wattenberg's, has never been raised.[60]

The public's image of business has become more positive in the 1980s. Certainly the Reagan administration's strong support for business interests and an upturn in the economy have been important factors in creating that change. But there is no doubt that corporate use of the media has had a significant impact on public opinion.

## BANKROLLING BALLOT ISSUES

Corporations and industries that were the subjects of the bad news of the 1970s also stepped up their use of the media to counter grassroot pressures to regulate them. Consumer advocates, environmentalists, and anti-nuclear groups responded to what they believed to be corporate abuses by attempting to regulate or curb corporate activities through state and local legislation. Citizen groups opposing corporate or industry practices had recourse to ballot issues (referenda and initiatives). Ballot issues were established specifically to serve as a means to bring controversial issues directly before the public. Ballot issues bypass state and local legislative bodies and thus theoretically circumvent undue influence of special interests. They are intended to counteract the influence of expensive lobbying efforts.

Referenda are initiated by the state or local legislatures, and a specific issue is submitted to the public for a vote. Some referenda (like a state constitutional amendment) must legally be submitted to the public before they may become law. On other referenda issues, the legislature could technically make a ruling, but it chooses, for various reasons, to let the public have a vote on the issue. Initiatives, on the other hand, are completely outside the legislative process and are created by the public. In order to get an initiative on the ballot, it is necessary to get a required number of signatures, specified by state and local law. Initiatives can be used in twenty-three states and in the District of Columbia.

Although there are limits placed on the amount of money a corporation may contribute to a campaign for public office, there are almost no limits on corporate or industry spending on state and local ballot issues. Initiatives which affect business interests have provoked very expensive campaigns. Where the battle lines are clearly drawn between corporations and citizen groups, business-backed interests typically have more money and more expertise. Most citizen groups are underfinanced and rarely can afford professional consultants.

Business interests rarely promote initiatives in their own interest, and, when they do, these initiatives are not especially successful. Traditional lobbying techniques are still most effective in promoting business interests. More typically, corporations and industries use their financial advantage to *oppose* electoral attempts to regulate their activities. Of the fourteen campaigns studied by Steven D. Lydenberg in 1980, where the business-backed side outspent its opponents, business interests won in eleven campaigns.[61] When we speak of outspending here, we mean outspending in ratios ranging from two to one to ratios of as much as 79 to one.[62] The average spending ratio in these fourteen campaigns was 27 to one. Money alone does not guarantee defeat of a ballot issue. However, almost unlimited funds for polling, media time, and media consultants are very powerful. Ballot issues tend to be dominated by those with financial superiority, a situation which obviously undercuts the very basis upon which the initiative and referenda process was founded.

Business-backed ballot campaigns are particularly effective because voters give less attention to ballot issues, in the same way that they give less attention to campaigns for local, state, and congressional offices. As we have pointed out, where a candidate for public office is well-known among the electorate, the effect of sophisticated campaign techniques is minimized. On the other hand, where the voter is less knowledgeable, expensive campaigns can be very effective. On ballot issues, positions with the greatest visibility tend to win. On ballot issues, money talks. However, when a ballot issue captures the attention of the electorate, the power of money can be weakened. As we shall see, before the Three Mile Island accident, the nuclear industry was very effective in opposing initiatives which would curb the development of nuclear plants. When nuclear accidents and cost overruns became front page news, the nuclear industry began to lose ballot issues, despite its financial advantage.

Corporations and industries directly affected by initiatives spend more financing opposition campaigns than they do on contributions to political candidates or on legislative lobbying. (On the federal level, corporations may not contribute directly to political candidates, but, since 1974, they have been able to set up Political Action Committees [PACs] whose funding comes from voluntary contributions of employees or members. The number of corporate PACs has steadily increased, as has the amount of money contributed by PACs to candidates.) However, corporations and industries involved in the initiative process spend more on initiative campaigns than on PACs. Once an issue is set before the public for a direct vote, the corporation is forced to spend its efforts on opposition to attempts at corporate or industry regulation. For example, R.J. Reynolds Tobacco spent $1,140,808 in 1980 to oppose two anti-smoking initiatives in California and in Dade County, Florida.[63] In contrast, R.J. Reynolds' PAC contributed $40,500 to federal candidates in 1979 and 1980. Westinghouse spent $251,692 in 1980 to oppose five anti-nuclear initiatives; its PAC spent $121,725.[64] Lockheed spent $213,000 to oppose an anti-nuclear weapons initiative in Santa Cruz County; its PAC spent $172,805.[65]

In much the same way, once an issue gets directly before the public, vigorous opposition to an initiative becomes a necessary substitute for traditional legislative lobbying. While total corporate spending on lobbying far exceeds spending on candidates and ballot issues, those companies involved in ballot issues spend more on ballot campaigns than on lobbying. For example, Pacific Power and Light spent $919,193 to oppose ballot issues in 1980, in contrast to $186,857 for lobbying. Portland General Electric spent $998,931 on ballot issues, compared to only $170,496 for lobbying.[66]

The major industries affected by ballot issue campaigns and the major contributors to these campaigns are the utilities, the tobacco companies, and the oil industry. In the seventeen ballot campaigns studied by Lydenberg in 1980, the ten biggest contributors spent $8,835,007, each contributing more than one-half million dollars. Of this total, $3,009,242 came from the utilities, $2,801,102 from the tobacco companies, and $3,024,623 from the oil industry. All but $25,000 of the tobacco companies' money went to oppose the anti-smoking initiatives in California and Dade County. The oil industry and the utilities combined resources to fight anti-nuclear initiatives. The oil industry waged a separate campaign to fight an oil tax, while the utilities fought the public takeover of utilities.[67]

When corporations or industries mount a ballot issue campaign, they use many of the same media consulting firms and pollsters used by politicians (described in Chapter 5). In fact, for many public relations firms, the ballot campaign is a major source of revenue. In initiative efforts, the political consultant is given more leverage, sinch there is no party involvement, and corporations often have little electoral experience and are in desperate need of expert guidance.

Winner-Wagner and Associates has made a national reputation for mounting successful campaigns against anti-nuclear initiatives. Their first case was Proposition 15 in California, in 1976. Proposition 15 sought to limit the construction of nuclear power plants. Big industry, oil companies, and the utilities opposed the measure. The backers of the initiative had a lot of popular support; they had almost twice as many signatures as were necessary to place the issue on the ballot. Given all the money they needed, Winner-Wagner set about to turn public opinion around. Since Winner-Wagner's research discovered that the public was relatively ignorant when it came to energy sources, they used an array of scientific experts, in 30- and 60-second commercials, stressing the need for nuclear power in the energy crisis, the need to end "our dependency on foreign oil," and the need to stop "foreign blackmail." While those who sought to limit nuclear power plants called Proposition 15 "the safeguard measure," Winner-Wagner called it "the shutdown initiative." They claimed that "shutdown" would cost the average family $375 per year in added energy bills. Proposition 15 was defeated, and Winner-Wagner went on to similar successes in Arizona and Montana.[68]

During the same year as Winner-Wagner's success, 1976, Media Access Project studied three propositions in Colorado that had drawn strong corporate opposition: a nuclear safety proposal, a bill promoting beverage container recycling, and a public utilities regulation reform proposal.[69] In each case, these propositions seemed headed for victory but lost on election day. In polls taken in September, each initiative had more than 50 percent support, with about 25 percent against and about 20 percent undecided. However, by November all three initiatives lost. In each case, corporate-backed interests significantly outspent the proponents of the initiatives (see Table 10-1).

Corporate dominance is even greater than the total dollar amounts suggest. For example, supporters of the nuclear safety initiative had 130 thirty-second television spots, while the opposition had 145 such spots. However, the opposition had most of their spots on during prime time or immediately before or after prime time. By outspending the proponents of the nuclear safety measure by four to one during prime time, the opposition gained significantly greater access to large numbers of voters.[70]

The disparity in media access was even more glaring in the other two races. In these cases, the Fairness Doctrine almost completely failed to

**TABLE 10-1**
COLORADO INITIATIVES 1976

| | Initiative | | |
|---|---|---|---|
| | **Nuclear Safety** | **Container Deposits** | **Utilities Regulation** |
| Poll (September): | | | |
| For | 55% | 57% | 55% |
| Against | 26% | 27% | 19% |
| Undecided | 19% | 16% | 26% |
| Election Day: | | | |
| For | 29% | 33% | 30% |
| Against | 71% | 67% | 70% |
| Contributions: | | | |
| For | $127,638 | $ 10,318 | $ 6,356 |
| Against | 593,195 | 587,842 | 284,774 |
| Ratio | (5 to 1) | (50 to 1) | (45 to 1) |

*Source:* Taken from: *Taking the Initiative: Corporate Control of the Referendum Process Through Media Spending and What to Do About It,* by Randy M. Mastro, Deborah C. Costlow, and Heidi P. Sanchez, Media Access Project, Washington, D.C., 1980, p. 12.

correct the obvious imbalance. In the container deposit campaign, opponents spent $69,415 on television ads; supporters had to rely on $13,850 worth of free television time. In the utility reform campaign, the opposition spent $67,180 in television ads, while proponents received $6,125 worth of free television time.[71] In both campaigns, two of the four television stations broadcast no messages supporting passage of the initiatives.[72] Similar patterns existed for radio advertising, and, naturally, the opponents of all three ballot issues outspent supporters in print advertising.

Since 1976, supporters of ballot issues have become more sophisticated in using the Fairness Doctrine, and ballot issues, particularly anti-nuclear initiatives, have received more media attention. More media attention, in the form of more across-media news coverage and in the form of public affairs programming, goes a long way to counter the imbalance created by the financial superiority of business-backed opposition. However, mounting levels of corporate spending still furnish a distinct advantage.

The nuclear industry provides an interesting case. The nuclear industry has been particularly affected by greater media attention. Between August of 1968 and March 28, 1979, the day before the Three Mile Island accident, the three television networks had allotted only one-quarter of 1 percent of their news time to news about the nuclear industry.[73] The Three Mile Island accident called into question the future of nuclear power. Getting more than halfway to meltdown, this nuclear accident cost an estimated $1 billion in damages and even more for extensive power replacements. The Nuclear Regulatory Commission ordered the plant to shut down for at least five years. More importantly, the Three Mile Island accident forced the press to focus attention on nuclear power.

Anti-nuclear initiatives became more newsworthy, and levels of corporate spending rose to counter negative public opinion. Table 10-2 shows the familiar pattern of corporate dominance and another Winner-Wagner victory. The before and after figures in this Missouri example are startling. In October of 1979, a year before the vote, 77 percent favored the initiative; by October of 1980, the figure had declined to 54 percent, and, on election day, the initiative lost. The corporate-backed side had outspent the supporters of the initiative by 30 to one. Union Electric, which had invested $900 million in the plant in question (the Callaway Nuclear Power Plant), had contributed $1,150,000 of the total $1,790,857 to fight the initiative. Over $900,000 was spent on television and radio advertisements showing doctors or scientists speaking in support of nuclear power and against the initiative. Under Winner-Wagner's guidance, direct mail appeals were sent to over 400,000 households. Based on replies, the opposition billed itself as a "citizen's committee of

**TABLE 10-2**
MISSOURI ANTI-NUCLEAR INITIATIVE 1980

Initiative: **Shall operation of nuclear power plants in Missouri be prohibited until there is a federally approved site for radio-active waste storage in operation?**

|  | November 1979 | October 1980 |
|---|---|---|
| Polls: |  |  |
| For | 77% | 54% |
| Against | 14% | 30% |
| Undecided | 9% | 16% |
| Election Day (November): |  |  |
| For | 39.1% |  |
| Against | 60.9% |  |
| Contributions: |  |  |
| For | $ 59,484 |  |
| Against | 1,790,857 |  |
| Ratio | (30 to 1) |  |

*Source:* Taken from: Steven D. Lydenberg, *Bankrolling Ballots Update 1980,* The Council on Economic Priorities, New York, 1981, p. 60.

over 25,000 Missouri men and women."* See Figure 10-5 for a list of the major expenditures in this Missouri campaign.

Although the initiative focused on the waste disposal issue, the opposition concentrated on economic arguments. They called the initiative "a gimmick . . . to shut Callaway down." The opposition argued that shutdown would damage the economy, create unemployment, cause energy shortages, and increase dependency on foreign oil. Apparently, the campaign did convince the voters that economics and shutdown were the real issues; even though the voters turned down the initiative, a poll taken after the vote showed that 68 percent still supported the concept of not allowing a nuclear reactor to operate until a federally-approved, high-level radioactive waste storage facility was in operation. Thus, the campaign did not really significantly change public opinion; rather, the campaign successfully redefined the issues.

If we look at other examples of anti-nuclear initiatives, some interesting patterns emerge. In Maine, during the same year, there appeared on the ballot the strongest of all anti-nuclear initiatives (see Table 10-3). The passage of the initiative would have meant the closing of an operating

*Winner-Wagner used this direct-mail technique in 1979 in Westchester County, New York, to oppose the public takeover of the utility company, Con Edison. Here, the opposition billed itself as "Westchester Citizens Against Government Takeover." Winner-Wagner did it again in Oregon, in 1980, for Portland General Electric and Pacific Power and Light, where the opposition was billed as "Oregonians Against Government Takeover."

**FIGURE 10-5**
EXPENDITURES IN THE MISSOURI CAMPAIGN

| Type of Expenditure | Date | Amount | Services provided by: |
|---|---|---|---|
| Direct Mail | 8/7 | $ 13,500 | Below, Tobe & Associates, Los Angeles, CA |
| | 8/19 | 20,000 | Same |
| | 8/22 | 40,000 | Same |
| | 10/17 | 41,531 | Direct Mail Corp., St. Louis, MO |
| | 10/27 | 53,037 | Below, Tobe & Associates, Los Angeles, CA |
| Postage | 8/22 | 40,000 | |
| | 9/10 | 4,480 | |
| | 9/25 | 2,650 | |
| | 10/23 | 43,000 | |
| | 10/27 | 48,000 | |
| Newspaper Advertisements | 10/16 | 6,250 | Union Communications, St. Louis, MO |
| | 10/20 | 1,600 | St. Louis Union Tribune |
| | 10/23 | 10,946 | Suburban Newspapers of Greater St. Louis |
| | 10/24 | 8,640 | St. Louis Argus Publishing |
| | 10/27 | 155,719 | Missouri Press Service |
| | 10/29 | 1,800 | St. Louis Review |
| Radio and TV Production | 8/12 | 37,000 | Churchill Films, New York, N.Y. |
| | 9/25 | 5,192 | Pacific Video, Los Angeles, CA |
| | 10/7 | 15,400 | Telemotion Productions, Denver, CO |
| | 10/7 | 4,793 | Churchill Films, New York, N.Y. |
| | 10/10 | 7,319 | Pacific Video, Los Angeles, CA |
| | 10/22 | 14,985 | Telemotion Productions, Denver, CO |
| | 10/22 | 5,500 | Laclede Communications, St. Louis, MO |
| | 10/24 | 4,500 | Video Production, Kansas City, MO |
| | 11/17 | 2,650 | Technisonic Studios, St. Louis, MO |
| TV and Radio Time Purchases | 8/14 | 200,000 | Mark II Media, Los Angeles, CA |
| | 8/29 | 6,000 | Same |
| | 9/12 | 18,992 | Same |
| | 9/15 | 20,000 | Same |
| | 9/22 | 8,000 | Same |
| | 9/25 | 99,621 | Same |
| | 10/3 | 35,000 | Same |
| | 10/6 | 125,000 | Same |
| | 10/8 | 140,000 | Same |
| | 10/16 | 136,501 | Same |
| | 10/23 | 144,223 | Same |
| Fee for Committee Coordinator and Expenses | 9/9⁻ | $ 14,275 | Winner/Wagner, Los Angeles, CA (fee) |
| | 9/9 | 7,392 | Same (expenses) |
| | 9/29 | 11,755 | Same (fee) |
| | 9/29 | 7,760 | Same (expenses) |
| | 11/5 | 7,341 | Same (expenses) |
| | 11/26 | 15,989 | Same (expenses) |
| Public Opinion Polls | 10/10 | 28,500 | Cambridge Reports, Cambridge, MA |
| | 11/3 | 4,750 | Market Opinion Research, Detroit, MI |
| | 11/28 | 8,000 | Cambridge Reports, Cambridge, MA |
| Literature Distribution | 10/29 | 2,200 | 20th Ward Democratic Org. St. Louis, MO |
| | 10/29 | 1,600 | 21st " " " " " " |
| | 10/29 | 1,300 | 1st " " " " " " |
| | 10/29 | 1,200 | 4th " " " " " " |
| | 10/29 | 1,000 | 22nd " " " " " " |
| | 10/31 | 800 | 5th " " " " " " |
| | 10/31 | 10,000 | Freedom, Inc., Kansas City, MO |

*Source:* Steven D. Lydenberg, *Bankrolling Ballots Update 1980,* The Council on Economic Priorities, New York, 1981, pp. 68–69.

**TABLE 10-3**
MAINE ANTI-NUCLEAR INITIATIVE 1980

**Initiative: Shall nuclear fission be prohibited as a means of generating electricity?**

|  | January | September |
|---|---|---|
| Polls: |  |  |
| For | 24% | 29% |
| Against | 65% | 61% |
| Undecided | 11% | 10% |
| Election Day (September): |  |  |
| For | 40.9% |  |
| Against | 59.1% |  |
| Contributions: |  |  |
| For | $159,311 |  |
| Against | 841,303 |  |
| Ratio | (5 to 1) |  |

*Source:* Taken from: Steven D. Lydenberg, *Bankrolling Ballots Update 1980*, The Council on Economic Priorities, New York, 1981, p. 56.

nuclear plant, Maine Yankee, which supplies 30 percent of the state's electricity. The focus here was directly on nuclear power, not on the more limited problem of nuclear waste disposal. Here was a situation in which the anti-nuclear groups were behind in the polls from the very beginning and were out-financed by five to one. Even though the initiative lost, it did draw 41 percent of the vote, and the opposition dropped from 65 percent to 59 percent. The proponents of the initiative used all the standard arguments against nuclear power: risks of meltdown, problems of evacuation, health risks of radiation, poor economics of nuclear power, and viability of other energy sources. The initiative received extensive media coverage, which helped overcome some of the disparity in spending. The proponents bought some air time, and they also received some free time by using the Fairness Doctrine.

The opposition, once again, presented itself as a citizens' group, even though its contributions came mainly from the utility companies (including Maine Yankee Atomic Power Co.) and large corporations: "Mainers from all walks of life and all regions of our state in [our] grassroots citizens committee." Once again, the opposition's argument was economic, citing the cost of replacing electricity lost from shutdown. Again, it worked. However, even though the initiative was voted down, public opinion was 62 percent to 28 percent against building more nuclear plants.

In 1980, two anti-nuclear initiatives won, despite the fact that proponents were significantly outspent by corporate forces. In Montana, the opposition outspent the proponents by 58 to one, yet the initiative passed, albeit by a very close margin. (Out of 345,402 votes cast, the initiative passed by only 416 votes.) The opposition succeeded in eroding the substantial lead that the proponents had had prior to the campaign (see Table 10-4). This initiative would have affected uranium mining operations, and the major issue in the campaign became whether or not this initiative would place a ban on uranium mining. Opponents, "Montanans for Jobs and Mining," argued that it would, because the cost of mining in Montana would be prohibitive. They argued that the initiative would mean the loss of jobs, would slow economic growth, would reduce the state's tax base, and would adversely affect national defense. Their slogan was: "Vote against Initiative 84 because our enemies would probably vote for it."

The proponents, as you can see in Table 10-4, spent very little on their campaign. Montana had a history of voting for anti-nuclear legislation and, in 1978, had passed an initiative requiring voter approval before any nuclear plant could be built in the state. Proponents received Fairness Doctrine time on seven out of twelve television stations and on twenty out of sixty radio stations.

In Oregon, we see a more dramatic win for anti-nuclear advocates. The proponents of this initiative won, even though they were outspent

**TABLE 10-4**
MONTANA ANTI-NUCLEAR INITIATIVE 1980

Initiative: **Shall the disposal of radioactive waste within the state of Montana be prohibited?**

|  | October 4 | October 28 |
|---|---|---|
| Polls: |  |  |
| For | 60% | 52–55% |
| Against | 40% | 45–48% |
| Election Day (November): |  |  |
| For | 50.1% (172,909) |  |
| Against | 49.9% (172,493) |  |
| Contributions: |  |  |
| For | $ 2,269 |  |
| Against | 131,894 |  |
| Ratio | (58 to 1) |  |

*Source:* Taken from: Steven D. Lydenberg, *Bankrolling Ballots Update 1980,* The Council on Economic Priorities, New York, 1981, p. 103.

by 18 to one. Again, the opposition succeeded in eroding the substantial lead that the proponents had had prior to the campaign. The 74 percent lead in late August and early September declined to 53.7 percent on election day (see Table 10-5). In this particular case, the anti-nuclear forces were very well organized. They had a campaign manager, a grassroots organizer, a media consultant, and a financial coordinator, and they hired professional pollsters. They made very effective use of the Fairness Doctrine and obtained free time during the last two days of the campaign on almost all radio and television stations. The supporters of this initiative were also helped by the fact that the electric utility companies, who were the major supporters of the opposition, had been concentrating on another initiative, which proposed the public takeover of the utilities. Opposition to this anti-nuclear initiative did not get started until mid-October.

However, the most interesting thing about this case is that the anti-nuclear advocates found a new tactic. Polls had indicated that the public thought that nuclear power was cheap. They began to fight the nuclear industry on its own ground. Unlike the wagers of other campaigns, the supporters of the initiative focused on the economic issue of inevitable rate increases that nuclear power would bring. As the media began to report nuclear plant cost overruns throughout the nation, the previous

**TABLE 10-5**
OREGON ANTI-NUCLEAR INITIATIVE 1980

| Initiative: Shall Oregon require operation of permanent radioactive waste storage and voter approval before permitting construction of nuclear plants? | | |
|---|---|---|
| | **August 1979** | **Late Aug./ Early Sept. 1980** |
| Polls: | | |
| For | 67% | 74% |
| Against | 26% | 17% |
| Undecided | 7% | 9% |
| Election Day (November): | | |
| For | 53.7% | |
| Against | 46.7% | |
| Contributions: | | |
| For | $ 34,262 | |
| Against | 625,561 | |
| Ratio | (18 to 1) | |

*Source:* Taken from: Steven D. Lydenberg, *Bankrolling Ballots Update 1980*, The Council on Economic Priorities, New York, 1981, p. 106.

nuclear industry argument that nuclear power would cost less became more and more untenable.

By 1981, the combined impact of the high costs of nuclear energy and the use of professional media consultants and pollsters by citizen groups began to undercut the nuclear industry's successful opposition to anti-nuclear initiatives. In Washington, Winner-Wagner's $1.3 million campaign lost to the Don't Bankrupt Washington Committee (DBW). It seems clear that Winner-Wagner's previous successes were largely based on successfully arguing the economic gains of nuclear power. The Washington Public Power Supply System (WPPSS)—recently known as Whoops!—was operating with enormous cost overruns, which made it an easy target. WPPSS had planned five nuclear plants, with an initial cost of $4 billion; by 1981, the cost had risen to $24 billion, and the construction of two plants had been cancelled. (WPPSS defaulted on its bonds in the summer of 1983.)

The Don't Bankrupt Washington Committee hired professional pollsters and Tony Schwartz, of political campaign fame, to create television commercials. DBW raised $230,000, a lot for anti-nuclear proponents, and bought $95,000 in radio and television time. (They obtained additional time under the Fairness Doctrine.) The anti-nuclear advocates were also significantly helped by the press, which widely publicized the fact that the primary contributors to the opposition campaign were construction contractors, aluminum companies, and Wall Street's biggest bond houses, including Merrill Lynch, Paine Webber, and Smith Barney.[74]

Although well-funded and professionally advised grassroots groups have been able to win against industry-backed opposition in some cases, this does not mean an overall drop in the effectiveness of corporate spending in initiative campaigns. The nuclear industry provides an interesting case, since it highlights what we observed earlier about the relationship between the corporation and the media. As long as an industry does not draw the attention of the news media by generating unfavorable news, the industry can control much of the news content and has, as we have just seen, a tremendous advantage in opposing ballot issues. However, when the media feel obliged to scrutinize an industry or a ballot issue, the corporate advantage is weakened. The nuclear industry became such an industry in the 1970s.

Despite these exceptions, where the corporate-backed side significantly outspends the other side, the corporate side usually wins. The tactics used by the nuclear industry are usually successful. Corporate America continues to successfully oppose anti-smoking initiative, handgun registration initiatives, proposals to increase corporate taxes, most container deposit initiatives, and the public takeover of utilities.

## CONCLUSION

During the 1970s, the relationship between the media and corporate America changed. The ability of the corporation to control business news through the judicious use of the press release, the pseudo-event, and patterns of secrecy was undercut by economic scandal and bad news; corporate control also suffered from government regulation and from attacks by consumerists, environmentalists, anti-nuclear plant advocates, and other citizens groups. The corporate response to what it perceived to be a hostile environment was to expand its public relations activities and attempt to mold public opinion in favor of business interests.

This issue advocacy, as we have seen, took many forms. One of the most visible techniques was the stepped-up use of advocacy advertisements in newspapers and on television and radio. Some corporations hired television journalists to anchor—and lend credibility to—television specials, which were given free of charge to television stations around the country. Many corporations and industries have begun a process of closely monitoring the news media for any negative stories, to which they can quickly respond. Corporate executives have been given training to deal with the media, and, in a fairly new practice, corporate executives have become available for interviews. The Chamber of Commerce has developed what amounts to a television network to foster and spread business values. Public Service Announcements have been used for corporate advocacy. Furthermore, Corporate America has taken to funding Public Television programs that support business interests. The efforts of an administration friendly to business have created a substantial change of climate. The corporate world is once again in a strong position to control the coverage it receives. For the time being, it has regained control of the agenda.

This upsurge in efforts by the corporation and industries to persuade the public about the business viewpoint on social issues raises the question of whether business advocacy campaigns, backed by multimillion dollar budgets, can overwhelm public communication space and drive out alternative points of view that do not have comparable financial support or media expertise. As we have seen, when corporate America mounts a media campaign to oppose initiatives placed on the ballot by groups of concerned citizens, few citizens groups can afford to respond in kind. As we have also seen, growing business spending adversely affects the public's right to hear arguments for both sides of a question.

Even when organized labor attempts to harness the power of the media in support of its goals, there is little hope that it can compete with business interests. Getting a late start in the war of ideas, in 1981 the AFL-CIO launched a media campaign reminiscent of the one established by the Chamber of Commerce, but on a much smaller scale. The federation's

Committee on Political Education began to develop sophisticated polling techniques in order to tap changes in public opinion. The AFL-CIO established the Labor Institute for Public Affairs, which provides nine hours a week of news, entertainment, and information to cable systems in Seattle, Pittsburgh, and Atlanta. It also has produced a series of eight half-hour programs called "America Works," which cover such issues as equal pay for women and occupational health hazards. "America Works" has appeared on thirty-six stations around the country. Each program includes advertisements promoting the social value of organized labor.

The AFL-CIO is planning to create a labor-oriented cable television network called "Solidarity Satellite Network," which would link ten to twelve cities that have large numbers of union members. The federation is also planning to use satellite technology to enable union leaders to confer by television, and it plans to produce more programs to improve the image of organized labor.[75] At present, the combined budget of the Committee on Political Education and the Labor Institute for Public Policy is about $5.5 million a year. When compared to the Chamber of Commerce budget of $70 million a year, and the vast resources of particular corporations and industries, this is meager indeed. Even as organized labor has stepped up its use of the media, it is no match for growing business spending, which calls into question the possibility of a free flow of ideas and raises serious challenges to a democratic society.

## NOTES

1 Joanne Ambrosio, "It's in The Journal. But Is This Reporting?" *Columbia Journalism Review*, March/April, 1980, pp. 34-36.

2 *New York Times*, September 16, 1973; *Newsweek*, January 13, 1975, p.66.

3 Peter Sandman, David Rubin, and David Sachsman, *Media*, Prentice-Hall, Englewood Cliffs, 1982, p. 154.

4 Ben Bagdikian, "Behold the Grass-Roots Press, Alas!" *Harper's*, December 1964, pp. 102-105; Mark Green, "How Business is Misusing the Media," *New York Times*, December 18, 1977.

5 A. Kent MacDougall, *Ninety Seconds to Tell it All: Big Business and the News Media*, Dow Jones-Irwin, Homewood, Illinois,1981, p. 102.

6 Nicholas Pileggi, "The New Flack Magic," *New York Magazine*, September 3, 1979, pp. 36, 38-41.

7 MacDougall, *Ninety Seconds*, p. 60.

8 Quoted in MacDougall, *Ninety Seconds*, p. 60.

9 MacDougall, *Ninety Seconds*, p. 2.

10 Nancy Needham Wardell, "The Corporation," *Dedalus*, vol. 107,1978, pp. 97-110.

11 Dom Bonafede, "The Bull Market in Business/Economics Reporting," *Washington Journalism Review*, July/Aug. 1980, p. 25.

12 Deirdre Carmody, "More Newspapers Are Starting Special Sections for Business News," *New York Times,* April 19, 1980, p. 25.

13 Bonafede, "Bull Market," pp. 24-26.

14 Ernest C. Hynds, "Business Coverage is Getting Better," *Journalism Quarterly,* Summer 1980, pp. 297-303, 368.

15 Quoted in MacDougall, *Ninety Seconds,* pp. 3-4.

16 Quoted in Joseph R. Dominick, "Business Coverage in Network Newscasts," *Journalism Quarterly,* Summer 1981, p. 179.

17 Dominick, "Business Coverage," p. 179.

18 Edwin McDowell, "The Reselling of the DC-10," *New York Times,* July 22, 1979, pp. F1, F11.

19 Irwin Ross, "Public Relations Isn't Kid-Glove Stuff at Mobil, *Fortune,* September, 1976.

20 Subcommittee on Administrative Practice and Procedure of the Committee on the Judiciary of the United States Senate, *Sourcebook on Corporate Image and Corporate Advocacy Advertising,* U.S. Government Printing Office, Washington, D.C., 1978, p. 60.

21 David B. Truman, *The Governmental Process,* Knopf, New York, 1951, p. 228.

22 Randall Poe, "Masters of the Advertorial," *Across the Board: The Conference Board Magazine,* vol. 17, no. 9, September, 1980, p. 20.

23 "The Corporate Image: PR to the Rescue," *Business Week,* January 22, 1979, p. 47.

24 "The Corporate Image: PR to the Rescue," p. 47.

25 *Sourcebook,* p. 1652.

26 MacDougall, *Ninety Seconds,* p. 128.

27 Joel Swerdlow, "Mobil Fables - Volume II," *Washington Journalism Review,* June 1980, p. 13.

28 Ross, "Public Relations."

29 Ross, "Public Relations."

30 Herbert Schmertz, "Advocacy Has Its Rewards," *Communicator's Journal,* May/June, 1983, p. 17.

31 Herbert Schmertz, "An Energy Story the Press Hasn't Told," *Fortune,* November 5, 1979.

32 Schmertz, "An Energy Story the Press Hasn't Told."

33 Schmertz, "An Energy Story the Press Hasn't Told."

34 *20/20* Transcript, ABC-TV, February 12, 1981.

35 Donald S. Stroetzel, "Is There a Future in Advocacy Advertising?" Speech before National Advertising Network, San Antonio, Texas, October 1, 1981.

36 *20/20,* ABC-TV.

37 Ross, "Public Relations."

38 Donald S. Stroetzel, "Why Mobil Uses Advocacy Advertising," *Public Affairs Review,* 1982, pp. 32-33.

39 Schmertz, "Advocacy Has Its Rewards."

40 MacDougall, *Ninety Seconds,* p. 120.

41 MacDougall, *Ninety Seconds,* p. 118.

42 MacDougall, *Ninety Seconds,* p. 113.

43 MacDougall, *Ninety Seconds,* p. 114.

**44** Ross, "Public Relations."

**45** MacDougall, *Ninety Seconds,* p. 125.

**46** MacDougall, *Ninety Seconds,* p. 123.

**47** *Wall Street Journal,* April 10, 1978.

**48** MacDougall, *Ninety Seconds,* p. 123.

**49** MacDougall, *Ninety Seconds,* p. 123.

**50** Poe, "Masters of the Advertorial."

**51** MacDougall, *Ninety Seconds,* pp. 122-123.

**52** MacDougall, *Ninety Seconds,* p. 121; *New York Times,* June 3, 1983.

**53** *New York Times,* October 1, 1983.

**54** *New York Times,* June 3, 1983.

**55** David Paletz, Roberta Pearson, and Donald Willis, *Politics in Public Service Advertising,* Praeger, New York, 1977, pp. 68-69.

**56** Cited by MacDougall, *Ninety Seconds,* pp. 129-130.

**57** MacDougall, *Ninety Seconds,* p.130.

**58** Paletz, Pearson, and Willis, *Politics in Public Service Advertising,* p. 17.

**59** MacDougall, *Ninety Seconds,* p. 131.

**60** MacDougall, *Ninety Seconds,* p. 132.

**61** Steven D. Lydenberg, *Bankrolling Ballots Update 1980,* The Council on Economic Priorities, New York, 1981.

**62** Lydenberg, *Bankrolling Ballots,* pp. 39-40.

**63** Lydenberg, *Bankrolling Ballots,* p. 192.

**64** Lydenberg, *Bankrolling Ballots,* p. 20.

**65** Lydenberg, *Bankrolling Ballots,* p. 20.

**66** Lydenberg, *Bankrolling Ballots,* p. 22.

**67** Lydenberg, *Bankrolling Ballots,* Appendix C.

**68** Larry J. Sabato, *The Rise of Political Consultants: New Ways of Winning Elections,* Basic Books, New York, 1981, pp. 136-137. Copyright © 1981 by Larry J. Sabato. Reprinted by permission of Basic Books, Inc., Publishers.

**69** Randy M. Mastro, Deborah C. Costlow, and Heidi P. Sanchez, *Taking the Initiative: Corporate Control of the Referendum Process Through Media Spending and What To Do About It,* Media Access Project, Washington, D.C., 1980.

**70** Mastro, Costlow, and Sanchez, *Taking the Initiative,* p. 14.

**71** Mastro, Costlow, and Sanchez, *Taking the Initiative,* p. 14.

**72** Mastro, Costlow, and Sanchez, *Taking the Initiative,* pp. 21-22.

**73** MacDougall, *Ninety Seconds,* p. 58.

**74** Steven D. Lydenberg, "Business Captures Few '81 Votes," *Council on Economic Priorities Newsletter,* July, 1982; Scott Ridley, "Money Meltdown," *The New Republic,* August 29, 1983, pp. 11-13.

**75** *New York Times,* October 12, 1983.

PART FOUR

## CONCLUSION

# CHAPTER 11

# MEDIA AND DEMOCRACY

## POLITICAL INFORMATION AND DEMOCRACY

Information is the fuel of democracy. In a society in which citizens are expected to participate in political decision making, it is essential. Without the availability of reliable, objective, and politically diverse information, citizens are without the raw material needed to exercise their political franchise intelligently. While good information will not, in and of itself, guarantee a healthy democracy, it represents an important step in that direction.

The difficulty of providing citizens with the information necessary to promote effective participation was never squarely faced by the early democrats. Jefferson, for example, put great faith in local institutions as a means for fostering dialogue and participation. In part, this faith was justified because America was largely an agrarian society, composed of thousands of small hamlets and villages, each with a local government. Participation in town hall meetings and local council sessions was a reliable means of getting information about issues affecting the community. But as America grew more industrialized and urban, many fewer citizens directly participated in local political activities. If they wanted to acquire political information, they had to find alternative sources.

In the past, the most widely available source for political information was newspapers. Even while town hall democracy flourished, newspapers were regarded as the means for citizens to learn about national and

**311**

international issues, which were unlikely to be debated at town meetings. Early democrats regarded newspapers as a panacea for the defects of democracy.[1] This faith is reflected in Jefferson's very strong stance in favor of press freedom and in the constitutional protections afforded the press. But newspapers were not available in many parts of the country, and many citizens were simply not able to read. While newspapers provided a direct source of information for the educated classes, the majority of the population had to depend on a "trickle down" effect for their information and news. At the time, politics was much more of a local grassroots activity than it is today, and there were a variety of opinion leaders who acted as conduits for political information. Consequently, there was a means for the citizen who could not read to acquire information. Despite this flow of information, the direct access and control of information enjoyed by the governing classes became an important tool for maintaining political power.

With the growth of the newspaper industry and the birth of the mass circulation newspaper, information became more widely available, but the innovations which held the promise of eliminating the inequality of access were radio and television. Soon after its invention, radio became an affordable commodity, and millions of Americans purchased radio sets. With the invention and subsequent mass production of television, the means to close the information gap, to democratize the dissemination of information, seemed available.

The early democrats' faith in the ability of newspapers was matched by the faith of those who heralded the electronic media as a means to revitalize the democratic process. At first, while newspapers, radio, and television were essentially local enterprises, there seemed reason for optimism. Decentralized ownership provided opportunities for greater and more diverse participation. However, local ownership and control of both electronic and print media had a rather short life span. Radio and television were quickly consolidated into the hands of a few giant corporations. Newspaper chains extended their empires. Media conglomerates, involved in all aspects of the production and dissemination of printed and electronic entertainment and news, became the growth industries of the sixties and the seventies. Today, the ownership of virtually all mass media is vested in fifty giant corporations.[2]

The political consequences of this centralized control are far-reaching. Several giant news organizations influence the portraits of reality that appear in all the national media. Another result of this consolidation has been a substantial change in the ratio of givers of opinions to receivers of opinions. "It is this shift in this ratio," wrote C. Wright Mills, "which is central to the problems of the public and public opinion in the latter-day phases of democracy."[3] The opportunities for access to the mass media are limited, and the costs are prohibitively high. The mass media have become the center of political action, but only a select number of groups and individuals are able to participate. The remainder of the population is confined to the role of receivers of information. It is impossible to have a political dialogue with television, radio, or newspapers.

## The Politics of Confusion

It is not that there is any lack of political information being sent through the mass media. Although television began as an entertainment medium, it has, over the years, become increasingly political. In the last five years, the amount of programming devoted to news has vastly increased. On the average, an affiliate television station will air 100 minutes of national news (minus commercials) and somewhere between 165 and 240 minutes of local news.[4] This increase is not the result of any hunger for news in the general population. In fact, the majority of Americans seem to have a limited interest in politics. There is more news on television because news has turned out to be a profitable enterprise, more profitable than a lot of entertainment programs.

If the sheer quantity of news produced greater competency in the citizenry, we would have a society of political masters. Yet, just the opposite is occurring. There has certainly been no significant increase in voting since television began delivering increasing quantities of news into American households. There is little evidence to support the claim that Americans are better informed politically than they were immediately before the advent of television news. In fact, the evidence seems to point in the other direction; political knowledge and interest seem to be continually declining. Of course, all the blame for limited participation cannot be laid at the door of the media. Television news may have actually created greater participation among some segments of the population. Black political participation may have been heightened by the attention given to the Civil Rights Movement during the sixties and seventies. And there is an increasing body of evidence which shows that television has had a significant impact on citizens' knowledge of, and attitudes toward, politics.

Television may not have created a better-informed public, but it has certainly created certain political effects in the viewing public. While Marshall McLuhan may have exhibited a flair for the dramatic when he coined the phrase "the medium is the message," there is surely a relationship between the form in which information is presented and the reaction of the receiver to that information. Television is essentially a passive medium. It requires less involvement than reading a newspaper. Because there is less effort involved in receiving and processing the message—a message which is dominated by visual symbols—there is less of a sustained reaction to the message being transmitted.

> Unless news is directly perceived as signaling a potential or actual personal threat, most people accept such information in the same manner as they accept the sounds of music they like. News is sensed rather than appreciated or analyzed. News has become so much background stuff.[5]

The continual use of a set of standard stereotypes further limits the involvement of the viewer. Many viewers eventually become bored and apathetic. Few take the time to evaluate critically the content of the messages. The very low level of involvement in the messages transmitted through television creates a large class of viewers who become increasingly more susceptible to subtle and not-so-subtle forms of manipulation. As Jarol Manheim explains, there is a direct relationship between one's involvement and one's susceptibility to change: "...the less an individual cares about, is interested in, and/or views as central to his personal well-being the holding of a particular attitude, the more easily he may be persuaded to change that attitude...."[6]

Some observers, such as Michael Robinson, strongly believe that individuals who watch television news become more confused and cynical in their attitudes concerning politics. The effects of a diet of television news are no longer a matter of speculation. Research on the effects of television found that those "...who rely upon television in following politics are more confused and cynical than those who do not. And those who rely totally on television are the most confused of all."[7] This cynicism and confusion are the result of a generally negative portrait of the political world painted on television news, according to Robinson. This negative portrait of politics influences the attitudes of those who choose to watch the news, as well as those who receive some news inadvertently.[8]

There is every reason to believe that the individual who depends on television to understand the political world stands a good chance of becoming confused and cynical. The recurring use of stereotypes and the fascination with dramatic and divisive issues create the image of a political world without an internal logic. When individuals try to relate what they see on the television news to concerns that permeate their everyday existence, the confusion is likely to multiply.

Despite the evidence indicating that regular watchers of television news are more cynical about politics, there is no reason to assume that television news will continually transmit the same values or have the same impact on the viewers. During periods when power brokers are able to exercise strong control over the agenda, they are better able to transmit their values through the media—values that generally reinforce the legitimacy of the basic power-sharing arrangements. Television is not simply a medium that manipulates; it is also easily manipulated. Even in periods when there are dissension and doubt, the media tend to give the basic political and economic arrangements a high degree of legitimacy. If we depend on television to educate the generations coming of age, there will not be enough people with political education and/or interest meet the demands placed on them as democratic citizens. Without knowledge of the political world, the democratic citizen is no longer an actor in the political system. Citizens devoid of information and wedded to a series of stereotypes are the potential victims of those who desire to bend reality to serve some personal, commercial, or political self-interest. No one saw these possibilities more clearly than Walter Lippmann, almost forty years ago:

> ... men who have lost their grip upon the relevant facts of their environment are the inevitable victims of agitation and propaganda. The quack, the charlatan, the jingoist, and the terrorists can flourish only where the audience is deprived of independent access to information. But where all news comes at second-hand, where all the testimony is uncertain, men cease to respond to truths, and respond simply to opinions. The environment in which they act is not realities themselves, but the pseudo-environment of reports, rumors, and guesses. The whole reference of thought comes to be what somebody asserts, and not what actually is.[9]

Further, there is no reason to believe that such new technologies as cable television, which have eroded the networks' share of prime-time audience, will upgrade the level of political discourse and overcome "the pseudo-environment of reports, rumors, and guesses." Most people who turn to cable television have changed for the movies and the sports, not for the news shows. Although some critics hail Ted Turner's Cable News Network as a more intelligent alternative to network news, the differences are not great enough to promote such enthusiasm. Cable is likely to produce some additional access for political groups. However, these increased opportunities will probably be absorbed by the better-funded and -organized single interest groups, who will use cable to mobilize the "believers."

> ... the main political impact of television's news devices may be, not to make ordinary citizens better informed, but to fragment the policy-making process of government even further.[10]

Finally, now that the FCC has permitted the networks to enter the cable market and intends to remove nearly all restrictions on ownership by 1990, it seems likely that small operators and minority groups will be driven out.[11]

## Social Class and Information

The effects of using the mass media to acquire political information are not evenly spread throughout the population. The attitude of the viewer plays a strong role in determining effects, as does the dependence of the individual on the media as a source of information. In addition, there are structural factors which determine the potential impact of political messages. One's socioeconomic status or class position conditions what information will be accessible and how it will be digested and used.

Information pumped into a stratified society will be received and used in different ways by different segments of the population. Information is a commodity which must, like other commodities, be purchased. Sometimes the costs are tangible, such as the purchase price of books, magazines, or specialized media. Often the cost is the time which must be invested to consume the information. In general, one's class position, determined by education, income, and occupation, will decide the "costs" one must pay to acquire information. Education, for example, has been found to be an important determinant of both costs and benefits.

> ... several studies have supported the hypothesis that as the flow of informa- tion into a social system increases, groups with higher levels of education often tend to acquire this information at a faster rate than those with lower levels of education.[12]

As the mass media make more information about particular issues available, the gap between the initial understanding of different groups does not narrow, as one might expect, but actually widens:

> As a result of the differential rates of acquisition, gaps in knowledge between segments with different levels of education tend to increase rather than decrease. Knowledge of space research is an example; after several years of heavy media attention to space rocketry and satellites, the gap in knowledge about that research across educational levels was greater than it had been before the space research program began.[13]

Income is an important factor in determining the "cost" of information. Of course, those with larger incomes are likely to have more education and reap the benefits of that differential. Income also determines whether an individual can purchase books, travel, and invest the time to become politically informed. The access to free information channels definitely rises with income. High-income individuals are not totally dependent on the mass media for political information. They have the time, the inclination, and the contacts to acquire specialized and diverse sources of information. But the factory worker, who has just completed another eight-hour day, does not have the energy, the time, or the re- sources to purchase this type of information. Because the average individual cannot afford to get information, he must depend, in most cases, on the mass media.

The political consequences are dramatic. Not only do high-income individuals better understand their political interests (an understanding which is partly derived from their ability to purchase information at lower costs), they also know how to recognize and use information consistent with those interests. The low-income individual must, according to Anthony Downs, a political scientist who has written a fascinating treatise on this subject, depend on the high-income individual, whose interests are often not the same as his own, to supply him with information.

> ... since the mass media of communications in many democracies are owned or dominated more by high-income interests than low-income ones, low-income citizens are more likely to receive data selected by principles conflicting with their own than are upper-income groups.[14]

Without the time and resources to make independent judgments about their interests, individuals are forced to rely on the mass media or to factor out interests as a basis for making political choices.

The dependence of much of the population on the mass media as a source of political information deepens the inequality of political resources by widening the information gap between certain classes. Certain groups are able to obtain the information necessary for them to understand their interests and make political choices based on those interests, while other groups are left to sort out the political world on their own. When these groups turn to the mass media for guidance in understanding the political world, they are left even more confused, and the information gap grows wider. Without a means to understand their interests and the impact of certain policies on those interests, much of the population makes political choices based on the lure of certain symbols or personality traits. The increasing use of images, symbols, and psychological appeals, a political tableau necessitated by the increased reliance on television, further confuses those without independent sources of information and further erodes the place of group interests in the political process. The information gap is a prime means by which the ruling class is able to win the allegiance of groups with antithetical interests. It may be foolish to believe that the news media can be much more perfect than the society in which they function. But the news media not only reflect some of the problems of American democracy (the inequality of opportunities, for example) but often magnify and intensify some of those problems as well.

## THE MEDIA AGE CAMPAIGN

Mass media have not only changed public attitudes toward politics but also have fundamentally restructured the way politics is practiced and the way power is distributed. These political changes occasioned by the burgeoning power of the mass media have, in turn, had a further impact on public attitudes about politics, the democratic system, and their role within the system. Elections are a prime example of a political transformation occasioned by the media. Theoretically, citizens in a democratic society are supposed to exercise considerable influence in the electoral process. Traditionally, elections were supposed to provide an opportunity and a focus for political debate and give various interests in the society an opportunity to have some impact on policy and election outcomes. Elections were to be an opportunity for citizens to become givers of opinion and, thereby, more directly participate in the formation of public opinion. They were to be a civic exercise that helped maintain the balance in the ratio of givers of opinion to receivers of opinion, which C. Wright Mills saw as essential to the maintenance of a healthy democracy.

Political parties were supposed to provide the vehicle for individual and group participation in the electoral process. Parties would have a central role in the electoral process, collecting campaign money and using the many volunteers to stimulate interest in the election. Historically, party bosses gained the leverage to exercise considerable influence over the candidates chosen to carry the party's banner.[15] Even more important than their role in selecting candidates, organizing participation, and raising money was the contribution they made in sorting out and making the political world intelligible.

> By inspiring "party identification" in most people they provided the main cognitive sorting devices that enable ordinary people to make sense out of politics and furnish them with a meaningful basis for voting on a wide variety of issues and in frequent elections.[16]

Parties provided the political glue which held together the very fragile and fragmented political and social systems. These parties not only gave people some reason to have political beliefs, they also gave them something to believe in.

Political parties were profoundly affected when the media, particularly television, became the arena for electoral contests. Certain politicians used television to overcome the power of the party to control the nomination of candidates and to shape the issues in the campaign. When television took over as the arena and arbiter of electoral contests, it was not only the party bosses that lost their traditionally powerful role but also the millions of party workers who brought the campaigns to the neighborhoods. It seemed to make little sense to cultivate and train volunteers to make telephone calls, knock on doors, discuss the campaign, or pass out leaflets at shopping centers when a 30-second television or radio commercial could reach far more people. The deemphasis on traditional grassroots campaigning fractured one of the few natural links between the political world and the public. Using television as the premier campaign tool not only dried up opportunities for participation and involvement by party regulars, volunteers, and members of various interest groups but also changed the nature of campaigning in ways that left citizens more confused about politics and about their obligation to participate.

When political campaigning moved from the streets and factories to the television studios, it was not merely a change of scene but also a change of characters and scripts. Media consultants took the lead in shaping the candidates' image and the themes for the campaign. They quickly disabused candidates of the notion that they could simply transplant the traditional political methods to television. If candidates were to use television effectively to get votes, they had to use the techniques which had a proven record of attracting interest. Candidates had to sell themselves. That's what people do in television commercials—they sell things—and they sell them by using provocative images, not by using appeals to principles and beliefs. An astute and sensitive political man like Adlai Stevenson, who ran as the Democratic candidate for President in 1952 and 1956, when television was first being used in presidential campaigns, could not help but observe that candidates selling themselves on television as a promoter sells a box of cereal would assuredly have a detrimental effect on the democratic process.[17]

If television commercials have not fully undermined traditional campaign dialogue, they certainly have trivialized the discussion. Incrementally, television transformed the language of politics and the logic of democracy. In order to use the medium of television to its fullest, politicians have, to a very large degree, abandoned the traditional discourse of politics. Political advertising does not contain political messages; it is simply a commercial message about something political. What was often special and significant about politics—the effort to confront and solve human problems and build a better, more just society, a notion that informed political dialogue since Plato and Aristotle—has been lost.

The drop in participation and party identification, not solely but importantly the result of television campaigning, has loosened democracy from its moorings. By nature, democracy can be an unwieldy political system. Periodic elections and the ebb and flow of political movements produce changes in a democratic society. These changes are not aberrations; they are vital to democracy. A political system built on mass participation must expect, and even encourage, change. It is the changing sands of democracy which allow it to evolve and remain vital. In order to weather these changes and provide a basis for political transitions, there must be some institutions that promote a degree of stability. Political parties have been an important source of that political stability.

Without parties to provide political focus or forge alliances among the multiple, overlapping, and conflicting interests that characterize the American political scene, the electorate has been fragmented into little pockets of single-interest groups. These small, narrowly-focused, single-interest groups promote a politics of selfishness, intolerance, and zealotry. This kind of politics reopens old wounds, separates rather than unites, and poses a mighty threat to the principles of democracy. Meg Greenfield, a writer familiar with the Washington political world, vividly describes the impact of these changes:

> I can't remember a time in Washington when interest group issues and politics so dominated events. And every day the units of protest and concern seem to be subdividing into even smaller and more specialized groupings.... By now, there can hardly be a cultural, racial, regional, economic or professional group for whom the lawmakers in Washington have not fashioned some special statutory blessing—a prerogative, a grant, an exemption, a reimbursement, something. It puts a premium on identifying yourself with the special subgroup and helps to thin, if not destroy, whatever feelings of larger national loyalty various citizens might have.[18]

If further confirmation of this political fragmentation is needed, there are ample illustrations in recent voting trends. Half the registered Democrats who cast their votes for Gary Hart in the primaries said they would vote for Ronald Reagan in the general election. Organized labor was not able to deliver its ranks to the Democratic party, despite a strong organizational effort. Candidates increasingly tailored their campaigns to cash in on this political fragmentation. The mayor of New York City ran on both the Democratic and the Republican lines. Candidates have commonly disassociated themselves from their political traditions and have run campaigns based on appeals to narrow interests or campaigns focused on seductive symbols of leadership, patriotism, and power. Party affiliations, or the support of traditional alliances based on political interests, are no longer a measure of a candidate's electoral chances. Candidates with the right formula and the means to project it are able to succeed in an electoral world that has been transformed by television. It is a world in which many voters make political choices using virtually the same criteria they use to make commercial choices.

If the existence of this large number of single-interest groups gives the impression that more people are involved in political activity, the impression is false. There are more groups, but there are fewer people politically participating. The number of citizens who choose even to vote, the easiest form of participation, declines with each election. The United States now has the lowest rate of voter turnout in the world. When the 1984 presidential votes were tallied, the African nation of Botswana, which traditionally had the world's lowest voter turnout, moved up a notch to yield sole possession of the cellar to the United States.[19] It is the political world's marriage with television that is one of the prime factors in this decline in voting. In much the same way that people are lulled into boredom and apathy by trying to disentangle and understand the political world presented in the news, they are tranquilized by the media's obsession with the vicissitudes of election campaigns and the drumbeats of politicians trying to sell themselves over the tube. It is not simply the quantity of information—although there certainly is an abundance of campaign news—that sends all but the political addict scurrying for relief but also the quality of that information, which deepens the apathy that is already far too pervasive.[20]

There are some theorists who are not particularly concerned about political apathy or its effects on the democratic process. They regard the decline in voting as the result of a "sorting out process." Those with the most interest in the results of an election are the ones who participate, which, according to these observers, is the way it should be.[21] But it is not a natural "sorting out" process which causes more individuals, particularly the young, to turn away from politics; it is their response to the pictures and realities in the political world. There is no reason to take comfort from the assertion, even if it were true, that those who vote have a high interest in the outcome. All this reveals is that fewer and fewer people feel as if they have a stake in the political system. And when fewer people feel as if they have a stake in the society in which they live and more people surrender their rights and ignore their obligations, there are political and social dues that must be paid.

Of course, not all Americans can devote large blocks of time to civic and political activities. For many, the difficulties in simply earning enough to satisfy basic needs and carving out a little time for leisure occupies most of their energy. Yet there are fundamental obligations and responsibilities that must be met if democracy is to be more than a word roundly celebrated but widely ignored or misunderstood. No matter what justifications some social scientists and propagandists give for the astonishing levels of political apathy, it means that the system is in a state of decay.

Yet there have been instances in which the population has shown surprising interest in political events. These flashes of interest confound some theorists. Observers wonder why 60 million people voluntarily watched the Carter/Reagan debate. They wonder why the speeches of Governor Mario Cuomo and the Reverend Jesse Jackson at the Democratic Convention stirred such political interest and emotion throughout the country. The answer is fairly simple. People tuned in on the debate because they expected to see a more authentic and spontaneous discussion of political issues, which they did not get, and they were moved by the speeches of Jackson and Cuomo because they were truly different from the normal political babble. There is a latent political interest in the country which is smothered by the banality of politics in the media age.

## GOVERNING THROUGH THE MEDIA

Television and other mass media are no longer solely used for the purpose of winning elections. Presidents and other political actors use the mass media to govern. In part, the realization that the mass media could be used for this purpose has required only a small extension of logic. However, the need to use the media to govern was created when candidates invested their political fortunes in television. Politicians' reliance on the mass media in elections withered the organic roots of power and so fragmented the electorate that it was much more difficult to get the consensus necessary to govern. Parties could not provide any real support. There were no enduring alliances and little cooperation among interest groups. With each new issue, it was necessary again to build a consensus. Politicians sought to enlist the vaunted powers of television to build this consensus. Using the mass media for one political purpose created additional needs and further incentives to use the media for other purposes. In a very real sense, it has created a dependence which will not be easily undone.

The mass media's coverage of the political world further contributes to the dependence of politicians on the technologies of mass communication. In the process of creating the stereotypes for news, the "good guys" and "bad guys," the winners and the losers, the rising and falling stars, the news media exert a pressure for immediate results. Through their exposure to the news, people come to believe that democracy should operate with the speed and efficiency of a network news broadcast.

> Television seldom covers the long, often dull meetings where democratic decisions are worked out. As a result, many viewers come to believe that great problems can be quickly resolved. T.V. has helped to produce a "turned on" generation that wants immediate experience and gratification at the flick of a switch.[22]

Entertainment programing, including the many political dramas and docudramas, has further reinforced this conception of the way problems get resolved:

> ...entertainment television is full of dramas and "docudramas" in which a problem of some sort, often social and political, is set forth, fought through, and resolved in an hour or two, minus commercials. One result is surely a spreading of the general assumption that life's problems can be understood

and resolved quickly, with no messy strings left dangling, if only people with vision and courage deal with them.[23]

In order to keep pace with the expectations created by television, politicians feel compelled to use television. There is, in their minds, no faster way to affect public perceptions. Since the success or failure of particular policies is a matter of interpretation, mass media provide a means for the power holders to provide their interpretation—to create an image of success or, if the need arises, to put the best face on failure.

This cycle has transformed and commercialized the policy-making process. At first, presidents and other political actors would determine policy and use the media to explain the policy and build support. These were largely separate processes. They are no longer quite so separate. The wisdom and advisability of particular policies are now considered in light of the potential for the policy to be successfully sold to the news media. The probability that the policy will produce some quick results, or can by portrayed as producing results, becomes a major concern. Whether a policy is good or bad, or whether a policy is necessary, is no longer the paramount concern. Leaders do not lead, they follow the changing tastes of the public opinion market. They listen to their pollsters and media and political consultants, who provide up-to-the-minute readings of the latest ideological fashion. Everything is calibrated and calculated. Since the news media are quick to define policies as strategies, the public is aware of the politicians' subservience to public tastes. Politicians who opportunistically change to benefit from some present ideological fashion cause people further to doubt the integrity and seriousness of political officials and the pronouncements of policy that they utter.

## OTHER POLITICAL ACTORS

It is not only the world of the president, the senator, the congressperson, the governor, and other political officials that has been transformed by "media politics"; corporations, interest groups, reform movements, and revolutionary movements, as well as others seeking to gain power, change the balance of power, or influence policy have been equally affected by the transformation in the political world.

For the corporation, these developments have proven to be something of an unexpected windfall. Politicians have legitimized using commercials and commercial devices to sell public policy. This has opened the door for the corporations to use precisely the same devices to sell their point of view on political issues to the public. Of course, the corporations have been using precisely these methods for years and are generally more sophisticated, better able to produce sustained information campaigns, and to pay the costs of enormously expensive advertising campaigns. In the view of many corporations, this new freedom could not have arisen at a more propitious time. Mobil Oil, which has broken the trail for many of its corporate brethren, is candid in its explanation of the importance of aggressively trying to influence public opinion:

> Mobil's overriding public relations strategy is simple: to improve the environment in which the company makes its money. In an era of shortage, advertising gasoline makes little sense; the profitability of a large oil company depends more on the freedom from both governmental and public skepticism. Insuring this freedom means trading in ideas rather than products.[24]

The freedom to use the airwaves and newspapers to persuade the public of the corporations' point of view provides the corporations with an incredibly strong political weapon. Because of their skill and resources for using the mass media effectively for persuasion, political advertising will undoubtedly become one of the strongest weapons in the corporations' political arsenal. One thing that American democracy does not need is an enormously wealthy corporate sector with even more power to determine the direction of the political agenda.

While the mass media will help to enhance corporate power, it may have the opposite effect on protest movements. Since most reform organizations do not have the resources to carry out advertising campaigns to inform the public of their ideas and positions, they are dependent on the mass media for an identity and a gateway to the public opinion arena. If a movement is able to gain the attention of the media, as the Civil Rights and antiwar movements were able to do, the media can be an enormous asset in focusing attention on the problems that the movement is seeking to redress and on the movement itself. Yet, without an independent means of conveying information about the activities and goals of a movement, even the most powerful movements are subject to definition by the mass media. "Mass media define the public significance of movement events," writes Todd Gitlin, who has extensively researched the media coverage of the organization called Students for Democratic Society. By ignoring certain events, or characterizing certain activities negatively, the media "... actively deprive them of larger significance."[25] In this way, the media help shape the direction of protest movements, which are forced to choose between accommodation to the values of the media or political obscurity. The choices made about which movements are given legitimacy are not random but reflect the ideological outlook of the media and the political establishment:

> *The more closely the concerns and values of social movements coincide with the concerns and values of elites in politics and in media, the more likely they are to become incorporated in the prevailing news frames. Since the sixties, for example, consumer organizations have been elevated to the status of*

regular newsmakers; they and their concerns are reported with sympathy, sufficiently so as to inspire corporate complaints and counter-propaganda in the form of paid, issue-centered advertising.[26]

While certain reform organizations can eventually get standing in the media, organizations that fundamentally threaten elite interests can, according to Gitlin, achieve standing only as deviants. Americans are systematically deprived of access to more radical ideas for social change. While the obstacles for organizations who hold such ideas are greater, even reform organizations must fight for a role in the democratic process:

> The routine frames... endure for reformists as well as deeply oppositional movements. Even reformist movements must work industriously to broadcast their messages without having them discounted, trivialized, fragmented, rendered incoherent.[27]

Within this spectrum of competing interests in American society, some interests are simply "more equal" than others. The media wield an enormous amount of influence in determining which interests will be heard and in creating the context within which they will be evaluated. The media respond to economic realities by selling space or air time only to those who can afford them. On the other hand, the media may respond with a genuine interest in reform movements like the Civil Rights Movement, consumerism, and environmentalism. However, the media also have the power to ignore, and often do ignore, those who cannot afford to buy space or time, those who represent a radical alternative, or those who are effectively disenfranchised through poverty, lack of education, and lack of the appropriate media skills.

The media have come to act as censors in determining which groups, ideas, and policies will be given public attention. As the media regulate the flow of political communication, they deprive the public of the right to learn and to determine independently the viability and merits of various groups' ideas. With the media acting as mediators, it becomes increasingly difficult for those seeking change to generate the necessary sparks and cultivate support for their interests. There are, of course, limitations on the number of groups and organizations that the media can cover. Yet there is a pressing need to broaden and deepen political discussion to include those who now stand outside the media's frame of reference.

## NOTES

**1** Walter Lippmann, *Public Opinion*, Free Press, New York, 1965, p. 19.

**2** Ben Bagdikian, *The Media Monopoly*, Beacon Press, Boston, 1983.

**3** C. Wright Mills, *The Power Elite*, Oxford University Press, New York, 1959, p. 302.

4 Austin Ranney, *Channels of Power*, Basic Books, New York, 1983, p. 67.

5 Bernard Rubin, *Media Politics and Democracy*, Oxford University Press, New York, 1977, p. 11.

6 Jarol B. Manheim, "Can Democracy Survive Television?" in Doris Graber (ed.), *Media Power in Politics*, CQ Press, Washington, D.C., 1984, p. 132.

7 Michael J. Robinson, "American Political Legitimacy in an Era of Electronic Journalism: Reflections on the Evening News," in Douglas Cater and Richard Adler (eds.), *Television as a Social Force: New Approaches to T.V.*, Praeger, New York, 1975, p. 101.

8 Robinson, "American Political Legitimacy"; see also Michael J. Robinson and Margaret Sheehan, *Over the Wire and on T.V.: CBS and UPI in Campaign '80*, Russell Sage Foundation, New York, 1983, p. 261.

9 Walter Lippman, *Liberty and the News*, Harcourt, Brace, and Hone, New York, 1920, pp. 54-55.

10 Ranney, *Channels of Power*, p. 167.

11 *New York Times*, July 27, 1984, p. 1; *New York Times*, July 29, 1984, p. E7.

12 Phillip J. Tichenor, George A. Donohue, and Clarice N. Olien, "Communication and Community Conflict," in Graber, *Media Power in Politics*, p. 93.

13 Tichenor, Donohue, and Olien, "Communication and Community Conflict," p. 93.

14 Anthony Downs, *An Economic Theory of Democracy*, Harper and Row, New York, 1957, p. 236.

15 See Ranney, *Channels of Power*, p. 105.

16 Ranney, *Channels of Power*, p. 106.

17 David Halberstam, *The Powers That Be*, Dell, New York, 1979, p. 322. Copyright © 1980 by David Halberstam. Reprinted by permission of Alfred A. Knopf, Inc.

18 Meg Greenfield, "Thinking Small," *The Washington Post*, April 19, 1978, p. A13.

19 Andrew Manatos, "U.S. Voter Turnout Now World's Worst," *New York Times*, Nov. 29, 1984.

20 Ranney is one who sees the quantity of information as the cause of apathy.

21 Ann Rawley Saldich, *Electronic Democracy*, Praeger, New York, 1979, p. 51.

22 Saldich, *Electronic Democracy*, p. 58.

23 Ranney, *Channels of Power*, p. 127.

24 Linda Charlton, "Upwardly Mobil," in *Channels*, vol. 1, no. 3, Aug./Sept., 1981.

25 Todd Gitlin, "Making Protest Movements Newsworthy," in Graber, *Media Power in Politics*, pp. 239-240.

26 Gitlin, "Making Protest Movements Newsworthy," p. 247.

27 Gitlin, "Making Protest Movements Newsworthy," p. 249.